*f*P

RITES OF AUTUMN

THE STORY OF COLLEGE FOOTBALL

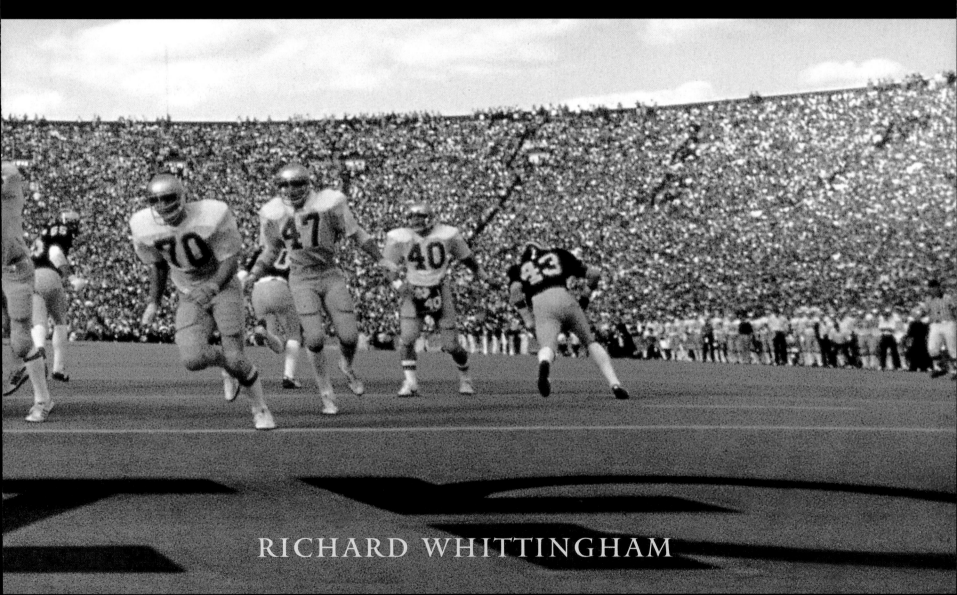

RICHARD WHITTINGHAM

*f*P

The Free Press
A division of Simon & Schuster, Inc.
Rockefeller Center
1230 Avenue of the Americas
New York, NY 10020

For information about special discounts for bulk purchases, please contact Simon & Schuster
Special Sales: 1-800-456-6798 or business@simonandschuster.com

Design by Vertigo Design, NYC
Manufactured in the United States of America
10 9 8 7 6 5 4 3 2 1
Library of Congress Cataloging-in-Publication Data
Whittingham, Richard.
   Rites of autumn: the story of college football/Richard Whittingham.
       p. cm.
   Includes index.
   1. Football—United States—History. 2. College sports—United States—History
   3.Football—United States—History— Pictorial works.
   4. College sports—United States—History—Pictorial works. I. Title.
   GV950.W46 2001
   796.332'63'0973—dc21   2001041084
   ISBN 0-7432-2219-9

Excerpt on page 94 is from Saturday's America, copyright © 1970 by Dan Jenkins; Little, Brown (Boston).
"The Play" on pages 112–113 is copyright © Weston W. George.
"Ten Great Things About College Football" on pages 142–143 is from Newspaper syndication, copyright © by Beano Cook, 1985.

ACKNOWLEDGMENTS

THE AUTHOR WISHES FOREMOST to extend his gratitude to the executive producers of the ESPN series *Rites of Autumn*, Don Sperling and Wayne Chesler, without whose efforts and foresight this project would not have come to pass, as well as to their staff at Pearl Entertainment.

TO ROGER STAUBACH for his participation and the fine Foreword he contributed.

SPECIAL APPRECIATION is extended to consultant Steve Fleming; to Beano Cook, Wes George, Dan Jenkins, and Bill McGrane for their contributions; and to NCAA statistician Rick Campbell, College Football Hall of Fame executive director Bernie Kish, and Pro Football Hall of Fame archivist Joe Horrigan for their cooperation and assistance.

THE AUTHOR AND PUBLISHER are deeply indebted to production coordinator Brad Bernstein and photo researchers Jason Sealove, Robyn Short, Joshua Kreitzman, Adam Hertzog, and Patricia Pfeifer. And, of course, to those at the film repositories of *Sports Illustrated*, ABC Sports, the Associated Press, and the other providers of photographs used in this book.

A VERY SPECIAL THANKS is extended to all the sports information directors and their staffs from the many universities whose cooperation was invaluable during the creation of this book. Scores of schools provided information, photographs, and guidance to the author. Appreciation is also extended to the Pasadena Tournament of Roses, the Sugar Bowl, the Cotton Bowl, and the Orange Bowl.

AS WELL, gratitude for the editorial guidance of Bill Rosen at Simon & Schuster and for the efforts and support of Peter Ginsberg of the Curtis Brown Ltd. literary agency.

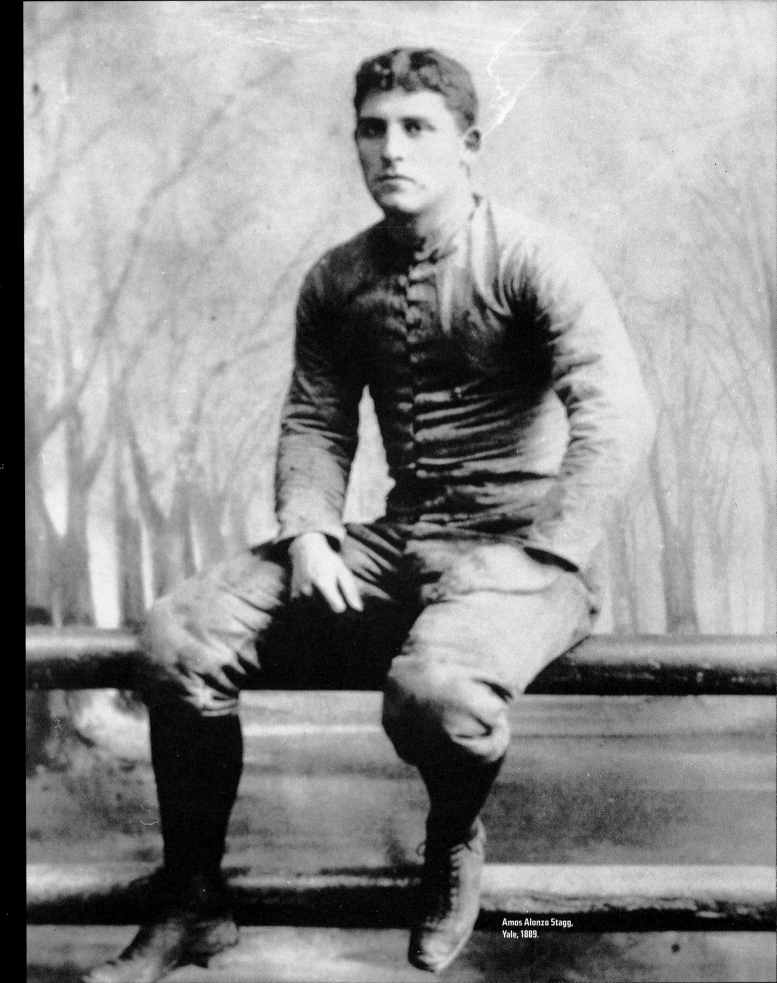

Amos Alonzo Stagg,
Yale, 1889.

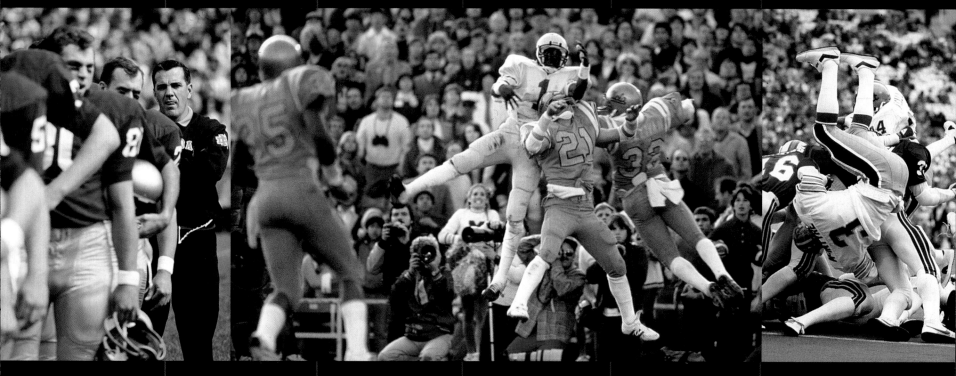

The game of football is to college life

what color is to painting. It makes

college life throb and vibrate.

BOB ZUPPKE
University of Illinois
Head Coach, 1913—41

FOREWORD

BY ROGER STAUBACH

Recently I went to an Army–Navy game. Both teams had poor records, no national ranking was on the line. Even so, the stadium was packed and the excitement was as feverish as if the national championship depended on the outcome. The pageantry and the tradition were as rich as ever, no different from my own time. As I watched the Cadets and the Midshipmen march onto the field before the game and watched how hard each team fought to win the game, all the chills came back. The only difference was this time I was in the crowd looking down at the field instead of standing on the field looking up at the crowd.

And it isn't just Army and Navy; it's the same everywhere throughout the country: Southern Cal and UCLA, Michigan and Ohio State, Texas and Oklahoma, as well as the smaller schools that have their own intense rivalries. They all compete just as fiercely; they all have their own colorful and cherished traditions. College football has always been something very special, with its heritage, its pageantry, and especially with the intensity of competition found on all levels. It has a spirit to it that lives; it has tradition that is unshakable.

As a boy in Cincinnati I followed college football, especially Ohio State and Notre Dame. I had my heroes: Hopalong Cassady at Ohio State, Johnny Lujack and Johnny Lattner at Notre Dame, Pete Dawkins at Army, Joe Bellino at Navy. I dreamed of playing in college myself, and the dream came true.

Not a day goes by that I'm not grateful for having had the experience of playing college football. When I finished high school, I had no idea whether I could compete on the next higher level. I deeply wanted to, but I knew it was going to be quite different than playing in high school. I was recruited by a number of teams—Ohio State, Purdue, Michigan—but the one that most caught my attention was Navy, and that came about by accident.

One of their assistant coaches, Rick Forzano, had come to our school to take a look at our center and co-captain Jerry Momper. While he was watching film on Momper he noticed me and said he'd like to talk to me as well. Rick was a dynamic guy—he later became head coach of the Detroit Lions—with a dry sense of humor. He gave me the recruitment pitch, and ended it with a smile and a shrug, saying, "We can't promise you anything other than that when you graduate you can have your own battleship."

At Navy I learned, fairly quickly, that I could compete at the college level, but I learned the primary objective even faster. Literally on the first day, after they clip your hair down to the scalp, you learn how to say "Beat Army." And as a plebe that year I remember sitting there watching the game, and all I could think was, "Next year I hope I get a chance to play in it." I'd never seen anything like it before.

The next year I did get the chance, and it's one of the greatest memories I have in football. The buildup to the game was so strong, so exciting. I have never been more nervous before a game than I was before that game. It was the only time I couldn't sleep the night before a game. I was more nervous than I ever was before a Super Bowl. I'll never forget going out onto the field; it was at Municipal (one year later renamed JFK) Stadium in Philadelphia and there were 102,000 people in the stands. It was an unforgettable experience, and would have been even if we hadn't won that day 34–14.

The next year was even better. We were in contention for the national championship, a rare posi-

tion for Navy. We had a terrific team: on it was Tom Lynch, a great captain, and players such as Pat Donnelly and Skip Orr. The four of us have remained very good friends over the years—a perfect example of how college football often creates meaningful and lifelong friendships. We had beaten Michigan and Notre Dame in 1963 and had only one loss, when we had been upset down in Dallas by Southern Methodist. But then, of course, there was Army, always the last game of the year and always the hardest fought no matter what the difference in the records of the two teams. It was also the year President Kennedy had been assassinated in Dallas. The country was in mourning and the Army–Navy game was suddenly cancelled. But at the request of the Kennedy family, who had great respect for tradition, the game was reinstated. Despite the sadness of the time, it turned out to be a great game. We led through most of it, but with only two seconds left and Navy ahead 21–15, Army was at our 2-yard line, needing a touchdown to tie and an extra point to win. But they had no time-outs left: their outstanding quarterback Rollie Stitchweh tried desperately to get a play off but time ran out before he could get the ball snapped. Pat Donnelly, incidentally, scored Navy's three touchdowns that day. And to illustrate that college football friendships can extend even to archrival opponents, Rollie Stitchweh and I have been good friends ever since that game.

As a result of beating Army, we got the invitation to the Cotton Bowl; we went down there ranked number two in the nation to play number-one Texas, and that's the way the year's rankings ended up as we lost 28–6.

Tens of thousands of people have experienced playing college football and their memories of it are as vivid and as dear-to-the-heart as mine. And there are many, many more who have watched and cheered, and to them it is just as cherished a memory, remembered as a great part of their college life. College is over for them now, but when they sit down on a Sunday morning in autumn to read the newspaper, the first thing they turn to is the sports pages to see how their school did the Saturday afternoon before. The spirit stays with you.

It's more than football really. The game helps cement the attachment of players, students, and alumni to the school they attended, to the college life that is such a wonderful experience in itself. It is an attachment that stays with you the rest of your life.

I'm pleased to have been asked to contribute to this book and the ESPN television series *Rites of Autumn*. Both celebrate in their own ways the history, the legacy, and the excitement of a grand sport, the one that is the closest to my heart. And I know it is to hundreds of thousands of others out there who share with equal devotion the same affection that the game brings out in me.

Saturday afternoons in autumn. For more than a century they have stood as the showcase for what has become a true American ritual, a time reserved for one of the most richly colorful, spirited, and vibrantly exciting sports in all the world—college football.

Baseball has its summer, pro football its Sundays and Monday nights, basketball its winters indoors, but tradition and college football's passionate following have indisputably claimed that first day of each autumn weekend.

The game's very birth was on a Saturday afternoon, three o'clock to be precise, November 6, 1869, when Rutgers took the challenge laid down by Princeton to meet in a football game that would pit one school's honor and skill against the other. It was really a game much more like soccer that they played that windy November afternoon, but it is considered the first intercollegiate football game to be played in America.

Soon after, games were being played between schools like Yale, Columbia, Harvard, Tufts, Amherst, Trinity, Pennsylvania, Williams, Wesleyan, as well as the two progenitors of the sport. By the 1880s, intercollegiate combat on the football field had become a common diversion in the Midwest, South, and Southwest, and the following decade even in the then remote and sparsely settled Far West.

In those infant days of college football, students decked out in coats, vests, ties, and bowlers crowded the boundary lines of the grassy malls or dirt fields where the games were staged. Clutching and waving handmade pennants, they devised spontaneous cheers to urge their compatriots to victory. From the very beginning, college football was as much—perhaps more—of a contest for its fans as for its players.

Schools eventually began erecting rickety wooden grandstands to accommodate the growing crowds, who chanted across the field at each other in derision and down at the field in support of their own. As time passed the sport began to develop its own pageantry with the infusion of cheerleaders, fight songs, mascots, marching bands, bonfires, pep rallies, and tailgate parties. The bleachers gave way to sturdy stadiums and massive bowls, and the fans eventually traded their derbies and greatcoats for flip-brim hats, raccoon coats, and saddle shoes. Alumni returned to their alma maters in droves to watch their school compete against lusty rivals, and townspeople joined the throngs for some of the best entertainment to be had. The intercollegiate sport that had once been witnessed by perhaps several hundred classmates had become a rite and the focus of hundreds of thousands of spirited spectators on any given autumnal Saturday afternoon.

The game itself—violent, tactical, demanding of skills, strength, and endurance—evoked the very essentials of classic drama: conflict, suspense, excitement, competition, triumph, and failure. It is hardly surprising then that it became such a fertile ground for the cultivation of legends. The fathers of the game were the early coaches, who developed it with a panoply of innovations and refinements; men like Walter Camp, Amos Alonzo Stagg, Glenn S. "Pop"

Warner, George Woodruff, Percy Haughton, John Heisman, Fielding Yost, Harry Williams, Gil Dobie, Bob Zuppke, Knute Rockne, and many others.

And the stars came out early on, sparkling on green fields across the country: a burly Pudge Heffelfinger at Yale, an imposing Hamilton Fish at Harvard, a fleet Willie Heston at Michigan, a corpulent but agile Pete Henry at Washington & Jefferson, a triple-threat Elmer "Ollie" Oliphant at Army, an awesome Jim Thorpe at Carlisle.

By the mid-1920s, more than 50,000 fans would fill Illinois's Memorial Stadium to watch the world's most famous ghost, Red Grange, gallop while professional football teams like the New York Giants and the Chicago Bears were thrilled if they drew more than 5,000 supporters on a Sunday afternoon. George Gipp died and a nation mourned the Notre Dame star's passing, but would never forget the name of the Gipper, thanks to Knute Rockne's now legendary locker room pep talk.

College football became a stage on which dramas of many natures have been played out, from last-second victories to Roy Riegels's wrong-way run, from Woody Hayes's tantrums to Doug Flutie's Hail Mary pass. Besides Grange and the Gipper, the game gave us Bronko Nagurski, Don Hutson, Tom Harmon, Sammy Baugh, Blanchard and Davis, Johnny Lujack, Doak Walker, Paul Hornung, Dick Butkus, Roger Staubach, O. J. Simpson, Archie Griffin, Randy White, Herschel Walker, Bo Jackson, and Barry Sanders, to name just a few of those skilled performers who left indelible marks on the history of the game. And, of course, there remains the wisdom and wizardries of the coaches who followed in the footsteps of the game's founders, such sideline geniuses as Wallace Wade, Fritz Crisler, Bob Neyland, Bernie Bierman, Frank Leahy, Earl

Blaik, Bud Wilkinson, Duffy Daugherty, Darrell Royal, Woody Hayes, Ara Parseghian, John McKay, Bear Bryant, Bo Schembechler, Barry Switzer, Eddie Robinson, Tom Osborne, Hayden Fry, Bobby Bowden, and Joe Paterno.

There are few spectacles in the sporting world to match the ceremony of an Army–Navy game, the color of a Rose Bowl pageant, the emotion when a chorus of thousands rings out with the Notre Dame fight song, the splendor of a tailgate party at a Texas–Oklahoma game, the beauty of the USC cheerleaders, or simply the great games that have been played and the extraordinary performances that have been given on college football fields over the years.

In the words of one of the game's finest coaches, Army's Earl "Red" Blaik, written back in the 1950s, college football is "a game that through the years has stirred a president to save it, Theodore Roosevelt; another to coach it, Woodrow Wilson; and a third to both play and coach it, Dwight D. Eisenhower." We might add subsequent president-players Richard M. Nixon, Gerald Ford, and Ronald Reagan, the latter having also portrayed the fabled Gipper on the silver screen. Blaik went on to explain that college football is "a game that numbers as legion statesmen, doctors, lawyers, men of finance and business, and thousands of just good citizens who have known the thrill of victory, have experienced the lessons of defeat and have felt, as few but football players can, the lasting satisfaction that comes from playing on a team."

What Coach Blaik neglected to mention were the particular pleasures of walking with a surging crowd across the fallen amber and red leaves of autumn into a cavernous stadium where one can cheer and sigh on a noble Saturday afternoon, and experience what has come to be the rites of autumn.

My definition of an
All-American is a player
who has weak opposition
and a poet in the press box.

BOB ZUPPKE
University of Illinois
Head Coach, 1913—41

GAME DAY HEROES
GREAT MOMENTS IN COLLEGE FOOTBALL

In the constantly unfolding drama of college football, it has been said, the coaches are the playwrights and the players the actors on stage. And just as in every good dramatic work there are starring roles, memorable lines, and unforgettable scenes, college football features stars of the first magnitude, the ones who have created memorable moments and unforgettable dramas. And, like the great performers they are, sometimes they achieved those moments by precise execution of a script, and sometimes by brilliant improvisation.

What makes college football such an enduring and vital sport are Saturday's heroes, the performances they have left behind and the games they have made so exciting. From breakaway runs and Hail Mary passes to game-winning field goals and game-saving tackles, the scrapbook of thrills in college football is one of the richest in all sports. The names are immortal: Thorpe, Gipp, Grange, Nagurski, Hutson, Harmon, Baugh, Blanchard and Davis, Trippi, Brown, Staubach, Simpson, Griffin, Dorsett, Elway, Flutie, Sanders (Barry and Deion) . . . their deeds legendary.

Greatness in college football is a rare thing, achieved by only a few; becoming a legend is quite another. A legend is recognized not merely by great performance but by his impact on the game as well. If ever there was an example, it was Harold "Red" Grange, the young man Grantland Rice dubbed the "Galloping Ghost." In November 1925, the Saturday before Thanksgiving, Grange, a senior, played his last football game for the University of Illinois, leading the Illini to victory at Ohio State before more than 70,000 fans. Then, with a swarm of reporters badgering him as he left the field and in the locker room with the burning question—Was the Galloping Ghost going to turn pro?—he escaped to

his hotel. The lobby there was awash with newspaper writers, too, so he snuck out of the hotel and, traveling incognito, boarded a train in Columbus for Chicago. Once there he registered in a midtown hotel under a false name and awaited word from his manager/agent/partner, C. C. Pyle, who was already sitting down with George Halas and Dutch Sternaman, co-owners of the Chicago Bears, in the process of pounding out a contract to make the fabled Grange a professional football player.

While still a college student, Grange had established his greatness on the football field, playing before crowds of 60,000 and often 70,000 or more. He was already a football legend, spoken of in the same sense of sports awe during the mid-1920s as one might Babe Ruth or Jack Dempsey. His next move was the most eagerly anticipated event in the sports world of 1925.

The entrepreneurial Pyle did sign Grange with the Bears and suddenly the then quite youthful National Football League (founded just five years earlier) got a tremendous boost in terms of respectability and economics. (Grange in fact played his first pro game as a Chicago Bear on Thanksgiving Day, five days after that last college game at Ohio State.) Over the next few months, with a special coast-to-coast football tour, Red Grange managed to put pro football on the proverbial map, in the process pocketing about $125,000 for his efforts on the field while picking up an almost equal amount from endorsements and personal appearances, not to mention contracts for three motion pictures—not bad for a college senior in those days before the income tax and when other pro football players were being paid only $300 or $400 a game. To put it in another perspective, the highest annual salary Babe Ruth earned during those years was $85,000, and he did not reach that figure until five years after the Grange tour. (A sportswriter at the time commented that Ruth's salary was greater than that of the president of the United States, to which the Babe famously replied: "I had a better year than he did.")

There have been a slew of greats over the years in college football: great players, great teams, great coaches, great games, great moments on the field. Today, when greatness is recognized on a college football field, it can lead to a pro contract calculated in the millions of dollars. And the ensuing recognition is almost unlimited. Where Red Grange had to rely mostly on print media to make his name known throughout the country, Saturday's heroes today are bolstered by cable and satellite television and the World Wide Web, which can instantaneously make their names and deeds known to tens of millions of people.

Greatness in college football, however, should not merely be measured by what it brings in worldly treasure or national acclaim. It should be recognized by the fabric from which it is woven: a com-

posite of raw talent, herculean effort, doggedness, concentration, the virtues and qualities threaded through the body and mind of an athlete.

Although greatness on the college football field is aspired to by all who put on the uniform, only a handful can lay claim to it. And when it is attained by a college football player, most still in their late teens or early twenties, it carries an enormous burden that some have found unbearable. More than a few Heisman Trophy honorees have failed to make it in the NFL, such college standouts as Johnny Lattner, Terry Baker, John Huarte, Gary Beban, Pat Sullivan, and Rashaan Salaam, to name a few. Why? No one really knows. Maybe they were a little too small, a step too slow. Maybe they suffered athletic burnout after three or four seasons as heroes on the college level. For some the college game showcased their talents or versatility that were in some cases assets not adaptable to the pro game. On the other hand, some college stars have simply opted to leave their gridiron greatness in their college lockers, channeling their talents in other directions: the military for Pete Dawkins and Joe Bellino, the business

Florida State's Charlie Ward (17) in action against Notre Dame in 1993. The Heisman Trophy winner that year, Ward opted for a professional basketball career after college. Closing in on him is Notre Dame tackle Jim Flanigan (44).

world for Jay Berwanger, Clint Frank, and Dick Kazmaier, or even another sport as the NBA's Charlie Ward chose.

College football is a sport that stands on its own, unique and special. In the early days, coaches like Amos Alonzo Stagg at Chicago and Bob Zuppke of Illinois strived to uphold the integrity of the college game, at least that's what they claimed. Stagg issued a press statement in 1923 in which he described the evils lurking in the shadows of the college game: "For years the colleges have been waging a bitter warfare against the insidious forces of the gambling public and alumni and against overzealous and shortsighted friends, inside and out, and also not infrequently against crooked coaches and managers, who have been anxious to win at any cost. . . . And now comes along another serious menace, possibly greater than all others, *viz*. Sunday professional football." Zuppke, upon learning his great star Red Grange was joining the pros, refused to speak to him for years after. The real reason they and other college coaches were trying so desperately to dissuade their players from joining the pros was that they were deathly afraid that the college game would eventually be overshadowed by the pro game, that it would become the equivalent of baseball's minor leagues, mere training grounds for the major leagues. It never happened; college football, with its elements like the wishbone offense and quarterback option, maintained its own distinctive character, its particular color, its unique identity—and its enormous following.

What follows here is a celebration of the great players, exceptional performances, and memorable moments on college football fields over the past century and a half.

ALL-AMERICANS

Grantland Rice once said it was a "mythical" thing to select "the very best" in college football, although he did just that for more than twenty years. There are other terms that come to mind: controversial or questionable, perhaps presumptuous. But almost since the game of college football began back in the mid-1800s, sportswriters, coaches, and other self-appointed pundits have been selecting All-America teams, singling out the heroes they have observed, the stellar figures who shone beyond all others, those who left an indelible mark on the game they played.

Here are the top players and coaches of their time, the best of those who played in the nineteenth century, and decade by decade through the twentieth century, selected by the author and a panel of experts and consultants to the *Rites of Autumn* project. You are welcome to agree, disagree, or even protest the selections, but one cannot deny that the marvelous athletes honored here stand as a roster of greatness in the game of college football.

Purdue quarterback Drew Brees literally tastes the rose, after the Boilermakers defeated Indiana 41—13 to secure an invitation to the 2001 Rose Bowl. It was the first time Purdue had made it to the Rose Bowl since 1966.

THE 1800s

First Team

POSITION	PLAYER	SCHOOL
E	Frank Hinkey	Yale
E	Charles Gelbert	Pennsylvania
T	Marshall Newell	Harvard
T	Arthur Hillebrand	Princeton
G	Pudge Heffelfinger	Yale
G	Truxton Hare	Pennsylvania
C	William Lewis	Harvard
B	Edgar Allan Poe	Princeton
B	Charles Daly	Harvard
B	Thomas McClung	Yale
B	Malcolm McBride	Yale
Coach	Amos Alonzo Stagg	Chicago

Second Team

POSITION	PLAYER	SCHOOL
E	Frank Hollowell	Harvard
E	Arthur Poe	Princeton
T	Langdon Lea	Princeton
T	Fred Murphy	Yale
G	Charles Wharton	Pennsylvania
G	Arthur Wheeler	Princeton
C	Peter Overfield	Pennsylvania
B	Knowlton Ames	Princeton
B	Frank Butterworth	Yale
B	George Brooke	Pennsylvania
B	Ben Dibblee	Harvard
Coach	George Woodruff	Pennsylvania

1900-09

First Team

POSITION	PLAYER	SCHOOL
E	Thomas Shevlin	Yale
E	John Kilpatrick	Yale
T	Hamilton Fish	Harvard
T	Jim Hogan	Yale
G	Dutch Goebel	Yale
G	Ham Andruss	Yale
C	Germany Schultz	Michigan
B	Walter Eckersall	Chicago
B	Willie Heston	Michigan
B	Ted Coy	Yale
B	Bill Hollenback	Pennsylvania
Coach	Fielding Yost	Michigan

Second Team

POSITION	PLAYER	SCHOOL
E	Casper Wister	Princeton
E	David Campbell	Harvard
T	Horatio Biglow	Yale
T	Jim Cooney	Princeton
G	William Warner	Princeton
G	Francis Burr	Harvard
C	Henry Holt	Yale
B	Foster Rockwell	Yale
B	Henry Torney	Army
B	Peter Hauser	Carlisle
B	Wallie Steffen	Chicago
Coach	John Heisman	Clemson/Georgia Tech

1910s

First Team

POSITION	PLAYER	SCHOOL
E	Tack Hardwick	Harvard
E	Guy Chamberlain	Nebraska
T	Fats Henry	Washington & Jefferson
T	Josh Cody	Vanderbilt
G	Stan Pennock	Harvard
C	Henry Ketcham	Yale
B	Jim Thorpe	Carlisle
B	Chic Harley	Ohio State
B	Elmer Oliphant	Army
B	Eddie Mahan	Harvard
Coach	Pop Warner	Carlisle/Pittsburgh

Second Team

POSITION	PLAYER	SCHOOL
E	Doug Bomeisler	Yale
E	Paul Robeson	Rutgers
T	Harold Ballin	Princeton
T	Wally Trumbull	Harvard
G	Clarence Spears	Dartmouth
G	Bob Fischer	Harvard
C	Bob Peck	Pittsburgh
B	Gus Dorais	Notre Dame
B	Fritz Pollard	Brown
B	Charlie Brickley	Harvard
B	Charles Barrett	Cornell
Coach	Bob Zuppke	Illinois

1920s

First Team

POSITION	PLAYER	SCHOOL
E	Bennie Oosterbaan	Michigan
E	Wes Fesler	Ohio State
T	Century Milstead	Yale
T	Ed Weir	Nebraska
G	Frank Schwab	Lafayette
G	Chuck Hubbard	Harvard
C	Ben Ticknor	Harvard
B	Benny Friedman	Michigan
B	Red Grange	Illinois
B	Ernie Nevers	Stanford
B	Bronko Nagurski	Minnesota
Coach	Knute Rockne	Notre Dame

Second Team

POSITION	PLAYER	SCHOOL
E	Brick Muller	California
E	Eddie Anderson	Notre Dame
T	Ralph Scott	Wisconsin
T	Frank Wickhorst	Navy
G	Jim McMillen	Illinois
G	Carl Diehl	Dartmouth
C	Mel Hein	Washington State
B	Harry Stuhldreyer	Notre Dame
B	George Wilson	Washington
B	Ken Strong	New York
B	George Gipp	Notre Dame
Coach	Wallace Wade	Alabama

1930s

First Team

POSITION	PLAYER	SCHOOL
E	Don Hutson	Alabama
E	Larry Kelley	Yale
T	Ed Widseth	Minnesota
T	Nick Drahos	Cornell
G	Ralph Heikkinen	Michigan
G	Bill Corbus	Stanford
C	Alex Wojciechowicz	Fordham
B	Sammy Baugh	Texas Christian
B	Tom Harmon	Michigan
B	Jay Berwanger	Chicago
B	Marshall Goldberg	Pittsburgh
Coach	Howard Jones	USC

Second Team

POSITION	PLAYER	SCHOOL
E	Wayne Millner	Notre Dame
E	Gaynell Tinsley	Louisiana State
T	Ed Beinor	Notre Dame
T	Ernie Smith	USC
G	Biggie Munn	Minnesota
G	Harry Smith	USC
C	Chuck Bernard	Michigan
B	Harry Newman	Michigan
B	Whizzer White	Colorado
B	Clint Frank	Yale
B	Marchy Schwarz	Notre Dame
Coach	Jock Sutherland	Pittsburgh

1940s

First Team

POSITION	PLAYER	SCHOOL
E	Leon Hart	Notre Dame
E	Hub Bechtol	Texas
T	George Connor	Notre Dame
T	Leo Nomellini	Minnesota
G	Alex Agase	Illinois
G	Bill Fischer	Notre Dame
C	Chuck Bednarik	Pennsylvania
QB	Johnny Lujack	Notre Dame
RB	Glenn Davis	Army
RB	Charlie Trippi	Georgia
RB	Doc Blanchard	Army
Coach	Frank Leahy	Notre Dame

Second Team

POSITION	PLAYER	SCHOOL
E	Barney Poole	Army/ Mississippi
E	Hank Foldberg	Army
T	Al Wistert	Michigan
T	Dick Wildung	Minnesota
G	Rod Franz	California
G	Joe Steffy	Army
C	Clayton Tonnemaker	Minnesota
QB	Bobby Layne	Texas
RB	Frank Sinkwich	Georgia
RB	Doak Walker	SMU
RB	Steve Van Buren	Louisiana State
Coach	Earl Blaik	Army

1950s

First Team

POSITION	PLAYER	SCHOOL
E	Bill McColl	Stanford
E	Ron Kramer	Michigan
T	Alex Karras	Iowa
T	Dick Modzelewski	Maryland
G	Les Richter	California
G	Jim Parker	Ohio State
C	Bob Pellegrini	Maryland
QB	Babe Parilli	Kentucky
RB	Billy Cannon	Louisiana State
RB	Johnny Lattner	Notre Dame
RB	Jim Brown	Syracuse
Coach	Bud Wilkinson	Oklahoma

Second Team

POSITION	PLAYER	SCHOOL
E	Ron Beagle	Navy
E	Dan Foldberg	Army
T	Bob Gain	Kentucky
T	Jim Weatherall	Oklahoma
G	Calvin Jones	Iowa
G	Bob Ward	Maryland
C	Jerry Tubbs	Oklahoma
QB	Jack Scarbath	Maryland
RB	Paul Giel	Minnesota
RB	Howard Cassady	Ohio State
RB	Alan Ameche	Wisconsin
Coach	Duffy Daugherty	Michigan State

1960s

Offense

POSITION	PLAYER	SCHOOL
E	Howard Twilley	Tulsa
E	Mike Ditka	Pittsburgh
T	Ralph Neely	Oklahoma
T	Ron Yary	USC
G	Rick Redman	Washington
G	Dick Arrington	Notre Dame
C	Lee Roy Jordan	Alabama
QB	Roger Staubach	Navy
RB	O. J. Simpson	USC
RB	Gale Sayers	Kansas
RB	Ernie Davis	Syracuse

Defense

POSITION	PLAYER	SCHOOL
DE	Bubba Smith	Michigan State
DE	Ted Hendricks	Miami (Florida)
DT	Bob Lilly	Texas Christian
DT	Carl Eller	Minnesota
MG	Jim Stillwagon	Oklahoma
LB	Dick Butkus	Illinois
LB	Tommy Nobis	Texas
LB	Steve Kiner	Tennessee
DB	Jack Tatum	Ohio State
DB	George Webster	Michigan State
DB	Johnny Roland	Missouri
DB	Buddy McClinton	Auburn
Coach	Ara Parseghian	Notre Dame

1970s

Offense

POSITION	PLAYER	SCHOOL
WR	Johnny Rodgers	Nebraska
WR	Lynn Swann	USC
TE	Ken MacAfee	Notre Dame
T	Jerry Sisemore	Texas
T	Chris Ward	Ohio State
G	Brad Beedde	USC
G	Mark Donahue	Michigan
C	Jim Ritcher	North Carolina State
QB	Jim Plunkett	Stanford
RB	Tony Dorsett	Pittsburgh
RB	Archie Griffin	Ohio State
PK	Chris Barr	Penn State

Defense

POSITION	PLAYER	SCHOOL
DE	Ross Browner	Notre Dame
DE	Hugh Green	Pittsburgh
DT	Randy White	Maryland
DT	Lee Roy Selmon	Oklahoma
LB	Mike Singletary	Baylor
LB	Jerry Robinson	UCLA
LB	Tom Cousineau	Ohio State
DB	Dennis Thurman	USC
DB	Tom Casanova	LSU
DB	Ken Easley	UCLA
DB	Dave Brown	Michigan
P	Ray Guy	Southern Mississippi
Coach	Paul Bryant	Alabama

1980s

Offense

POSITION	PLAYER	SCHOOL
WR	Anthony Carter	Michigan
WR	Tim Brown	Notre Dame
TE	Keith Jackson	Oklahoma
T	Bill Fralic	Pittsburgh
T	Tony Mandarich	Michigan State
G	Dean Steinkuhler	Nebraska
G	Mike Pitts	Alabama
C	Dave Rimington	Nebraska
QB	Jim McMahon	Brigham Young
RB	Herschel Walker	Georgia
RB	Marcus Allen	USC
PK	John Lee	UCLA

Defense

POSITION	PLAYER	SCHOOL
DE	E. J. Junior	Alabama
DE	Billy Ray Smith	Arkansas
DT	Ken Sims	Texas
DT	Tracy Rocker	Auburn
LB*	Lawrence Taylor	North Carolina
LB*	Derrick Thomas	Alabama
LB	Brian Bosworth	Oklahoma
LB	Chris Spielman	Ohio State
DB	Deion Sanders	Florida State
DB	Bennie Blades	Miami
DB	Ronnie Lott	USC
DB	David Fulcher	Arizona State
P	Reggie Roby	Iowa
Coach	Joe Paterno	Penn State

*Tie

1990s

Offense

POSITION	PLAYER	SCHOOL
WR	Raghib Ismail	Notre Dame
WR*	Desmond Howard	Michigan
WR*	Keyshawn Johnson	USC
TE	Chris Gedney	Syracuse
T	Orlando Pace	Ohio State
T	Chris Samuels	Alabama
G	Aaron Taylor	Nebraska
G	Will Shields	Nebraska
C	Jim Pyne	Virginia Tech
QB	Peyton Manning	Tennessee
RB	Eddie George	Ohio State
RB	Ricky Williams	Texas
PK	Sebastian Janikowski	Florida State

*Tie

Defense

POSITION	PLAYER	SCHOOL
DE	Grant Wistrom	Nebraska
DE	Corey Moore	Virginia Tech
DT	Steve Emtman	Washington
DT	Warren Sapp	Miami
LB	Marvin Jones	Florida State
LB	LaVar Arrington	Penn State
LB	Trev Alberts	USC
DB	Charles Woodson	Michigan
DB	Terrell Buckley	Florida State
DB	Chris Canty	Kansas State
DB	Antoine Winfield	Ohio State
P	Shane Lechler	Texas A&M
Coach	Bobby Bowden	Florida State

Record-Setters

David Klinger of Houston set three NCAA Division I-A records in a game against Arizona State on December 2, 1990, when he accounted for 11 touchdowns (passing) and a total of 732 yards gained (716 passing, 16 rushing).

The standard for most passes completed in a game, 55, was set by Rusty LaRue of Wake Forest, October 28, 1995, against Duke. The mark was tied by Purdue quarterback Drew Brees, October 10, 1998, against

Texas Christian's LaDainian Tomlinson

Wisconsin; in the same game Brees broke the record for most passes attempted, when he threw 83.

Texas Christian running back LaDainian Tomlinson set the single-game rushing record when he carried the ball for 406 yards against University of Texas El Paso on November 20, 1999.

The record for the most total yards gained in a single season was posted by David Klinger of Houston in 1990: 5,221 (5,140 passing, 81 rushing).

Quarterback Ty Detmer of Brigham Young holds both career records of three years and four years for yards gained passing: 1989–91, 13,779; 1988–91: 15,031.

Barry Sanders of Oklahoma State set the mark for most yards rushing in a season in 1988 when he gained 2,628 (344 carries in 11 games).

Ty Detmer of Brigham Young

Georgia's Herschel Walker holds the record for the most yards gained rushing in a 3-year career: 1980–82, 5,259 (994 carries).

Ron Dayne of Wisconsin set the standard for yards rushing in a 4-year career, 1996–99, when he brought his total to 6,397 (1,115 carries).

Tim Couch of Kentucky posted a new record for passes completed in a season in 1998: 400 (11 games, 553 attempted).

Chris Redman of Louisville set the record for pass completions in a 4-year career, 1996–99: 1,031 (1,679 attempted).

Most yards gained passing in a season:

    11 games: David Klinger of Houston,
    1990, 5,140 (completed 374 of 643)

    12 games: Ty Detmer of Brigham Young,
    1990, 5,188 (completed 361 of 562)

The record for most passes caught in a game, 23, was set by wide receiver Randy Gatewood of UNLV in a 1994 game against Idaho.

Manny Hazard of Houston holds the single-season mark for passes caught, 142 in 1989.

Most passes caught in a career:

    3 years: Howard Twilley of Tulsa,
    1963–65: 261 (3,343 yards gained)

    4 years: Trevor Insley of Nevada,
    1996–99 (5,005 yards gained)

Troy Edwards of Louisiana Tech set the record for most yards gained on pass receptions in a game, 405, against Nebraska in 1998 (21 receptions).

The most yards gained on pass receptions in a season, 2,060, was recorded by Trevor Insley of Nevada in 1999 (134 receptions). Insley also holds the mark for most receiving yards gained in a 4-year career, 5,005 (1996–99, 298 receptions).

The records for most points scored by nonkickers:

    Game: Howard Griffith of Illinois,
    48, vs. Southern Illinois, 1990 (8 TDs)

    Season: Barry Sanders of Oklahoma State,
    234, 1988 (39 TDs)

    3-year career: Ricky Williams of Texas,
    404, 1996–98 (67 TDs, 1 2-point conversion)

    4-year career: Travis Prentice of Miami (Ohio),
    468, 1996–99 (78 TDs)

The record for most field goals kicked in a game, 7, is shared by Mike Prindle of Western Michigan, vs. Marshall in 1984, and Dale Klein of Nebraska, vs. Missouri in 1985.

John Lee of UCLA holds the record for most field goals kicked in a season, 29, in 1984 (33 attempts).

Jeff Jaeger of Washington set the mark for the most field goals kicked in a 4-year career (1983–86), 80 (99 attempts).

Washington's Al Worley holds the record for most interceptions in a season, 14 in 1968.

The record for most interceptions during a career, 29, is held by Al Brosky of Illinois (1950–52)

Wisconsin's Ron Dayne,
winner of the 1999 Heisman Trophy

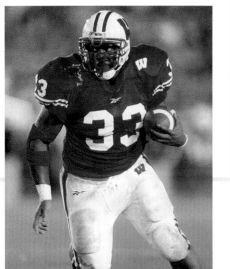

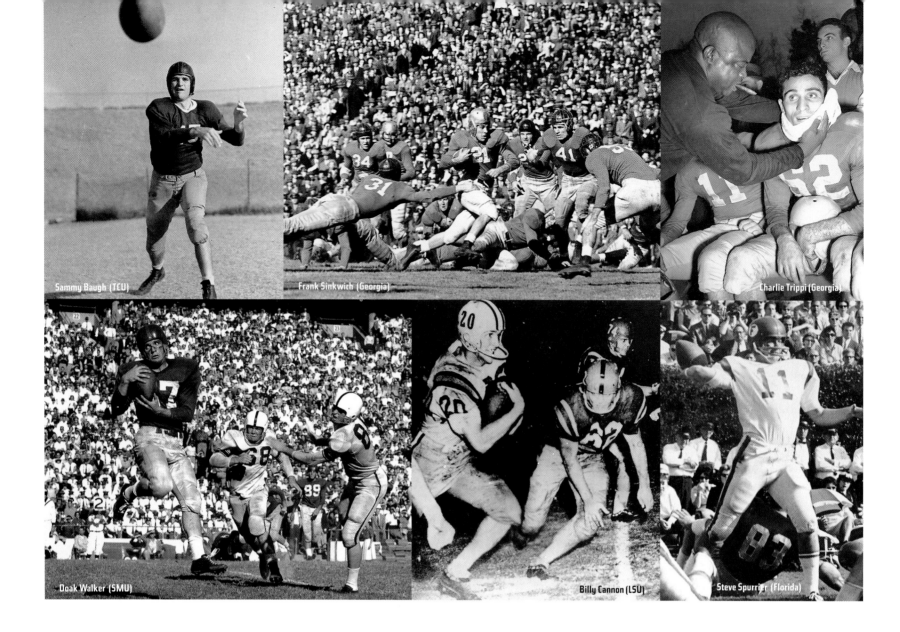

Sammy Baugh (TCU)

Frank Sinkwich (Georgia)

Charlie Trippi (Georgia)

Doak Walker (SMU)

Billy Cannon (LSU)

Steve Spurrier (Florida)

GAME DAY HEROES

ABOVE, CLOCKWISE FROM LEFT
"Slingin'" Sammy Baugh targets the camera in this 1936 photograph. Playing out of the single wing, the Texas Christian tailback (1934—36) was a two-time All-American and one of the first great passers in college football (completing 274 of 599 passes). Baugh was also one of the greatest punters of his time (8,108 yards on 198 punts) and an outstanding defensive back.

Frank Sinkwich of Georgia bursts through the Tulane defense in this 1942 game, which the Bulldogs won 40—0. Sinkwich, who was nicknamed "Fireball Frankie," was a triple-threat tailback and led the nation in rushing in 1941 with 1,103 yards, and in to-

tal offense in 1942, gaining 2,187 yards. He led the Bulldogs to victories in the Orange Bowl, 1942, over TCU, and the Rose Bowl, 1943, defeating UCLA.

Georgia All-American Charlie Trippi gets a little attention from trainer "Squab" Jones after a 66-yard touchdown run against Georgia Tech in 1946. The 35—7 win that day clinched an invitation for the Bulldogs to the Sugar Bowl, where they defeated North Carolina to end a perfect 10-0-0 season. Trippi, who played for Georgia in 1942 and 1945—46, was a great running back and one of the best safeties in the game, as well as a fine punter. Trippi won the Maxwell Award in 1946 and was runner-up to Army's Glenn Davis for the Heisman.

Florida's All-American quarterback Steve Spurrier unloads here against Missouri in the 1966 Sugar Bowl, a game in which he set a bowl record with 27 completions, although the Gators lost that day 20—18. The next season Spurrier became the sixth quarterback to win the Heisman Trophy. In his three years at Florida (1964—66), Spurrier completed 392 of 692 passes for 4,848 yards and 36 touchdowns. He also had a career punting average of 40.3 yards.

Billy Cannon of Louisiana State finds a hole in the Mississippi defense in this 1959 game, which LSU won 7—3. Cannon starred for the Tigers from 1957 to 1959, the two-time All-American halfback rushing for 1,867 yards and scoring 154 points, and was a

feared kick returner. Cannon won the 1959 Heisman Trophy and after an illustrious career in the American Football League, pursued a career in dentistry.

SMU's Doak Walker gathers in a pass in this game against Texas. Only five-foot-eleven inches and 170 pounds, Walker was a giant in the eyes of football fans in Texas. As a 19-year-old freshman in 1945 he was Southeastern All-Conference; over his career, which extended to 1949, the versatile halfback gained for the Mustangs 3,582 yards in total offense (1,928 rushing, 1,654 passing, including 38 rushing touchdowns and 14 passing). "The Doaker," as he was called, won the Heisman Trophy in 1948.

Anthony Davis (USC)

Johnny Rodgers (Nebraska)

Tony Dorsett (Pittsburgh)

Joe Montana (Notre Dame)

Kordell Stewart (Colorado)

ABOVE, CLOCKWISE FROM LEFT
Southern Cal's Anthony Davis streaks toward one of the six touchdowns he scored against Notre Dame in 1972, which included kickoff returns of 97 and 96 yards, leading the Trojans to a 45—23 victory. In his career (1972—74) Davis earned a place among the long line of great USC running backs, which included Frank Gifford, O. J. Simpson, Charles White, and Marcus Allen, among others. He was runner-up to Ohio State's Archie Griffin for the Heisman Trophy in 1974.

One of the game's most electrifying runners, Johnny Rodgers slashes through the Notre Dame defense for a Nebraska touchdown in the 1973 Orange Bowl. This was one of four touchdowns Rodgers scored that evening, an Orange Bowl record, in leading the Cornhuskers to a 40—6 victory. In his three-year career (1970—72), Rodgers broke or tied four NCAA records and set 28 Nebraska marks. A two-time consensus All-American, he was the Heisman Trophy winner for 1972; he also led the Cornhuskers to three consecutive Orange Bowl wins (over LSU in 1971, Alabama in 1972, Notre Dame in 1973).

All-American Tony Dorsett had a record-breaking day carrying the ball for Pittsburgh in this 1975 game against Notre Dame, gaining 303 yards. Chasing him is another All-American, Notre Dame defensive end Ross Browner (89). As a freshman, Dorsett was the nation's second leading rusher with 1,586 yards; when he left Pitt four years later he held every school rushing record. He was awarded the Heisman Trophy for 1976.

Colorado's Kordell Stewart unleashes a 64-yard Hail Mary pass as time expires in this 1994 game against Michigan. Moments later a helmetless Shay Davis (22), who caught Stewart's pass to give Colorado a 27—26 win over the Wolverines, is about to embrace his battery-mate as other jubilant Buffalo players celebrate in the end zone.

Joe Montana throws for Notre Dame in the 1979 Cotton Bowl against Houston. Split end Kris Haines catches it in the end zone with only seconds remaining, tying the game 34—34; moments later the Irish won it with the point after touchdown.

PREMIER ALL-AMERICANS

The first All-America team was selected in 1889 by Caspar Whitney and Walter Camp and published in a journal called The Week's Sport. Those first honorees:

POSITION	PLAYER	SCHOOL
E	Amos Alonzo Stagg	Yale
E	Arthur Cumnock	Harvard
T	Hector Cowan	Princeton
T	Charles Gill	Yale
G	Pudge Heffelfinger	Yale
G	Jesse Riggs	Princeton
C	William George	Princeton
B	Edgar Allan Poe	Princeton
B	Roscoe Channing	Princeton
B	Knowlton Ames	Princeton
B	James Lee	Harvard

Pudge Heffelfinger, one of the greatest of the early players, was a guard on Yale teams from 1888 to 1891. Best known for his ferocious assaults on the lead man in the "Flying Wedge," the most popular offensive tactic of the time, he was a member of Walter Camp's first All-American team in 1889. Heffelfinger is also acknowledged as the first professional football player after he received $500 for playing in a game in Pittsburgh the year after he graduated from Yale.

THE FIRST LEGEND: JIM THORPE

His Indian name was *Wa-Tho-Huk*, which translates "Bright Path," but to the world he was known as Jim Thorpe, and he was among the first acknowledged sports legends in America. He made his athletic debut when he took to the football field in 1907 for Carlisle, a school for American Indians in Pennsylvania with an enrollment then of about 250, to play for the already legendary Glenn "Pop" Warner. He would go on to stardom as an Olympic gold medalist in track and field and as a major league baseball player, but in the game of college football in the early years of the twentieth century he inscribed his first mark.

Thorpe was of Sac and Fox heritage, with a little Irish and Welsh blood thrown in, born in a one-room cabin in Prague, Oklahoma, in 1888. He stood six foot tall (give or take an inch or two on either side, depending on who was describing him) and weighed between 175 and 180 pounds during his playing days at Carlisle, and by 1911 (he had returned home to Oklahoma in the spring of 1909, but was coaxed back by Warner a year later) had established himself, with his wonderful combination of speed and power, as the most punishing running back the game had yet seen. He was a quintuple threat: ball-carrier, passer, kicker, savage blocker, and brutal tackler.

In 1911, tiny Carlisle, with Thorpe starring, took on the giants of the era, defeating teams like Penn, Georgetown, Harvard, and Pittsburgh, losing only to Syracuse. In the summer of 1912, Thorpe represented the United States in the Olympic Games held in Stockholm, Sweden, where he won gold medals in track and field's two most demanding events, the pentathlon and decathlon. Returning to Carlisle for the 1912 football season, Thorpe led the Indians to 12 wins again against much larger schools while losing to only one and tying another. John Heisman observed in an article for *Collier's* magazine a number of years later: "At Carlisle in 1912, that Indian scored twenty-five touchdowns [a total of] 198 points. No player has equaled that. Jim had everything. He was a star punter, a star drop kicker, a star passer. At blocking and end running certainly we've not produced his master."

Against Harvard that year, Thorpe drop-kicked four field goals, including a 48-yarder, and ran for a touchdown to give Carlisle an 18–15 victory; in the Indian's win over Penn he had touchdown runs of 60, 75, and 85 yards. But the biggest triumph that year occurred at West Point where Carlisle, a con-

Jim Thorpe, the first true college football legend, played for Pop Warner at the Carlisle Indian School in Pennsylvania in 1908 and 1911-1912. A halfback, he won All-America honors in both 1911 and 1912, the latter year single-handedly overwhelming opponents by scoring 198 points, including 25 touchdowns.

siderable underdog, traveled to take on the Army cadets, a team renowned for its impregnable defense. As reported the next day in the *New York Times*, "Standing out resplendent in a galaxy of Indian stars was Jim Thorpe, recently crowned the athletic marvel of the age [referring to his performance at the Olympics]. The big Indian captain added more lustre to his already brilliant record, and at times the game itself was almost forgotten while the spectators gazed on Thorpe, the individual, to wonder at his prowess. . . . He simply ran wild while the Cadets tried in vain to stop his progress. It was like trying to to clutch a shadow." Pop Warner's Carlisle team, behind the dazzling performance of Thorpe, won that day 27–6, the most points scored on Army's vaunted defense since Harvard tallied 29 back in 1900.

Jim Thorpe left Carlisle after the 1912 academic year. He played professional football for the Canton Bulldogs and various other early pro teams, and major league baseball for the New York Giants (under legendary manager John McGraw), Cincinnati Reds, and Boston Braves. The first true legend, Thorpe, in 1950, was selected in an Associated Press poll as the greatest male athlete of the first half of the twentieth century; fifty years later he was honored as ABC's Wide World of Sports Athlete of the Century.

Thorpe Defined

After awarding Jim Thorpe gold medals in the 1912 Olympic Games for his victories in the pentathlon and decathlon, King Gustavus of Sweden said: "You, sir, are the greatest athlete in the world."

To which Thorpe famously, if apocryphally, responded, "Thanks, King."

THE TWO SIDES OF THE GIPPER

There really isn't any competition for the title of the most famous locker room pep talk of all time; it is Knute Rockne's halftime tearjerker during the Notre Dame–Army game of 1928, associated forever with the urging: "Win one for the Gipper." Paul Gallico and Grantland Rice, two of America's greatest sportswriters, however, had the legendary halfback pocketed in different areas of their memory banks.

Rice immortalized George Gipp as the lead in a melodrama. He wrote in 1928 of sitting with Knute Rockne the night before the game with favored Army, "sipping 'Tennessee milk' and watching the rest of the world go to hell." Rice told the story this way:

That evening, sitting by the fire, Rock said he expected to be up against it—but good, next day.

"You recall Gipp," said Rock. "He died—practically in my arms—eight years ago next month. He's been gone a long time but I may have to use him again tomorrow.

"You saw Gipp on one of his better days—against Army in 1920," continued Rock—not in that staccato voice but in a quiet, hushed tone. "He fell sick later that same season. In our final game against Northwestern, at Evanston, he climbed out of bed to make the trip. I used him

One of the very few photos of George Gipp in action, the Notre Dame star halfback is captured here on one of his patented breakaway runs. Gipp played for the Fighting Irish in 1917 and 1919–20, and was as famous for his off-field carousing as he was for his on-field heroics. In his freshman year, Gipp drop-kicked a 62-yard field goal, and his career rushing record of 2,341 yards was not broken until 1978.

very little that day. We were away and winging—the final was 33 to 7. But in the last quarter the fans chanted Gipp's name so loud and long that I finally sent him in for a few plays—on that ice-covered field with the wind off Lake Michigan cutting us all to the bone. I got him out of there, quick; but after returning to school with a raging fever, Gipp went back to his sickbed. He never got up. Pneumonia had him backed to his own goal line. He lived barely two weeks. Shortly before he went, Father Pat Haggerty baptized him into the church. After the little ceremony, I sat with him on his bed. His face seemed thinner than the Communion wafer he'd just taken—and just as white . . . but his forehead was strangely cool.

"Gipp looked up at me and after a moment, he said, 'Rock, I know I'm going . . . but I'd like one last request . . . some day, Rock . . . some

time—when the going isn't so easy, when the odds are against us, ask a Notre Dame team to win a game for me, for the Gipper. I don't know where I'll be then, Rock, but I'll know about it and I'll be happy.'

"A moment later Gipp was gone. Grant, I've never asked the boys to pull one out for the Gipp. Tomorrow I might have to."

The following day that '28 Army–Notre Dame game played, as always, to an overflow sell-out. At the half it was 0–0. The rest is history.

A sobbing band of Fighting Irish raced out for the third quarter. When Notre Dame lined up for the kickoff, I knew they were playing with a 12th man—George Gipp. . . .

Notre Dame carried that day, 12–6. Somewhere George Gipp must have been very happy.

Paul Gallico's George Gipp is an iconoclastic antihero. Gallico had heard the story of Gipp's famous deathbed plea, and he had a different slant on the Gipper's legend. Gallico wrote it this way:

The whole thing sounds apocryphal, but quite classical for our times and the kind of treacle we loved to swallow. Actually, the real deathbed story was quite different. Rockne, holding the boy's hand said, "It must be tough to go, George," to which Gipp replied unequivocally, "What's tough about it?"

What was not common currency was that George Gipp, in addition to being a brilliant football player, was a very bad little boy. He was everything that a Notre Dame college boy ought not to be, a womanizer, a pool shark, a card player, a gambler, and a drunk, and Rockne was attached to him. And with this love for a sinner who could deliver the goods on the football field, any phoniness in Rockne's morality falls away and he stands exposed to us as a genuine human being.

How the great Gipp regarded [Rockne's] dressing room orations was told to me privately by a contemporary of those days when, in 1920, Rockne found himself ten points behind Indiana at the half, after an undefeated season in 1919.

The coach went into his locker room oration and was in full swing when he noticed that Gipp was not anywhere around. He finally located him standing in a doorway, leaning against the sill, looking bored as he flicked cigarette ashes outside.

Rock was speechless but the Gipper said, "Aw, these pep talks are O.K., Rock, I guess, but I got two hundred bucks bet on this game and if you think I'm lying down out there, you're crazy"

It was one of the few times when Knute Rockne was struck dumb. In the second half Gipper went out, scored two touchdowns, and

drop-kicked the [extra] points. His two hundred dollars was safe.

But the story of how Gipp was able to place a wager, an act which today would have gotten him disqualified not only from amateur but from professional football as well, is even better. He had "agents" who did his betting for him, and they reported that for the Indiana game at Bloomington, the gamblers wanted no part of Notre Dame or brother Gipp. The "agents" were planted in the local betting emporium where, the night before the game, a tall muffled figure with his overcoat collar turned up, marched in and shakily demanded a Bromo Seltzer, in those days a popular cure-all for hangover. He shivered, and with trembling fingers raised the glass to his lips, swallowed, coughed, gagged, and finally after downing it, staggered out of the door. Someone asked, "Who the hell was that wreck?"

Here, an "agent" volunteered the reply, "Why, don't you know? That's George Gipp. He's been like that just about all week. I doubt if he'll get into the game at all tomorrow. It won't even be a contest without him."

The whole thing, of course, was an act. Gipp hadn't had a drop, got his bet down, and collected the money.

The Gipper could make a living out of pool room hustling and did. He bet heavy sums of money on games in which he played and spent more time carousing in off-limit South Bend hangouts and saloons, and card-playing, and eventually he was expelled from Notre Dame. But upon Rockne's plea and the passing of a stiff oral examination, he was readmitted.

And so the legend of the Gipper runs on, its direction depending, of course, on who is telling the story.

GRANGE'S GREAT DAY

Michigan had not lost a game in three years when Fielding Yost brought his Wolverines to Champaign, Illinois, to face Bob Zuppke's Illini in 1924. It was a special day at Illinois, the dedication of their brand-new stadium, and 66,609 fans jammed it for the festivities.

The experience of a new stadium was nothing, however, in comparison to the desire to watch the Illini's marvelous halfback Harold "Red" Grange run with the football. Perhaps he could bring down mighty Michigan, which had not tasted defeat since 1921.

Harold "Red" Grange of Illinois. On his great day against Michigan in 1924, the Galloping Ghost scored five touchdowns—four in the first quarter—and gained 402 yards carrying the ball. He also completed six passes, one for a touchdown. Illinois crushed the Wolverines that day 39–14.

Fielding Yost, however, was unimpressed. "All Grange can do is run," he said with a note of condescension. Just how well he could run, Yost found out to his ultimate dismay shortly after the game got underway. Warren Brown, who wrote for the *Chicago Herald-American* and was one of America's finest sportswriters of the 1920s, 1930s, and 1940s, captured the ambiance of that crisp October afternoon in 1924 in this remembrance:

The Wolverines would stop Grange! They'd knock him into the end zone seats the first time he carried the ball. He wasn't going to be running against Smackover Institute this time. Michigan went to Illinois for the game prepared to put him who was now known as the "Galloping Ghost" in his proper place. . . .

There was no blather about Michigan's fearing Illinois or Grange. No phony psychological gloom designed to build up the enemy that he might be torn down easier.

There was to be no question of keeping the ball away from Grange. Michigan's kicker was instructed to aim one at him, first chance that came along. He was to be stopped right away.

So Michigan kicked to Grange almost as the game began. The ball soared high and far down the field, five yards from the Illini goal, where it settled into Grange's grasp. Red was away from his mark like a trained sprinter at the starter's gun. The Michigan men were closing in on him from every angle. Many of them were cut down by Illini blockers. The others the Ghost sidestepped, dodged, or otherwise evaded, and in less time than it takes to read it he was in the clear and racing, unstoppable, for the Michigan goal. Six points for Grange before you could say Fielding Yost, and a ninety-five yard run through the entire Michigan team.

Well, after all, that might happen to anybody. No one ever said that Grange couldn't run fast, or that Zup's blockers didn't know their stuff. But let's see what the guy will do next time. . . .

Grange shortly thereafter took off around right end and raced 67 yards for a score. Just minutes later he streaked 55 yards for still another, and then 44 for his fourth touchdown of the first quarter.

I'll give Michigan credit for one thing. Its men and its coaches were stubborn. They still wanted to see what Grange would do once he was in the grasp of an opponent.

But Coach Zuppke was a merciful man. After twelve minutes and twenty-four points, he took Grange from the game, amid the greatest ovation I have ever heard given a football player on any field.

Grange returned to score one more touchdown later in the game. At day's end, he had accounted for all of the Illini's touchdowns, running for five and throwing a pass for the sixth. He gained 402 yards in the 21 times he carried the ball and completed six passes, one for a touchdown. It was, in the words of Amos Alonzo Stagg, "the most spectacular single-handed performance ever delivered in a major game."

Grange Lyricized

Grantland Rice penned this poetic description of the man he named the "Galloping Ghost":

A streak of fire, a breath of flame,
Eluding all who reach and clutch;
A gray ghost thrown into the game
That rival hands may never touch;
A rubber bounding, blasting soul
Whose destination is the goal — Red Grange of Illinois!

THE FOUR HORSEMEN

"Outlined against a blue-gray October sky, the Four Horsemen rode again," Grantland Rice wrote in the *New York Herald Tribune* after Notre Dame defeated Army in 1924. "In dramatic lore they are known as famine, pestilence, destruction and death. These are only aliases. Their real names are: Stuhldreyer, Miller, Crowley, and Layden. They formed the crest of the South Bend cyclone before which another fighting Army team was swept over the precipice at the Polo Grounds this afternoon as 55,000 spectators peered down upon the bewildered panorama spread out upon the green plain below."

Seeing the publicity potential from this poetic tribute, Knute Rockne's student publicity aide, a youngster named George Strickler (who later would become sports editor of the *Chicago Tribune*), photographed the four backs in their uniforms on four plow horses he dredged up from a nearby farm.

The wire services picked up the photo, and soon the Four Horsemen were immortalized as the most famous backfield in the history of college football. It helped, of course, that Notre Dame went on to win the national championship that year and that three of the Four Horsemen were consensus All-Americans (Miller probably would have made it also had Red Grange not been playing for Illinois that year).

The four young men who personified the stalkers from the Apocalypse were small even by the football standards of the 1920s—none weighed more than 162 pounds—but they were molded by Rockne into an explosive backfield that proved to be

FACING PAGE
Knute Rockne looks upon his most famous backfield, "The Four Horsemen," in 1924. From the left: Don Miller, Elmer Layden, Harry Stuhldreyer, and Jim Crowley.

unstoppable, destroying ten consecutive opponents by the collective score of 285–54, including a 27–10 demolition of Stanford in the Rose Bowl that year.

Harry Stuhldreyer, five-foot-seven and 151 pounds, came from Massillon, Ohio, and as quarterback was the field leader. The best blocker of the four, Stuhldreyer was also a quick, shifty runner and the team's chief passer that year (he completed 25 of 33 for 471 yards and 4 touchdowns). After graduating he played a year of pro ball in 1926 with the Brooklyn franchise in the short-lived American Football League, then coached at Villanova for twelve years and Wisconsin for eleven after that. Later he became an executive of the U.S. Steel Corporation.

Left halfback Jim Crowley came down from Green Bay, Wisconsin, and acquired the nickname "Sleepy Jim" because of his drowsy appearance. At five-foot-eleven, 158 pounds, he was far from a lethargic runner and was Notre Dame's leading scorer that year with 71 points (9 touchdowns, 17 extra points). Crowley was an assistant at Georgia before taking the head coaching job at Michigan State in 1929; he moved to Fordham in 1933, where he developed one of college football's most heralded defensive lines, the "Seven Blocks of Granite," which featured Alex Wojciechowicz and Vince Lombardi. After service in the Navy during the war, Crowley served first as commissioner of a new pro league, the All-American Football Conference, and later as a member of it, as coach and part owner of the Chicago Rockets. He then left football to pursue a business career.

Right halfback Don Miller, five-foot-eleven, 160 pounds, was the team's most dangerous open-field runner, and his career rushing average of 6.8 yards a carry is still a Notre Dame record. From Defiance, Ohio, he was elected Notre Dame's class president his senior year. After college, Miller went to law school, then coached at Ohio State and Georgia Tech before being appointed U.S. district attorney for northern Ohio by President Franklin Roosevelt.

Fullback Elmer Layden stood six feet tall, weighed 162 pounds, and was considered the fastest of the four and the best defensive back on the team. From Davenport, Iowa, Layden proved to be the hero of the 1925 Rose Bowl game, scoring three touchdowns, two on interception returns of 78 and 70 yards. Layden coached first at Columbia (now Loras) College in Dubuque, Iowa, then at Duquesne, before taking over the head coaching duties at his alma mater in 1934. He led Notre Dame through the 1940 season, then resigned to take the job of commissioner of the National Football League, where he served through 1946. After that he went into business with the General American Transportation Company in Chicago.

The Four Horsemen stands as football's most famous nickname. Don Miller summed it up later in talking with Rice. "Granny," he said, "Rock put us together in the same backfield but the day you wrote us up as the Four Horsemen, you confirmed an immortality on us that gold could never buy. Let's face it. We were good, sure. But we'd have been just as dead two years after graduation as any other backfield if you hadn't painted that tag line on us. It's twenty-nine years since we played. Each year we run faster, block better, score more TDs than ever! The older we are, the younger we become—in legend . . . [it] has meant more to each of us in associations, warmth, friendship and revenue, than you'll ever know."

SCHOLAR ATHLETE

Johnny Blood McNally, who played for St. John's of Minnesota and had a very brief stint at Notre Dame in the early 1920s before going on to stardom as a pro, felt his contribution to the Fighting Irish was more academic than athletic. He tells it this way:

> I got in some trouble around St. Patrick's Day, some pretty good celebrating for the saintly Irishman, and then went AWOL. They didn't take to it that well and, as I used to call it, I became a double-dipped dropout at Notre Dame. I'd tried out for football while I was there. Knute Rockne was the coach and they had the Four Horsemen on the varsity that year. I ended up on the freshman team because it was my first year of eligibility there, even though I'd played at St. John's before. But I didn't do anything on the football field at Notre Dame. I always like to say that my one contribution to Notre Dame football was that I used to write Harry Stuhldreyer's English poetry papers for him.

THE BRONK

No football name personified raw power more than Bronko Nagurski, who starred for Minnesota in the late 1920s as both a fullback and a tackle on defense. He was big: six-foot-four, 230 to 240 pounds of solid muscle, at a time when a big lineman might tip the scales at 200 pounds; an incredible mixture of size, strength, speed, and agility. In his time, the Bronk was to college football what the Sherman tank became to the U.S. Army.

His coach at the University of Minnesota, Clarence Spears, often told this story of how he recruited the Bronk. "I went up to International Falls to look at another kid named Smith who was supposed to be a good prospect. Just outside of town I saw this young, high-school-age boy in a field pushing a plow. There was no horse or anything else, just this kid pushing the plow. I asked him where I could find the Smith kid, and the other boy—who happened to be Bronko—just picked up the plow and pointed it in the direction. I decided then and there to get the kid with the plow for Minnesota."

Bronko Nagurski, the most powerful back of his time (and certainly one of the most punishing tacklers), played for Minnesota from 1927 to 1929, fullback on offense, tackle on defense. "He's the only man I've ever seen who runs his own interference," George Halas once said of Nagurski.

JIM BROWN'S RECORD DAY

The year was 1956. Oklahoma was at the height of its dynasty under Bud Wilkinson; the Ivy League where the deepest roots of college football were implanted was finally organized into an athletic conference; Paul Hornung became the first (and only) Heisman Trophy winner to come from a school with a losing record (Notre Dame won only 2 of 10 games). And at Syracuse that year, another running back by the name of Jim Brown astounded the college football world on a Saturday afternoon in mid-November.

Jimmy Brown, as he was better known in college days, ended his regular season college career on a note unparalleled in the history of the game. Number 44 had been carrying the ball and booting extra points for the Orangemen since 1954, and by his senior year Brown was a consensus All-American.

In the last game of the season, Syracuse, in the running for a bowl bid, was entertaining Colgate on a cold, gray afternoon at what was then known as Archbold Stadium. A crowd of 39,701, including New York Governor Averell Harriman, turned out for the game. Early in the first period, Brown set the tone for the day when he burst in from the 1-yard line, then kicked the extra point to give Syracuse a 7–0 lead. By halftime, he had scored another three

touchdowns—on 15-, 50-, and 8-yard runs—and booted two more extra points, prompting the announcement over the public address system: "The score is now Brown 27, Colgate 7."

In the second half, he was equally destructive, scoring two touchdowns and converting four extra points. Brown left the game in the fourth period with Syracuse ahead 55–7. He had contributed a total of 43 points, six touchdowns, and seven extra points, a new NCAA scoring record, eclipsing the mark set by Arnold "Showboat" Boykin of Mississippi in 1951, and a record that would stand until 1990.

Brown accounted for 197 yards rushing on 22 carries that day, and brought his season total of rushing yards to 986, both new Syracuse records. The final score was Syracuse 61, Colgate 7 . . . or, if you will, Brown 43, Colgate 7.

As a result, Syracuse did get an invitation to the Cotton Bowl that year (where they lost on New Year's Day to TCU 28–27 despite Brown's three touchdowns and three conversions), after which Jim Brown went on to a legendary NFL career.

FLUTIE'S GREAT MOMENT

It was a game specially arranged for national television and staged at the Orange Bowl on Thanksgiving weekend 1984, Boston College versus Miami (Florida), appropriately billed as the "Battle of the Quarterbacks." A meeting of Mutt and Jeff—Doug Flutie, the five-foot-nine-and-three-quarter-inch quarterback of Boston College, was going against his counterpart from Miami, six-foot-five-inch Bernie Kosar.

Seldom in the annals of college football have two passers as spectacular as these taken the field during the same 60 minutes and fared so well. It was a game that was all offense; more precisely, aerial warfare. When it was over, Flutie and Kosar had thrown the ball 84 times for a total of 919 yards. Total offensive yardage for the day was 1,282 yards, surprisingly not an NCAA record (Arizona State and Stanford had racked up 1,436 in 1981). A total of 92 points were scored. And the winner was decided on the momentous last play of the game.

Flutie, a senior who clinched the Heisman Trophy with this performance, completed his first 11 passes in a row, guiding the Boston College Eagles to a 14–0 lead in the first quarter over the team that, the year before, had snagged the national championship.

Doug Flutie celebrates after the Boston College quarterback threw one of the most famous Hail Mary passes in college football history to defeat Miami in 1984, 47–45. Lifting Flutie in triumph is his brother Darren.

Kosar, undismayed, came out in the second quarter and tossed 11 consecutive completions, guiding the team to three touchdowns to put the Hurricanes right back into the ball game. But Flutie was far from idle, and his passing and some strong Eagle rushes enabled BC to post another two touchdowns. The score at the half: Boston College 28, Miami 21.

At the start of the second half, Kosar launched a drive from Miami's own 4-yard line that stormed the length of the field, ending when fullback Melvin Bratton smashed in from the 2 for the touchdown, with the conversion evening the score.

Each team kicked a field goal later in the period. Then BC booted another to give them a 34–31 edge in the fourth quarter. Miami, however, bounced right back with, surprise of surprises, a breakaway 52-yard touchdown run by Bratton, giving Miami its first lead of the game 38–34.

Flutie went right to work, starting at BC's 18-yard line. With just under 4 minutes remaining, he had driven the Eagles to the Hurricanes' 1-yard line. Fullback Steve Strachan vaulted over the Miami defense and plopped into the end zone to regain the lead for Boston College 41–38.

There were two and a half minutes remaining when the Hurricanes, after the kickoff, were stranded on their own 10. It was third and a distant 19 yards for the first down. Kosar dropped back, but BC rushers converged on him at the Miami goal line. He scrambled, somehow got free, and tossed a little floater to Darryl Oliver, who raced 20 yards for the first down. With that catalyst and later a fourth-and-one conversion, Kosar moved the Hurricanes to the Eagle 1-yard line. Melvin Bratton got the call again and burst in for his fourth touchdown of the game. It was now Miami 45, Boston College 41.

There were only 28 seconds on the clock when Miami kicked off, but there was no movement in the aisles of the Orange Bowl, as the more than 30,000 wildly entertained fans stood together to see what might happen next. And they were rewarded.

Using up 22 precious seconds, Flutie got the Eagles out to their own 48-yard line. With 6 seconds left, he called in the huddle for a "Flood Tip," a desperation play, a Hail Mary pass. Three wide receivers lined up to the right, their mission to race like hell down the field, get in the end zone, and, in the maelstrom, catch the ball.

Flutie took the snap and dropped back. There was only a two-man rush, but one of them got through. The diminutive quarterback sidestepped him and rolled out to his right. He was all the way back at his own 37-yard line and still under pressure when he set himself and hurled the ball toward Miami's end zone. The ball traveled 64 yards in the air, just over the hands of three Miami defenders who leaped in unison, banged into each other, but did not touch the ball. And just behind them was Flutie's roommate, wide receiver Gerard Phelan, who caught the ball just before falling to the turf. For the 12th time that afternoon, the referee reached for the sky to signal a touchdown.

As the *New York Times* reported, it was "the last spectacular play of a spectacular game." Or, as described in *Sports Illustrated*, "one wildly wonderful play, punctuating a wildly wonderful game."

The final score was 47–45, and Boston College was triumphant in one of the most pyrotechnical games in college football history. As for the aerial warfare: Flutie had thrown 34 completions in 46 attempts for 472 yards, while Kosar completed 25 of 38 passes for 447 yards, but it is that one desperate pass for which the game will always be remembered.

> "Then strip, lads, and to it, though sharp be the weather,
> And if, by mischance, you should happen to fall,
> There are worse things in life than a tumble on heather,
> And life is itself but a game at football.

SIR WALTER SCOTT,
The Lord of the Isles, "Song," 1815

2

SEASONS OF CHANGE
COLLEGE FOOTBALL EVOLVES

The origin of the sport that eventually evolved into what we know as football can never be precisely determined. But people likely started playing an ancestral version somewhere between the time they came out of their caves and the age when they began building things like pyramids and Parthenons.

Hieroglyphic records show a game like soccer was played in ancient Egypt and that it had something to do with fertility rites, although the exact relationship has never been fully ascertained. The Chinese, it is also recorded, began playing a similar game somewhere around 300 B.C., using a ball stuffed with hair.

In ancient Greece, the game was a popular diversion, written of and played everywhere from Athens to Sparta. Their game was called *harpaston* ("hand ball") and involved two teams, each trying to move a ball-like object across a goal line by kicking or throwing it. The Romans, who conquered the Greeks in the second century before Christ, adopted the game and the name, Latinizing it to *harpastum*.

It is generally believed that marauding Roman legions spread the game through Europe and to the British Isles (note: many years later, marauding British soccer fans returned the favor). In England, it acquired the name "mellay," a predecessor to the term "melee." It was appropriate because the game as it was played then was riotous and violent, a mob-action scene with no visible restraints or rules of conduct. Legend has it that the first ball used in an English football game was actually the head of a Danish pirate.

Both in Great Britain and on continental Europe the game thrived. Mellays eventually became part of medieval festivals, taking place alongside such activities as jousting and other knightly pursuits. It became a tradition at the Roman-founded village of Chester—from the Latin *castra*, for camp—in England on Shrove Tuesday, commemorating a day long past when the people of the area had formed a great wedge and driven the legionnaires out of the village. So, on the day before the formal start of Lent, all work was halted and the townsmen of Chester and the farmers from the surrounding area met on an improvised field of play next to the village's common hall. The event soon became part of the pre-Lenten celebrations in other English towns, which would take on one another in the game, which still resembled a raucous mix of kickball and hand-to-hand combat. The ball that was used in those days was ordinarily the inflated bladder of a pig, but later, village shoemakers produced balls from hides.

As time passed and pressure was applied by governments and churches to make the game more civilized, it gradually emerged from mayhem to sport and by the eighteenth century it vaguely resembled the modern version of soccer. It became popular as an intramural activity at most of the secondary schools, from the famous ones like Eton and Harrow to the lesser-known ones in rural England. Up to that time the game had mostly been the domain of commoners, and was frowned on as undignified by the upper classes. But with its acceptance on the greens of academe, football gained respectability in England. There were no rules, however, nor any governing body, and the game itself varied considerably from campus to campus. The only hard-line rule was that the ball could not be carried in the hands or arms. But even that tacit regulation would eventually fall.

The iconoclast responsible for it was a youngster named William Webb Ellis, a student at the Rugby secondary school. The story is told that one day in 1823 in the closing moments of a game of football, the end of which was signaled by the tolling of the five o'clock bell in the school tower, Ellis caught a long kick and in some flight of mad desperation took off running with the ball toward the opposing team's goal.

At first, everyone was stunned at such a breach of tradition, but then players began racing to stop him and knock him down before he could reach the goal line. The would-be tacklers never did bring down the revolutionary running back, it is told, although the score was not allowed.

The sport that was to become known as rugby was not born on the spot as the five o'clock bell rang out that afternoon. But afterward, the idea of running with the ball was discussed frequently around the school and in a while became part of the football games that were played there; and, of course, the school imparted its name to the new game.

In the middle of the nineteenth century, soccer and rugby moved up to the university level in England, and in the cities independent clubs were formed to field teams and compete with each other. From these developments emerged the first sets of

Noteworthy Points from *Beadle's Dime Book of Cricket and Football* (1866)

Technical Terms Used in Football (Selected)

Free Kick—The privilege of kicking the ball in such a manner as the kicker may think fit.

Hacking is kicking an adversary on the front of the leg, below the knee.

Tripping is throwing an adversary by the use of the legs, and without hacking or charging.

Laws of the Game (Selected)

#9. If a player make a *fair catch*, he shall be entitled to a free kick, provided he claim it by making a mark with his heel; and in order to take such a kick, he may go as far back as he pleases, and no player on the opposite side shall advance behind his mark until he has kicked.

#14. No player is to wear projecting nails, iron plates, or gutta-percha soles or heels to his boots or shoes.

With regard to the ball. Opinions are divided between the claims of the bladder confined in a leather bag, and the stronger India-rubber sphere sold in the shops: we incline to the latter. The ball should not be too large nor too light, as in windy weather too large a ball is a nuisance, and the kick can not be fairly and effectually made.

The Eton Game

The players close up, each side forming a semicircle, with their strongest men in front. They meet each other the ball being in the center of these, and then push, kick, and struggle, till the weaker side gives way and goes down, the other side falling on the top of them, and the ball being somewhere beneath. In this position they carry on the battle, and continue to writhe and struggle, trying on the one side to creep through the goal and drag the ball with them, on the other to drive it away. These struggles sometimes continue for ten minutes. Players get exhausted, and creep out; wipe the beads of perspiration from their faces; and plunge down again with renewed vigor.

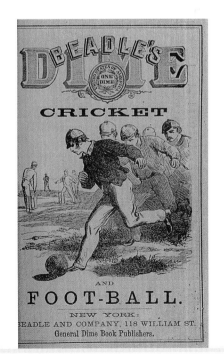

BEADLE'S DIME CRICKET AND FOOT-BALL.

NEW YORK:
BEADLE AND COMPANY, 118 WILLIAM ST.
General Dime Book Publishers.

organized rules for the games. In October 1863, a set of laws for the soccerlike game of football was written and published at Cambridge. That same year, a similar code of rules was drawn up by representatives of various independent clubs at a meeting at the Freemasons Tavern in London. Shortly thereafter the two codes were combined into a uniform "Rules of the London Football Association" (which, incidentally, is how the term "association football" became synonymous with soccer).

Those clubs and university groups that preferred to play the form of football that allowed running with the ball, which was becoming increasingly popular in the larger cities like London, Manchester, and Liverpool, then took to organizing themselves. The first association of note was the Oxford University Rugby

The First College Game: Rutgers vs. Princeton

John W. Herbert of the Rutgers class of 1872 and a member of the Rutgers team that participated in the first intercollegiate football game in the United States, played in 1869, wrote this account many years afterward (reprinted from the football program for the 1968 Cornell–Rutgers game):

The game was called at 3 o'clock and started with a free kick-off from the tee, the same as now. It was played on the commons (where the Rutgers gymnasium now stands). On the arrival of the players, a few minutes before the game was called, they laid aside their hats, coats and vests. Neither team was in uniform, although some Rutgers players wore scarlet stocking-caps.

The players lined up on each side, the organization of the twenty-five being the same on both sides. Two men were selected by each team to play immediately in front of the opponent's goal and were known as captains of the enemy's goal.

The remainder of each team was divided into two sections. The players in one section were assigned to certain tracts of the field which they were to cover and not to leave. They were known as "fielders." The other section was detailed to follow the ball up and down the field. These latter players were called "bulldogs." They were easily recognizable in the evolution of the game as the forerunners of the modern rush line. I played in this division as I was a good wrestler and fleet of foot.

The toss of the coin for advantage gave Princeton the ball and

Rutgers the wind. Amid a hush of expectancy among the spectators Princeton "bucked" or kicked the ball, but the kick was bad and the ball glanced to one side.

Parke H. Davis in *Football, the American Intercollegiate Game*, then describes the game as follows:

The light, agile Rutgers men pounced upon it like hounds and by driving it by short kicks and dribbles, the other players surrounding the ball and not permitting a Princeton man to get near it, quickly and craftily forced it down to Old Nassau's goal, where the captains of

Rutgers—Princeton game, 1869: An artist's rendering of the historic Rutgers—Princeton football game of 1869, considered to be the first intercollegiate football game played in America. Princeton challenged Rutgers and the two teams met on a field in New Brunswick, New Jersey, on November 6. More a game of soccer than the football we know today, Rutgers prevailed 6 goals to 4.

Football Club, which was founded in 1869. Two years later representatives of various clubs and three universities met at the Pall Mall restaurant in London and formed the Rugby Football Union, drafting bylaws and drawing up a uniform set of rules.

Both soccer and rugby, now organized, flourished in Great Britain. The particulars of soccer were then brought to America by early colonists, and those of rugby by the immigrants of the mid-nineteenth century. Elements from the two games were gradually blended and out of the matrix came a new and distinct sport, American football, which would grow from casual intramural games on the malls of the Eastern colleges in the mid-1850s to the complex and compelling sport played in the cavernous stadiums of today.

the enemy's goal were waiting and these two latter sent the ball between the posts amid great applause.

The first goal had been scored in five minutes of play. During the intermission, Captain Gummere (William S. Gummere, who later served as Chief Justice of the Supreme Court of New Jersey from 1901 until his death in 1932) instructed Michael (the late Jacob E. Michael, Princeton '71, who was to become Dean of the Faculty at the University of Maryland), a young giant of the Princeton 25, to break up Rutgers' massing around the ball. Sides were changed and Rutgers "bucked." In this period the game was fiercely contested. Time and time again Michael, or "Big Mike," charged into Rutgers' primitive mass play and scattered the players like a burst bundle of sticks. On one of these plays Princeton obtained the ball and by a long accurate kick scored the second goal.

The third goal or "game," as it was then called, went to Rutgers, and the fourth was kicked by Princeton.

"Big Mike" again bursting up a mass out of which Gummere gained possession of the ball and, with Princeton massed against him, easily dribbled the ball down and through the Rutgers goal posts, making the score once more a tie.

The fifth and sixth goals went to Rutgers, but the feature of this latter period of play in the memory of the players after the lapse of many years is awarded to "Big Mike" and Large (the late State Senator George H. Large of Flemington, a Rutgers player). Someone, by a random kick, had driven the ball to one side, where it rolled against the fence and stopped. Large led the pursuit for the ball, closely followed by Michael. They reached the fence, on which the students were perched, and, unable to check their momentum, in a tremendous impact struck the fence, which gave way with a crash, and over went its load of yelling students to the ground.

Every college probably has the humorous tradition of some player who has scored against his own team. The tradition of Rutgers dated from

this first game, for one of her players, whose identity is unknown, in the sixth period started to kick the ball between his own goal posts. The kick was blocked, but Princeton took advantage of the opportunity and soon made the goal. This turn of the game apparently disorganized Rutgers, for Princeton also scored the next goal after a few minutes of play, thus bringing the total up to four-all.

At this stage Rutgers resorted to that use of craft which has never failed to turn the tide of every close battle. Captain Leggett had noticed that Princeton obtained a great advantage from the taller stature of their men, which enabled them to reach above the others and bat the ball in the air in some advantageous direction. Rutgers was ordered to keep the ball close to the ground. Following this stratagem the Rutgers men determinedly kicked the ninth and tenth goals, thus winning the match six goals to four and with it the distinction of a victory in the first game of intercollegiate football played in the world.

1820

A form of association football (soccer) called "ballown" is played at Princeton.

MID-1800s

A new form of football, combining elements of soccer and rugby, is played at various colleges in the Northeastern United States but not on an intercollegiate basis. There are no uniform rules nor any set number of players on a team.

1860

Football is banned at Harvard as being too violent a sport. (The ban is lifted in 1871.)

1866

Beadle's Dime Book of Cricket and Football, the first book on American football, incorporating a definition of terms related to the sport and the "laws" of the game (as well as rules for betting on it), is published in New York City.

1869

Princeton challenges Rutgers to a football game. Played on November 6 in New Brunswick, New Jersey, it is considered the first intercollegiate football game to be played in the United States. Each team is allowed 25 players on the field, and it is agreed that the first team to score six goals will be declared the winner. Rutgers wins the game 6–4.

1873

Yale plays in the first international intercollegiate football game, defeating England's Eton, 2 goals to 1. The first formal rules for intercollegiate football are adopted at a meeting of representatives from Princeton, Yale, Rutgers, and Columbia, held in New York on October 19. Included among the rules:

- Scores can only be made by kicking or butting the ball with the head across the opponent's goal line and under the crossbar.
- Players cannot run with the ball.
- Passes can only be made laterally or backward.
- Tackling below the waist is prohibited.
- The field of play is to be 140 yards in length and 70 yards wide.
- There are to be two 45-minute periods of play.

Yale and Princeton meet in New Haven on November 15 for the first game played under the new set of rules. Princeton wins 3–0. The first intercollegiate football game in the South is played between Virginia Military Institute and Washington & Lee. Each squad fields 50 players.

1874

Harvard plays three games of football against McGill University of Canada, two in Cambridge and one in Montreal. The second of the three games is the first college game played under Rugby Union football rules by an American college. Running with the ball, which is oblong instead of round, is permitted and touchdowns are counted differently. The game ends in a scoreless tie. Also among the rugby rules is the provision for a free chance to kick a goal after having scored a touchdown, the equivalent of the modern extra point, although in 1874 it has a higher scoring value than the touchdown itself.

In the games with McGill, Harvard players wear sweaters and tie handkerchiefs around their heads to distinguish themselves from their opponents. Members of the McGill team wear white trousers, striped jerseys, and turbans.

1876

Representatives of Harvard and Yale meet at the Massasoit House, a hotel in Springfield, Massachusetts, to form the Intercollegiate Football Association. The rugby-type rules, which permit running with the ball, are formally adopted, and the round soccer-type ball is replaced by a more oval-shaped one.

Walter Camp is know as the "Father of American Football." A halfback at Yale (1876–79, 80–81, eligibility being what it was in those days), he is best remembered as the game's first true innovator: introducing rules, developing formations and strategies, and inaugurating and maintaining the All-America selections.

1879

The first intercollegiate game in the Midwest is played in the spring between the University of Michigan and Racine (Wisconsin) College at a baseball park in Chicago. Michigan wins, 1 goal and 1 touchdown to 0.

1880

Princeton is awarded a 1–0 victory over Columbia in the first forfeited game on record.

Walter Camp of Yale develops major rules changes that send American football on a path clearly divergent from that of rugby. Definite possession of the ball by one team is established, instead of the battle for possession after each play, which is the rule in rugby. The scrum line is made a line of scrimmage. However, there is no neutral zone between opposing lines at the line of scrimmage.

With definite possession of the ball as the prevailing mode, the position of quarterback is born and so named. (The terminology reflects the position of the backs from the line of scrimmage—in an I formation—quarterback, halfback, full-back.) The quarterback receives the ball from a holder who stands at the line of scrimmage and snaps the ball back with his foot.

Other rules changes include the reduction of the size of the playing field to 110 yards in length and 53 1/3 yards in width, and restricting the number of players on a side to 11.

1882

A system of downs is instituted, also by Walter Camp, with teams required to gain 5 yards in three downs or give up possession of the ball. Previously one team would control the ball for an entire period and the other team would have it for the second period. Now teams have to kick the ball to the opposing team on third down or turn over possession if the 5 yards is not made.

White lines at 5-yard intervals running the width of the field are required. As a result of the pattern, the playing field is called a "gridiron."

Camp's system of signals is adopted by the IFA Rules Committee. Usually coded words or phrases, the signals are shouted to the other players to tell them which play is to be run. (Camp may have used signals as early as 1880, and the University of Michigan may have used them in 1881.)

1883

At the now annual Rules Committee meeting, Walter Camp introduces and obtains enactment for a new numerical scoring system: 5 points for a goal kicked from the field during play, 4 for a goal on the free kick after a touchdown, 2 for a touchdown, and 1 for a safety.

1884

The "V-Trick," also known as the wedge, is used by Princeton in a game against Pennsylvania. At the kickoff of a game the two teams line up 10 yards apart. To put the ball in play, however, the kicker does not have to kick it 10 yards. With the V-Trick, the kicker merely nudges the ball forward, which sets it in play, and he maintains possession. His teammates quickly scramble to form a V-shaped wedge in front of him, providing interference as he advances the ball. The V-Trick is also used by Lehigh the same year.

The point value of a touchdown is raised to 4, and the goal on a free kick after the touchdown is lowered to 2 points.

continued on page 36

Father of the Game

Walter Chauncey Camp, a "townie" from New Haven, graduate of Hopkins Grammar School there, was seventeen years old when he walked onto the campus at Yale in 1876. A handsome, serious-looking young man, his face adorned with a full mustache and muttonchop whiskers, he stood just under six feet tall, weighed somewhere in the vicinity of 160 pounds, and was wiry, strong, fast, and very athletic. His plan was to finish undergraduate work, attend Yale's respected medical school, and then forge a career in the curative arts as a physician. But the game of football got in the way of that plan, and instead Camp, through his innovations and devotion to the game, became the true founding father of American football.

In the 1870s football was just becoming a popular diversion at colleges in the Eastern United States, played mostly as an intramural sport. The form of the game was a derivative from Europe of soccer, or on occasion, the more physical and violent game of rugby. In the four years before Camp's matriculation at Yale, the school had occasionally engaged in football games with other colleges like Rutgers, Princeton, Columbia, and Wesleyan, but they were random encounters.

In 1876, however, the sport suddenly took on the veneer, if not the substance, of formal organization with the creation of the Intercollegiate Football Association (IFA).

A call for volunteers came from Yale upperclassman Eugene Baker to flesh out a football team that he would be captain of, and Walter Camp was among the first to offer his manifold talents.

Camp earned a starting position as halfback his freshman year on the then 15-man Yale squad, and he quickly proved to be one of the most adroit players on the field. It was the beginning of his lifelong marriage to the sport.

The game that emerged from the IFA's first "rules convention" in 1876 was really rugby: the action initiated from a scrum line where the two teams battled for possession of the ball on each play. It would not, however, continue as such because during the next six years Walter Camp would become the guiding force of the IFA Rules Committee and would sponsor new rules that would radically change the nature of the game and create a unique sport.

Foremost among Camp's divergences was the establishment of a line of scrimmage, instead of a scrum line, from which a team would have definite control of the ball. The team in possession of the ball would snap it into the backfield to set play in motion, and the new position Camp created to receive the snap he called "quarter-back." Within just a few years he added more shape and substance to the sport: the size of a team was reduced to 11 men (seven linemen and four backs); a system of downs was introduced with a set

yardage that had to be gained in order to maintain possession of the ball; signals were devised for the quarterback to communicate with his teammates at the line of scrimmage; and a scoring system was designed that eventually evolved into the point values that exist today for touchdowns, field goals, extra points, and safeties.

When Walter Camp was not inventing rules and guiding them to fruition, he was on the field playing the game. For six years, during the last two of which he was in medical school, he was Yale's premier halfback, and twice was honored as the team's captain. He was also captain and pitcher on Yale's baseball team, a member of the school's swimming and tennis teams, a hurdler on the track team, and he held a seat on the crew.

A knee injury in 1882 ended Camp's playing career, but certainly not his life in football. By that time the call of the medical profession had paled considerably, and Camp dropped out of medical school and took a job in sales with the New Haven Clock Company, the firm in which he would eventually rise to the presidency and board chairmanship.

Despite leaving Yale, he never strayed too far from the Eli football field. He remained an active member of the IFA Rules Committee and then returned in 1888 as the school's first head football coach. Previously the captain had handled the coaching of a team. With

Camp's return in 1888, that changed forever. There was no recompense for the job in those days, but Camp remained there through the 1892 season.

He developed as a coach what came to be called the "Camp System," which he later described to Grantland Rice as being "very simple and very sound. At the end of a season I'd call a meeting at which we'd determine who was graduating and who wasn't. Then we'd screen the returnees. Were they fast? Did they pack power? The type material we would have pretty much determined our mode of offense. We moved the ball with more authority because, as a team, we worked much harder on signals than our adversaries. As far as I know we also had the distinction of being the first team to develop the cutback—where a back starts at one point in the rival line and hits at another. This got us many, many yards. Remember, however, that everything and anything we tried in those days was new."

It was also improvisational and definitely informal. Just how much so is evident in the words of William "Pudge" Heffelfinger, one of the most luminous of Yale's early football stars, quoted by sportswriter John McCallum in his book *Ivy League Football Since 1872:* "In 1888, Yale actually had *two* coaches—Camp and his earnest young bride, Allie. . . . They were newlyweds and Walter was sales manager in the New York office of the New Haven Clock Company. His superiors

wouldn't let him attend our afternoon practices, so he sent his wife to stand in for him. I can still see her pacing up and down the sideline, taking notes of our scrimmages. Walter kept in touch with our progress by reading her notebook. Then, several nights a week some of us on the team would go over to the Camps' home in New Haven for a review of strategy.

"Allie Camp could spot the good points and the weaknesses in each man's play. Her woman's intuition helped Walter suggest the right man for the right position to the team captain. Remember, in those pioneer days at Yale, the head coach made no decision without first consulting the captain."

Walter Camp's name is, of course, deeply associated with the All-America teams that he selected, starting in 1889, when he collaborated with Caspar Whitney (whose byline appeared on the listings). Camp started making the selections by himself in 1897 when Whitney went abroad. Two years later, Whitney took over again at *Harper's Weekly*, and Camp started publishing his picks under his own name in *Collier's* magazine. From that point forward, Camp's choices were considered the standard for outstanding performance on the gridiron, the last word, so to speak, until his death in 1925.

Among Camp's pupils in the game of American football were Amos Alonzo Stagg, Henry Williams, and Howard Jones, all Yale graduates who in turn

went out and established themselves as legends when they coached, contributing creatively to the sport. Camp also wrote three books about the game he loved so dearly; they became the gospel of the sport in their time: *Football: How to Coach a Team* (1886), *American Football* (1891), and *Walter Camp's Book of College Sports* (1893).

The man who gave American football unique character died on the evening of March 14, 1925, while he was attending a Rules Committee meeting in New York City. Being there was hardly new for him; he had attended the meetings regularly since 1878, guiding the actions and polishing the product. He was indeed Father of the Game.

Birth of the Forward Pass

Allison Danzig, sportswriter for the *New York Times* for 45 years, made this observation some years ago: "The earliest mention of the use of a forward pass in a game is found in *Athletics at Princeton—A History* (1900), as pointed out by Dr. L. H. Baker. In the 1876 Yale–Princeton game, it states, Walter Camp, when tackled threw the ball forward to Oliver Thompson, who ran for a touchdown. Princeton protested and claimed a foul. The referee tossed a coin to make his decision and allowed the touchdown to stand."

1888

Tackling below the waist is allowed for the first time. To protect the newly vulnerable ball handler, offensive lines, which previously lined up randomly apart, line up shoulder to shoulder. With this potential for mass interference, line plunges become an integral part of the game. The backs also line up close together for added protection, setting the stage for Walter Camp's T formation, which he introduces in 1889 at Yale.

1889

Caspar Whitney of *Harper's Weekly* magazine selects the first All-America team, published in a New York periodical called *The Week's Sport.* It includes such notables as Amos Alonzo Stagg of Yale at end, William "Pudge" Heffelfinger, also of Yale, at guard, and Edgar Allan Poe (a grand-nephew of the famed poet) of Princeton at quarterback. Although his name does not appear, football historians have suggested that Walter Camp assisted Whitney in the selection.

1890

Amos Alonzo Stagg, coach at Springfield (Massachusetts) College, introduces the "Ends-back" formation. The ends line up a few steps into the backfield, often in tandem with the tackles, to protect the backfield's flanks.

1891

The first game of college football to be played at night is staged under arc lights at Yale.

Coach Stagg devises the "Turtleback" formation for Springfield College. In his words: "This was a formation executed by massing the team into a solid oval against the tackle, and at the snap of the ball into the interior of the oval, rolling the mass around an end and unwinding the runner into a clear field."

1892

Lorin F. Deland of Harvard creates the "flying wedge," a play he first uses in a game against arch-rival Yale. At the kickoff, five players on the kicking team line up at each sideline about 20 yards behind the kicker. On a signal, they race toward the kicker and, as they converge on him, form a wedge in front. With the wedge moving at full speed, the kicker nudges the ball into play and follows his flying wedge interference into the opposing team.

The first intercollegiate game in the West is played between the University of California and Stanford.

1893

Amos Alonzo Stagg, with Henry L. (Harry) Williams, writes *A Scientific and Practical Treatise on American Football for Schools and Colleges,* published by the Case, Lockwood & Brainard Company of Hartford, Connecticut.

BELOW LEFT
A youthful Amos Alonzo Stagg at Yale. Playing end, Stagg led the Elis through four seasons, from 1886 through 1889, two of which they were national champions (1887, 1888). After leaving Yale, he served as a head coach for 57 years: Springfield (Mass.) College, 1890–91; Chicago, 1892–32; College of the Pacific, 1933–46.

BELOW RIGHT
The University of Pennsylvania and Cornell face off in an 1893 game at Manheim Cricket Grounds in Manheim, Pennsylvania. Penn won 53–0.

1894

The Southern Intercollegiate Athletic Association (SIAA), forerunner of the Southern Conference, which later spawns both the Atlantic Coast Conference and the Southeastern Conference, is formed at a meeting called for and directed by Dr. William L. Dudley of Vanderbilt. Charter members of the conference are Alabama, Auburn, Georgia Tech, Sewanee, and Vanderbilt.

The flying wedge is in effect outlawed when a new rule requires a kickoff to travel at least 10 yards before the ball is deemed to be in play.

Playing time is reduced from two 45-minute periods to two 35-minute periods. Linemen, who heretofore could line up in the backfield for interference on what were then called "mass momentum plays," are required to remain on the line of scrimmage.

1895

What will become the Big Ten conference is organized. At its inauguration, the conference has seven charter members: Chicago, Illinois, Michigan, Minnesota, Northwestern, Purdue, and Wisconsin.

1897

The touchdown is given a point value of 5, and the goal after touchdown is reduced to 1 point.

1898

The first of Walter Camp's "official" All-America teams is published in *Collier's* magazine and will appear in that periodical annually and be recognized as the official selection through 1924.

1902

The first Rose Bowl game is played on New Year's Day at Tournament Park in Pasadena, California. Michigan, coached by Fielding Yost, with a regular season record of 12-0, defeats Stanford, coached by Charles Fickert and with a record of 3-1-2, by the score of 49–0. Wolverine fullback Neil Snow scores five touchdowns.

A backfield formation shift is devised by Amos Alonzo Stagg for his University of Chicago team, considered to be the first use of a shift. Some historians suggest, however, that Harry Williams may have used his Minnesota shift a year or two earlier.

1903

John Heisman, coach of Clemson, recommends to Walter Camp that the forward pass be legalized, but the Rules Committee rejects it.

The hidden ball trick, or "hunchback play," is used by Pop Warner's Carlisle team against Harvard for the first time on record. It results in a touchdown.

Harvard builds a concrete stadium seating 30,000 for football games.

1905

The publication of statistics on the violent nature of the game of football causes a nationwide furor. According to the reports, 18 deaths and 159 serious injuries were directly attributable to the sport.

1906

Pop Warner, coaching now at Cornell between stints at Carlisle, begins developing the single wing formation. The next year he moves to Carlisle and uses it often, and it becomes known as the Carlisle formation. A few years later Warner improvises

further, bringing the other halfback up in line with the wingback to create the double wing formation.

President Theodore Roosevelt summons representatives of Princeton, Yale, and Harvard to the White House for a meeting at which he insists they take steps to reform the sport to make it less brutal and dangerous. If not, he warns, it might be banned altogether.

Representatives of 28 colleges that are not members of the Intercollegiate Football Association meet in New York City to establish their own rules committee. Called simply the "Conference Committee," it is headed by Captain Palmer E. Pierce of Army. Subsequently Pierce meets with Walter Camp, leader of the IFA Rules Committee, and the two agree to

continued on page 40

The Way It Was

John W. Heisman, one of the forefathers of college football and the man for whom the Heisman Trophy was named, played five years at Brown and Pennsylvania from 1887 through 1891. He described what it was like in those days:

Players of my time had to be real iron men, because we played two games each week—Wednesdays and Saturdays.

Once a game started, a player could not leave unless he actually was hurt, or, at least, pleaded injury. Accordingly, whenever the captain wanted to put a fresh player into action, he whispered, "Get your arm hurt, or something." In one game my captain whispered to me, "Get your neck broke, Heisman."

We wore jerseys and shorts of great variety. We had no helmets or pads of any kind; in fact, one who wore home-made pads was regarded as a sissy. Hair was the only head protection we knew, and in preparation for football we would let it grow from the first of June. Many college men of that day, especially divinity and medical students, permitted their beards to grow. Often they were referred to as "Gorillas." . . .

We didn't have many sweaters in those days, but we all wore snug-fitting canvas jackets over our jerseys.

You see, the tackling in that day wasn't clean-cut and around the legs as it is today. All too often it was wild, haphazard clutching with the hands, and when runners wore loose garments they were often stopped by a defensive player grabbing a handful of loose clothing. Some players wore pants, or jackets, of black horsehair. When you made a fumble grab, you lost your fingernails.

In those pioneer years, arguments followed most every decision the referee made. The whole team took part, so that half the time the officials scarcely knew who was captain. More than that, every player was privileged to argue as much as he pleased with any and every player of the opposition. The player who was a good linguist always was a priceless asset. . . .

In the old days, players of one side were permitted to grab hold of their runners anywhere they could and push, pull or yank them along in any direction that would make the ball advance. Sometimes two enemy tacklers would be clinging to the runner's legs, and trying to hold him back, while several teammates of the runner had hold of his arms, head, hair, or whatever they could attach themselves to, and were pulling him in the other direction. I still wonder how some of the ball carriers escaped dismemberment.

John Heisman, who would later lend his name to college football's most prestigious trophy, played quarterback on offense and safety on defense for Brown, 1887—88, and Pennsylvania, 1889—91. Later he was a head coach for 36 years: Oberlin, 1892, 1894; Akron, 1893; Auburn, 1895—99; Clemson, 1900—03; Georgia Tech, 1904—19; Pennsylvania, 1920—22; Washington & Jefferson, 1923; Rice, 1924—27.

The Hidden Ball Trick

Famed coach Glenn S. "Pop" Warner of Carlisle in 1903 claims to be the first to have used the hidden ball trick, perpetrated on the opening kickoff in a game against Harvard. He described it in an article he wrote for *Collier's* magazine in 1931.

> The ball sailed far and high down the center of the field, and was caught on the five-yard line by Jimmie Johnson, our little quarterback, who was an All-America that year.
>
> The Indians gathered at once in what now would be called a huddle, but facing outward, and Johnson quickly slipped the ball under the back of Charlie Dillon's jersey. Charlie was picked as the "hunchback" because he stood six feet and could do a hundred yards in ten seconds. Besides, being a guard, he was less likely to be suspected of carrying the ball.
>
> "Go!" yelled Johnson. And the Carlisle players scattered and fanned out toward the side lines, each back hugging his helmet to his breast, while Dillon charged straight down the center of the field. Talk about excitement and uproar! The Indian backs were chased and slammed, but when the tacklers saw that it was only headgear they were cuddling, not the ball, they began to leap here and there, yelping like hounds off the scent. Nobody paid any attention to Dillon, for he was running with both arms free, and when he came to Carl Marshall, safety man, the Harvard captain actually sidestepped what he thought was an attempt to block and dashed up the field to join the rest of his team in a frantic search for the ball.
>
> The stands were in an uproar, for everybody had seen the big lump on Dillon's back, but the Harvard players were still scurrying wildly around when Charlie crossed the goal line. One of his mates jerked out the ball and laid it on the turf and, as I had warned the referee that the play might be attempted, he was watching carefully and ruled that the touchdown had been made within the rules.

Letterman Glenn S. "Pop" Warner played guard for Cornell, 1892—94 (he was also the school's heavyweight boxing champion in 1893). Nicknamed "Pop" because he was older than most of the other Cornell players (he was 20 in 1892), Warner went on to become one of the winningest coaches in college football history, at Georgia, 1895—96; Cornell, 1897—98, 1904—06; Carlisle, 1899—1903, 1907—14; Pittsburgh, 1915—23; Stanford, 1924—32; Temple, 1933—38.

merge. The resulting organization is called the Intercollegiate Football Rules Committee (IFRC), the forerunner of the National Collegiate Athletic Association (NCAA).

The IFRC formally adopts a set of new rules designed to make the game safer. Among them are:

- Legalization of the forward pass (with a variety of restrictions).
- Creation of a neutral zone at the line of scrimmage.
- Raising the yardage required for a first down from 5 to 10 yards.
- Reducing the playing time of a game from two 35-minute periods to two 30-minute periods.
- Calling for the disqualification of players guilty of "fighting with or kneeing" an opposing player.

1908

Amos Alonzo Stagg devises the "Statue of Liberty" play for his Chicago team. The quarterback raises his arm as if to throw a forward pass, but instead a halfback runs behind him, snatches the ball from his uplifted arm, and races around end. The Statue of Liberty play, from a forward pass formation, was based on the principles of the "Old 83" play, an end-around play from a "semipunt" formation, developed by Fielding Yost at Ohio Wesleyan in 1897.

1909

The value of a field goal is reduced from 4 to 3 points.

1910

The Intercollegiate Football Rules Committee changes its name to the National Collegiate Athletic Association.

The NCAA offers some new rules. Among them:

- Changing the segments of play from two 30-minute periods to four 15-minute periods.
- Outlawing the flying tackle.
- Making only backs and ends eligible to receive a forward pass (formerly, any lineman could receive one if he lined up behind the line of scrimmage).
- Requiring seven men on the line of scrimmage at the start of any play.
- Banning interlocked interference, wherein linemen interlocked arms to form a single block of interference.

A scrumlike pile of players in the Yale–Harvard game of 1901, played at Harvard.

1911

Jack Marks, new head coach at Notre Dame, designs and uses what is to become known as the "Notre Dame box formation," adapted from a formation Marks developed as a coach at Dartmouth with head coach Frank Cavanaugh, in which the four backs form the corners of a box. Two years later, Notre Dame's new head coach, Jesse Harper, introduces the Notre Dame shift, which he had developed with Amos Alonzo Stagg at Chicago, in which the backfield lines up in a T formation and on a signal shifts into the box.

1912

A touchdown is given the value of six points and the onside kick is eliminated.

The length of the football field is reduced to 100 yards, with the provision of a 10-yard end zone behind each goal line. Teams are allowed four downs instead of three to gain the 10 yards necessary for a first down.

Some restrictions on the forward pass are removed, except that only one such pass can be thrown during a single four-down series of plays, and the pass has to be thrown from at least 5 yards behind the line of scrimmage.

1914

The Southwest Conference is founded, with eight charter members: Arkansas, Baylor, Oklahoma, Oklahoma A&M (today Oklahoma State), Rice, Southwestern, Texas, and Texas A&M.

1916

The conference that will become the Pac-10 is formed; charter members are California, Oregon, Oregon State, and Washington.

The most lopsided victory in college football history is posted by Georgia Tech, under Coach John Heisman, when his prolific 11 drub Cumberland 222–0. In that game, Tech kicker Jim Preas boots 18 extra points in the first half alone.

1917

Coaching from the sideline, which includes sending in a substitute with a play, is prohibited.

1925

The first East–West Shrine game is played in San Francisco; each team is composed of selected college all-stars. The West wins 6–0.

1926

The first electronic scoreboard is installed by the University of Wisconsin, premiering in their game against Iowa.

1927

The goal posts are moved 10 yards back from the goal line to the end line.

Illegal use of the hands by a defender is defined to include striking a player. The penalty for such an infraction is disqualification of the player from the game and a penalty of half the distance to the goal line, regardless of where the line of scrimmage is.

1928

The Big Six conference (later to become the Big Seven, then the Big Eight, and, later still, the Big 12) is formed at a meeting in Lincoln, Nebraska. Charter members include Iowa State, Kansas, Kansas State, Missouri, Nebraska, and Oklahoma.

1932

The Southeastern Conference comes into being. Its original members: Alabama, Auburn, Florida, Georgia, Georgia Tech, Kentucky, Louisiana State, Mississippi, Mississippi State, Sewanee, Tennessee, Tulane, and Vanderbilt.

1934

The first College All-Star game is played at Soldier Field in Chicago. More than 79,000 people watch the college stars under coach Nobel Kizer of Purdue battle to a scoreless tie against the 1933 NFL champs, the Chicago Bears, coached by George Halas.

continued on page 44

Red Grange sweeps left end for Illinois against Michigan in 1924, a game in which he turned in one of the greatest individual performances in college football history. Grange's five touchdowns running and one passing enabled the Illini to triumph over the undefeated and favored Wolverines, 39–14. It was also the dedication day of Illinois's new stadium, and 66,609 were in attendance to watch Grange's marvelous performance.

Halas Remembers

Prior to his more than 60-year career in professional football as a player, coach, and owner of the Chicago Bears, George Halas served his apprenticeship as an end, first at Illinois and, after World War I broke out, with the Great Lakes Naval Base team, which played against college teams in 1917 and 1918. He wrote of a particularly memorable experience in his autobiography, *Halas by Halas:*

One of the games I remember best from those days was when I was at Great Lakes. We traveled to Annapolis to play the Naval Academy team. They had a lot of pride and looked on us as a bunch of upstarts.

Navy scored on us and were leading six to nothing. Much later in the game, they were about to score again. They were near our goal and their fullback Bill Ingram tried to smash through. But we hit him on the one yard line and he fumbled the ball. It popped right into the arms of one of our players, Dizzy Eilson.

Well, Dizzy took off toward the other end of the field. Jimmy Conzelman [who would go on to become a great pro player and coach] and myself blocked for him. By the time he reached midfield, there wasn't a player between him and the goal line. Jimmy and I, at this point, just turned around to protect him, to stop anybody who might be chasing him.

Gil Dobie, the Navy coach that year, almost went insane as he saw his game slipping out from under him. "Stop him! Stop him!" he shouted.

Bill Saunders, a substitute who later went on to coach at Denver, was alongside Dobie waiting to enter the game. He took Gil at his word, dashed onto the field, and made a perfect tackle of Eilson. There was a big to-do on the field, everybody shouting at everybody else—coaches, players, referees.

Finally the Academy superintendent, a man named Captain Edward Eberle, came marching out onto the field and demanded order. He wanted to know what in hell was going on. The officials told him they had decided that Navy would be penalized halfway to the goal for the infraction. We were all screaming that we should be awarded a touchdown.

The captain decreed that we should be given the touchdown. The officials said that was not the rule. The rule was a penalty, halfway to the goal. Captain Eberle said that was a ridiculous rule, and he didn't give a damn about it. "It would have been a touchdown if that idiot hadn't run onto the field," he said. "I run this place and a touchdown it is."

Well, we made the conversion and won the game 7–6. Captain Eberle went on to become an admiral and chief of naval operations.

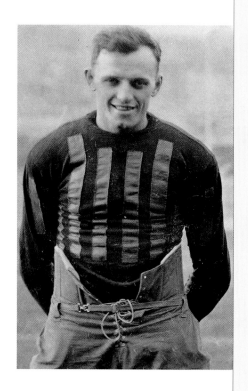

George Halas played end for Illinois, 1915—17, and the Great Lakes Naval Training Center team (outside Chicago), 1918, which defeated the Mare Island Marine Base team (outside San Francisco) in the 1919 Rose Bowl 17—0. He later was one of the founding fathers of the National Football League, and the longtime owner and coach of the Chicago Bears.

The Watch-Charm Guard

If ever there was a football player who symbolized the difference between college football as it was played in the days prior to World War II and the modern game, it had to be Bert Metzger of Notre Dame. He played guard from 1928 through 1930, made All-America his senior year, although he stood only five-foot-nine inches tall and weighed 145 pounds (it was reported he occasionally got up to 149 pounds).

He was called the "Watch-Charm" guard because of his diminutive size, not presence. Metzger held forth in the line like a 275-pounder today, played 60 minutes a game, and in 1930 was one of the key figures, along with Frank Carideo and Marchy Schwarz, who brought an unofficial national championship to Notre Dame. The Watch-Charm Guard came to be one of Notre Dame's most famous players from the Rockne era, right up there with the likes of George Gipp and the Four Horsemen.

Despite his consensus All-America recognition, Metzger chose—perhaps for safety's sake—to forego professional football after graduation. He was inducted into the College Football Hall of Fame in 1982.

Not much is certain in life, but it is a safe bet there will never again be a 145-pound All-America guard in college football.

1935

The first Heisman Trophy (although it will not be called that until the following year) is awarded by New York's Downtown Athletic Club to Jay Berwanger, a halfback for the University of Chicago.

The first Coach of the Year Award, selected by a vote of the American Football Coaches Association, goes to Lynn "Pappy" Waldorf of Northwestern.

The first official Orange Bowl game is played in Miami, with Bucknell demolishing Miami (Florida), 26–0.

1937

The first Sugar Bowl game is played at Tulane Stadium in New Orleans, where Tulane defeats Temple by the score of 20–14.

Official national statistics rankings for college football are instituted.

The first Cotton Bowl game is held in Dallas, where Texas Christian defeats Marquette 16–6.

1938

The first official Blue-Gray game, with selected all-stars from Northern colleges on the Blue and those representing Southern colleges on the Gray, is played in Montgomery, Alabama. The Blue win 7–0.

1940

On October 5, Maryland meets Pennsylvania in the first televised college football game. (The first television coverage of college football actually occurred the year before when NBC telecast a Fordham practice session in New York, with Bill Stern handling the commentary.)

1941

Free substitution is allowed, and substitutes are permitted to communicate immediately with their teammates on the field, and therefore can bring in plays from the sideline.

1945

Cecil Isbell of Purdue becomes the first coach in history to direct his team from the press box, and his Boilermakers defeat Ohio State 35–13.

1946

The first Gator Bowl game is played in Jacksonville, Florida, with Wake Forest beating South Carolina by the score of 26–14.

The Outland Award, a trophy to honor the outstanding interior lineman of the year, with the selection made by a vote among the members of the Football Writers Association of America, is instituted. The first recipient is George Connor, tackle for Notre Dame.

1947

The Tangerine Bowl begins in Orlando, Florida, with Catawba beating Maryville 31–6. (In 1983, the name of the game is changed to the Florida Citrus Bowl.)

1949

Tom Nugent, head coach at Virginia Military Institute, introduces the I formation, which features all the running backs lined up in a row behind the quarterback. Nugent goes on to success at Florida State and the University of Maryland, while his new formation gains fame when used by Frank Leahy at Notre Dame in 1951.

1951

The televising of college football games on Saturday afternoons is approved by the NCAA, but restricted to only one game in each area per Saturday.

1953

The Atlantic Coast Conference is founded with seven charter members: Clemson, Duke, Maryland, North Carolina, North Carolina State, South Carolina, and Wake Forest.

Free substitution is eliminated, and the game of college football reverts to one of single platoon.

FACING PAGE LEFT
Pittsburgh sophomore halfback Marshall Goldberg finds a lot of running room in the 1937 Rose Bowl game against Washington. The Washington defenders closing in on Goldberg are Chuck Bond (72), Steve Slivinski (34), and Jimmie Johnston (18). Pitt won 21—0. Goldberg would win All-America honors in both 1937 and 1938.

1956

The Ivy League is formally organized as an athletic conference, consisting of eight universities: Brown, Columbia, Cornell, Dartmouth, Harvard, Pennsylvania, Princeton, and Yale. Winner of the first Ivy League crown is Yale, under head coach Jordan Olivar, with a conference record of 7-0 and an overall record of 8-1.

FACING PAGE RIGHT
Triple-threat halfback Bob Fenimore of Oklahoma State picks up 7 yards here in the 1946 Sugar Bowl game against St. Mary's College (California). Fenimore, an All-America that season, scored two touchdowns in leading the Aggies to a 33—13 victory. No. 11 is St. Mary's star halfback Herman Wedemeyer.

1958

The two-point conversion after a touchdown in lieu of the kicked extra point is introduced.

1959

The first Bluebonnet Bowl is held in Houston, Texas, on December 19. Clemson easily defeats Texas Christian 23–7.

The first Liberty Bowl game is played on December 19 in Philadelphia, Pennsylvania, as Penn State beats Alabama 7–0. By 1965 the game makes a permanent home for itself in Memphis, Tennessee.

1962

The Western Athletic Conference is inaugurated, initially comprising Arizona, Arizona State, Brigham Young, New Mexico, Utah, and Wyoming.

1964

Unlimited substitution is restored, and platooning becomes the accepted mode of play.

BELOW LEFT
Howard "Hopalong" Cassady of Ohio State bursts through the Michigan line to score the final touchdown in the Buckeyes' 21—7 win in 1954 at Columbus. Trying to get a hand on him are Michigan defenders Ted Cachey (65) and Dan Cline (44). Cassady, a consensus All-American in both 1954 and 1955, won the Heisman Trophy in 1955.

1968

Coach Darrell Royal of Texas perfects the wishbone, or triple option, offense. A staple of college football in the 1970s and early 1980s, the formation gives the quarterback the option of handing off to the fullback or rolling out with the ball and running it himself or pitching out to the halfback.

Atlanta, Georgia, hosts the first Peach Bowl game on December 30, as LSU beats Florida State 31—27.

BELOW RIGHT
A loose ball becomes the focus of attention of two legendary rivals, UCLA and Southern Cal, in 1958, in a game that ended in a 15—15 tie.

1969

The Pacific Coast Athletic Association is formed. Charter members: California/ Long Beach, California/ Los Angeles, California/ Santa Barbara, Fresno State, Pacific, San Diego State, and San Jose State.

Intercollegiate football celebrates its 100th anniversary. Commemorations of the event include a special stamp, issued in a ceremony in New Brunswick, New Jersey, site of the first game.

At the close of the 1968 season, the Associated Press changes the timing of its selection of a national champion, waiting until the bowl games, played in January 1969, are over instead of making the pick at the end of the regular season. The first winner under the new system is Ohio State.

1970

The NCAA restricts the regular season schedule of major college football teams to 11 games (postseason competition not included).

1971

The first Fiesta Bowl game is held on December 27 in Tempe, Arizona. The local favorite prevails as Arizona State beats Florida State 45–38.

1973

At a special NCAA convention, a three-division reorganization plan is adopted. Teams classified as "Major College" are placed in Division I; "College-division" teams are assigned to Division II or Division III.

1975

UPI joins AP in waiting until after the bowl games are over to select a national champion for 1974. They don't agree on their selections though, as UPI picks USC and AP chooses Oklahoma. The AP poll is determined by the vote of sportswriters and broadcasters; the UPI poll by coaches.

1976

The first Independence Bowl game is played in Shreveport, Louisiana, on December 13. McNeese State edges Tulsa 20–16.

1978

The NCAA divides the existing Division I (for football only) into Division I-A and Division I-AA.

San Diego, California, hosts the first Holiday Bowl, on December 22. The visitor from the East, Navy, beats Brigham Young 23–16.

Oklahoma's Greg Pruitt (30), running out of the Sooners' patented wishbone T formation, breaks loose against Colorado in 1971. Pruitt, a consensus All-American, was instrumental in Oklahoma's 11-1 season and No. 2 ranking at the end of the year.

1982

On December 29, Alabama defeats Illinois 21–15 in the Liberty Bowl, giving coach Paul "Bear" Bryant his final triumph. With 323 career victories, Bryant retires as the winningest Division I-A college football coach ever.

On Christmas Day the first Aloha Bowl game is held in Honolulu, Hawaii. Washington ekes out a 21–20 victory over Maryland.

BELOW LEFT
Michigan and Ohio State at war in 1980. The fabled rivalry between the two Big Ten teams goes back to 1897 when the Wolverines triumphed in Ann Arbor 34–0. In this contest at Columbus, Ohio, Michigan again prevailed 9–3.

1985

The Missouri Valley Conference, forerunner of the Big Eight, announces it will no longer sponsor college football after the 1985 season. Only two schools, Tulsa and Wichita State, will remain in Division I-A, as the others move to I-AA level competition.

1991

USA Today Poll takes over the Coaches Poll.

The Big East Conference is founded. Charter members: Boston College, Miami (Florida), Pittsburgh, Rutgers, Syracuse, Temple, Virginia Tech, and West Virginia.

1992

The College Football Bowl Coalition, featuring four bowl games (Cotton, Fiesta, Orange, and Sugar), is introduced.

1995

The Bowl Alliance, involving three bowls—Fiesta, Orange, and Sugar—on a rotating basis replaces the Bowl Coalition.

Eddie Robinson, after 55 seasons at Grambling, retires with the distinction of having won more college football games (408) and head-coached in more games (588) than anyone in the history of college football.

1996

The Big 12 Conference is founded by merging the Big Eight Conference and four teams from the Southwest Conference. Charter members: Baylor, Colorado, Iowa State, Kansas, Kansas State, Missouri, Nebraska, Oklahoma, Oklahoma State, Texas, Texas A&M, and Texas Tech.

1997

USA Today and ESPN combine to distribute the Coaches Poll nationally.

1998

The Bowl Championship Series (BCS), designed to match the nation's No. 1 and No. 2 ranked teams in a bowl game to determine the national champion, is launched. In the first BCS championship game, played at the Fiesta Bowl, Tennessee defeats Florida State 23–16.

2000

A passer is allowed to intentionally ground the football without penalty if he is 5 yards or more toward the sideline from the original position of the ball at the snap.

BELOW RIGHT
Miami's All-American defensive tackle Warren Sapp (76) grabs at the leg of a Central Florida ballcarrier in a 1994 game.

3

> " To me, the coaching
> profession is one of
> the noblest and most
> far-reaching in building
> manhood. No man is
> too good to be the
> athletic coach for youth. "
>
> AMOS ALONZO STAGG
> *University of Chicago*
> *Head Coach, 1892–1932*

INNOVATORS AND MOTIVATORS
THE GAME'S GREATEST COACHES

A college football coach is a strategist, a leader, an exhorter, an inspirer, sometimes a surrogate father and usually an orator as articulate or abrasive as the situation may require. And whatever his size, he must also be someone with the ability to scare the hell out of a six-foot-five-inch, 290-pound defensive tackle.

His profession puts undue pressure on the heart, mind, and emotions; occupational hazards include ulcers, sleepless nights, butterflies in the stomach and throbbings in the skull, and occasional paranoia. It is a life of anguish and ecstasy, one in which he is dogged by evangelistic alumni and petulant sportswriters, sometimes adulated, sometimes hung in effigy, and always given a sense of job security similar to that of the leader of a Central American nation.

Despite the pressures and talents that all coaches share, the profession has attracted an incredibly diverse group of personalities over the years. From a laid-back Amos Alonzo Stagg to a melodramatic Knute Rockne to a more-than-loquacious Woody Hayes, the locker rooms and sidelines on a Saturday afternoon in autumn have often been as interesting as the events on the playing field.

When football was first played in the United States, however, there were no coaches. The leader was the team captain, and he determined who would play and what strategies, if any, the team would use. The first officially designated coach of a major school appears to be Lucius N. Littauer of Harvard, who guided the Crimson, it is recorded, in 1881. After that year, however, Harvard went back to being coached by its captains, until Frank A. Mason was appointed coach in 1886.

Princeton actually called upon the services of various alumni in those early days, who provided some organization and guidance from the sideline but weren't considered coaches either. Yale, presciently, signed on the first of the soon-to-be famous coaches in 1888, Walter C. Camp, although he was not paid for his efforts.

Amos Alonzo Stagg, who had taken on the coaching chores at Springfield College in Massachusetts in 1890 (the same school, incidentally, where, the following year, Dr. James Naismith invented the game of basketball), turned coaching into a paid profession in 1892. That was the year he was hired by the University of Chicago and became the first coach to earn official faculty recognition (he was titled associate professor and director of the Department of Physical Culture as well as head coach) and be paid a salary.

As colleges started employing coaches for their teams, the game of football began to change significantly. Tactics, new formations and plays, and organization were incorporated into the sport. Besides Camp and Stagg, the great innovators of the earlier days of the game included Percy Haughton at Harvard, George Woodruff of Pennsylvania, Harry Williams at Minnesota, John Heisman, Pop Warner, Fielding Yost—the list is long and impressive.

It was from these imaginative minds that American football developed into the game as it is known today. As technically complex and sophisticated as football is in the twenty-first century, with cadres of coaches, encyclopedic playbooks, films, communications systems, computers, scouting programs, aids ad infinitum, the basics of the game are really no different from the formations, shifts, and plays that were dreamed up in the late 1800s and early 1900s by the game's first masterminds.

There have been so many wonderful coaches in the first century of college football, so many contributions to the game by them, such imprint on the players they have guided. We have chosen some for special recognition here, the criteria including not just their successes in the won-loss column but also the impact each has had on the game. Their football creativity truly bequeathed unique legacies to college football.

Unprofiled, but not overlooked either in anecdotes, statistics, or the heart of the author, are such legends in their own right as (in no particular order and identified with the schools they were most associated with): Jock Sutherland (Lafayette, Pittsburgh), Jess Neely (Clemson and Rice), Warren Woodson (Arkansas State, Hardin-Simmons, Arizona, New Mexico State), Dana Xenophon Bible (Texas A&M, Nebraska, Texas), Dan McGugin (Vanderbilt), John Vaught (Mississippi), Carl Snavely (Cornell, North Carolina), Gil Dobie (Washington, Navy, Cornell, Boston College), Ben Schwartzwalder (Syracuse), Eddie Anderson (Holy Cross, Iowa), Frank Thomas (Alabama), Bernie Bierman (Minnesota), Fritz Crisler (Princeton, Michigan), Jim Crowley (Michigan State, Fordham), Andy Smith (California), Frank Cavanaugh (Dartmouth, Boston College, Fordham), Lou Little (Columbia), Clark Shaughnessy (Stanford), Lynn Waldorf (Northwestern, California), Duffy Daugherty (Michigan State), Wally Butts (Georgia), Jim Tatum (Maryland, North Carolina), Bill Roper (Princeton), T.A.D. Jones (Yale), Bobby Dodd (Georgia Tech), Red Sanders (UCLA), Frank Howard (Clemson), Bob Devaney (Nebraska), Ray Eliot (Illinois), Frank Kush (Arizona State), John McKay (Southern Cal), Dan Devine (Missouri, Notre Dame), Frank Broyles (Arkansas), Vince Dooley (Georgia), Barry Switzer (Oklahoma), Tom Osborne (Nebraska), Johnny Majors (Tennessee, Pittsburgh), Hayden Fry (Southern Methodist, North Texas, Iowa), LaVell Edwards (Brigham Young), Carmen Cozza (Yale), and Lou Holtz (Notre Dame, South Carolina).

Rice on Sutherland

Jock Sutherland's brilliant coaching career spanned more than 20 years, at Lafayette from 1919 to 1923 and Pittsburgh from 1924 to 1938. His record at Pitt was an impressive 111-20-12, with four Rose Bowl appearances.

On the occasion of Sutherland's demise, Grantland Rice composed this poem in eulogy to the famous Pittsburgh coach:

*There's a fog now over Scotland,
  and a mist on Pittsburgh's field;
There's no valiant hand to flash the sword
  or hold the guiding shield.
There's a big, braw fellow
  missing from the golden land of fame.
—For Jock Sutherland has left us—
  and the game is not the same.*

*We hear the roaring chorus—
  and we get the age-old thrill;
But when a pal has left us,
  there's a gap that none can fill,*

*There's a shadow on the thistle
  and the Panther's growl is low—
As the bagpipes send their message
  to the friend we used to know.*

*The laurel fades—the olive dies—
  the cheers are silent now,
No more the chaplet from lost years
  adorns the master's brow.
But here's to Jock, through fog and mist,
  beyond the final score.
—As we turn down an empty glass
  to one we'll see no more.*

AMOS ALONZO STAGG

"All modern football stems from Stagg," said Knute Rockne, who came to know and admire football's Grand Old Man when Stagg was at the University of Chicago, in the first decade of his 57-year tenure as a college football coach. Few will disagree with the Rock's assertion.

Amos Alonzo Stagg was a pioneer in developing so many elements of the game, including diagrammed playbooks, the huddle, various backfield shifts, men in motion, the spiral pass, onside kick, fake kick, and reverses, among many others. He was also the first coach to take a team cross-country to play a game.

He began his coaching career at Springfield College in Massachusetts in 1890 and moved on to the University of Chicago in 1892. At Chicago, for 41 years, Stagg battled other legendary coaches from the Big Ten, such as Fielding Yost of Michigan and Bob Zuppke of Illinois.

Born when Abe Lincoln was president, and still an active part of college football during the Eisenhower administration, he outlasted generations of competitors, and did not finally retire from the game until 1960, at the age of 98. At the time, he was the second winningest coach in the history of college football, his 314 victories just short of the 319 of Glenn "Pop" Warner.

Stagg's career and teams were a testament to clean living. As both a star pitcher and a football mainstay at Yale, he refused to drink, smoke, or swear. He rejected a flurry of professional baseball offers after graduation because he objected to the sale of alcoholic beverages at professional baseball games. "The whole tone of the game was smelly," he said some years later.

Even during the heat of many gridiron battles, Stagg never swore. His strongest epithet to a player was "jackass," and, in particularly flagrant situations, "double jackass." Many of his players felt that their college careers could not be complete until they had joined, at least once, the coveted "Jackass Club."

Throughout his career, Stagg felt that sportsmanship and honor were more important than victories. A longtime member of college football's Rules Committee, he once refused to send in a substitute with a badly needed play when Chicago's offense had faltered on its opponent's 1-yard line. "The Rules Committee deprecates the use of a substitute to convey information," he explained. Chicago went on to lose the game. During his tenure at Chicago, from 1892 through 1932, the school won only six Big Ten titles.

FACING PAGE
Amos Alonzo Stagg directs his University of Chicago football team from an electric car in 1930. The then 68-year-old Stagg said, "I got so mussed up scrimmaging with the boys, I couldn't get around very well." In the car with him is Mrs. Stagg. The coaching career of the Grand Old Man of College Football extended from 1890 to 1946.

RIGHT
A scheduling letter in 1891 to Stagg, then head coach at Springfield College in Massachusetts.

At the age of 70, Stagg was forced to obey university rules and retire. But the very next year he became head coach at the College of the Pacific in California where, until the age of 84, he compiled a respectable record against often larger and more powerful rivals. Two other positions there kept him active in college football until the age of 98.

Stagg's 100th birthday was celebrated from coast to coast in 1962, a time when football's Grand Old Man was finally beginning to feel the effects of advancing age. "I would like to be remembered," he said at the time, "as an honest man."

Record

Schools: Springfield (1890–91), Chicago (1892–1932), Pacific (1933–46)

Totals: Won 314, Lost 199, Tied 35; Percentage .605

GLENN S. "POP" WARNER

Until Bear Bryant came along, no coach had won more football games than Glenn Scobey Warner, known to the football world as "Pop." In coaching assignments at Georgia, Cornell, Carlisle, Pittsburgh, Stanford, and Temple, he compiled a record of 319 victories against 106 losses and 32 ties.

Like Stagg, Warner is known as one of the great innovators of the game. He introduced the single wing and double wing formations, numbers on players' jerseys, the spiral punt, rolling body blocks, and blocking dummies. In his career of nearly half a century, he coached 47 consensus All-Americas, including two of football's greatest players, Jim Thorpe at Carlisle and Ernie Nevers at Stanford.

Also like Stagg, Warner was a stickler for good sportsmanship. "You cannot play two kinds of football at once, dirty and good," he once said. The esteemed sportswriter Red Smith described him as a "gruff old gent, kind and forthright and obstinate and honest."

Warner was also spectacularly successful. Between 1915 and 1918, his teams at Pittsburgh went undefeated for four consecutive seasons. By the early 1920s, his nationwide reputation attracted considerable interest even on the West Coast, where Stanford officials began courting his services. When he accepted the Stanford head coaching position prior to the 1923 season, Warner insisted on honoring the remaining two years of his contract at Pittsburgh. In the interim he sent assistants Andy Kerr and Tiny Thornhill to Stanford to begin implementing his system.

At Stanford, Warner coached some of his greatest players and engaged in one of college football's all-time great rivalries. His finest athlete was All-America back Ernie Nevers, still regarded as perhaps the greatest player ever to wear a Stanford uniform. Comparing Nevers to Thorpe, Warner gave

Glenn S. "Pop" Warner gives a chalk-talk to his 1937 Temple team. The legendary Warner coached for 44 years, beginning at Georgia in 1895 and ending his career at age 67 at Temple in 1938. He was also the head coach at Cornell, Carlisle, Pittsburgh, and Stanford.

Warner on the Record

Writing to football historian H. A. Applequist in 1943, Pop Warner tried to set straight the innovations in the game that he claimed as his own:

The things which I *did* originate are as follows:

The crouching stance of the backs on offense. In 1908 I started this innovation, having the backs stand with one or both hands on the ground. This practice has since been almost universally used by teams with the exception of the teams using a shifting backfield. This stance gives nearly the same advantage in starting as that used by modern trackmen over the old standing start of early days.

The unbalanced line. I am quite sure that I was the first coach of football to use the *four* and *two* line which is so commonly used by teams today. I started this offensive method in 1906.

The single wing formation. I started this type of offensive formation in 1906, when the rules prohibited helping the ball carrier by pushing or pulling of a player in order to advance the ball. This formation was alluded to by Walter Camp and other noted writers and coaches of football as the "Carlisle Formation." This formation or its variations is probably used at the present time by at least three-fourths of all the football teams in the country.

The two wing-back formation. In 1911, I carried the wing-back idea a step further and started the double wing-back formation which I used almost exclusively throughout the rest of my coaching career.

The direct pass from the center to the ball carrier. I am quite certain that I was the first to use this method of getting the ball to the runner instead of having the quarterback handling the ball on every play.

The screen forward pass. I used such a pass very successfully along about 1920, and it is my belief that I was the first football coach to make use of this type of forward pass. Such a pass, as you know, becomes illegal except when the screen is formed on or behind the scrimmage line.

the edge in overall performance to Nevers. Thorpe, he felt, did not always give his best effort. "If their skill is about the same," he once said, "I'll take the all-outer over the in-and-outer every time."

Stanford's historic rivalry with the University of Southern California began in 1925, coach Howard Jones's first season at USC. Warner won the first two meetings and tied the third, but beginning with the fourth contest, USC took five straight games from Stanford.

Depressed and disgusted by his inability to defeat Southern Cal, Pop Warner resigned from Stanford at the end of the 1932 season. In a move he later described as "the worst mistake of my life," he became head coach at Temple, where his teams never achieved glory. But his legacy at Stanford, subsequently directed by Tiny Thornhill, thrived with the famed "Vow Boys," who pledged never to be defeated by USC.

Despite his lackluster years at Temple, Warner is regarded as one of the most influential collegiate coaches of all time. Grantland Rice once observed that it would be difficult to determine whether Pop Warner or Knute Rockne had the greatest overall effect on the game of college football.

Record

Schools: Georgia (1895–96), Cornell (1897–98, 1904–06), Carlisle (1899–1903, 1907–14), Pittsburgh (1915–23), Stanford (1924–32), Temple (1933–38)

Totals: Won 319, Lost 106, Tied 32; Percentage .729

FIELDING YOST

"You're not movin' out there. Ya think we got all day?" he would holler, clapping his hands at a player who dared to enter a scrimmage somewhat slower than the speed of light. "Hurry up! Let's go! Hurry up!" To his parents, Peremenus and Elzena Yost, he was known by the name of Fielding, but to everyone connected with college football, he was Hurry Up Yost, the master of rapid motion on and off the field.

"Horrible Nightmare" screamed a West Virginia newspaper headline after Yost's Michigan team destroyed West Virginia by the devastating score of 130–0 at a game played in Ann Arbor in 1904. Unabashed even in this most lopsided of games, Yost was quick to point out that 40 or more players had participated in the drubbing.

Hurry Up Yost's coaching career developed early. After earning a law degree from either Lafayette or West Virginia (historians are not certain which school holds the honor), Yost began coaching college football teams. In the next four years, he won four championships with four different schools,

Fielding "Hurry Up" Yost made his biggest mark at the University of Michigan where he coached for 25 years, beginning in 1901. Yost's 1901 Wolverines were known as the "Point-a-Minute" team, outscoring their opponents that year 501–0; they also won the very first Rose Bowl game on January 1, 1902, defeating Stanford 49–0. Yost began his college coaching career at Ohio Wesleyan in 1897 and also coached at Nebraska, Kansas, and Stanford before coming to Michigan.

Ohio Wesleyan, Nebraska, Kansas, and Stanford. By the time he reached California, a single coaching job during the football season was simply not enough for his restless nature. So, in 1900, he guided the Stanford varsity, the Stanford freshman team, the Lowell high school team, and assisted at San Jose College. All four teams won championships, but by the close of the season Yost apparently grew

Yost and Lardner

Fielding Yost, Michigan's fabled coach, was not always the easiest man to get along with. Ring Lardner, while traveling with Yost in the early 1920s, got caught in a little argument regarding the Michigan–Pennsylvania game of 1906.

"Penn won that one, 17–0," Lardner said.

"No, Michigan won it," Yost said. "That was the year we had Garrels, a great fullback."

"Penn won it," Ring repeated. "That was the year they had Scarlett and Greene."

Finally Yost bet Lardner $5, a tremendous bet for Yost. They looked it up in a record book. Score: Pennsylvania 17, Michigan 0.

"I told you Pennsylvania won," Yost said. And then he told Lardner it was not necessary for him to pay up.

bored with the pace of life in California. With three of his top players in tow, he moved to the University of Michigan in 1901, where he established one of the great dynasties in the history of Big Ten football.

Yost's Wolverines responded immediately, all but destroying their opponents, ending the season with a crushing victory over Stanford on New Year's Day 1902 in what was the first Rose Bowl Game. When C. M. Fickert, the overwhelmed Stanford coach, asked that the game be stopped, Yost replied, "No sirree, let's get on with it." But the Michigan captain finally agreed to end the rout with nearly 10 minutes left to play, the score standing at 49–0.

Yost was named athletic director at Michigan in 1921 and retired as head coach after an undefeated season in 1923. When the Wolverines committed the unspeakable sin of losing two games in the 1924 season, however, Yost was back at the helm in 1925. That year, Michigan defeated everyone but Northwestern (to whom they lost 3–2; these were the only points the Wolverines gave up all season), shutting out even the Illinois team led by Red Grange. Yost regarded that 1925 team as his greatest and retired again in 1926, but for several years, the head coach's position would be "questionable," with Yost always ready to step back in.

There could be little question, however, about Yost's remarkable record at Michigan: 164 victories against only 29 defeats; eight undefeated teams, seven Big Ten titles, and four national championships.

Record

Schools: Ohio Wesleyan (1897), Nebraska (1898), Kansas (1899), Stanford (1900), Michigan (1901–23, 25–26)

Totals: Won 196, Lost 36, Tied 12; Percentage .828

Howard Jones, one of the great innovators in the early days of college football, is best remembered for the years he led the Southern Cal Trojans, 1925–40. He brought Southern Cal two national championships, seven conference titles, and five Rose Bowl victories. Jones's first head coaching job was with Syracuse in 1908, and he also guided teams at Yale, Ohio State, Iowa, and Duke before coming to USC.

HOWARD JONES

Until the last decade of his life, Howard Harding Jones was an unsung hero, an innovative and highly successful coach known chiefly by football experts. It shouldn't have been so. After relatively brief coaching experiences at Syracuse, Yale, and Ohio State, the onetime Yale end became Iowa's head coach in 1916. By 1922 he could boast of two undefeated and untied seasons for the Hawkeyes and two consecutive Big Ten championships, the second of which was shared with Michigan.

At Iowa, Jones developed his first superstar, quarterback Aubrey Devine, who the coach described as "the greatest all-around backfield man I have ever coached or seen in the modern game." Howard Jones's innovations at Iowa included an offensive shift in which both ends dropped back into the backfield to block for the quarterback and the fullback rush, a move that caused considerable confusion among opponents. Before Illinois finally defeated Iowa in the fourth game of the 1923 season, the Hawkeyes had won 20 consecutive games. Jones then left for Duke at the end of the season, where he won only four of nine games.

In 1925 he was installed as the head coach at the University of Southern California where, half a decade later, he finally established a national reputation. At Southern Cal he won seven Pacific Coast Conference titles, two national championships, and his teams were invited to the Rose Bowl five times, winning on each occasion. But even before his second appearance in the Pasadena classic, the *New York Times* would describe him as "the most underrecognized coach, from a national standpoint, the game has had in many years. It seems incomprehensible that Jones should have received so little attention as has been accorded him."

By leading his Trojans to three Rose Bowl victories in four years, however, Jones became a phenomenon that no one could ignore. One of his quarterbacks at USC, Ambrose Schindler, described Jones this way: "He was just such a genius at football. He believed in knowing the opponent by having them well scouted. That way his team could properly set up a defense. And by controlling them, his team could beat them with their own selected offensive patterns. He preferred to win with his system. . . . He liked to win by seeing that his techniques prevailed, and that his methods were superior. . . . Howard Jones believed in running directly at the other team's best linemen. Jones would pick their All-American and concentrate the attack on him to prove to his own men that you had to beat their best man, and that when you did, you had the game. He had us do that against everybody."

After his Rose Bowl victories in 1930, 1932, and 1933, Jones's teams were eclipsed in 1934 and 1935 by the Vow Boys at Stanford. But his strict, often unforgiving, demands never ceased. A player for Jones always knew that if he made one critical mistake, a chance for redemption might never come.

The 1938 and 1939 teams, called the "Thundering Herd," made a strong comeback, winning the Rose Bowl in each season. After a 3-4-2 record in 1940, Jones died suddenly of a heart attack at the age of 46. He left behind several books on football and libraries of memories for Southern Cal fans.

Record

Schools: Syracuse (1908), Yale (1909, 1913), Ohio State (1910), Iowa (1916–23), Duke (1924), Southern Cal (1925–40)

Totals: Won 194, Lost 64, Tied 21; Percentage .733

KNUTE ROCKNE

"The Rock," as he was known to every football fan in America, masterminded one of football's most memorable dynasties, bringing Notre Dame national championships in 1924, 1929, and 1930, and guiding some of the most famous players ever to wear college football uniforms, among them George Gipp and the fabled Four Horsemen.

In 1913, playing end for Notre Dame, he teamed with quarterback Gus Dorais to develop the use of the forward pass in a game against Army. But it is his coaching genius and inspirational pregame and halftime talks that are best remembered.

The Rock would say whatever he felt was needed to inspire—or goad—his Irish on to victory. Actor Pat O'Brien immortalized Rockne's "Win one for the Gipper" speech in the film *Knute Rockne, All American*, but there were dozens of other inspired anything-for-a-win locker room talks. It is said Notre Dame's locker room still rings with his pregame chants: "Go out there and hit 'em," he would yell. "Crack 'em! Fight to live! Fight to win! Fight to win, win, win, WIN!"

FACING PAGE
Knute Rockne leads the 1930 Fighting Irish of Notre Dame in calisthenics at old Cartier Field in South Bend. It was the last team the Rock would coach, killed in a plane crash the following year. As famous for his locker room pep talks as his championship teams, Rockne's winning percentage of .881 (105-12-5) is still the best in the history of major college football. He coached at Notre Dame from 1918 through 1930.

A Moral Force

Paul Gallico, writing for the *New York Daily News*, described how the force of college football was pervasive enough to influence the social structures in which it existed. As proof, he told this story of Knute Rockne in the Roaring Twenties:

He closed down a *maison de joie* known as "Sally's," above a feed store on LaSalle Street in South Bend, as having a deteriorating effect on the neighborhood. The police dragged their feet when requested to cooperate, since apparently some kind of profit-sharing plan was in operation. When repeated

appeals failed, Rockne made another suggestion. Either Sally's closed, or he would bring his football team down and take the place apart. The threat of this kind of publicity shook the city fathers to the soles of their shoes, and Madame Sally's establishment took over premises in another town.

He frequently used sarcasm to bring his troops to life. Opening the locker room door after a disappointing first-half performance, he peered in at his team, shook his head, and said, "I beg your pardon. I thought this was a Notre Dame team." That was all. Rock's halftime invectives could evoke passion and pain. "Remember girls," he once said to his team after another lackluster first half, "let's not have any rough stuff out there." But when the game was over, Rockne always showed his team that there was nothing personal in his remarks. After berating the team as a whole, he would then shower with the players, forsaking his personal locker room. Few of his troops missed the point. But, by the next game, he would be back at work, exhorting them to win, bending the truth if necessary, threatening to quit, even using the phlebitis that plagued him late in his career to explain why a loss might kill him.

From the sidelines, squeezing an unlit cigar and often gesticulating wildly with it, Rockne marshaled the Irish's winning strategy. His innovations included the "Notre Dame shift," a refinement of a system that he inherited from former Irish coach Jesse Harper, in

which the backfield lined up in a T formation and shifted into a single wing. He developed the "Shock Troop" system, using his second-string players to start the game to absorb the initial blows of the opponents, then bringing in his first string to face a tired opponent. He was the first to advocate and implement what was then known as a "suicide schedule," a game with a major opponent every week.

The Rock was also a master of situational tactics. In a game against Nebraska in 1919, the Irish were ahead 14–9 in the fourth quarter but the players were exhausted. Slow down the game, Rockne told his star halfback, George Gipp. According to a Notre Dame publication, "The resourceful George used every legitimate time-waster in the book; and some which the officials seemed to think had a slight odor of illegality. The Cornhusker crowd booed; the Cornhusker players raged." But it worked and the game ended with Notre Dame still ahead by 5 points. Afterward a furious Nebraska coach, Henry Schulte, said to Gipp, "What course do you take at Notre Dame?" To which the Gipper replied, "Watch repair."

Rockne was highly respected throughout the country for his public speaking skills, inspirational thoughts and suggestions, and his legion of friends and followers, establishing him as a legend in his time.

"Rockne sold football to the men on the trolley, the elevated, the subway," said pupil Harry Mehre, "to the baker, the butcher, the pipe fitter who never went to college. He made it an American mania."

Many of his players went on to become successful coaches themselves, including Frank Leahy, Eddie Anderson, Jim Crowley and Adam Walsh. Rockne was killed in an airplane crash in Kansas several months before the start of the 1931 season, and a nation mourned.

Record

Schools: Notre Dame (1918–30)

Totals: Won 105, Lost 12, Tied 5; Percentage .881

BOB ZUPPKE

It is hard to imagine a less likely candidate than Bob Zuppke for coaching stardom. Born in Berlin, Germany, in 1879, he spoke with a thick accent. At the University of Wisconsin, he majored in philosophy (throughout his career he would quote Schopenhauer and Kant, often to the bewilderment of his players), and fine art was his avocation. He weighed a mere 140 pounds and stood five-feet-seven inches tall. He never played a minute of varsity football, although he did play on the Wisconsin scrub teams, helping out the varsity during scrimmages.

A talented painter, Zuppke launched a career in commercial art soon after graduating. Before long he was teaching art at Hackley Manual Training

School in Muskegon, Michigan, where he also became the football coach. His obvious coaching talent led shortly to assignments with several high school football teams, most notably at Oak Park in Chicago, where he developed a string of Illinois state champions. By 1913, a number of colleges actively sought his services, but it was the University of Illinois athletic director George Huff who won the young coach's allegiance.

The year after his arrival, Zuppke led the Illini all the way to the national title. During his three decades in Champaign, Zuppke won, or shared, seven Big Ten titles, produced four unbeaten teams, and secured three national championships.

"My definition of an All-American is a player who has weak opposition, and a poet in the press box," is a typical Zuppke remark. There was no denying, however, at least one athlete who starred for Zuppke was a true, unadulterated All-America, running back Red Grange (called "Grench" by Zuppke, with his German accent), who became one of the greatest stars the game has ever known, rock-

Illinois coach Bob Zuppke (right) poses with his most famous player, Red Grange, in 1924. Zuppke came to Illinois in 1913 and remained there through the 1941 season, winning or sharing three national titles and seven Big Ten championships. Four of his Illini teams were undefeated. Zuppke introduced such innovations as the screen pass, the modern huddle, the onside kick, the spiral pass from center, and the "Flea Flicker" play.

eting out of the Illinois backfield throughout the glory-filled seasons of 1923, 1924, and 1925.

"I will never have another Grange," Zuppke said at the time, "but neither will anyone else. They can argue all they like about the greatest player that ever lived. I'm satisfied I had him when I had Grange."

Zuppke developed great rivalries with Chicago's Stagg, over whom he held a dramatic 12-4-3 lifetime edge, and Michigan's Fielding Yost, against whom he was only 2-4. Still, Zuppke seemed to find considerable solace in one of his favorite nonathletic activities, something he called "Yost-baiting."

The highlight of this off-the-field rivalry occurred in 1924 at the American Football Coaches Association meeting in New York. With characteristic modesty, Yost, who had relegated himself to the post of athletic director at Michigan, prepared a speech to nominate himself for president of the organization. But Zuppke would not allow Yost to speak. "This organization is for coaches only," Zuppke announced. "Yost is not a coach. He's an athletic director." Adding to the insult, Zuppke then nominated himself and won the election—after casting the only vote for Yost. Such were the times.

Throughout the 1930s, the fortunes of the Illini declined, but a number of attempts to oust the head coach were thwarted. He finally retired at the end of the 1941 season to pursue, with considerable success,

Zuppke on the Record

In a letter written in 1943 to football historian H. A. Applequist, Bob Zuppke claimed the following as his own significant contributions to the game:

The spiral pass from center to the backs. The first was used by my teams in 1906 at Muskegon High School and Hackley Manual Training School. Lester Nelson my youthful center suggested the idea and together we made it practical.

The screen pass. This type of pass play was first developed at Oak Park High School by the aid of skillful ball handlers. This took place in the years 1910 and 1912 inclusive. I showed the plays from coast to coast. The American Rules Committee later legislated against the stratagem thus making it obsolete. That led to the development of the University of Illinois "kettle screen" which was difficult to execute, but legal and effective.

The guards protecting the forward passer. This was developed at the University of Illinois in 1914 and 1915.

The forward and backward lateral passes. This type of pass play was first attempted at Oak Park High School in 1910, and later refined at the University of Illinois. It was then known as the "flea flicker." At the University of Michigan–University of Pennsylvania game in 1901 I saw a backward pass followed by a forward pass. This maneuver suggested to me the reverse pass, namely, the so called "flea flicker." A variation of this play, also, at Oak Park High School was called the "Whoa Buck." Both of these plays were employed successfully by the University of Illinois football teams, together with an additional attraction, namely, the "Flying Trapeze" as used by my teams in 1933 to 1936 inclusive.

The huddle. The huddle formation was first used by the University of Illinois in 1921–22. This formation caused considerable controversy, because of its deviation from the orthodox method of calling signals. At the time the "huddle" was introduced, the innovation was called the "Ring around the Rosie," because the players arranged themselves in propinquity around the signal caller.

Wallace Wade turned two losing football programs in the South into winners. In 1923, he took over as head coach at Alabama and the following year produced a team that went undefeated. He took the Crimson Tide to Rose Bowls in 1926, 1927, and 1931. After the last he moved to Duke and turned the North Carolina school into a winner as well, including two trips to Rose Bowl games. He retired after the 1950 season.

his suspended art career as well as to raise prize hogs, another hobby he picked up along the way. But he left a lasting mark on the game of college football: the design of the modern, streamlined football, which would, of course, facilitate the passing game. "I cut the design out of leather in my own workshop," he claimed. Among other innovations for which Zuppke claimed responsibility were the onside kick, the spiral snap from center, the screen pass, guards pulling back to protect the passer, and what was later to be called the "flea flicker," where the quarterback hands off to a running back, who then laterals back to the quarterback for a pass downfield.

Record

Schools: Illinois (1913–41)

Totals: Won 131, Lost 81, Tied 13; Percentage .628

WALLACE WADE

"We were nothing but little country boys when we started, then Coach Wallace Wade made something out of us," said Alabama halfback Johnny Mack Brown just before the 1926 Rose Bowl game. Johnny Mack Brown went on to become a well-known movie star, and Wallace Wade established a football dynasty at Alabama, before moving on to Duke.

For the head coach of the Crimson Tide, the road to stardom had not been an easy one. When coach Dan McGugin was commanding the Vanderbilt powerhouses of the early 1920s, Wade was a virtually unknown assistant. Resigning this role to seek a head coaching spot of his own in 1922, Wade applied for the top job at the University of Kentucky. After a lengthy wait during the selection

proceedings, sitting outside the closed committee hearing, Wade became angered and stormed out, never again to offer his services to Kentucky.

Fortunately for the Crimson Tide, McGugin recommended his former assistant to Alabama, which was also seeking a new head coach. Within two years, Wallace Wade pounded a second-rate Alabama team into a winner. In 1924, he led the Crimson Tide to a perfect season and the Southern Conference championship. Undefeated again the following year, Alabama became the first Southern team to play in the Rose Bowl, defeating Washington 20–19.

Wade had a long and storied history in the Pasadena classic. His first Rose Bowl appearance had been as a guard, playing for Brown University in 1916. As head coach, he brought Alabama to Pasadena in 1926 (the one-point win over Washington), 1927 (a 7–7 tie against Stanford), and 1931 (when the Tide walloped Washington State 24–0).

Wade moved to Duke after the 1931 Rose Bowl game and was back in Pasadena in 1939, where his Blue Devils were defeated by USC. But it was the 1941 Duke team, and the weird Rose Bowl game that culminated the season, that is best remembered by football historians.

Wade's 1941 Duke team, led by quarterback Tommy Prothro (later to become an eminent coach himself), had destroyed every opponent by at least two touchdowns. For the second time in three years, an undefeated team under Wallace Wade seemed destined for Pasadena until, three weeks before the scheduled game, the Japanese attacked Pearl Harbor. Fearing Japanese attacks on crowded stadiums, Lieutenant General John DeWitt demanded the cancellation of all major sporting events in Southern California. But Percy Locey, the athletic director of Oregon State, refused to abide by the cancellation of his team's first Rose Bowl invitation.

Locey called Wade and asked if the game could be held in Durham, North Carolina, site of the Blue Devils' stadium. "The game's all yours," Wade said to Locey. "Manage it in Durham, as you see fit. You handle the gate receipts and everything else." So, for the only time in its history, the Rose Bowl game (in name only) was held outside California. Wade was happy to play in friendly territory—after his 1939 defeat, he had refused to shake hands with USC's coach Howard Jones, and then had compounded the insult by reputedly making remarks critical of the state of California.

Unfortunately for Wade he found further embarrassment right at home in Durham as his heavily favored team fell to Oregon State 20–16. Nevertheless, Wallace Wade will be remembered as the man who developed the Crimson Tide's winning football tradition, an ancestral thread of sorts to the glory they were to experience later under Bear Bryant.

Record

Schools: Alabama (1923–30),
Duke (1931–41, 46–50)

Totals: Won 171, Lost 49, Tied 10;
Percentage .765

BOB NEYLAND

His name was Robert Reese Neyland III, and he rose to the rank of brigadier general in the U.S. Army; he also became one of the most successful and respected coaches in the history of college football, a veritable institution at the University of Tennessee.

After graduating from West Point in 1916 where he had starred as an end on the football team, as a pitcher with a 35-5 record on the baseball team, and as the school's heavyweight boxing champion three years in a row, Neyland seemed intent on making a career of the Army. After graduation, he turned down major league baseball offers from the New York Giants, Philadelphia Athletics, and Detroit Tigers; as a lieutenant in the Corps of Engineers (he also earned a graduate degree in engineering from MIT), Neyland served with the American Expeditionary Force in France before returning to West Point in 1921 as an aide to academy superintendent Douglas MacArthur. He took on the additional duties of an assistant coach for both the Cadets' football and baseball teams. In 1925, he was transferred to the University of Tennessee to run the school's ROTC program; he also chose to sign on as an assistant football coach. The next year he was asked to take over as head coach, and Neyland decided to change professions.

Tennessee's football program was a disaster when Neyland took over: losing was the norm and the Volunteers were considered the doormat of the South. Worse, however, than the general failure of the team was the very specific embarrassment of the Vols' perennial defeat by intrastate rival Vanderbilt, a team they had not beaten since 1916 and to whom they had lost 18 of 21 games since the two schools began playing each other back in 1892. Neyland's mission, he was told emphatically, was to turn the tide against arch-enemy Vanderbilt. In 1927 Neyland's Volunteers tied Vanderbilt; the following year they defeated them and began a domination that would last for more than two and a half decades.

Neyland not only turned the football program around down in Knoxville, he created a dynasty. During his first six years at Tennessee, his teams won 52 games, lost only 1, and tied 5. In the three seasons from 1938 through 1940, Tennessee was 31-2, including a 22-game winning streak. When he retired after the 1952 season, he had won one national championship (1951), and shared two others (1938 and 1940), won five SEC championships, took his teams to all four of the major bowls, posted eight undefeated seasons, and had held opponents scoreless in 42 games.

Defense was Neyland's specialty, coupled with a highly effective kicking game. In 188 games during the first 19 of his 21 years as head coach at Tennessee, Neyland's teams gave up an average of only *five* points a game, which prompted Herman Hickman, a former Tennessee star and later coach of his own renown, to observe: "If Neyland could score a touchdown against you, he had you beat. If he could score two, he had you in a rout."

Neyland's career at Tennessee was twice interrupted when the Army called upon his services: for a year in 1935, to command a battalion of army engineers in Panama, and five more during World War II (1941–45), where he earned a Distinguished Service Medal among other military honors for his service in the China-Burma-India theater of operations.

He was a demanding coach, and not an easy one to play for, but his players held him in high esteem and basked in the success he brought to the teams they represented. Sportswriter and historian Tim Cohane described him this way: "The side of

Robert Reese Neyland that the public saw was cool, aloof, self-centered, autocratic, proud, sometimes arrogant. But to a chosen few he revealed a side that was warm and charming."

His influence as a coach was broad. His trademark defense was widely copied; he was credited with being the first to have a telephone hookup from the press box to the bench and to have his running backs wear light "tear-away" jerseys and low-cut shoes. Many of his players went on to impressive coaching careers themselves, including Herman Hickman, (Yale), Bobby Dodd (Georgia Tech), Bowden Wyatt (Wyoming, Arkansas), Murray Warmath (Minnesota), and Beattie Feathers (North Carolina State)

Record

Schools: Tennessee (1926–34, 1936–40, 1946–52)

Totals: Won 173, Lost 31, Tied 12; Percentage .829

Bob Neyland (hand extended) of Tennessee gives some last-second instructions to quarterback Buist Warren (21) before sending him into the 1940 Rose Bowl game, which the Volunteers lost to Southern Cal 14—0. General Neyland (he attained the rank of brigadier general in the Army Corps of Engineers as well) coached at Tennessee for 21 years, producing eight undefeated teams before retiring after the 1952 season.

EARL "RED" BLAIK

In the late 1930s at West Point, Army football had fallen into a state of disrepair, hastened by the reform of loose eligibility requirements (earlier some players had been recruited just to play football, some of whom never graduated much less served in the Army, while others played for four or five years). President Franklin D. Roosevelt (a former assistant secretary of the navy) had demanded in 1938 that the Army restrict its players to three years of varsity competition, including previous experience at civilian schools. The restriction has-tened West Point's slide into football oblivion. In 1939 and 1940, the once proud Cadets—a heritage that went back to the great teams captained by Elmer Oliphant just before World War I and Chris Cagle in the 1920s—could muster a total of only four victories.

In the meantime, Earl "Red" Blaik, a former Cadet player (1918–19, after playing at Miami of Ohio from 1914 to 1917—eligibility requirements being somewhat looser in those days), was leading Dartmouth to spectacular victories in the hills of New Hampshire. When Brigadier General Robert Eichelberger became the West Point superintend-

Earl "Red" Blaik looks on with disbelief at Baker Field as his Army team's 32-game winning streak is brought to an end by the extra point that gave Columbia a 21—20 victory in 1947. Blaik took over at West Point in 1941 and guided the Army dynasty through the 1940s: two national championships and three undefeated seasons. He retired after the 1958 season. Before coming to Army, Blaik had been the head coach at Dartmouth for seven years.

ent in late 1940, he quickly went to work trying to lure Blaik back to the Academy as head coach. Blaik needed considerable coaxing. Eichelberger had to promise to liberalize the Cadets' recruitment policy, to build a new house for the head coach, and to keep the line of command clear and streamlined.

Blaik soon realized the rare opportunity he was being offered at West Point. "A coach who comes in at the bottom of a curve," he said later, "has a pronounced advantage over one who succeeds to a going or even half-going operation. In 1941, there was no place to go at West Point but up. And we went up at a rate of speed that surprised a lot of people."

When Blaik took command of the West Point team, Europe was already at war and the service academies in America were attracting an enriched flow of students. But for the varsity players at West Point, the first taste of battle came not in Europe but on the scrimmage fields of the Army campus. Few of the Cadets on the 1941 varsity team were prepared for the thunder that Blaik brought to the Hudson Valley. His uncompromising demands strained every athlete to his limits.

While the world was at war, Army's football fortunes soared. Following three years of extraordinary rebuilding, Blaik's teams went on to three undefeated seasons, with national championships in 1944 and 1945. The offense of those championship teams was spearheaded by two phenomenal running backs, fullback Felix "Doc" Blanchard (Mr. Inside) and halfback Glenn Davis (Mr. Outside). In 1945, the Heisman Trophy was awarded to Blanchard, with Davis finishing second. In 1946, Davis won that honor. Blaik's Cadets were masters of all they surveyed.

Only a scoreless tie against Frank Leahy's Irish spoiled an otherwise perfect season for Blaik in 1946.

Even in 1947, with Blanchard and Davis gone, Army's winning ways continued until a monumental 21–20 upset by Columbia ended Blaik's undefeated streak at 33 games. After a bad loss to Notre Dame, Blaik masterminded another remarkable unbeaten streak of 28 games. Army's golden years of 1944 to 1950 were among the most impressive in the annals of college football—during seven full seasons, Blaik's Cadets were defeated only two times.

During the 1950s, Army's success was never quite the same, although in 1958 they were once again in contention for a national championship. Part of the reason was the play of that year's Heisman Trophy winner, halfback Pete Dawkins; another part was a newly installed Blaik innovation that came to be known as the "Lonesome End." With a wide receiver flanked out near the sideline, far from the ball, Blaik succeeded in spreading out defenses, which helped Army's passing game tremendously. (A standard sports trivia question: Who was Army's Lonesome End? Answer: Bill Carpenter, who was also a consensus All-America in 1959.) A great mystery that puzzled sportswriters throughout the 1958 season was, how did the Lonesome End, who seldom entered the huddle, know which play was being called? Blaik took his secret into retirement after the 1958 season; later, however, he revealed that the cue to Carpenter was the positioning of the quarterback's feet. Red Blaik left behind a fine winning record and a tradition of Cadet football excellence that remains a proud memory.

Record

Schools: Dartmouth (1934–40), Army (1941–58)

Totals: Won 166, Lost 48, Tied 14; Percentage .759

FRANK LEAHY

"To him there was only one way to play football," a sportswriter once said of Knute Rockne's greatest student: "The Frank Leahy way. His system was simple: You won."

No one except Rockne himself led the Irish to so many victories and honors as Frank Leahy. In a career spanning the years 1941 to 1953, shortened by ill health and two years in the Navy during World War II, Leahy's teams amassed four national championships and six undefeated seasons.

Despite that enviable record, Leahy never achieved his personal goal, "to go through ten seasons without a loss." On the other hand, neither has anyone else. During one remarkable streak, 1946–49, Leahy's Notre Dame teams went 39 games without a loss, yet even that astounding feat fell short of the coach's lossless 10-season ambition. "I still think we would have done it," Leahy pointed out later, "if our scholarships hadn't been cut down in 1948."

A tackle on Rockne's last team, Leahy's playing career was cut short by a knee injury in 1930. He tried unsuccessfully to hide the torn ligaments from his coach, especially when Leahy and Rockne ended up rooming together at the Mayo Clinic, both recuperating from leg surgery.

Leahy's determination to play is illustrated by a famous story from the 1929 season. Sidelined for several games by a fractured elbow, Leahy was intent

Wojciechowicz on Leahy

Alex Wojciechowicz, one of Fordham's "Seven Blocks of Granite," a two-time All-America there and later one of the finest centers ever to play professional football, remembers well Frank Leahy, who was a line coach at Fordham before becoming head coach at Boston College:

I liked Jim Crowley, our coach at Fordham, but my personal coach there was Frank Leahy, his assistant who handled the center and the guards. Every day with him it was snap the ball and block, snap the ball and block, hours on end.

There's a little story about Leahy and myself which happened my senior year [1937]. The way we used to practice, I'd center the ball and he'd go after me and bang me around the head, really give me a whack. After an hour of it, I'd have a headache. Well, in my last year, I said to him, "Frank, if you keep hitting me around the head like that, I'll probably flunk all my courses." Then I told him, "You know, coach, I never block against you in practice like I do in a game. I go easy on you. In a game I block like a wild man."

He looked at me very astonished. "What?" he shouted.

"What the heck, you're older and my coach. I don't want to hurt you."

He was furious. "From now on, you go after me just like you do in a ball game. Even more so!"

Well, I didn't for the next three or four blocks, and he knew it, and he reminded me of it. "Are you really sure?" I asked. He was, he said.

So I went at him as hard and as fast as I could. I don't think he knew what hit him. I got him just right. They carried him off the field, and for a long time after that he had to go up to Mayo Clinic for treatments for his back. I felt bad about that but that's the way Frank Leahy was. We remained good friends after I left Fordham and he went on to Notre Dame.

on taking the field against USC. After insisting to a skeptical Rockne that his arm had healed, he rolled up his left sleeve and flexed his elbow repeatedly, showing no pain or stiffness. Convinced, Rockne allowed him to play, forgetting that Leahy had fractured his right elbow, not his left.

As a coach, Leahy expected the same uncompromising effort from his players as he had given Rockne years earlier. Although his approach was more understated than his mentor's, he often used subtle wit and sarcasm to make a point, giving the impression that no amount of effort was quite enough.

Quarterback Frank Tripucka once told the story of how receiver Leon Hart made a remarkable catch, finally brought down with at least six players hanging on to him. Leahy's only comment, in his often exaggerated Irish brogue, was, "Oh, Leon, at Notre Dame, we not only catch the ball, but we run with it after we catch it."

After two years leading Boston College, Leahy came to Notre Dame in 1941. During the glory years of 1946 through 1949, Leahy's unbeaten national championship teams were famous for confusing defenses with highly unorthodox offensive patterns. His T formation gave way to the I formation, in which the backs lined up directly behind the quarterback, ready to break either way. On a number of occasions, he used a system of dual quarterbacks, lined up side by side and pivoting in opposite directions as the ball was snapped. Even the best-coached defenses withered in confusion.

Leahy always had a host of trick plays tucked well up his sleeve, such as his controversial fake injury play, to use when his time-outs were expended. "A team feels better if it believes it has something in reserve," the master pointed out. Perhaps the most notorious use of this tactic was in the Notre Dame–Iowa

game of 1952, carried out by tackle Frank Varrichione, who collapsed in a dead faint near the Iowa goal line with just seconds left before the half and the Irish trailing 7–0. He later explained his action on a television show hosted by fellow Notre Damer Regis Philbin: "If you were on the ground and looked at the scoreboard and saw your team trailing with time running out, wouldn't you feel sick?"

When emotional strain and poor health forced Leahy to retire in 1953, it took the Irish more than a decade to fully recover. Not until 1964 and the start of the Ara Parseghian era would the Irish get back on the track to glory.

Record

Schools: Boston College (1939–40), Notre Dame (1941–43, 1946–53)

Totals: Won 107, Lost 13, Tied 9; Percentage .864

CHARLES "BUD" WILKINSON

He owns one of the game's most prestigious records, a standard that may never be broken. It started during the third game of the University of Oklahoma's 1953 season, when the Sooners, coached by Charles "Bud" Wilkinson, defeated Texas 19–14. That victory started a record-shattering streak would not end until November 10, 1957, with a 7–0 upset by Notre Dame—the Wilkinson-coached Sooners won 47 games in a row. No other college team has ever come close.

It is hard to describe how completely Bud Wilkinson's team dominated college football in both the Midwest and the entire United States. But here's

Bud Wilkinson is carried triumphantly from the field after one of the 145 victories his Oklahoma teams logged. Wilkinson guided the Sooners to a win streak of 47 games from 1953 to 1957, by far the longest ever in college football history. Known for his powerful running game, his teams at Oklahoma prevailed in more than 82 percent of their games during his 17-year tenure there.

percentage of .826. Normally dressed in a white shirt and loosely knotted tie, the gray-haired wizard of Norman, Oklahoma, looked more like a business executive than a football coach as he paced up and down the sidelines during Sooner games.

On the field he was noted for popularizing a number of split-T modifications, but to the delight of his fans and the chagrin of his opponents, there was little mystery to his crushing ground attacks. Four of the great running backs who played under Wilkinson—Billy Vessels, George Thomas, Tommy McDonald, and Clendon Thomas—had the distinction of scoring more than 100 points in a single season. Oklahoma football was a testament to the efficacy of bone-jarring power, and Wilkinson had a natural ability to inspire desire and effort from his players. His all-business style, devoid of affectations, seemed just right for his time and place.

Had Wilkinson continued his college coaching career, he would probably rank among the winningest coaches of all time. While still at Oklahoma, Wilkinson was appointed to oversee President John F. Kennedy's pet Physical Fitness Program. He left the coaching profession after the 1963 season at age 50 to make an unsuccessful bid for the U.S. Senate in 1964, and later served in an executive post for President Richard Nixon.

Despite his relatively brief career, Wilkinson left behind a memorable legacy: three national titles, a 6-2 bowl record (including four Orange Bowl victories), and the longest winning streak in the history of college football.

Record

School: Oklahoma (1947–63)

Totals: Won 145, Lost 29, Tied 4; Percentage .826

a hint. Between 1948 and 1957, the Big Seven Conference (now the Big 12) had but a single champion—Wilkinson's Oklahoma Sooners. And his teams claimed three national championships: 1950, 1955, 1956.

Wilkinson was no stranger to winning streaks, having played guard on the undefeated Minnesota team coached by Bernie Bierman in 1934. During his playing days at Minnesota, he lined up against a stocky but powerful center for Ohio State named Gomer Jones, who made such an impression that Wilkinson later hired him as an assistant and saw to it that Jones eventually succeeded him as the Oklahoma head coach.

At Oklahoma, Wilkinson compiled one of the best winning records of modern times: 145 wins against 29 losses and 4 ties, for an enviable winning

PAUL "BEAR" BRYANT

"This must be what God looks like," said George Blanda describing the towering six-foot-three-inch Bear Bryant, his coach at Kentucky. The Bear went on to become a living legend with Alabama's Crimson Tide, and, although Penn State's Joe Paterno is relentlessly stalking his record, Bryant, with 323 victories, has reigned as the winningest coach in the history of major-college (Division I-A) football since his retirement in 1982.

What is it that separates Bryant from mere mortals in his profession? "I'm just a plow hand from Arkansas," he said in a *Time* magazine article near the end of his final season. "But I've learned over the years how to hold a team together. How to lift some men up, how to calm down others, until finally they've got one heartbeat together, a team."

Bryant had played at Alabama from 1933 through 1935, the "other end" on the Crimson Tide team that featured the legendary Don Hutson. With those two at ends and Dixie Howell at tailback, Alabama went undefeated in 1934, capping the season with a victory over Stanford in the Rose Bowl and a national championship.

Although he coached such high-spirited superstars as Kenny Stabler and Joe Namath, his ability to mold a team out of raw individual talents was the secret of his success. The awe he inspired in his players must have made the formidable task somewhat easier. Once before a game with Texas A&M, John David Crow, who went on to win the Heisman Trophy, stood outside Bryant's closed office door for more than an hour, anxious for a brief talk with his coach, but afraid to knock. People around Bryant treated him with the sort of respect usually reserved for divinity. Once when the coaching staff was

Bear Bryant watches as his Alabama team takes on Rutgers at the New Jersey Meadowlands in 1980. The Crimson Tide prevailed 17–13. A true coaching legend, Bryant joined Alabama in 1958 and brought the Tide five national titles and a share of another during his 25 years as head coach. He had previously coached at Maryland, Kentucky, and Texas A&M before coming to Alabama.

ordered to appear in his office for an early morning meeting, the story is told, an assistant coach slept on the office floor the night before because he was unsure of the exact hour of the appointment.

Although his presence may have hinted at the deific, his reputation was less godlike. Bryant's personal life was filled with contradictions. While many of the game's greatest coaches emphasized clean living and total sportsmanship, the Bear followed a more tortuous path. He fought a long but eventually successful battle against alcohol; he was also a gambler, and spent many hours at the craps tables in Las Vegas. While coaching at Texas A&M, he was at the center of a recruitment scandal involving cash payments and gifts of cars to athletes. In 1963, he and Georgia coach Wally Butts were accused in a *Saturday Evening Post* article of fixing the 1962 Alabama–Georgia game. Both sued and were exonerated, winning large cash settlements from the magazine. At all times, however, he seemed to test the limits of the rules so fiercely that NCAA officials kept a constant and concerted eye on him.

His technical coaching was not original. The Bear added a passing attack to the wishbone formation, which he borrowed from Darrell Royal. When he challenged NCAA rules with his tackle-eligible pass play, officials banned it. But he won football games, more often than anyone else. Another colorful coach, Bum Phillips, once said that Bryant won "because he coached people, not football."

Late in his career, the Bear insisted that when he stopped coaching football he would die. During the 1982 season, the Tide lost four games. "I'm going to alert the president of the university and anybody who wants to know that we need to make some changes, and we need to start at the top, and I'm at the top," Bryant said before the season was over. And, true to his prediction, Bear Bryant passed away less than a month after his final game, a 21–15 victory over Illinois in the Liberty Bowl.

Record

Schools: Maryland (1945), Kentucky (1946–53), Texas A&M (1954–57), Alabama (1958–82)

Totals: Won 323, Lost 85, Tied 17; Percentage .780

DARRELL ROYAL

The coach who found fame with the University of Texas Longhorns understood well the potential dangers of the forward pass. As an All-America defensive back for Oklahoma in the late 1940s, Darrell Royal played on two Sugar Bowl winners and set a school career record with 17 interceptions.

"When you pass, three things can happen, and two of them are bad," Royal said, after he had been firmly installed at Texas. Little wonder then that his

teams were noted for their outstanding rushing attacks. But when Royal first came to Texas, few people realized what kind of glory-maker had arrived.

One who seemed to understand Royal's talent early on was Bear Bryant. In 1956, while Bryant was still at Texas A&M, a sportswriter asked the Bear if he could see any stars looming on the college coaching horizon. "There are three great young ones right now," Bryant answered, "and one of them is Darrell Royal."

Following brief assignments at Mississippi State and Washington, Royal came to Texas after the Longhorns' disastrous 1-9 season in 1956. He quickly provided a glimpse of things to come when Texas upset previously top-ranked Arkansas in 1957, thus igniting what would become a great Southwest Conference rivalry.

By 1959, the Longhorns shared the conference championship with Arkansas and TCU, and went on to the Cotton Bowl. Royal always regarded the 1961 Texas team as one of his finest, comparing it favorably with his 1963 national championship team, the first ever for Texas. In 1961, the Longhorns sported Royal's new "flip-top" offense, which featured running back James Saxton, who, helped along considerably by Royal's novel plays, averaged almost 8 yards per carry and won All-America honors. Throughout much of the season, Texas was ranked first in both the AP and UPI polls, but Royal's dreams of a national title were dashed when underdog TCU defeated them in a defensive battle. Much to Royal's chagrin, TCU's only score came on a 50-yard touchdown pass.

For Royal, of course, there would be plenty of conference championships and No. 1 rankings in the future. The 30 consecutive victories he put together between 1968 and 1970 ranks as the 10th longest winning streak in college football history. He took Texas to six straight Cotton Bowls (1969–74). And he found considerable support for his prejudice against the forward pass when the Longhorns defeated Joe Namath's top-ranked and hitherto undefeated Alabama team 21–17 in the Orange Bowl on New Year's Day 1965. His 1969 Texas team was Royal's second undisputed national champion, while his Longhorns of 1970 shared the national title with Nebraska.

Royal's most lasting contribution to football strategy was unquestionably the wishbone offense, which he introduced in 1968 and used to propel the Longhorns to the top of the college ranks. In the wishbone, the quarterback could pass—if he had to. Bear Bryant was so impressed by the triple option the formation afforded the quarterback that he almost immediately installed the wishbone at Alabama, as did other coaches across the country.

Despite his obvious misgivings about the forward pass, a Royal-coached Texas team could use it effectively "when it was absolutely necessary," as he was once quoted. Still, Darrell Royal's personal philosophy was perhaps best summed up in his own words, when he saw a magazine illustration of his bitter 1961 defeat to TCU. "There's that damn pass," he said.

Record

Schools: Mississippi State (1954–55), Washington (1956), Texas (1957–76)

Totals: Won 184, Lost 60, Tied 5; Percentage .749

ARA PARSEGHIAN

When Ara Parseghian assumed command at South Bend in 1964, the fortunes of Notre Dame football were at an all-time low. The Fighting Irish had compiled a pathetic record of 19 wins against 30 losses from 1959 through 1963. Even the announcement of Ara's new role at South Bend began on a sour note.

With an impressive record of 75-41-2 at Miami (Ohio) and Northwestern University, including four consecutive victories against Notre Dame, Parseghian was negotiating for the head coaching position with the Irish when he walked out of a press conference called, it was thought by all, to announce his appointment. Apparently, a last-minute disagreement with one of the school's athletic administrators, Father Edmund Joyce, had brought about the debacle. The flustered coach, son of an Armenian father and French mother, returned for several days to Northwestern. A week later, however, Parseghian was back in South Bend to accept a new agreement,

Ara Parseghian is hoisted in triumph after his first victory as Notre Dame head coach in 1964, his Fighting Irish having just defeated Wisconsin 31–7. In the foreground is quarterback and that year's Heisman Trophy winner John Huarte (7). During his 11 years at Notre Dame, Parseghian won two national championships (1966 and 1973) and barely lost out on another (his first year, 1964). He retired from coaching after the 1974 season at age 51. Before Notre Dame, Parseghian was the head coach at Miami (Ohio) and Northwestern.

refusing forever to divulge the true nature of the previous row. "Father Joyce wanted a shamrock on the new helmets," Ara joked later about the incident, "and I wanted a camel crossing the desert."

"He should be with us for a long time," said athletic director Moose Krause, "after all, he signed twice." Parseghian seemed to agree, because he immediately departed from the conventional wisdom of new head coaches and built a house in Indiana.

From his very first season, Ara fashioned a new dynasty in South Bend, at once rekindling the beloved memories of Knute Rockne and Frank Leahy. Taking control of essentially the same team that had managed only two victories the previous season, Parseghian juggled assignments until he had an imposing passing attack and a solid defense. Then he began a series of tough drills for every member of the team, including workouts at four o'clock on Sunday afternoons, which, it is said, made the golden dome and spires shake around South Bend. An example of Parseghian's skillful development of talent: John Huarte went from being a third-string quarterback in 1963 to winning the Heisman Trophy in 1964.

Parseghian came to Notre Dame with a plan to make the lackluster team into national champions in four years, and came within seconds of doing the impossible in his first season. After winning their first nine games in 1964, only USC stood between Notre Dame and a national championship. When the showdown came, the Irish took a 17–0 lead into the locker room at halftime. But with less than two minutes to go in the game, the Trojans managed to pull out a 20–17 victory. "I prefer to think of our record as 9 3/4 to 1/4," the new Irish coach said of his first season, "not 9 and 1."

For another full decade, his teams pounded out the victories, showing totally new offensive looks virtually every season, and winning a national championship in 1966 (one year ahead of Parseghian's bold prediction) and again in 1973. Notre Dame had not been to a bowl game since 1925 when Parseghian brought his 1969 team to the Cotton Bowl, where they succumbed to Texas 21–17; the following year, however, he brought them back to trounce Texas 24–11. In his last three years at the helm of the Fighting Irish, Parseghian's teams played in two Orange Bowls and one Sugar Bowl.

The pressure-packed job finally took its toll on the high-strung coach. Parseghian had frequently fought the pressure by scrimmaging right along with his players, absorbing the blows along with the youngsters. By the end of his 11th season, however, he had had enough. After one of the most successful coaching careers in the proud Fighting Irish history, he resigned at the relatively young age of 51.

Record

Schools: Miami (Ohio) (1951-55), Northwestern (1956-63), Notre Dame (1964–74)

Totals: Won 170, Lost 58, Tied 6; Percentage .739

WOODY HAYES

For three decades at Ohio State, Wayne Woodrow Hayes was the winningest coach in the Big Ten. Considering his attitude, it is only surprising that he wasn't the winningest field general since Alexander the Great. "Without winners," he flatly asserted once, "there wouldn't be any civilization."

Despite his gleaming success on the field, many detractors found it odd that Hayes, of all people, should talk about being civilized. He was a loner, who one associate said "lived without friends happily." Woody's career was characterized by his frequent, and often violent, explosions of temper. During a 1971 game against arch-rival Michigan, Hayes demonstrated his anger against the officials by grabbing the yard markers and breaking them over his knee, then tossing the scraps onto the field.

Often, Hayes also used living targets to vent his displeasure. In 1973, a *Los Angeles Times* photographer claimed that the Ohio State coach shoved the camera back into his face when he tried to take a picture at a practice session before that season's Rose Bowl game, and then shouted, "That ought to take care of you, you son-of-a-bitch." The photographer dropped a criminal battery charge after Hayes sent him "an appropriate communication." In 1977, near the end of a game with Michigan, after a crucial Ohio State turnover, which in effect gave the game and a Rose Bowl trip to the hated Wolverines, an impetuous television cameraman stepped in front of Hayes to capture a close-up of the coach's anguish. Hayes punched him in the face.

The Buckeye coach often treated the working press, even the locals from Columbus, as wartime enemies. He was notorious for making them wait inordinately long for interviews, threatening them

with physical violence on occasion, and sometimes even following through on the threat if things were going badly. His aggressive instincts and legendary temper were not just reserved for sportswriters, but extended to everyone, players included.

Partly because of his stormy relationship with the press, Hayes was surrounded by criticism as well as accolades throughout his career. Some people complained that his "three yards and a cloud of dust" style of offense was outdated, and more than one writer called Ohio State's play monotonous. Other critics pointed to an Ohio State schedule that year after year excluded such nonconference power-

Woody Hayes, doused in the shower after his Buckeyes defeated Iowa in 1957 to clinch an invitation to the Rose Bowl. Temperamental and explosive, as well as the winningest coach in Big Ten history, Hayes became a legend at Ohio State during a career that spanned 1951–78. He brought the school two national championships (1954 and 1968) and a share of another (1957) as well as 14 Big Ten titles (some shared).

houses as Notre Dame, Oklahoma, and Nebraska. But by the end of 1978, Hayes could point to three national championships: 1954 (AP), 1957 (UPI), and 1968 (AP and UPI), and 14 Big Ten titles (a number of them shared with his nemesis, Michigan). In the history of the sport of college football he proved to be one of the winningest coaches, and even his harshest critics had to admit that there was nothing outdated about being a winner.

For all his success, Hayes lived a simple, spartan life. Although he made considerable money from a television show, hundreds of lectures and clinics, and three books, he rejected several offers of a raise in pay, insisting that the additional money go to his assistants instead. "I had a Cadillac offered to me a couple of times," he recalled. "You know how that works. They give you a Cadillac one year and the next year they give you the gas to get out of town."

The gruff genius of Ohio State football doomed his career at the Gator Bowl in late December 1978. In the last two minutes of that game, with Woody's Buckeyes trailing 17–15, Clemson linebacker Charlie Bauman intercepted an Ohio State pass and was knocked out of bounds not far from where Hayes was standing. Enraged at the turn of events, Woody rushed at Bauman, shouting, and took a swing at the linebacker, striking him on the face mask. When a Buckeye player tried to restrain Hayes, Woody turned and punched him just below the face mask. The next day Hayes was fired, bringing to an end his often successful, usually controversial, and always frenetic 28-year career at Ohio State.

Record

Schools: Denison (1946–48), Miami (Ohio) (1949–50), Ohio State (1951–78)

Totals: Won 238, Lost 72, Tied 10; Percentage .759

BO SCHEMBECHLER

Michigan has an illustrious football history, going back all the way to Fielding Yost's dominant teams in the first two decades of the twentieth century and carried on through the successful tenures of Harry Kipke in the 1930s, Fritz Crisler in the 1940s, Bennie Oosterbaan in the 1950s, and Chalmers "Bump" Elliott in the 1960s. But the winningest coach of all arrived in 1969, Glenn E. "Bo" Schembechler.

An offensive tackle in college, he played under Woody Hayes at Miami of Ohio, the school that has come to be known as the "Cradle of Coaches" because of the extraordinary number of its players who have gone on to famous football coaching careers in college and the NFL. Bo began his career as a line coach for Presbyterian College in Clinton, South Carolina, in 1954, taking a similar position the next year at Bowling Green in Ohio. From there he joined Ara Parseghian's staff at Northwestern for a year before moving on to serve the next five seasons as an assistant to Woody Hayes at Ohio State. In 1963 Schembechler was appointed head coach at his alma mater, Miami (Ohio), where he won two Mid-American Conference championships before coming to Michigan in 1969.

When he took over at Michigan, one of the great coaching rivalries in all college football was launched: Schembechler's Michigan and Hayes's Ohio State. Bo beat his former mentor the very first year 24–12 in an upset of major proportion, and then took his team to the Rose Bowl where they lost to Southern Cal 10–3. During the 10 years that Schembechler and Hayes went head-to-head in the Big Ten, Bo prevailed five times, Woody four, while the 1973 game ended in a 10–10 tie. In the 21 years

Bo Schembechler poses with some of his players on Media Day 1988. Schembechler won the most games of any coach in Michigan football history, 194, and captured or tied for 13 Big Ten championships. He took the Wolverines to 17 postseason bowls during his 21 years at Michigan.

that Schembechler's teams faced Ohio State, Bo won 11 against 9 losses and 1 tie.

The most memorable of the early matchups between Bo and Woody, however, were pleasant only to Hayes's Buckeyes: Michigan was undefeated in 1970 until they lost to Ohio State in Columbus; again in 1972 Ohio State spoiled a Wolverine perfect season; and again in 1974 the Buckeyes dealt Michigan its only loss of the season, this time additionally denying the Wolverines a trip to the Rose Bowl. But in 1976, Bo got some satisfaction by drubbing the Buckeyes 22–0, the only shutout in the years the two coaches faced each other. Even more so, however, in 1978, Hayes's last year at the OSU helm, with the Rose Bowl bid in the balance: Michigan went to Columbus and defeated the Buckeyes 14–3, and got the bid to Pasadena.

In his 21 years guiding the Wolverines, Schembechler compiled a record of 194-48-5, a winning percentage of .796. His record against Big Ten opponents was even better: 143-24-3. Thirteen of his

21 teams either won or tied for the Big Ten title; 17 went to bowl games, 10 of which were played at the Rose Bowl. Despite being in contention several times, Schembechler never captured the one thing he often said he wanted most (after defeating Ohio State, of course), a national championship.

After the 1989 season, Bo retired (he had also served as Michigan's athletic director the final two years). Changing sports, he took the job as president of the Detroit Tigers from 1990 to 1992, but kept a voice in football as a broadcaster and studio analyst for ABC Sports.

Upon retiring he was asked what his coaching philosophy had been. Bo gave a wry smile: "The Team, The Team, The Team," he said.

Record

Schools: Miami (Ohio) (1963–68), Michigan (1969–89)

Totals: Won 234, Lost 65, Tied 8; Percentage .775

JOE PATERNO

Harry Truman was president of the United States when Joe Paterno began his coaching career at Penn State; Joe DiMaggio and Ted Williams were still playing baseball, Ezzard Charles was the heavyweight champion of the world, Ben Hogan and Sam Snead ruled the golf world. More than 50 years and 10 presidents later, and in a new century, Joe is still at Penn State, primed to become the winningest coach in major college football history.

He was born in Brooklyn, New York, raised in New Jersey where he played football at St. Cecelia's High School in Englewood under a young coach just getting started in the business by the name of Vince Lombardi. In 1949 Joe graduated from Brown where he was a backfield star along with his brother, George, the two leading the Ivy League school to an 8-1 record his senior year.

After graduation, Paterno joined the staff of Rip Engle at Penn State as backfield coach and would remain under Engle for 16 years. In 1966, he became the Nittany Lions' 14th head coach; in 2001 he remains the state school's 14th head coach. With his successes over the years, Joe Paterno has easily established himself as one of the game's greatest coaches. But his impact has gone far beyond merely turning out winning teams and outstanding players. As Shane Conlan, one of those outstanding players—an All-America linebacker in college and an NFL standout—described his former coach, "He's tough as hell, but he does things the way they're supposed to be done. He follows the rules. He believes you're there for an education. He teaches you more than football. He teaches you about life." Paterno himself wrote in his autobiography, *Paterno: By the Book*, "The purpose of college football is to

serve education, not the other way around. . . . Ten years from now I want them to look back on college as a wonderful time of expanding themselves—not just four years of playing football."

But play football his teams did. As the 2001 football season got underway, Paterno had won more major college football games, 322, than any coach save Bear Bryant, the record holder at 323. He had captured two national championships (1982 and 1986) and produced four other uncrowned yet undefeated teams (1968, 1969, 1973, 1994). He has taken his team to 30 bowl games and won 20 of them; for trivia buffs he is the only coach in history to claim victory in each of the four major bowls: Rose, Sugar, Cotton, and Orange. In the first eight years alone, Paterno posted a record of 74-13-1.

There are many highlights close to Paterno's heart, the following are some he admits to. The dramatic 15–14 win over Kansas on New Year's Day 1969 at the Orange Bowl (a 2-point conversion with 15 seconds left). The 30–6 romp over Texas in the 1972 Cotton Bowl, which he called "one of the greatest

Joe Paterno victorious: his Nittany Lions have just defeated Georgia in the Sugar Bowl, 27–23, to claim the 1982 national title. Going into the 2001 college football season, Paterno trailed Bear Bryant as major college football's winningest coach by a single game. Since taking over the Nittany Lions in 1966, he has won 322 games to Bryant's 323. His taking Penn State to 30 postseason bowls and triumphing in 20 of them are both NCAA records. Paterno also posted five undefeated seasons at Penn State: 1968, 1969, 1973, 1986, and 1994.

victories in school history." Going undefeated on the running of Heisman Trophy winner John Cappelletti in 1973. Defeating Georgia 27–23 in the Sugar Bowl to clinch Penn State's first national championship. His defense intercepting Vinny Testaverde five times while beating Miami (Florida) 14–10 at the Fiesta Bowl to reap a second national championship in 1986. Posting his 200th victory on September 5, 1987, with a 45–19 win over Bowling Green. Claiming his first Big Ten title in 1994 with a come-from-behind 35–31 win over Illinois (Penn State joined the conference in 1993). Becoming only the sixth coach in NCAA history to win 300 games when his Nittany Lions rolled over Bowling Green 48–3 in 1998.

Milestones, however, are not what motivate him, Paterno once said. There is much more to it than that. "My motivation has to come not only from what I want to do but my ability to get some other people to do some things the right way. If I have a strong suit, it has been the fact that I have set a standard. I can't expect other people to follow if I have not set a standard myself."

Besides endowing Penn State with a wonderful football reputation, Joe and his wife, Suzanne, have returned much of the money he has received as a result of his coaching there, most prominently a gift of $3.5 million in the late 1990s. Penn State president Graham Spanier perhaps got to the heart of it when he said of the coach who has done so much for his school: "I have a theory that Joe coaches not so much for what he can do for football as for what he can do for the university and the community."

Record

Schools: Penn State (1966–)

Totals: Won 322, Lost 90, Tied 3; Percentage .780

EDDIE ROBINSON

On the warm evening of September 25, 1982, a chant echoed back and forth in Florida A&M's Bragg Stadium. "Not here, Eddie, not here! Not here, Eddie, not here!" the fans taunted. But it did happen there. When Eddie Robinson's Grambling Tigers came from behind in the fourth quarter to defeat the home team, Coach Robinson joined the most select club in the proud annals of collegiate football. That night, he won his 300th game. Only Stagg, Warner, and Bryant had done it before. He was far from finished, however.

The name of Eddie Robinson is not listed in the major college coaches' section of the NCAA Official Record Book because Grambling, the small, pre-dominantly black university in northern Louisiana where he coached for 55 years, is not a Division I-A member. By the time he retired after the 1997 season, however, Robinson had coached in more games (588) and won more (408) than any coach in college football history.

At age 22 in 1941, Robinson became the head coach at Grambling, when the enrollment at that institution was a mere 320 students and only shortly after it had been renamed from Louisiana Negro Normal and Industrial Institute. His starting salary was $63.75 per month. He suffered a losing season that first year but came back with a vengeance the next, posting a 9-0 record and shutting out every opponent. It was the beginning of a dynasty. Since the early 1950s, Grambling has won more than 75 percent of its games.

Some may quibble with Robinson's record because of the NCAA's varying classifications of Grambling over the years, which have included Small College, Division II, and Major College, and

Grambling's longtime coach and college football legend, Eddie Robinson talks with two of his players on the sideline of this 1971 game against Mississippi Valley, which proved to be his 200th college coaching victory. Robinson began his career at Grambling in 1941; after 55 seasons as head coach he had guided the Tigers to 408 victories, the most by any coach in all college football history. He retired after the 1997 season, having coached in more games (588) than any coach ever had before.

the smaller college opposition his teams have faced. Grambling is currently in Division II and a member of the Southwestern Athletic Conference.

But all NCAA officials do not necessarily share such qualms or prejudices. On the occasion of his 300th victory, NCAA associate director of statistics Steve Boda said, "If he gets to 324, we'll consider him the winningest college football coach of all time, regardless of division, pure and simple." When he reached 408, most everybody considered him the winningest coach in college football history, but still his mark escapes the NCAA Official Record Book. Those who would accuse Robinson of winning at least a portion of his honor in the bush leagues might, however, consider that Eddie Robinson has surely sent as many players to the pros as any other coach; he can claim more than 200.

For all his success, Robinson changed little over nearly half a century of coaching. He continually cautioned his students about the dangers of drugs, loose women, and a lackadaisical attitude toward education. At 6:00 A.M. on most school days, he walked up and down the corridors of the Grambling dorm, ringing an old-fashioned school bell to be certain that all students woke early enough to attend their first class.

The tradition remembered best by Grambling players, however, was Robinson's ritual of bringing back former students to help train newcomers each year. "When I was at Grambling," USFL star wide receiver Trumaine Johnson said, "I got to work with former players like Frank Lewis, Sammy White, and Charlie Joiner." Another insight into the man can be found in this story related by sportswriter Tony Barnhart. "When Grambling did not field a team in 1943 and 1944 due to World War II, Robinson coached the local high school football team. One day the father of Robinson's star running back came to practice wanting to take his son home to pick cotton. Robinson responded by taking his whole team to the fields. Once the cotton was picked, the running back [and the rest of the team] was allowed to return to practice."

All of his former players remember with a touch of reverence Eddie Robinson, the carefully dressed, patriotic, raspy-voiced football genius who made history in the profession of coaching college football. According to Penn State coach Joe Paterno, "No one has ever done or ever will do what Eddie Robinson has done for this game. . . . Our profession will never be able repay Eddie Robinson for what he has done for the country and the profession of football."

Record

School: Grambling (1941–42, 1945–97)

Totals: Won 408, Lost 165, Tied 15; Percentage .707

COACH OF THE YEAR

Each year the American Football Coaches Association (AFCA) and the Football Writers Association of America (FWAA) poll their members to determine a Coach of the Year. The AAFC began its poll in 1935, the FWAA in 1957. When the two organizations differ in their selection, both are given.

YEAR	COACH	TEAM	YEAR	COACH	TEAM	YEAR	COACH	TEAM
1935	Lynn Waldorf	Northwestern	1962	John McKay	USC	1980	Vince Dooley	Georgia
1936	Richard Harlow	Harvard	1963	Darrell Royal	Texas	1981	Danny Ford	Clemson
1937	Ed Mylin	Lafayette	1964	Ara Parseghian (AFCA & FWAA)	Notre Dame	1982	Joe Paterno	Penn State
1938	Bill Kern	Carnegie Tech				1983	Ken Hatfield (AFCA)	Air Force
1939	Eddie Anderson	Iowa	1964	Frank Broyles (AFCA)	Arkansas	1983	Howard Schnellenberger (FWAA)	Miami (Florida)
1940	Clark Shaughnessy	Stanford	1965	Tommy Prothro (AFCA)	UCLA			
1941	Frank Leahy	Notre Dame	1965	Duffy Daugherty (FWAA)	Michigan State	1984	LaVell Edwards	Brigham Young
1942	Bill Alexander	Georgia Tech	1966	Tom Cahill	Army	1985	Fisher DeBerry	Air Force
1943	Amos Alonzo Stagg	College of the Pacific	1967	John Pont	Indiana	1986	Joe Paterno	Penn State
1944	Carroll Widdoes	Ohio State	1968	Joe Paterno (AFCA)	Penn State	1987	Dick MacPherson	Syracuse
1945	Bo McMillin	Indiana	1968	Woody Hayes (FWAA)	Ohio State	1988	Don Nehlen (AFCA)	West Virginia
1946	Earl Blaik	Army	1969	Bo Schembechler	Michigan	1988	Lou Holtz (FWAA)	Notre Dame
1947	Fritz Crisler	Michigan	1970	Charles McClendon (AFCA)	Louisiana State	1989	Bill McCartney	Colorado
1948	Bennie Oosterbaan	Michigan	1970	Darrell Royal (AFCA)	Texas	1990	Bobby Ross	Georgia Tech
1949	Bud Wilkinson	Oklahoma	1970	Alex Agase (FWAA)	Northwestern	1991	Bill Lewis (AFCA)	East Carolina
1950	Charlie Caldwell	Princeton	1971	Paul Bryant (AFCA)	Alabama	1991	Don James (FWAA)	Washington
1951	Chuck Taylor	Stanford	1971	Bob Devaney (FWAA)	Nebraska	1992	Gene Stallings	Alabama
1952	Biggie Munn	Michigan State	1972	John McKay	USC	1993	Barry Alvarez (AFCA)	Wisconsin
1953	Jim Tatum	Maryland	1973	Paul Bryant (AFCA)	Alabama	1993	Terry Bowden (FWAA)	Auburn
1954	Red Sanders	UCLA	1973	Johnny Majors (FWAA)	Pittsburgh	1994	Tom Osborne (AFCA)	Nebraska
1955	Duffy Daugherty	Michigan State	1974	Grant Teaff	Baylor	1994	Rich Brooks (FWAA)	Oregon
1956	Bowden Wyatt	Tennessee	1975	Frank Kush (AFCA)	Arizona State	1995	Gary Barnett	Northwestern
1957	Woody Hayes	Ohio State	1975	Woody Hayes (FWAA)	Ohio State	1996	Bruce Snyder	Arizona State
1958	Paul Dietzel	Louisiana State	1976	Johnny Majors	Pittsburgh	1997	Lloyd Carr (AFCA)	Michigan
1959	Ben Schwartzwalder	Syracuse	1977	Don James (AFCA)	Washington	1997	Mike Price (FWAA)	Washington State
1960	Murray Warmath	Minnesota	1977	Lou Holtz (FWAA)	Arkansas	1998	Phillip Fulmer	Tennessee
1961	Paul Bryant (AFCA)	Alabama	1978	Joe Paterno	Penn State	1999	Frank Beamer	Virginia Tech
1961	Darrell Royal (FWAA)	Texas	1979	Earle Bruce	Ohio State	2000	Bob Stoops	Oklahoma

THE CRADLE OF COACHES

One university, Miami (Ohio), has an unparalleled record in turning out successful football coaches. All the following played football for Miami, then went on to make their mark as head coaches with major colleges or NFL teams, with the exception of Paul Brown, who did not play and merely cheered the team on while an undergraduate there.

COACH	GRADUATED FROM MIAMI	BEST KNOWN FOR COACHING
Earl Blaik	1917	Dartmouth (1934—40)
		Army (1941—58)
Paul Brown	1930	Cleveland Browns (1948—62)
		Cincinnati Bengals (1968—73)
Weeb Ewbank	1930	Baltimore Colts (1954—62)
		New York Jets (1963—73)
Ara Parseghian	1947	Miami (1951—55)
		Northwestern (1956—63)
		Notre Dame (1964—73)
Paul Dietzel	1948	Louisiana State (1955—61)
		Army (1962—65)
		South Carolina (1966—74)
Bill Arnsparger	1950	Kentucky (1954—61)
		New York Giants (1974—76)
Bo Schembechler	1951	Miami (1963—68)
		Michigan (1969—89)
John Pont	1951	Miami (1956—62)
		Indiana (1965—72)
		Northwestern (1973—77)
Carmen Cozza	1952	Yale (1965—96)
John McVay	1953	Dayton (1964—71)
		New York Giants (1976—78)
John Mackovic	1966	Kansas City Chiefs (1983—86)

Other coaches who served their apprenticeships on Miami coaching staffs include Woody Hayes (above) of Ohio State, Stu Holcomb of Purdue, and Sid Gillman of the San Diego Chargers.

> "Football is only a game.
>
> Spiritual things are eternal.
>
> Nevertheless,
>
> Beat Texas!"
>
> A sign outside the First Baptist Church
> of Fayetteville, Arkansas, circa 1980

4

BRAGGING RIGHTS
THE RIVALRIES

College football is home to so many rivalries, hot and frenetic, that at times it seems there isn't a game listed on a given Saturday that could not be described as a rivalry. Every team has at least one arch-rival, some several. These deep-rooted antipathies often crop up within a conference, or merely because the schools are within the same state. But some heated rivals are continentally divided, such as Notre Dame and Southern California; historically nurtured, witness Williams–Amherst; or professionally at war, like Army and Navy.

Whatever the reason, rivalries exist all over the nation's gridirons and they add a certain something to college football. Beyond the bitter battles on the field of play, they give students reasons to rage and party and alumni something to savor, gloat over, or suffer through.

Harvard and Yale is perhaps the oldest rivalry in college football lore . . . that is, if you don't count Princeton and Rutgers or Rutgers and Columbia, both of whom began playing each other with special fervor a few years before Harvard and Yale first met in full football combat in the autumn of 1875.

Army and Navy put on the most picturesque show with their precision-marching Cadets and Midshipmen and all the brass from the Pentagon and other VIPs from Washington who routinely come for the game. It has been said that the specially scheduled Saturday morning trains from Washington to Philadelphia on the day of this illustrious contest carry more scrambled eggs on Army and Navy hat peaks than were served to the invading American forces on D-Day morning. Tradition also requires that the president of the United States attend the game, sitting on the Army side for one half and the Navy side the other. The commander-in-chief is supposed to favor neither service academy, but no one believes Dwight D. Eisenhower could summon a scintilla of pleasure following a Navy score. And most observers found John F. Kennedy inordinately quiet while he sat his half on the Army side of the field.

Certainly the most extravagant display of alumni riches is in evidence when Texas and Oklahoma get together each year and the Longhorn and Sooner oilmen and ranchers invade with their squadrons of private planes and convoys of limousines. Tailgate parties outside the Cotton Bowl have featured everything from silver bowls of Beluga caviar and magnums of Dom Perignon to Tex Mex chili and barbecued ribs. At the same time it is not unknown to see alums partying off the rear of a Rolls-Royce or Bentley before a Harvard–Yale game.

Rivalries have also given birth to a breathtaking range of imaginative pranks, many clever, others mean-spirited . . . and some, of course, both The fertile minds of the students of Stanford and California have long been tested to see who could outdo whom in the way of pranking. Notre Dame and USC fans ache to humiliate each other in new and creative ways every fall.

We have selected some especially fervid rivalries to chronicle here. But there are dozens more that are part of the rich tradition of college football, between big schools, between small colleges, teams that reside in the same state and those that are almost a continent apart. How could we forget:

Pittsburgh–Penn State
Tennessee–Vanderbilt
Purdue–Indiana
Texas–Texas A&M
Louisiana State–Tulane
Missouri–Kansas

Alabama–Georgia

Florida–Florida State

Michigan–Michigan State

Mississippi–Mississippi State

North Carolina–North Carolina State

Oklahoma–Nebraska

Georgia–Georgia Tech

Washington–Washington State

Clemson–South Carolina

Cornell–Colgate

Texas–Arkansas

Notre Dame–Army

Minnesota–Michigan

Nebraska–Oklahoma

Oregon–Oregon State

California–Stanford

Texas–Arkansas

Williams–Amherst

Lehigh–Lafayette

Bates–Colby

Wabash–Depauw

The list goes on and on . . .

Halfback Clint Frank (14) gains a few yards for Yale in their 1937 meeting with Harvard at Cambridge. Despite the efforts of Frank, who would win the Heisman Trophy that year, the Elis fell to the Crimson that day 13–6. The Harvard–Yale rivalry began on a Saturday afternoon, November 13, 1875, in New Haven, with 20 players on each side and a soccer-like scoring system; Harvard won that game, too, 4–0.

HARVARD–YALE

T.A.D. Jones, one of Yale's more storied coaches, stood before his team in the Eli dressing room one day in the mid-1920s and said: "Gentlemen, you are about to play football for Yale against Harvard. Never in your lives will you do anything so important."

Years later, at the Yale Bowl on a Saturday afternoon in November of 1983, Harvard and Yale met to play the 100th game in their august Ivy League rivalry. Although it had been many a decade since either team had seriously pursued anything as unscholarly as a national football championship, the event hardly went unnoticed. Seventy thousand fans cheered, presumably not all at the same time, as more than 60 former Harvard and Yale captains were introduced before the game. The eldest was 94-year-old Hamilton Fish of Harvard, two-time All-American tackle (1908–09), who could also boast of having tackled Jim Thorpe. Harvard won the most ancient alumnus contest by a mere two years over Yale's Henry Ketcham, age 92, center, and another two-time All-American (1911–12). Harvard also went on to win the ensuing game that day 16–7.

Not surprisingly, no one at the 1983 game had been present at the very first Harvard–Yale contest,

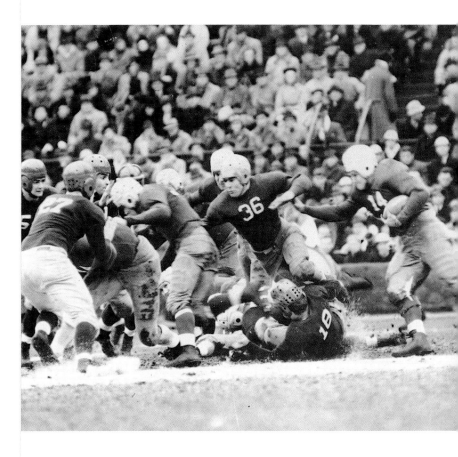

which was held more than a century earlier in 1875. A milestone in the history of American football, that original battle commenced with pregame negotiations—necessary because each team played a different form of the game: Harvard's version was based loosely on rugby, while Yale's had its roots in soccer, so the two schools had to resolve their conflicting styles of play.

Two delegates from each school convened at Springfield, Massachusetts, to agree on a series of "concessionary rules." As Harvard's newspaper, the *Crimson*, would report after the game: "The adopted rules were not fully understood by either team, and the Yale men said that they differed from theirs more than from Harvard's." Yale had consented to play Harvard's rugby-style rules, and Harvard had agreed to play the game at Yale.

So, on a Friday evening in November 1875, the Harvard team, accompanied by about 150 students, boarded a train to New Haven for the game the following afternoon. On Saturday morning, Yale students obligingly led members of the Harvard team on a tour of New Haven's major sights. The spirit of good-natured camaraderie was even carried over to the game, with rooters for either side applauding good plays, regardless of who made them.

That Saturday was a perfect day for football, slightly overcast with virtually no wind. Approximately 2,000 people crowded into the grandstands at Yale's Hamilton Park for the game, scheduled at 2:30. One of the fascinated fans was Walter Camp, who would attend Yale the following year, and later do so much to establish the modern rules of American football.

Football and the Poet

Archibald MacLeish, noted poet, essayist, and dramatist, Librarian of Congress, Boylston Professor at Harvard, and three-time recipient of the Pulitzer Prize, played football while a student at Yale. In the following excerpt from a speech of his, he recalls those days:

It is historically true that I played football at Yale. It is historically true that I won my freshman numerals. It is even historically true that I won my Y—as an all-purpose, all-position substitute on a series of Yale teams which never beat Harvard. . . .

I have only one glorious memory of those four years and its setting is not Soldiers' Field in Cambridge but the bar of the long-vanished Tremont Hotel in Boston. We— we being the Yale freshman team of the fall of 1911—had just held the best Harvard freshman team in a generation (Brickley, Bradlee, Hardwick, Collidge, Logan) to a nothing–nothing tie in a downpour of helpful rain and we were relaxing, not without noise, when the coach of that famous Harvard freshman team approached us, looked us over, focused (he had had a drink or two himself) on me and announced in the voice of an indignant beagle sighting a fox that I was, without question, the dirtiest little sonofabitch of a center ever to visit Cambridge, Massachusetts. It was heady praise. But unhappily I didn't deserve that honor either: I was little but not that little.

Pep Talk

Hefty Herman Hickman, Yale's colorful coach from 1948 to 1951, known as the "Poet Laureate of the Great Smokies" (he was from Tennessee), was noted for his unique pep talks, which included quoting the classics in stentorian tones. This memorable one delivered before a Harvard game was preserved by John McCallum in his book *Ivy League Football Since 1872*:

"Ye call me chief," he [Hickman] declaimed, "and ye do well to call me chief. If ye are men, follow me! Strike down your guard, gain the mountain passes, and there do bloody work as did your sires at old Thermopylae!" His voice impassioned now, his features grim with determination. "Is Sparta dead? Is the old Grecian spirit frozen in your veins, that you do crouch and cower like a belabored hound beneath his master's lash? O, comrades, warriors, Thracians! If we must fight, let us fight for ourselves. If we must slaughter, let us slaughter our oppressors! If we must die, let it be under the clear sky, by the bright waters, in noble, honorable battle!"

Then, having concluded his rendition of *Spartacus to the Gladiators*, he snapped his fingers. "Whadya say, men," he growled. "Let's go, gang. Whadya say, let's go chew up those Harvards."

Harvard won the toss and Yale kicked off. The players from Cambridge scored the first touchdown six minutes after the game began and kicked a goal a few minutes later. Before the first of the three half-hour periods ended, Harvard kicked a second goal. In the second period, Harvard scored a touchdown after an attempted kick for a goal hit the uprights. According to the rules of the day, a kicked goal was worth more than a touchdown.

When Yale was threatening to score in the third period, one of its players was thrown on the ball, which deflated. The ball was pumped up and put in play again, but Yale's chances for victory had burst. The final score was 4 goals and 4 touchdowns for Harvard, none for Yale.

Until about 1910 or so, what are now known as Ivy League teams, especially Yale, Harvard, and Princeton, dominated college football. Yale and Harvard contests were always well-fought battles, but the overall crown for the Golden Age of the Ivy League, the late 1800s and the first decade of the twentieth century, must be handed to Yale. By 1910, after 31 meetings, Yale had triumphed in 23 of the games, Harvard only 5, and 3 ended in ties.

There were some grand names on the roster in those days. Walter Camp began his remarkable football career as a player at Yale in 1876: he coached the Eli from 1888 through 1892. Playing end from 1885 through 1888 was Amos Alonzo Stagg. In the Harvard–Yale games of 1888 through 1891, spectators watched the legendary strongman Pudge Heffelfinger bolster the Yale line. Debuting in 1891 was Frank Hinkey, one of the school's all-time great ends, called the "Football Freak" because at a fragile 150 pounds, with a noticeably anemic pallor, he hardly appeared to be what he was—the most brutal and feared tackler of his time. In the early 1900s, Yale could also claim such other early luminaries as T.A.D. Jones and Ted Coy.

Harvard had its share of stellar lights as well around this time, backs like Charles Daly, Benjamin Dibblee, Percy Wendell, Charlie Brickley, and Eddie Mahan, among others.

Yale's dominance in the rivalry came to an end when Percy Haughton took over the head coaching duties at Harvard in 1908. During his nine-year tenure, Yale won only two of the nine contests. By the mid 1920s, Harvard–Yale matches no longer carried the possibility of propelling either team to a national championship. Over the years, quite a few people destined for prominence in other fields participated in the annual brawls, such as Archibald MacLeish and John Hersey from Yale and Bobby and Ted Kennedy from Harvard, the latter best remembered as having scored Harvard's only touchdown in their 1955 loss to Yale.

The most memorable modern installment of the old rivalry came in 1968, when, by a somewhat miraculous turn of events, both teams had undefeated seasons going into the big game. That year Harvard had developed a defensive powerhouse, while Yale, led by quarterback Brian Dowling (who was later and forever after immortalized as the never-without-his-helmet B.D. of Garry Trudeau's comic strip *Doonesbury*) and halfback Calvin Hill, produced its best offense in many years.

With 42 seconds to go, the Yale Bulldogs were ahead 29–13. Sportswriters were already wrapping up their stories describing the ruination of the Crimson's heretofore perfect season. But in that 42 seconds, Harvard scored a touchdown, a 2-point conversion, and another touchdown just as time expired. Then, with the game clock at zero, Harvard racked up another 2-point conversion to tie the score. The *Crimson* captured the miracle finish with its proud headline: "Harvard Beats Yale, 29–29."

Army captain and All-American halfback Pete Dawkins (left) calls attention to the Cadets' most fervent wish for 1958, posted on a campus building at West Point. A few days later he made that wish come true, leading Army to a 22–6 victory over Navy at Municipal Stadium in Philadelphia. With Dawkins is fellow back Joe Caldwell. Dawkins won the Heisman Trophy in 1958.

ARMY–NAVY

What remains one of college football's most colorful rivalries began more than a century ago. In 1890, the Naval Academy at Annapolis, Maryland, challenged West Point's Military Academy to a game of soccer-style football with, of course, the bruising body contact that had become an integral part of the American game. The mere fact that Army had no football team at the time was hardly an excuse to ignore the challenge.

Rushing to fill the void, a young cadet named Dennis Michie gathered some of the best athletes at West Point and gave them a crash course in the sport. Near the end of November, Navy's Midshipmen sailed up the Hudson and marched across the plains at the Point to meet the inexperienced Army team.

While en route, the Middies commandeered a goat that was grazing in a yard and brought it along to the contest to serve as the team mascot, launching a tradition that remains to this day. Whether because of the goat, or their great familiarity with

blocking and tackling, Navy trounced the Cadets in their first football encounter. The final score was 24–0. Enraged by the lopsided defeat, Army issued an immediate challenge to meet again the following year at Annapolis. When the two teams reassembled in 1891, Army, with a year of rigorous practice behind them, defeated Navy by a score of 32–16. The historic rivalry was underway, but not for long.

After the fourth meeting in the series, in 1893, an Army brigadier general and a Navy rear admiral got into a terrific argument over some game detail and challenged each other to a duel. Shortly thereafter, President Grover Cleveland issued an edict banning games between the two military academies. The ban was observed until 1899, when officials at both academies agreed to renew the series (and presumably instructed their officers to refrain from dueling about it).

The Army team, never to be outdone by Navy, by now had adopted a mule as their mascot. The creature selected to counter Navy's goat, which was now known as Billy, was relieved of its duties hauling an ice wagon; then it was curried, groomed, bedecked in leggings, and, with black and gold

Stop the War

Coach Earl Blaik received this telegram just after the 1944 Army–Navy game, which Army won 23–7 to cap an undefeated season:

The greatest of all Army teams.
We have stopped the war to celebrate
Your magnificent success.

DOUGLAS MACARTHUR

streamers fluttering from its ears and tail, brought to the Army sideline. It must have had the desired effect because the Cadets pummeled the rival Middies 17–5 that day in 1899.

Once the rivalry resumed, it continued to grow in popularity and intensity, despite a number of brief hiatuses: in 1909 after the death of an Army player during a game; in 1917 and 1918 because of World War I; and in 1928 and 1929 when Annapolis and West Point disagreed on eligibility requirements for their players.

In the twentieth century, the yearly Army–Navy game evolved into a national phenomenon. A number of sports historians have claimed that the series produced football's first ticket scalpers. To accommodate the huge number of spectators seeking tickets for the classic confrontation, the game has been held throughout much of its history in Philadelphia, first at Franklin Field, then Municipal Stadium, and since 1980 at Veterans Stadium (though the 1983 game was played at the Rose Bowl).

In 1926, the schools helped to dedicate Chicago's Soldier Field. Before a crowd estimated at 110,000, Army, led by All-America Chris "Red" Cagle, and an undefeated Navy team battled to a 21–21 tie in what many consider one of the greatest college football games of all time.

Two decades later, an equally memorable game was played at Philadelphia's Municipal Stadium. Going into the final game of the 1946 season, Earl "Red" Blaik's Cadets were undefeated, cursed only by a tie with Notre Dame; in fact that magnificent Army team had not lost a game in three seasons. They were in contention with Notre Dame for the national championship, and it was the final game for Army's famous one-two punch, "Mr. Outside" Glenn Davis and "Mr. Inside" Doc Blanchard.

War of Words

Dan Jenkins, *Sports Illustrated* staffer, wrote about the furtive goings-on at the 1949 Army–Navy game in his book *Saturday's America:*

> Not only did the Cadets whomp Navy 38–0, but they took advantage of some espionage to embarrass the Midshipmen before all of their admirals. An Army officer on duty at Annapolis had learned of a Navy plan to hoist some banners poking fun at Army's 1949 schedule and to parody "On, Brave Old Army Team," the West Point fight song. Soon after both student bodies had done their usual pregame march-on, drills and salutes, they took their places across the field from each other and Navy cheerfully sang the parody:
>
> *We don't play Notre Dame.*
> *We don't play Tulane*
> *We just play Davidson*
> *For that's the fearless Army way.*

Then the Midshipmen lofted a huge banner that said:

When Do You Drop Navy?

Navy was mortified when the Army cheering section immediately unrolled a banner that said:

Today!

Thinking this had to be a coincidence, or incredible bad luck, the Middies quickly tried again with another of their banners. This one said:

Why Not Schedule Vassar?

And Army countered with a sign that produced one of the biggest laughs Municipal Stadium ever heard. It read:

We Already Got Navy.

By contrast that year, Navy's fortunes had sunk as dramatically as a PT boat hit by a torpedo. Beaten only by Army the previous year, Navy found its course reversed in 1946 when a series of resignations following the end of World War II and serious injuries to no fewer than five running backs had left the team in a state of disrepair. After winning their opening game that season, Navy proceeded to lose the next seven. In desperation, the Midshipmen decided to import a new mascot in an effort to change their luck, finding what was reported to be the "smelliest, nastiest goat in all Texas." The 11th in the great line of goats to grace the Navy sideline, Billy XI, as he was dubbed, was formally greeted by the commanding officer at Annapolis and promptly tethered next to his predecessor, the disgraced Billy X. Then with an almost divine sign that Navy was down but not out, Billy X responded by kicking the starch out of the upstart replacement and, as a result, was given a last-minute reprieve.

Billy X and the Middies traveled to Municipal Stadium as 28-point underdogs. President Harry S. Truman and 100,000 other fans (the game had been sold out before the start of the season) saw the festivities open with a large group of Army cheerleaders pulling an enormous wooden goat out onto the field. To the surprise of all, a trapdoor opened in the belly of the "Trojan Goat," and Billy X walked down a ramp onto the field. The cheerleaders then pulled off their Army outfits to reveal their Navy uniforms.

The game began as expected, Army on the march almost without resistance. Doc Blanchard surged into the end zone for the Cadets' first touchdown. By halftime, the score was Army 21, Navy 6, and it looked likely to turn into a rout. But the scenario didn't go as predicted when the two teams reconvened. Navy scored early in the third quarter, but for the second time in the game missed the extra point. Army's next drive stalled at its own 35-yard line when Blanchard failed to gain the half-yard needed on fourth down.

A newly inspired Navy drove down to the Army 5-yard line as the third quarter ended. Moments later, Navy passed for another touchdown, but once again missed the point after. The score stood at Army 21, Navy 18. The Cadets appeared exhausted and were unable to sustain a drive of any kind during the fourth quarter. After several exchanges, the Midshipmen drove all the way to Army's 3-yard line, where it was first down and goal with about a minute and a half to play.

Two Navy rushes into a desperately revived Army line failed to gain an inch. With the crowd roaring and surging from the stands to the sidelines, and the Middies with no time-outs remaining, Navy coach Tom Hamilton sent in a substitute with a play, but it took too long to explain in the huddle, and the Middies were penalized 5 yards for delay of game. On the next snap with time now running out, Hamilton's play sent Navy back Lynn Chewning around end. He got back to the 3-yard line but couldn't get out of bounds to stop the clock, and time expired. So Army maintained its three-year undefeated streak and stretched its lead in the historic rivalry to 24 triumphs against 19 defeats and 3 ties.

Despite the setback of an honor code scandal at West Point in the early 1950s, the Cadets had a few more impressive years. Their 1958 team, featuring Heisman Trophy winner Pete Dawkins, vied for a national championship with an unbeaten season.

And after Earl Blaik retired in 1958, Army had several respectable seasons under Tom Cahill.

Navy also thrived in the late 1950s and early 1960s. The 1957 Midshipmen squad, led by All-America candidate quarterback Tom Forrestal, ranked fifth in the nation. In the 1959 Army–Navy game, halfback Joe Bellino became the first Midshipman ever to score three touchdowns in a single game against Army as the Middies won 43–12. The following year Bellino won the Heisman Trophy after leading Navy to another win over Army, 17–12 this time. And Roger Staubach, yet another Heisman winner, brought Navy to national prominence in the early 1960s, quarterbacking them to victories over Army in 1962 and 1963.

The annual Army–Navy game continues to this day, the last of each school's season, still a sellout, still a marvelous spectacle with uniformed Cadets and Midshipmen parading before the start of it, still the goat and the mule, and as always a bitterly contested football game.

TEXAS–OKLAHOMA

"It's college football's equivalent of a prison riot—with coeds," wrote *Sports Illustrated*'s Dan Jenkins, describing the annual autumnal madness in Dallas when the Oklahoma Sooners battle the Texas Longhorns. But few of the spectators are as impoverished as the average prison inmate. After all, this is oil country, the land where real-life J. R. Ewings leave their private airplanes at Love Field and their long limos at the gate and make their way to private boxes where they can cheer their alma mater, be it Texas or Oklahoma. "Give a Texas oilman two drinks," Jenkins also wrote, "and he'll bet you every

TEXAS GAME

home field is in Austin, 180 miles to the south) nor Oklahoma plays in unless they are invited there for a New Year's Day appearance. Nor is there a crowd advantage. Sooner fans by the thousands flock to Dallas from Norman and other Oklahoma locales to watch the annual brawl, no fewer in number, devotion, or boisterousness than the Longhorn fans. The action in the stands has sometimes been as bruising as the play on the fields.

The kinetic energy that fills the stadium is all the more remarkable considering the percentage of spectators who must be suffering from the year's biggest hangover. Mass arrests in downtown Dallas the night before the gridiron war are routine, sometimes totaling as many as 700 overzealous fans. On a more reserved note, the occasion also brings together a cavalcade of affluent alumni who could probably wipe out the national debt of Brazil if they had a desire to do so. One writer once observed that "there are more lizard-skin cowboy boots at this game than there are lizards in all of Texas."

The classic rivalry also contains a few ironies. Though the game is no longer an intraconference affair, Oklahoma, now a member of the Big 12, was in fact the Southwest Conference's first champion. During the first 11 years of Bud Wilkinson's reign at Oklahoma, from 1947 through 1957, the Sooners dominated the rivalry, often beating the Texans with key players who had been recruited from the Lone Star State. Wilkinson's Sooners demolished the Texans in 9 of those 11 contests, and once, in 1956, by the embarrassing score of 45–0.

There was some irony on the other side of the Red River as well. After Texas posted a humiliating 1-9 record for the 1956 season, predictably a new coach was in demand down in Austin. Following a brief search, the Longhorns found just the savior

offshore well he's got (and some that he hasn't got) that the Longhorns will whip Oklahoma. It takes about the same for an Oklahoma oilman to wager every dust bowl well he's got that the Sooners will whip Texas."

Texas first played Oklahoma at the turn of the century, and a while later the game became integrated into the Texas state fair activities. It has become as vital a part of the Texas football scene as chili, chicken-fried steak, and Pearl beer are to the Longhorn diet. There is no home field advantage because the game is traditionally played at the Cotton Bowl, a stadium that neither Texas (whose

A group of Oklahoma fans, known as the "Roughnecks," travel in a style of their own in 1940 to cheer on the Sooners against archrival Texas at the Cotton Bowl in Dallas. They were in for a letdown, as the Longhorns defeated Oklahoma that year 19–16.

they needed to reverse the disastrous state of football affairs. His name was Darrell Royal, who in the late 1940s had been an All-America back at none other than Oklahoma. Under this former Sooner, the dominance in the rivalry would shift to Texas. During the seven years that Darrell Royal strode the sideline across the field from Bud Wilkinson (1957–63), his Texas teams won six of the encounters, losing only in his first year.

Over the years meetings between these schools have frequently involved more than simple bragging rights. In 1950, for example, the national championship was on the line when the two teams met. In

the fourth quarter, Texas was leading 13–7, punting from their own 11-yard line, but the punter fumbled and the Sooners recovered. Then a pair of All-Americas came through with crucial points: Billy Vessels slashed off tackle for the touchdown and Jim Weatherall booted the extra point, giving Oklahoma a 1-point victory and the national championship.

Another important game, the confrontation of 1958, concluded with a taste of irony. That year, for the first time in nearly half a century, the NCAA Rules Committee had approved a change in the scoring system. The optional 2-point conversion was introduced in an attempt in reduce the number of tie games. One of the coaches who vigorously opposed this change was Darrell Royal of Texas. But that very year; Royal's Longhorns used it to defeat Wilkinson's Sooners by a score of 15–14, and in so doing they not only served Oklahoma its only loss of the season, but also knocked them out of the running for the national championship.

Even though both the old masters are no longer coaching, the annual battle between the two heated rivals hasn't mellowed, as the following will attest.

It was a dark, rainy Saturday in Dallas when the Sooners visited the Cotton Bowl for the 1984 edition of the rivalry. It was the fifth game of the season for both teams, and they had identical records of 3-0-1, with Texas clinging precariously to a No. 1 ranking.

In the first half, the Longhorns took a 10–0 lead on a Todd Dodge touchdown pass and a 40-yard field goal from Jeff Ward. With the playing field soggy and slippery from the rain, the lead appeared to be a most comfortable one. In the third quarter, however, the Sooners recovered a fumble by Texas tailback Terry Orr and went on to score a touchdown two plays later. Less than 2 minutes after that, Oklahoma forced a safety, narrowing the score

to 10–9. The inspired Sooners then took the free kick and marched downfield, adding another score on a 24-yard touchdown pass from Danny Bradley. With a lead of 15–10, Oklahoma went for the 2-point conversion but failed. Then things began to get a little weird.

With less than 6 minutes to play in the game, a third-string Texas tailback, freshman Kevin Nelson, scampered 60 yards through the puddles and was not brought down until he reached the Oklahoma 2-yard line. But there the Longhorns stayed for four nightmarish downs, unable to advance an inch against a fortresslike Sooner defense.

When the ball exchanged hands at the 3, Oklahoma found that on three successive downs they couldn't gain an inch either. With a call that would endear him forever to second-guessers, Oklahoma coach Barry Switzer decided to take an intentional safety rather than risk a kick from deep in the end zone, because, as he explained later, the Sooners' kicking game had been poor throughout the contest. The safety brought the Longhorns to within 3 points of the Sooners.

After the free kick, there were 2 minutes to go, and Texas had the ball at their own 44-yard line. With a precision passing attack, Todd Dodge brought the Longhorns to the Oklahoma 15-yard line with 10 seconds remaining in the game. Now it was Texas's turn to gamble. Coach Fred Akers decided they had time for one pass to try for a game-winning touchdown. If it was incomplete, they should still have time for a field goal. But Todd Dodge's pass was tipped and appeared to be intercepted at the sideline by a Sooner defender. Television replays showed that the ball certainly seemed to be caught and controlled before the Oklahoma defender fell out of bounds. But to the

consternation of Sooner fans everywhere, the play was ruled an incomplete pass. Texas then lined up and kicked a field goal as time expired, and the game ended in a 15–15 tie. That year, at least, no Texas or Oklahoma oil wells changed hands.

NOTRE DAME–USC

The greatest cross-country, or almost cross-country, rivalry in the history of college football has done much to nurture the popularity of the sport, and, in its earliest contests, brought together two of the game's most legendary coaches, Notre Dame's Knute Rockne and Southern Cal's Howard Jones.

In 1924, the Fighting Irish, under Rockne and with the legendary Four Horsemen, provided the catalyst for the great rivalry by traveling to Pasadena to make their first appearance in the Rose Bowl. Their defeat of Pop Warner's talented Stanford team made Notre Dame the undisputed national champion. When Howard Jones came to Southern Cal in 1925, he brought with him his "beat the best" philosophy. So Southern Cal invited Notre Dame back to the West Coast in 1926, and some of the most exciting moments in intercollegiate football have been provided by the clash of the two teams ever since.

The first two games in the series, 1926 and 1927, were closely fought contests, with Notre Dame winning each by a single point. In 1928, Rockne fielded the only mediocre team he ever had at Notre Dame, his "Minutemen," he called them. "They'll be in the game one minute and the other team will score," the Rock joked. Well, the Trojans scored often enough that year to defeat the Irish for the first time 27–14. It was part of USC's 9-0-1 season, which earned for Howard Jones's 11 the nickname "Thundering Herd."

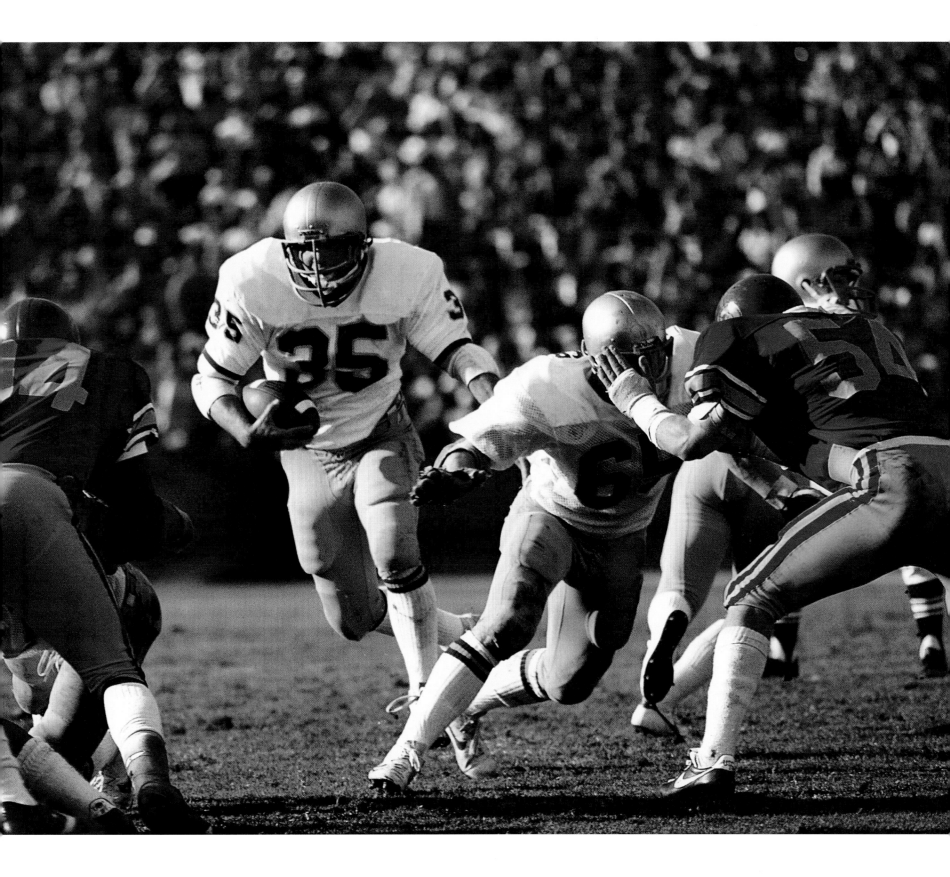

Notre Dame avenged the loss with a 1-point victory the following year, but it was the 1930 game between the two that is remembered by many as one of the great surprises of the series. The Fighting Irish had defeated everyone they encountered that year, but the victories, especially the bruising 7–6 win over Army in the next-to-last game of the season, had taken a toll. Several key players were injured, and powerful running back Joe Savoldi had been expelled after it was learned that he was married (which was against Notre Dame rules in those days). On the other hand, the Trojans were completely healthy, and had outscored their nine opponents so far that season by a total of 382–39. The oddsmakers predicted a close game, giving the edge to a healthy USC.

Rockne knew he had to do something to fire up his team. En route to California for the game, the Irish stopped in Tucson, Arizona, where he scheduled a scrimmage. He deemed it a lackluster practice and told his team as much. Then he shook his head, looked at them balefully, and told them that he could not be a part of a team that was so lethargic, could not accompany them to a sure slaughter in Los Angeles. In fact, he said he was quitting as coach and returning to South Bend. His horrified team then begged him to stay, pledging full fervor when they met USC.

The Rock agreed to stay on and continuously reminded them of their promise until they took the field. It had its effect. Notre Dame held the explosive offense of Southern Cal scoreless, and put 27 points on the scoreboard themselves. It gave them their second undefeated season in a row. "That was the greatest Notre Dame team I've ever seen,"

Notre Dame's Bad Move

In 1931 Notre Dame had gone undefeated in three seasons, a total of 25 wins and 1 tie (in a mudbath at Northwestern). And they were hosting Southern Cal in South Bend where, incredibly, they had lost only 1 game in 27 years (to Carnegie Tech in 1928).

Knute Rockne was gone by then, and replacing him that year was one of the Rock's former All-America linemen, Hunk Anderson. Howard Jones was at the helm for USC. In the stands were such luminaries as Mayor Jimmy Walker of New York and Mayor Anton Cermak of Chicago, both avid Notre Dame fans. Everyone thought it was to

be the conclusion of another undefeated season for the Irish.

It certainly seemed so. With a strong running attack Notre Dame built a 14–0 lead, which they maintained into the fourth quarter. But then the Trojans decided the time had come to change things. Two long marches, engineered by Orv Mohler, Southern Cal's quarterback, ended in touchdowns, both capped by scoring runs by Gus Shaver. But a missed extra point left Southern Cal a point behind Notre Dame.

Notre Dame, however, had made a big mistake. Earlier in the quarter, before Southern Cal began to move so

effectively, Coach Anderson, confident that his team would prevail, had taken most of his regulars out of the game. Now, according to the rules of the day, they could not return during that quarter. The hapless Irish had unintentionally set the stage for their own demise. The reserves could not move the ball, nor could they stop the inspired Trojans. With a minute left, Southern Cal was again within striking distance of the Notre Dame goal. On came Johnny Baker to boot a game-winning 33-yard field goal as Anderson and his first-stringers watched dismally from the Irish sideline.

Howard Jones said after the game. It was also Rockne's last game. He was killed in an airplane crash before the start of the 1931 season.

Throughout the remainder of the 1930s, Notre Dame searched for another coach as great as Rockne, but didn't find one, and in confrontations with arch-rival Southern Cal managed only 4 victories against 5 losses and 1 tie.

But the glory that once was Notre Dame's was restored in the 1940s. Frank Leahy, hired as head coach in 1941, finally proved the worthy successor to Rockne. Leahy, who had played for Rockne in 1929 at Notre Dame, led the Irish to two successive triumphs in his first two encounters with the Trojans. Not everyone at the time was thrilled with Notre Dame's revival, nor with the extraordinary zeal Leahy imparted to his players. Said one Trojan player after losing to the Irish, "They'll give you the knee, they'll hold you, they'll clip you, and they'll belt you with an elbow every chance they get. Maybe Leahy doesn't tell them to do it, but he sure doesn't tell them not to do it."

There may have been some truth to the remark (Leahy's "anything for a win" style of coaching was legendary), but whatever a Trojan said about the Fighting Irish during the Leahy years must have been served up with a full bowl of sour grapes. In the 10 games that the Leahy-coached teams played against Southern Cal, Notre Dame won 8, lost only 1, and tied the other.

One of the most thrilling endings to any game in the rivalry occurred in 1948. Undefeated Notre Dame, in the running for the national championship, met USC in the last game of the season. Trailing by a touchdown with a little more than two minutes remaining, Irish halfback Bill Gay ran the kickoff back 87 yards, to the USC 12-yard line. Leahy

planned on a quick touchdown followed by an onside kick. But it took four plays before Emil Sitko could carry it in for the score—as a result, there was not enough time left for another drive. The tie ruined Notre Dame's perfect season and the national title went to Michigan.

Under John McKay, Southern Cal finally turned the tables on Notre Dame. Probably the greatest single joy for USC fans of that era came in 1964 when an unheralded Southern Cal team upset Ara Parseghian's bid for an undefeated season and a national championship in the last game of the year. Notre Dame was an overwhelming favorite to win that game; with consensus All-Americas like quarterback John Huarte and end Jack Snow, the Irish had the nation's No. 2 ranked offense, and they also laid claim to the best defense in the country.

Southern Cal had lost 3 games and appeared fresh for the slaughter. "I studied the Notre Dame–Stanford film for six hours last night," coach John McKay said, "and I have reached one conclusion: Notre Dame can't be beaten."

A few days later, he added, "I've decided that if we play our very best and make no mistakes whatsoever, we will definitely make a first down." His ploy in the Rockne tradition, to arouse his Trojans to a pitched anger, would ultimately prove successful.

No one was surprised when Notre Dame took a 17–0 lead into the locker room at halftime. But everyone was astounded at the events of Act Two. Southern Cal roared right back into the game as Mike Garrett carried the ball in for a touchdown on the first Trojan drive of the second half. Quarterback Craig Fertig led a second Trojan touchdown march, and suddenly they were a mere 4 points behind the vaunted Irish. Southern Cal's defense was impenetrable, playing its best half of the year. Then they got the ball back in the final minutes, and Fertig passed them down the field. With 2 minutes to play on fourth down, he rifled a shot to Rod Sherman in the end zone. And that was it; Southern Cal had come up with an amazing rally and beaten top-ranked Notre Dame, which dropped to No. 3 in the national rankings behind undefeated Alabama and Arkansas. It was a precedent Parseghian would wish had never been set. In an otherwise stellar career of successful coaching, his Notre Dame teams lost to Southern Cal 6 times, managing only 3 wins and 2 ties. But that's the way it is with a rivalry.

In fact, the reversal of momentum between the two schools carried much beyond Parseghian's tenure. After having prevailed for so long, Notre Dame lost 13 games to USC over the next 20 years, tied 2, and won only 5.

And one of those losses was a special disillusionment. It was 1978, and the national championship was on the line. The year before, Notre Dame, coached by Dan Devine, had won the coveted crown. Now Southern Cal, guided by John Robinson, was at the top, only a victory away from taking the title. The Trojans built a 17–3 lead by the half, and Notre Dame, with its two chief running backs, Vagas Ferguson and Jerome Heavens, out with injuries, seemed doomed. But the Fighting Irish put on a splendid comeback in the fourth quarter. Losing 24–6, quarterback Joe Montana suddenly erupted. First it was a 57-yard bomb to Kris Haines for a touchdown. Then, throwing both long and short, Montana marched the Irish 98 yards for another touchdown, with Pete Buchanan finally carrying it in for the score. Notre Dame again got the ball and moved all the way to the Trojan 2-yard line where, with 48 seconds on the clock, Montana tossed a little bullet to Pete Holohan on a slant-in

pattern in the end zone, and the Irish took a 25–24 lead. There were only 41 seconds left when the Trojans got the ball on their own 30-yard line. Paul McDonald, the Southern Cal quarterback, reacted swiftly and with Montana-like precision. With two passes he moved Southern Cal to Notre Dame's 25-yard line. A handoff to Heisman Trophy candidate Charles White picked up 5 more yards and positioned the ball in the center of the field. Southern Cal then stopped the clock with 2 seconds left, and Frank Jordan came on and coolly booted a field goal to give the Trojans a 27–25 victory. *New York Times* columnist Red Smith called it the "gaudiest game in the 50 years of the rivalry."

MICHIGAN– OHIO STATE

When Ohio State enjoyed its greatest success in the Big Ten, while Woody Hayes reigned stout and supreme from the early 1950s to his dismissal in 1978, the Buckeyes entered each year with a special goal, right up there in importance with winning the national championship or spending New Year's Day in Pasadena. Their sharp-tongued, ill-tempered coach fueled it annually. Many a sportswriter and Big Ten fan had noticed over the years a peculiar impediment when a certain word came up in interviews or discussions. That word seemed to always twist his tongue into knots and alter his expression to a snarling grimace. The word, of course, was Michigan. And the special goal was simply: beat Michigan.

There was legitimate cause for Hayes to want to conquer his neighbors to the north. For half a century before he came to Columbus, the Wolverines

Ohio State fullback Jim Otis dives in for a touchdown in the 1969 meeting with Michigan at Ann Arbor. Otis's TD was not enough, however, the Wolverines coming out on top that afternoon 24—12. The Michigan— Ohio State rivalry can be traced back to 1897, when the two teams met in Ann Arbor, with Michigan winning 34—0.

of Michigan had routinely humiliated Ohio State football teams in their annual battles.

The earliest recorded game between Michigan and Ohio State took place in 1897, and was won by the Wolverines 34–0. The next game, held in 1900, was played to a scoreless tie, and that was Ohio State's best showing against Michigan for a decade. During that interim, Fielding "Hurry Up" Yost was establishing his coaching reputation and building a dynasty at Ann Arbor, one that would deal out more than a few indignities to rival Ohio State.

In 1902, Michigan fans were especially confident. Their team the year before was not only undefeated and untied, but not one opponent had scored a single point in 11 games. And they still had All-America back Willie Heston, among other gems, on a team that was once again undefeated. To rub it in

even deeper, Wolverine rooters chorused a parody of a Buckeye cheer throughout the game:

What will we do?
What will we do?
We'll rub it into OSU,
That's what we'll do.

And that's precisely what the Wolverines did that afternoon, by a score of 86–0.

Ohio State lost to Michigan, often by lopsided scores, until 1910, when they finally managed a 3–3 tie. Following two more years of defeats, Ohio State finally solved the Wolverine whammy by joining the then Western Conference (a forerunner of the Big Ten conference) and dropping Michigan from its schedule (the Wolverines had left the conference five years earlier).

By 1919, Hurry Up Yost's Wolverines were back in the conference and were undefeated when they faced the Buckeyes, who had breakaway runner Chic Harley and another superb back in Pete Stinchcomb.

For the first time in Yost's illustrious career, however, his Wolverines could not match up to the Buckeyes, and Ohio State, after 16 encounters, finally beat Michigan, by the score of 13–3.

Yost's teams fell again in 1920 and 1921 to OSU, and some alumni organized themselves and called for his ouster as head coach. But Yost managed to hold on and, to the horror of Ohio State fans, the old master had at least one more thunderbolt to hurl at the gents from Columbus.

It was the era of great Michigan punters, but there were critics who sometimes mocked Yost's defensive style of play. And quite a few of the critics were from Ohio State. Yost shrugged them off: "At Meecheegunn [as he always pronounced the name of his team] we play percentage. By this I mean we let the other fellow rush the ball on the wrong side of midfield and waste his energy in his own territory. Many people don't realize that football games are usually lost rather than won. Meecheegunn's consistent record over a span of years is largely due to our policy of letting the enemy take the risk of fumbling inside his forty yard line. We then cash in on his mistakes. Cynics call our method the 'punt, pass, and prayer' system, but we generally have the last laugh."

Ohio State fans were the ones laughing before the 1922 encounter between the two rivals, reflecting on the wins in three previous meetings and poking fun at Yost's philosophy. On top of that, they were fired up about the opening of their brand-new football stadium.

But the hero of the day turned out to be Michigan's Harry Kipke. Punting no fewer than 11 times, Kipke averaged 47 yards per kick. And of the 11 boots, seven skittered out of bounds, while the remaining four rolled dead. Not one was returned for a single yard. Capitalizing on that, Michigan handed OSU their worst defeat in years 19–0. The sour note of Yost's last laugh reverberated through the new Buckeye stadium for quite some time.

Over the next 28 years, until the start of Woody Hayes's regime at Ohio State, Michigan again dominated the series with 17 victories against 9 losses and 2 ties. But then the momentum was reversed. Hayes, during the next quarter century, bulldogged his Buckeyes to 16 victories against only 8 defeats and 1 tie.

By the close of the 1975 season, Woody's best years were over, and Michigan, under Bo Schembechler, who had played for Hayes at Miami (Ohio) and later served as an assistant to him at OSU from 1958 to 1962, swept the last three games before Hayes was dismissed for hitting a Clemson player during the 1978 Gator Bowl.

The 1977 loss was especially painful because riding on the game was a trip to the Rose Bowl. Each team had a Big Ten record of 7-1, tied for the conference title (in the event of a tie, however, Ohio State would get the bid). At mammoth Michigan Stadium, a crowd of 106,024 gathered while another 30 million people watched on television. Bo Schembechler's Wolverines, led by quarterback Rick Leach, moved smoothly and built a 14–6 lead, which they carried into the fourth quarter. But Ohio State was dogged. With 4 minutes remaining, they marched from their own 10-yard line to the Michigan 8. A touchdown and a 2-point conversion would send them to Pasadena. On the next play,

Buckeye quarterback Rob Gerald started to pitch out to Ron Springs but was hammered by Michigan's John Anderson; the ball squirted loose, and Anderson's teammate Derek Howard fell on it to squelch the OSU drive. Woody Hayes was so enraged at the turn of events that he stormed along the sideline and suddenly punched a television cameraman who was trying to record the tantrum.

Ohio State got its revenge two years later, however, in another meeting of the rivals that would decide the 1979 Big Ten title, and the Rose Bowl bid. Again the Buckeyes traveled to Ann Arbor, and this time 106,255 fans turned out, the largest crowd ever to attend a college football game since official attendance statistics were first taken in 1948.

Ohio State, now coached by Earle Bruce, was a different kind of team than the ones led by Woody Hayes. Gone was the grind-it-out ground game, and in its place was a passing attack led by sophomore sensation Art Schlichter, an offense good enough to carry the Buckeyes through the season without a defeat.

For Michigan, Bo Schembechler started a freshman quarterback, Rich Hewlett, who had virtually no college experience. "Our offense had been tailing off," Schembechler explained, "and we wanted to do something about it."

Neither young quarterback got anything going in the first quarter or for most of the second period. The lone score was a Buckeye field goal. But then John Wangler came off the bench to guide the Wolverines, throwing a stunning 59-yard touchdown pass to All-America wide receiver Anthony Carter.

Schlichter got OSU moving immediately after, passing into the heart of the Michigan prevent defense and moving his team 72 yards in eight plays. But the Buckeyes had to settle for a field goal. Schlichter came right back in the third period and hit split end Chuck Hunter for a touchdown. A try for a 2-point conversion failed, but OSU now had a 12–7 lead.

Michigan responded in kind. Wangler dropped back and found his favorite receiver, Anthony Carter, for a 66-yard gain. Moments later the Wolverines made it into the end zone. Their try for a 2-pointer was successful, giving them a 3-point lead.

But then, with just over 11 minutes to play in the game, disaster struck the Wolverines. With Michigan set to punt from their own 38-yard line, Ohio State put 10 men on the line of scrimmage in a fateful effort to block the kick. And they did, the ball bounding around deep in Michigan territory until it was picked up by OSU's Todd Bell at the 18, who then carried it in for the score. Ohio State controlled the ball for most of the remaining 5 minutes of the game and came out of it with their first win in the rivalry in four years and a ticket to the Rose Bowl.

"The point is that our kicking game has been disastrous," said Michigan's Bo Schembechler after the game. A Michigan team with an awful kicking game? Mingled with the noise of the 106,000-plus fans in Ann Arbor that day, you could probably hear old Hurry Up Yost moaning in his grave.

USC–UCLA

America's premier intracity rivalry has been fought at the close of every recent football season in Los Angeles, pitting the preppy private school of Southern California (USC) against the enormous state school just west of Beverly Hills, known best by its initials, UCLA. At stake is often the Pac-10 (formerly the Pac-8) title and the right to visit the Rose Bowl on New Year's Day.

Not unlike the Harvard–Yale rivalry, which has showcased a number of its future poets and politicians on the field of play, USC and UCLA can boast their own kinds of celebrities-to-be. Marion Morrison played tackle for USC before he took up movie acting and changed his name to John Wayne. Two other future actors have played in the game between the two rivals, both tackles as well: Ward Bond for USC and Gary Lockwood for UCLA. Before he exchanged his football cleats for a pair of Brooklyn Dodger spikes, UCLA had a fleet halfback in the late 1930s named Jackie Robinson. And marching at halftime was USC band member Herb Alpert.

The rivalry was slow to develop, perhaps because during its first decade UCLA fans were happy just to put the game out of their minds—as one would do with any nightmare. In their first meeting in 1929, the USC Trojans annihilated UCLA's Bruins 76–0; the following year they let up a little and beat them only 52–0. The teams did not meet again for six years, when the Bruins managed a 7–7 tie. UCLA could not claim a victory over USC until 1942, when they finally prevailed 14–7.

One of the problems was that when coach Howard Jones began building his dynasty at USC in 1925, UCLA was a mere six years old and consisted of just a few buildings on Vermont Avenue in downtown Los Angeles. In those early days of the then Southern California Conference, UCLA's record in their first six years was 4 wins, 30 losses, and 4 ties.

In the first two decades of the rivalry, from 1929 through 1949, the teams faced each other 19 times, with USC claiming 13 victories, UCLA winning twice, and four games ending in a tie. It was not until the 1950s when Red Sanders brought UCLA an old-fashioned but highly successful single wing attack that the Bruins began to make a game of it against USC and a name for itself in the Pac-10.

From 1950 through 1959, the momentum changed hands, with the Bruins taking seven of the contests, the Trojans only two, and one ending in a tie. The lowlight of an otherwise fulfilling decade for the Bruins came in 1952. Both teams were unbeaten and untied when nearly 100,000 fans jammed the Los Angeles Coliseum to see which team would earn the right to represent the Pac-10 in that year's Rose Bowl. But USC, behind the running of All-America back Jim Sears, eked out a 14–12 win.

The rivalry reached its greatest intensity after John McKay took over the head coaching chores at USC in 1960, and Tommy Prothro did the same at UCLA. The first half of the 1960s belonged to USC, who won four of the five encounters, but in 1965 and 1966, with both teams national powerhouses, UCLA took command and set the Trojans down in two hard-fought battles. All of it led to a classic showdown in 1967 that turned out to be one of the most memorable games in college football history.

That year both teams were at the top of the AP and UPI rankings when they squared off in Los Angeles. The Bruins were quarterbacked by All-America Gary Beban, and the Trojans had the mercurial running back O. J. Simpson.

USC had been ranked No. 1 in the nation up to the week before meeting UCLA, but a squeaker of a loss to Oregon State, 3–0, knocked them out of that spot as their record went to 8-1. Replacing them was UCLA, which had also won 8 games, lost none, but had been tied once—by dream-wrecker Oregon State. On the line was the national championship, the Rose Bowl bid, and quite likely the Heisman Trophy for either Beban or Simpson.

There were 93,000 spectators in the Coliseum that sunny Saturday, expecting a great game. And that is surely what they got. In the first quarter, Beban, playing with severely bruised ribs, guided

The Tale of Tommy Trojan

When two teams as gifted as the USC Trojans and UCLA Bruins are situated so close together (their campuses are about 10 miles apart), it's not surprising that the gridiron rivalry might extend to off-field pranks and other undergraduate mischief.

USC's statue of a Trojan warrior, dubbed "Tommy Trojan" by all who know him, has served as a target for Bruin fans ever since it was first unveiled in 1930. For many years, UCLA students were content merely to steal Tommy's sword or, under cover of night, to paint him some garish color. However, as the gridiron wars heated up between the two schools, so did attacks on the Trojan. The most odorous highlight came when two UCLA students flew over the stat-ue in a helicopter, trying to bomb it with cow dung.

Students at USC responded with pranks of their own. One evening a group of Trojan supporters used bricks and cement to seal all the doors and windows of a UCLA sorority house.

Some of the pranksterism, however, got dangerously out of hand. One year USC students planted dynamite under the rival campus's homecoming bonfire. The explosion was heard over much of Westwood and Beverly Hills, but fortunately no one was hurt. Another year a spectator planted dyna-mite in one of the end zones and sat in his Coliseum seat clutching a detonator until security guards removed him and the dynamite from the stadium.

Tommy Trojan has survived it all.

Tommy Trojan. Revered at USC; reviled by UCLA.

the Bruins on a drive to the Trojan 12-yard line, then handed off to Greg Jones, who ran it in for the score. UCLA was again on the march as the quarter was ending, but then Beban threw short, and USC's Pat Cashman picked it off and raced 55 yards for a touchdown. In the second quarter, UCLA drove again, Beban by this time appearing unstoppable. But when he got the Bruins to the 15-yard line he took a shot to his injured ribs and gasped all the way to the sidelines. Without him, the Bruins' drive flagged, and Zenon Andrusyshyn came on for the field goal, but missed it. Now, however, USC's offense came alive. End Earl "The Pearl"

McCulloch, on a flashy end-around reverse, broke away for 52 yards. Then O. J. Simpson, playing with an injured right foot that was encased in a foam-covered shoe, took a handoff and sped 15 yards into the end zone to give USC the lead. A pained and somewhat slowed Gary Beban got UCLA moving again, the highlight a 48-yard pass play to Joe Nuttall. But he couldn't get them beyond the Trojan 15-yard line. Andrusyshyn came on to try for another field goal, but this one was blocked.

Trailing 14–7 in the third quarter, Beban un-leashed a long pass to George Farmer, a game-tying, 47-yard touchdown play. Later in the period, Beban moved the Bruins to within field goal range again, but again the attempt was blocked. In the final period, Beban, playing remarkably well with his bruised ribs, hurled another touchdown pass, but Andrusyshyn's conversion try was blocked, leaving the score at 20–14. With time now an imposing factor, USC had the ball at their own 36-yard line, third down and 8 yards to go. With UCLA expecting a pass, the Trojans called an audible "23 Blast," a hand-off to O. J. Simpson. Gimpy foot and all, O.J. blasted off tackle at full speed. He headed toward the sideline, then broke back across the field, threading his way through the UCLA secondary, which tried valiantly but vainly to bring him down. For 64 yards he raced to the background of a standing, stomping, screaming crowd of 93,000, crossed the goal line, and casually dropped the ball in the end zone. The tumultuous crowd became eerily silent as Rikki Aldridge lined up for the extra point; then pandemonium broke as the ball sailed through the uprights. That was it for the day: USC 21, UCLA 20—USC No. 1 in the nation; USC on to the Rose Bowl.

But the gutsy performance of UCLA's battered quarterback did not go unnoticed. Beban won the Heisman Trophy for 1967; Simpson would have to wait until 1968.

ALABAMA–AUBURN/ AUBURN–ALABAMA

"People talk about the Alabama–Auburn game [or Auburn–Alabama game, depending on who the people are] on New Year's Day. They talk about it on Christmas Day. They talk about it on the Fourth of July. It's the only game I've ever heard of where people talk about it 365 days a year." So Alabama coach Gene Stallings is quoted in Tony Barnhart's book, *Southern Fried Football*. And then he adds the insightful postscript, "And if you don't live here, you couldn't possibly understand."

The intrastate rivalry is indeed one of the most rabid in all of college football; and the game, the last each plays every season, is itself much like the finale of a Fourth of July fireworks extravaganza. For the impassioned fans of each team, everything else is a prelude to the season's climactic moment when the two teams square off for bragging rights to football in Alabama.

It is also one of the oldest rivalries in the history of college football, dating back to 1893, although in the first half of the twentieth century there was a 41-year intermission during which the schools ignored each other. It all began back when Grover Cleveland was president of the United States, the population of Alabama had yet to hit 1.5 million, and intercollegiate football in the South was only a few years old. The game was played on neutral ground, at Lakeview Park in Birmingham, a fairly long buggy ride from Tuscaloosa and a goodly long one from the town of Auburn. The Auburn Tigers won 33–22 that day in 1893, which strangely enough happened to be in February. The two teams met again in the fall of that year, this time at the state capital, Montgomery, with Auburn winning 40–16. But in 1894 Alabama prevailed at another meeting in Montgomery, shutting out the Tigers 18–0.

The first game to be played in Tuscaloosa was 1895, and home field proved to be no advantage with the Crimson Tide humbled 48–0. According to the *Birmingham Age Herald*, "It was apparent to the spectators that when the two teams came on the field, Auburn greatly outclassed the University team in a matter of size and when the playing began it was a battle of seasoned veterans against fresh recruits. The

University boys put up a plucky game, but it was to no avail." Actually the Birmingham newspaper devoted more space to the party and dance that took place after the game, observing that "even though the hometown boys got crushed, nobody could accuse them of being spoilsports. The University boys gave a brilliant hop in the red 'Mess Hall' in honor of their victorious rivals. In the elaborate decorations of the hall, the Orange and Blue of the visitors was as much in evidence as the Crimson and White of the home team."

After that game, the burgeoning rivalry was brought to a halt, reportedly because of "a few unspecified disagreements" between the two institutions and not resumed until 1900. Alabama could not have been all that pleased with the resumption because they lost 53–5, in what would prove to be the second widest margin of victory ever between the two teams. The two teams met seven more times, with Alabama winning three of the games, Auburn three, and the teams tying the last before once again suspending play after the 1907 game. This interlude would last just over four decades.

According to an offical publication of the University of Alabama, the reason for the suspension of competition between the two schools was twofold: "Auburn insisted that their next meeting be officiated by an umpire from outside the South. Alabama thought this request to be ludicrous, and that became the first matter of disagreement between the two schools.

"The second conflict, which was over per diem, essentially amounted to $33. Each team was allowed 22 players on its roster. Auburn wanted each player to receive $3.50, while Alabama thought the amount should only be two dollars."

The dispute went on for months and the teams did not schedule each other in 1908. The issues eventually faded into the Alabama night, but reconciliation was long in coming, 41 years to be precise. Finally, in 1948, the two schools agreed to meet again on the field of play, once again in neutral Birmingham. Not only did they agree to do combat, a trophy was created to serve as the spoils of victory. The chapters of Omicron Delta Kappa, a national leadership honor society, at

At the bottom of the pile is Auburn's All-American running back Bo Jackson, scoring a touchdown in 1982 to give the Tigers their first win over Alabama in 10 years, the final score 23—22. The first contest between the two intrastate rivals took place on November 23, 1892, in Birmingham, both teams with records of 0-4 going into the game; Auburn annihilated the Crimson Tide that day 48—0.

Alabama and Auburn joined to sponsor a trophy "devoted to sportsmanship" (the fraternity chapters more compatible apparently than either the schools' football teams or administrations), possession of which would be maintained for a year by the contest winner. Today the traditional award is known as the ODK–James E. Foy V Sportsmanship Trophy, honoring both the fraternity and Foy, a beloved dean of students (1950–78).

Once again the resumption of play was one that would be less than cherished in hearts of Crimson Tide fans; Auburn defeated Alabama 55–0, *the* largest margin of victory in the rivalry's history.

Since 1948, however, the rivalry has continued (festered?) uninterrupted, the game traditionally played in neutral Birmingham until Auburn hosted it in 1989 (it would not be played in Tuscaloosa again until the year 2000). With the renewal of hostilities, momentum swung back and forth, at least until Paul "Bear" Bryant arrived in Tuscaloosa in 1958. Alabama won four games in a row (1950–53); then Auburn won the next five consecutive, the last, 40–0, in 1957, which also ensured Auburn, under coach Shug Jordan, the school's only national championship. It was so galling to Alabama that they enticed Bryant away from Texas A&M to change the Tide's destiny (defined as defeating Auburn at each season's end).

Bryant lost his first encounter with Auburn in 1958, 14–8, but then won the next four. After a loss in 1963, Alabama strung together another five straight wins. The longest win streak of the series, however, was the nine victories Bryant-led teams tallied between 1973 and 1981. Auburn put together a string of its own, defeating the Tide each year from 1986 through 1989. Through the 2000 football season, Alabama holds the rivalry lead, having won 36 to Auburn's 27 with only 1 tie.

In the hearts and minds of Alabamans of either loyalty, there have been many memorable moments from the confrontations of these two avowed enemies. Auburn fans remember vividly the day in 1983 when Bo Jackson rushed for 256 yards to help the Tigers to a 23–20 triumph. On the other hand, Tide fans still gloat over the season-ender in 1967 when quarterback Kenny Stabler scrambled through a muddy field for the game-winning touchdown (7–3). In 1969, Bama quarterback Scott Hunter set Tide records galore when he completed 30 of 55 passes for 484 yards; still, Alabama lost that day to Auburn 49–26. Two years later, Auburn's Pat Sullivan, Heisman Trophy winner of 1971, was stopped cold by Alabama, held to the lowest yardage total of his college career, as the Crimson Tide crushed the Tigers 31–7.

The 1972 matchup has to stand as one of the most memorable, at least to Auburn fans. In the fourth quarter, the Tigers trailed favored Alabama, ranked No. 2 in the nation at the time, 16–3. Auburn's Bill Newton, however, blocked a punt and David Langer scooped it up and ran for a touchdown. Minutes later, the two Auburn heroes of the day teamed up again, Newton blocking another Bama punt and Langer running it back for the game-winning touchdown, the final score Auburn 17, Alabama 16.

In 1989, Auburn again spoiled Alabama's season. The undefeated Tide, No. 2 in the nation going into the Auburn game, had a shot at the national championship that year. Even though they were playing in the first game of the rivalry ever to be staged in Auburn, and the Tigers were 9-1, Alabama was still clearly favored. The Tide knew they had to get by the Tigers if they were to prevail in the national polls. They didn't. Auburn won 30–20. It cost otherwise successful Alabama head coach Bill Curry (26-10-0 and three bowl appearances in three years) his job. Tells you something about the heat of the rivalry between the two titans of Alabama football.

The Play

The most incredible, most uproarious ending to a college football game took place November 20, 1982, within a cavernous arena in Strawberry Canyon on the rim of the University of California (Berkeley) campus. As John Crumpler of the *San Francisco Examiner* wrote: "What 75,662 people saw, what 22 people participated in, and what six officials ruled on, could not possibly have happened yesterday at Memorial Stadium, but it did. In the most bizarre ending imaginable, California used five laterals on a kickoff return with no time left to turn certain defeat into unbelievable victory over Stanford."

It was the 85th meeting of the two staunch rivals, an event as near and dear to Northern Californian hearts as the Texas–Oklahoma matchup is to Southwesterners or the Yale–Harvard contest to their devoted alumni. It is a spectacle each year, with elaborate tailgate parties, fans flaunting their school colors (Cal, blue and gold; Stanford, red and white), and the most vocal, frenzied spectators found this side of a European soccer match. The game is often a cliff-hanger; the victor's reward possession of a trophy known as the Stanford Axe. On the two campuses, it is simply known as "The Big Game." Now, however, its lore contains "The Play."

The following account of The Play is described by Weston W. George, a devoted Cal fan, who attended the Big Game that year with his wife, Jennie, and their children:

The Stanford band, involuntarily included in the action of the 1982 game against California—"The Play"—dressed appropriately for the following year's game between the two long-time antagonists.

In the fourth quarter with 1:27 remaining, we [California] were ahead 19–17 and had Stanford on their own 20-yard line. We'd been to enough Big Games to know Cal didn't quite have it in the bag, but our defense had held them scoreless for the entire first half, so doing the same thing for less than a minute and a half didn't seem too much to ask. Most Cal fans sensed a victory.

A play later, we were even more confident. On first down, their All-American quarterback John Elway threw a screen pass to Vincent White, and he slipped and lost seven yards. Then on second down Elway passed again, and this one was broken up by noseguard Gary Plummer. Elway's third pass attempt was batted down by defensive back Richard Rogers. Fourth and 17. Breathing easy now. No way could they score from their own 13. I tossed the confetti we brought for the occasion and hugged Jennie.

But then Elway took the snap, stepped back in the pocket, and threw a bullet 29 yards down the middle to split end Emile Harry. First and ten on their 42. There were 43 seconds left on the clock. Again Elway went back, this time rifling one to fullback Mike Tolliver on the sideline for 19 yards. The Stanford fans were roaring, and I suddenly felt a sick feeling creeping into my guts. They were now at our 39.

One more completed pass and they'd be in field goal range. Everyone on the field and in the stands had their eyes drilled on Elway. But it wasn't a pass. Instead he handed off to halfback Mike Dotterer, who ran to his left and picked up 19 more yards, the ball now at our 18. The red-and-white part of the stadium was in an uproar; we sat in quiet disbelief.

There were eight seconds on the clock when Stanford called a time-out. Mark Harmon, their placekicker, came on the field. It was unbearable to watch.

He made it, the scoreboard showing the horror: Stanford 20, California 19, four seconds remaining.

Stanford had been assessed a 15-yard penalty after the field goal because their players had rushed elatedly but prematurely onto the field, so Stanford had to kick from their 25. It all seemed academic. We'd lost. Harmon booted a low-bouncing squibber so there would be little chance for a runback. With that, the Stanford band and some fans surged onto the south end of the field.

But wait a second, a Cal player was running with the ball . . . being tackled . . . No, he lateraled the ball and someone caught it and was now running with it . . . then he pitched it back. Where the hell were my binoculars? We were straining to see. It looked like this runner threw the ball back again and the new ball carrier was now running right into the Stanford band down there. The stadium was a madhouse. We couldn't tell just what had happened. Then suddenly the scoreboard lights flickered and switched. It read Stanford 20, California 25. We jumped. We screamed. We hugged strangers. We moved as a mass down onto the field. We kept looking at the scoreboard to see if it was an illusion or if it would change.

What actually happened, we learned later, was that Kevin Moen scooped up the squib kick on the Cal 43-yard line and carried it to the 48 where, surrounded by red jerseys, he lateraled back to Richard Rogers, who kept the ball only briefly and then tossed it to running back Dwight Garner. Garner carried the ball to the Stanford 48 where the Stanford defenders caught up with him. In their grasp, he pitched it back to Rogers, who began running again with it. When Rogers was about to be hit, he lateraled to Mariet Ford, who continued the astonishing trek to the 25 and, as he was about to be brought down, arched a crazy flip over his shoulder to the guy who had started it all, Kevin Moen. By this time they were in the midst of the Stanford band that had spilled onto the playing field. Moen bowled over the Stanford trombone player, the last person to touch him before he went into the end zone for the game-winning touchdown.

The week following the Big Game of 1982, Stanford students in pursuit of some measure of revenge produced an exact replica of the Cal student newspaper, the *Daily Californian*, its text a well-conceived hoax, carrying the headline, "NCAA Awards Big Game to Stanford." The undergrads from Palo Alto took several thousand copies over to Berkeley, then followed the legiti-

mate distributors of the *Daily Californian* on their rounds, scooping up copies of the real paper and replacing them with their bogus issue. It caused consternation throughout the campus and gained recognition as one of the better practical jokes in college football lore.

Florida and Florida State meet in 1998 in Tallahassee. Florida State won 30–23. The intrastate rivalry goes back to 1958 when the two teams first met on Florida Field in Gainesville; the Gators defeated Florida State that time 21–7.

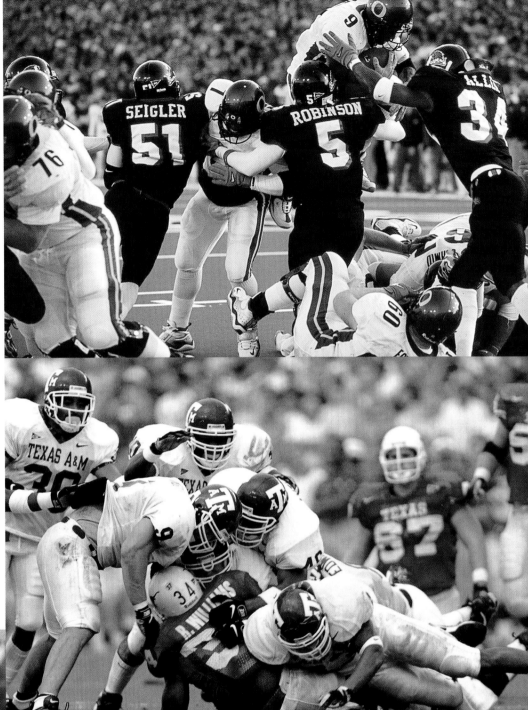

FACING PAGE
Action from the 2000 game in the long-standing rivalry between Georgia and Georgia Tech. The rivalry got underway in Athens in 1893, with visiting Georgia Tech winning that first game 28–6. In 2000, Georgia Tech again defeated the Bulldogs, this time 27–15.

ABOVE RIGHT
Oregon–Oregon State, 2000. Oregon's Maurice Morris tries to go up and over; Oregon State's Darnell Robinson tires to prevent him. Oregon State triumphed that day 23–13, in what was the 104th meeting between the two intrastate rivals.

BELOW
Michigan–Michigan State, 2000. Wolverine All-American wide receiver David Terrell adds a few more yards after catching a pass against the Spartans. Michigan won the game 14–0. The two teams first met in 1898.

RIGHT
Texas–Texas A&M, 1998. The A&M "Wrecking Crew," as they were known, smothered Texas All-American running back Ricky Williams in 1998. But Texas won that day 26–24. It was in 1894 when the Longhorns and the Aggies first battled, a game also won by Texas 38–0.

The Biggest Little Game in America

Amherst and Williams first met on a college football field in 1884 to begin one of the longest rivalries in college football history. On that windswept afternoon in Williamstown, Massachusetts, the Ephs of Williams triumphed 15–2, although it is said that the game was cut short so that the Lord Jeffs could catch the last train back to Amherst.

The confrontation has come to be known as "The Biggest Little Game in America," and in its own right, it has become an essential part of college football tradition. As Larry Dorman wrote in a feature for the *New York Times* in 1995, "To come here [an Amherst-Williams game] is to breathe clean air once again. This has less to do with the remote location of these colleges than with their priorities. It is here that the nomenclature 'student-athlete' is no oxymoron. . . .

"It is really the essence of what college athletic competition can be. It is Division III, but it is first-rate. Football is not a business here. It might be a very important piece of the fabric that is woven into the whole way of life at Williams, and down the road at Amherst. But it is only a piece. There are no scholarships, no red shirts, no pressures on the coach to win or leave, no pending investigations by the National Collegiate Athletic Association, no slush funds, no failed drug tests, no bowl games and no agents lurking in doorways."

But it is college football, and in its own way it provides a bridge from the game that was played without helmets in the 1800s to the one staged with all the electronics of the 2000s. As ESPN commentator Beano Cook observed: "It's quaint. It's scenic. It's the way college football probably looked 60 to 80 years ago, back when it was supposed to be a game. And they play just as hard as the players at Ohio State and Michigan. It may not mean as much to the rest of the country, but to these guys it means a lot."

"These guys," of course, include not just the players but the student bodies of the moment and the alumni of both schools as well.

By the end of the 2000 season, Williams had won 64 of the Biggest Little Games in America, Amherst 46, and five ended in ties.

FACING PAGE
Amherst vs. Williams, the year
2000. Quarterback Jake Moore
(23) carries the ball for Williams
against Amherst in the 115th
meeting of the two
Massachusetts schools. The
Amherst Lord Jeffs broke a
12-game losing streak to arch-
rival Williams (a 0—0 tie, in
1995, was sandwiched in that
streak) by defeating the Ephs
20—12 in 2000.

ABOVE
Wabash and Depauw come
together in midair here in the
year 2000, in one of the longest
running rivalries in small
college football, as a DePauw
defensive back picks off a
Wabash pass to help his team
to a 27—17 victory. The first
meeting between the two
Indiana schools was in 1890.
And it has always been close:
by 2001 Depauw had won
50 times, Wabash 48, while nine
games ended in ties.

RIGHT
Lehigh and Lafayette square
off in the late 1800s on the
grass in front of Pardee Hall on
the Lafayette campus in Easton,
Pennsylvania. The Lehigh-
Lafayette rivalry can be traced
back to 1884.

Treasured Traditional Trophies

When two rivals go at it on the field, there's often more at stake than mere victory. To the victor go the spoils, which, in college football, often include some prized old piece of bric-a-brac that has been given trophy status.

There are two especially famous trophies, both long on tradition and both from the Big Ten. The first, the Little Brown Jug, goes each year to the winner of the Michigan–Minnesota game. But it should be noted that North Dakota and South Dakota also play for a Little Brown Jug, Montana and Idaho for a Little Brown Stein, and Gettysburg and Dickinson for a Little Brown Bucket. The second is the Old Oaken Bucket, the annual prize for the winner of the Indiana–Purdue game.

An Oaken Bucket, however, isn't the only "Old" treasure. Brigham Young and Utah State vie for the Old Wagon Wheel, Appalachian State and Western Carolina for the Ol' Mountain Jug, while Southern Methodist and Texas Christian once vied for the Old Frying Pan, as Morehead State and Eastern Kentucky used to compete for the Old Hawg Rifle.

Six intrastate rivalries offer a Governor's Cup as a prize: Kansas–Kansas State, Florida–Florida State, Colorado–Colorado State, Louisville–Kentucky, Georgia–Georgia Tech, and Brown–Rhode Island (as does one game between out-of-state teams: Dartmouth–Princeton). Three pairs of schools vie for a Victory Bell

each year: UCLA and USC, Duke and North Carolina, and Cincinnati and Miami (Ohio); three others for a Peace Pipe: Missouri and Oklahoma, Miami (Ohio) and Western Michigan, and Bowling Green and Toledo; and two for a Brass Spittoon: Indiana and Michigan State, and New Mexico State and University of Texas El Paso.

Notre Dame plays for a Shillelagh every time it confronts either USC or Purdue. And at stake in each Alabama and Auburn game is the trophy with the longest name, the ODK–James E. Foy V Sportsmanship Trophy.

The following are sundry other treasured trophies, the spoils of traditional college football combats.

LEFT
Triumphant Michigan players hoist the Little Brown Jug. The treasured trophy is claimed each year by the winner of the Michigan—Minnesota game.

RIGHT
The Old Oaken Bucket. Possession of it is taken each year by the winner of the Purdue—Indiana game.

TROPHY	SCHOOLS	TROPHY	SCHOOLS	TROPHY	SCHOOLS
Anniversary Award	Bowling Green—Kent	Fremont Cannon	Nevada—UNLV	Paul Bunyan Axe	Minnesota—Wisconsin
Apple Cup	Washington—Washington State	Gem State	Boise State—Idaho	Paul Bunyan-Governor of Michigan	Michigan—Michigan State
Axe	Stanford—California	Golden Boot	LSU—Arkansas	Ram-Crusader Cup	Fordham—Holy Cross
Band Drum	Kansas—Missouri	Golden Egg	Mississippi—Mississippi State	Ram Falcon	Air Force—Colorado State
Battle for the Bell	Marshall—Ohio			Rusty Old Cannon	Princeton—Rutgers
Bayou Bucket	Houston—Rice	Golden Hat	Oklahoma—Texas	Schwartzwalder Trophy	Syracuse—West Virginia
Bell	Missouri—Nebraska	Governor's Flag	Arizona—Arizona State	Silver Shako	Citadel—VMI
Bell Clapper	Oklahoma—Oklahoma State	Grizzly-Bobcat Painting	Montana—Montana State	Steel Tire	Akron—Youngstown State
Big Game	Arizona—Arizona State	Illibuck (wooden turtle)	Illinois—Ohio State	Team of Game's MVP	Lafayette—Lehigh
Bill Knight	Massachusetts—New Hampshire	Indian Princess	Dartmouth—Cornell	Telephone	Iowa State—Missouri
		Jefferson-Epps Trophy	Florida State—Virginia	Textile Bowl	Clemson—North Carolina State
Black Diamond	Virginia Tech—West Virginia	Keg of Nails	Cincinnati—Louisville		
Brice—Colwell Musket	Maine—New Hampshire	Kit Carson Rifle	Arizona—New Mexico	Tomahawk	Northwestern—Illinois
Bronze Boot	Colorado State—Wyoming	Land Grant Trophy	Penn State—Michigan State	Top Dog	Butler—Indianapolis
Cannon	Illinois—Purdue	Mayor's Cup	Rice—SMU	Wagon Wheel	Akron—Kent State
Commonwealth Cup	Virginia—Virginia Tech	Megaphone	Notre Dame—Michigan State	Williams Trophy	Rice—Tulsa
Cy—Hawk	Iowa—Iowa State				
Floyd of Rosedale	Iowa—Minnesota	Monon Bell	Depauw—Wabash		
		Paniola Trophy	Hawaii—Wyoming		

The Monon Bell, the treasured trophy that each year goes to the winner of the DePauw—Wabash game: DePauw carries it off here after defeating Wabash in 2000. The 300-pound bell has traded hands between the rivals since 1932; before that it graced a Monon Railroad locomotive that ran between the Indiana cities in which the schools are located, Greencastle (DePauw) and Crawfordsville (Wabash).

5

"Watching college football is the most fun I ever had as a youngster. Covering college football is the most fun I ever had as a fully employed grownup."

DAN JENKINS
I'll Tell You One Thing, 1999

PASSION AND PAGEANTRY

THIS IS COLLEGE FOOTBALL

College football is a spectacle. The game began on open fields on college campuses with only a handful of the curious standing on the sidelines wondering what their classmates were doing out there on the grass or in the mud. But more and more got curious and soon it was not just a game to be played but one to be watched as well, and even heard, with orchestrations of cheers and sighs, chants, songs, and blaring bands.

In 1903, Harvard became the first school to build a stadium for its football team, a concrete edifice that would seat 30,000. Today, stadiums like those at Michigan and Tennessee can easily accommodate crowds of well over 100,000—the largest crowd at a college football game since attendance figures were first officially recorded back in 1948 is the 111,794 who jammed into Michigan Stadium in 1999 to watch the Wolverines defeat Northwestern 37–3. As evidence that there is something to home

field advantage, the 12 largest crowds in college football history were recorded at Michigan, and Michigan won all 12 of those games; the next 10 largest attendance figures were posted at Neyland Stadium in Knoxville, Tennessee, and the Volunteers were victorious in each of those 10. Before attendance figures were routinely counted, Notre Dame played in two games at Soldier Field in Chicago where the crowds were estimated at more than 120,000; the Fighting Irish—the nominal home team—defeated Southern Cal in the first 7–6 in 1927, and Navy the following year 7–0.

Cheerleaders were among the first of college football's accoutrements. Team mascots were soon to follow. Some, like the Notre Dame leprechaun and Southern Cal's Trojan, Army's mule and Navy's goat, have become as recognizable and as famous as the greats who have performed on the field. Marching bands have grown into spectacles them-

LEFT
W for Wisconsin, at the 1999 Rose Bowl.

FACING PAGE
The Golden Domes of Notre Dame.

John Wayne

Dwight D. Eisenhower

Byron White

Richard M. Nixon

Gerald R. Ford

ABOVE, CLOCKWISE FROM LEFT
Marion Morrison, aka John Wayne, was a six-foot-four, 185-pound tackle for Southern Cal in 1925.

Dwight D. Eisenhower, showing his punting form here, lettered for Army in 1912. A halfback, he played in the famous Army—Carlisle game of that year in which the Indians, led by Jim Thorpe, demolished the Cadets 27—6. Eisenhower was one of four U.S. presidents who played college football; the others: Richard Nixon, Gerald Ford, and Ronald Reagan.

Colorado halfback Byron "Whizzer" White (24) breaks free on a touchdown run against Rice at the Cotton Bowl on January 1, 1938, but Rice still won 28—14. White, an All-American and a runner-up for the Heisman Trophy that season, went on to a distinguished career on the U.S. Supreme Court, appointed by President John F. Kennedy in 1962 and serving as a justice on the nation's highest court for 31 years.

Center Gerald R. Ford played for Michigan three years (1932—34); he was good enough to be invited to play in the second of the traditional College All-Star games, played at Soldier Field in Chicago in 1935.

Richard M. Nixon (23), with some of his teammates at Whittier College in California in 1934. At 155 pounds, Nixon played both end and tackle.

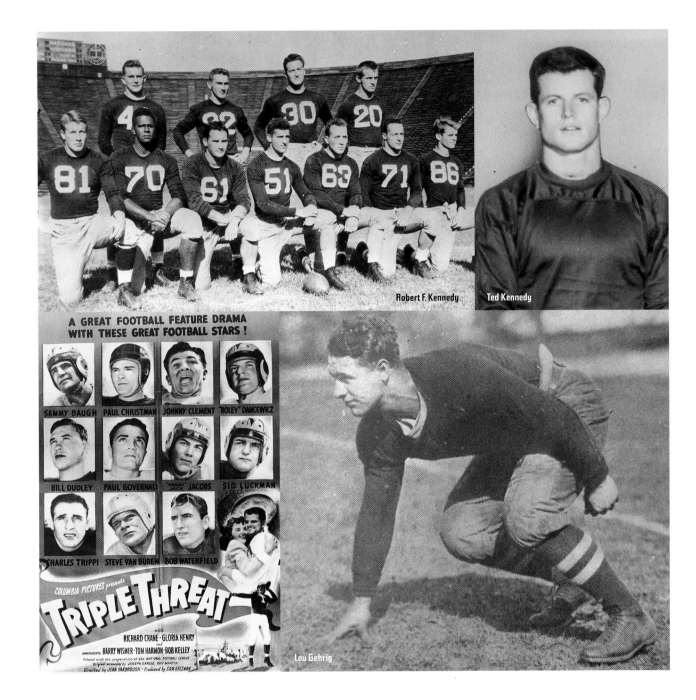

Robert F. Kennedy   Ted Kennedy

A GREAT FOOTBALL FEATURE DRAMA
WITH THESE GREAT FOOTBALL STARS !

SAMMY BAUGH   PAUL CHRISTMAN   JOHNNY CLEMENT   "BOLEY" DANCEWICZ

BILL DUDLEY   PAUL GOVERNALI   JACOBS   SID LUCKMAN

CHARLES TRIPPI   STEVE VAN BUREN   BOB WATERFIELD

COLUMBIA PICTURES presents
TRIPLE THREAT
with
RICHARD CRANE · GLORIA HENRY
and
announcers HARRY WISMER · TOM HARMON · BOB KELLEY
Filmed with the cooperation of the NATIONAL FOOTBALL LEAGUE
Original screenplay by JOSEPH CAROLE, DON MARTIN
Directed by JEAN YARBROUGH · Produced by SAM KATZMAN

Lou Gehrig

ABOVE, CLOCKWISE FROM LEFT
The Harvard squad of 1947. No. 86 is left end
Robert F. Kennedy.

Ted Kennedy, acknowledged as the most
talented of the football-playing Kennedys,
scored Harvard's only touchdown in the
Crimson's 21–7 loss to Yale in 1955.

Baseball legend Lou Gehrig. Before joining
the New York Yankees, Gehrig, pictured here
in 1922, played halfback for Columbia.

Some college greats of the 1940s who took—
briefly—to the silver screen: "Slingin'"
Sammy Baugh (Texas Christian), "Pitchin'" Paul
Christman (Missouri), Johnny "Zero" Clement
(Southern Methodist), Frank "Boley" Dancewicz

(Notre Dame), "Bullet" Bill Dudley (Virginia),
Paul Governali (Columbia), "Indian" Jack Jacobs
(Oklahoma), Sid Luckman (Columbia), Charlie
Trippi (Georgia), Steve Van Buren (LSU), and Bob
Waterfield (UCLA).

selves, magnificent in their range and performance, from huge schools like Ohio State and Michigan to the much smaller black colleges of the South.

Cole Porter wrote Yale's fight song. Herb Alpert marched with his trumpet in Southern Cal's band.

Other celebrities played college football, from presidents to movie stars. Dwight D. Eisenhower played for Army, so did Omar Bradley, Gerald Ford at Michigan, Richard Nixon for Whittier, Ronald Reagan at Eureka College. Supreme Court Justice Byron "Whizzer" White was an outstanding running back at Colorado. Both Bobby and Ted Kennedy played for Harvard; F. Scott Fitzgerald made the freshman team at Princeton. Lou Gehrig was on Columbia's football team, Jackie Robinson on UCLA's; John Wayne was a tackle at Southern Cal, Johnny Mack Brown a running back for Alabama, Burt Reynolds played for Florida State.

The pageantry, the color, the drama, the traditions, they are truly instrumental in making college football the unique spectacle it is today.

HOW TO ENJOY A FOOTBALL GAME
By Franklin P. Adams

This excerpt from an article appeared in *Liberty Magazine*, December 4, 1937, written by Franklin P. Adams, noted wit, philosopher, and charter member of New York's fabled Algonquin Round Table.

You can have your football games. I'm through. Too much trouble, for one thing. And too vicarious. I'm funny that way. I'd rather play my own tenth-rate—oh, all right, eleventh-rate—tennis than watch [Don] Budge pass [Gottfried] von Cramm at the net. I'd rather play The Battle Cry of Freedom on my harmonica than listen, all dressed up, to Jascha Heifetz play anything in Carnegie Hall. I don't say that I don't like to see Budge or to hear Heifetz; but if it's a choice, I'll do something I participate in.

That is one of the things the matter with the United States: vicariousness. It's a big subject; it's why people listen to the radio, go to see movies that they may live somebody else's romance, read book reviews instead of books, and go to games that they don't play and never have played. The bigger the crowd and the more they pay for tickets, the more vicarious are the spectators. . . .

The football crowd, audience, or aggregation of spectators is the worst of the whole vicarious lot. It is true that many of the crowd are alumni of the universities twenty-two of whose students are out there jousting. To a boy playing a game I can see that it makes a big difference—too much, I think—whether his team wins or loses. But what difference does it make to an alumnus?

The standard of scholarship may be twice as high at Atwater as at Bingham, to swipe a couple of names from George Ade's *The College Widow*. Bingham beats Atwater year after year. To hear a Bingham alumnus talk, you would think that he personally made all those tackles and runs—an alumnus from fifty to sixty years of age.

I'm not guessing. I have two brothers-in-law who have been out of Princeton at least thirty-five years. From September to Thanksgiving they have no other thought and no other conversation but football. Take it from their wives, they are at their boringest during the football season. All their talk is last Saturday's game or next Saturday's game. Multiply those two by millions.

My diagnosis is not that such football fans are just Great Big Boys; they are puerile, they are immature; they are not perennially youthful, they are incurably childish. Do they ever voice their pride, night after night, when or if their college acquires

FACING PAGE
The heralded University of Southern California marching band.

somebody on the faculty? Do they all get together and say, "All together now: Three short cheers for Einstein!"? . . .

Bored though you might be by alumni who re-play every game, you don't know punishment until you attend a game with somebody who used to play, particularly on one of the teams contending out there on the field. The only thing comparable to it is going to a play with a lad who designed the scenery. He takes all the fun out of it. You enjoy the play and the acting; this fellow tells you that the desk in the left corner is all wrong, and is ruining the play; it is an 1831 item, and the play's period is 1830. "What an anachronism!" he whispers. . . .

I blame the newspapers as much as the alumni.

About Tuesday you read the ballyhoo. Harvard, spurred by last Saturday's staggering defeat, has a fighting chance against Yale. Thursday one of the Yale stars has galloping rigor mortis and may be out of the game
ten days.

Saturday morning he is on crutches or in a wheel chair, and that afternoon he plays the Game of His Life. The sporting writers, in their forecasts, say that Yale may win; on the other hand, if Harvard, etc. They are the greatest of the However boys.

Well, by some miracle you have tickets. The papers last night said that all seats had been sold, and that somebody had offered $100 for a pair of the Coveted Pasteboards. Incidentally, I never met anybody who paid more than the printed price of $3.30 or $4.40 for a ticket. Saturday morn-ing is Fair and Warmer, known as Ideal Football Weather for the spectators. You are going from New York to New Haven, and by train—the most favorable conditions. You are ready at ten, and the Little Woman, a prey to Speed Madness, is ready at 10.45. Accoutered with two lap rugs, you board the train at 11.05, and you get seats. The train leaves at 11.20; you settle down to read. Every time

you get interested an unpleasantly voiced man comes through the car with "Buy or sell football tickets." And another, with a nastier, louder voice yells, "Get choah winnink cullahs heah." These lads are nuisances. . . .

At two the Bowl is reached; at 2.10 we find our Portal, near the goal posts. The game is on; no score yet. But there are two alumni behind us complain-ing loudly. "They make me sick," says one. "Been out twenty-six years and I get these seats! The longer you're out the worse the seats. I suppose in 1950 they'll give me seats in Bridgeport." "Shut up, the play'll all be down here. It's the Harvard goal line this quarter." This goes on during the first half.

The game is no good. It ends Harvard 13, Yale 0. But in the third quarter the sun vanishes; it is raining and snowing. "I wore my good coat, like a fool," says the Little Woman. "This'll ruin it." P.S. It ruined it. The game ended in a concoc-tion half rain, half snow, and a jigger of bitter-ness, mine about having to get her a new coat or have this one dyed or something, and hers because I didn't tell her to wear the old one. "You wouldn't have done it." "I would." "And then you'd have met somebody on the train, and said to me: 'Me in that old coat! I felt like a fool.'" "That," I said, "is no coincidence."

We arrived home at 7.40, tired, angry, still wet, hungry. "The cook is out, and no dinner will I get," she cooed. So we went to a good place where you can get all you can eat and more than you want to drink for forty-five dollars. First thing I knew it was two o'clock of a Sunday morning.

Football isn't worth the candle to me. This season I'm sleeping of a Saturday morning, hav-ing lunch at home, listening to a broadcast of the game I'm most interested in, but lying on a couch near the fireplace, with a stein on the taboret. And at 4.22, when the game is over, there I am, warm and at peace with the universe, no residents of which I have seen for three hours.

THE FIRST HOMECOMING

Homecoming, that grand tradition which is so much a part of college football, originated at the University of Illinois in 1910. Two seniors, Elmer Ekblaw and C. F. Williams, were waxing sentimental that spring as their graduation neared, and wondering if ever they would return to their alma mater.

Between them they came up with the idea of designating a certain weekend in the autumn, focused around an Illini football game, on which all grads would be invited back to socialize with one another and cheer on the old Orange and Blue. Enterprising youngsters that they were, the two mustered support from some of the university's honorary societies and fraternities and took their case to the school authorities.

Permission was granted to stage a Homecoming the following autumn on a trial basis. Word of the plan went out and on October 14, 1910, approximately 5,000 Illinois grads returned to campus to watch their team defeat the University of Chicago 3–0. Among the other festivities devised for that first Homecoming weekend were a hobo parade and a stunt show.

The first homecoming game ever held at Notre Dame. The year was 1920, and the Fighting Irish, with coach Knute Rockne patroling the sideline and George Gipp featured on the field, defeated Purdue 28–0.

FAVORITE FIGHT SONGS

"NOTRE DAME VICTORY MARCH"

University of Notre Dame
Lyrics by John F. Shea
Music by Reverend Michael I. Shea

(Chorus)

Cheer! Cheer for old Notre Dame

Wake up the echoes cheering her name

Send the volley cheer on high

Shake down the thunder from the sky

What tho' the odds be great or small

Old Notre Dame will win over all

While her loyal Sons are

Marching onward to Victory.

"THE VICTORS"

University of Michigan
By Louis Elbel

Now for a cheer, they are here triumphant!

Here they come with banners flying,

In stalwart step they're nighing,

With shouts of vict'ry crying,

We hurrah! hurrah!

We greet you now, Hail!

Far we their praises sing,

For the glory and the fame they've brought us,

Loud let the bells then ring,

For here they come with banners flying;

Far we their praises sing,

For the glory and the fame they've brought us;

Loud let the bells then ring,

For here they come with banners flying,

Here they come! Hurrah!

(Chorus)

Hail to the victors valiant

Hail to the con-q'ring heroes!

Hail! Hail! to Michigan,

The leaders and best — Hail to the victors valiant!

Hail to the conq'ring heroes! Hail

Hail to Michigan, the Champions of the West!

We cheer then again, for Michigan!

We cheer with might and main,

We cheer, cheer, cheer,

With might and main we cheer!

Hail to the victors valiant!

Hail to the con-q'ring heroes! Hail!

Hail! to Michigan, the leaders and the best,

Hail! to Michigan, the Champions of the West.

Notre Dame's mascot, the Leprechaun, leads the Fighting Irish onto the field in South Bend.

"RAMBLIN' WRECK FROM GEORGIA TECH"

Georgia Institute of Technology
By Frank Roman

Oh, if I had a daughter, sir,

I'd dress her in white and gold,

And take her on the campus, sir,

To cheer the brave and bold,

But if I had a son, sir,

I tell you what he'd do,

He would yell to hell with Georgia

Like his daddy used to do.

(Chorus)

I'm a rambling wreck from Georgia Tech,

And a hell of an engineer,

A hell of a hell of a hell of a hell

Of a hell of an engineer,

Like all good jolly fellows,

I drink my whiskey clear,

I'm a rambling wreck from Georgia Tech

And a hell of an engineer.

I wish I had a barrel of rum,

And of sugar three thousand pounds,

A college bell to put it in,

And a clapper to stir it round,

I'd drink to ev'ry fellow

Who comes from far and near,

I'm a rambling wreck from Georgia Tech,

And a hell of an engineer.

Coach Earl Blaik with the core of his "Brave Old Army Team" backfield of the mid-1940s: halfback Glenn Davis (left), fullback Doc Blanchard (second from right), and quarterback Arnold Tucker (right).

"ON, BRAVE OLD ARMY TEAM"

U.S. Military Academy
By Philip Egner

The Army team's the pride and dream

Of ev'ry heart in gray.

The Army line you'll ever find

A terror in the fray:

And when the team is fighting

For the Black and Gray and Gold,

We're always near with song and cheer

To "sound off" strong and bold:

The Army team —

Rah! Rah! Rah! Boom!

(Chorus)

On, brave old Army team!

On to the fray.

Fight on to victory

For that's the fearless Army way.

Cole Porter and the Yale Fight Song

Cole Porter was an undergrad at Yale in 1913 when he wrote the school's fight song, "Bulldog." He later, of course, went on to write such hit Broadway musicals as *Anything Goes, Kiss Me, Kate, Can-Can,* and *Silk Stockings* as well as a host of songs that have become American classics.

THE GRAMBLING BAND

The Grambling Band, it has been said, is the best show in college football. After they performed at a San Diego Chargers game in the American Football League back in 1964—their first appearance at a truly major event—one San Diego sportwriter observed, "That band looked better getting on the bus than most bands do on the field."

It all began on a most modest scale back in 1926. That was the year Grambling president Charles P. Adams asked one of the new faculty members, Ralph Waldo Emerson Jones, to form "a group of marching musicians." Jones wrote to Sears, Roebuck & Company, asking for a line of credit so they could buy some instruments, and the company complied, enabling the school to obtain 17 instruments. And Jones and his band were off and marching.

While guiding his newly formed marching band, Jones, who would have a 50-year career at

Grambling, also taught and coached the baseball team. In 1936, he was elevated to the school's presidency and among his first acts was to hire a full-time band director. Also in the latter part of the 1930s, the Grambling Band took its act off the football field and local parade routes and began performing at concerts and dances in nearby Louisiana towns. When Conrad Hutchinson, Jr., took over in 1952, he vowed to "make the Grambling College Marching Band the best in the land." Over the next 40 years he would make good on that vow.

The big break did not come, however, until 12 years later, when Hutchinson finagled an invitation to provide halftime entertainment at that San Diego Chargers game in 1964. Transportation was not provided, so Prez Jones dug into his own pocket to pay for the chartering of buses to get the band members from Grambling to Southern California. It was a worthwile investment because it launched the Grambling College Marching Band on a path that would lead to unparalleed national acclaim and later international prominence.

Since then Grambling's band, 250 strong in the twenty-first century, has entertained at Super Bowls (including Super Bowl I), the 1976 official Bicentennial celebration in Washington, D.C., and U.S. presidential inauguration ceremonies. They have cut records, performed in a prize-winning commercial for Coca-Cola and later for ESPN, Procter & Gamble, Fox Sports TV, and the Louisiana Bureau of Tourism, as well as entertained at jazz festivals, outdoor concerts, and USO shows. Besides appearing on fields from the Los Angeles Coliseum to Yankee Stadium and practically every major football stadium in between, the band has traveled to such distant places as Japan and Liberia . . . fulfilling Bandmaster Hutchinson's vow of making the Grambling Band the best in the land.

FOOTBALL CORRESPONDENTS

CRISLER WRITES . . .

Before his legendary years as head coach at Michigan, Fritz Crisler led Princeton's Tigers from 1932 to 1937. He was an inveterate correspondent, regularly writing to his present and former players. The following is taken from a letter sent to his players before the beginning of a school year in the mid-1930s, outlining exactly what was expected of a Princeton football player.

The following qualities are demanded of the candidates for the Princeton University football team of 1934. Unless you can offer these qualities on a hundred percent basis do not come out for practice for I do not want anybody on the field who cannot give one hundred percent interest, one hundred percent enthusiasm, and one hundred percent fighting courage while on the squad. Further, a fellow who becomes self-satisfied and thinks that he is so good that he cannot improve will be better off not to report. We must have:

1. Men who are loyal, who are fighters, who have a superabundance of courage, determination and perseverance.

2. Men who are conscientious, serious-minded, hard workers.

3. Men who have continuous interest, prolonged enthusiasm, and unending ambition to make the team.

4. Men who have the capacity to think, study and work to develop every feature of their position and technique of play and imagination to translate it into team work.

5. Men who will be supremely interested in perfecting the technique of their own play, but will be

equally interested in cooperating for the perfection of team play results.

6. Men who will work to understand and perfect every detail of their assignment on every play.

7. Men who are selfish to produce the highest rate of individual performance of play but absolutely unselfish where the team's interests are concerned.

8. Men who will have a broad friendship and companionship with the other men on the squad and be interested in the development of the team's morale and esprit de corps.

9. Men who have predominant will power to do their level best and to stimulate others to give their best in order to produce team spirit, team enthusiasm, and the will to win.

10. Men who are masters of themselves who will make personal sacrifices in eating, smoking, sleeping, drinking, and in social events in order to train honestly and faithfully to get themselves in the best physical condition possible so that individually and cooperatively they can always do their best.

11. Men who have an earnest desire to strive for perfection and realize that there is always something that can be done to improve themselves.

FITZGERALD RESPONDS...

F. Scott Fitzgerald dabbled in football at Princeton, although he soon gave it up for other interests. So, when he received a letter and questionnaire in 1934 from Princeton head coach Fritz Crisler sent to former players requesting suggestions for the betterment of the football program, Fitzgerald felt obligated to answer. His letter:

> *Dear Fritz:*
> *You write me again demanding advice concerning the coming season. I hasten to answer—again I insist that using a member of the Board of Trustees at left tackle... would be a mistake. My idea is a backfield composed of Kipke, Eddie*

Mahan, President Lowell and anybody we can get for the left side... and then either bring back Light-Horse Harry Lee, or else you will fill in yourself for the last place....

> *Now Fritz, I realize that you and Tad know more about this thing than I do—nevertheless I want to make my suggestion: all the end men and backfield men and members of the Board of Trustees start off together—then they all reverse their fields, led by some of the most prominent professors and alumni—Albie Booth, Bob Lassiter, etc.—and almost before we know it we are up against the Yale goal—let me see, where was I? I mean the Lehigh goal—anyhow some goal, perhaps our own. Anyhow the main thing is that the C.W.A. is either dead, or else just beginning, and to use again that variation of the "Mexican" shift that I suggested last year will be just disastrous. Why? Even I can follow it! Martineau comes out of the huddle—or perhaps topples back into it—he passes to some member of past years' teams—(who won't be named here because of the eligibility rules) and then—well, from there on we go to practically anything.*

> *But not this year, Fritz Crisler, if you take my advice!*

> *Best,*
> *F. Scott Fitzgerald*

DARTMOUTH'S TWELFTH MAN

Perhaps the most famous interloper in college football history made his appearance in the 1935 Princeton–Dartmouth game before 56,000 fans who braved the snow and cold of Hanover, New Hampshire, and were, according to their persuasion, either amused or outraged. Asa Bushnell III, Princeton class of 1947, wrote of the incident 25 years after the fact for the *Princeton Athletic News*:

> Strange as it may seem, it was a young architect from Cranford, N.J.—a refugee from the University of Cincinnati, no less—who immortalized the activities in Palmer Stadium on November 23,

1935. It was he who, midway through the fourth period that tingling afternoon, left the other 55,999 spectators in their seats to assist the Dartmouth Indians in a determined goal-line stand. It was he who lined up with the Hanoverians on the two-yard stripe and prevented Jack White from scoring—and White boasted interference from the awesome likes of Johnny Weller and Homer Spofford. It was the daring "twelfth man" who, though escorted unceremoniously off the field and out of the stadium without further ado, gained a nationwide football reputation in a single play.

"I remember the incident as if it had happened only yesterday," Stuart W. McFadden of Cranford reminisced just last week. (McFadden is the not-so-famous thirteenth man who deserves recognition, as you will see very soon.) "I suppose there was no stopping it. It was one of those spontaneous things that takes place before you're sure what's going on."

The traditional bonfire at Texas A&M. The tradition was suspended after a tragic accident in 1999 when tons of lumber collapsed during the preparation of the bonfire; 12 students were killed.

McFadden, now a lumber materials salesman, was peddling new cars in Westfield, N.J., the morning of November 23, 1935. "I got a telephone call from an old Cranford High buddy, George Larsen, who insisted that we attend the Princeton–Dartmouth game in Princeton that afternoon. I was hesitant because of the bad weather and the lateness of the hour, but George insisted because he had free tickets from a newspaper friend and we had sufficient reason to root for Dartmouth—my brother-in-law went there."

When Larsen arrived to pick up McFadden, the former was "a little under the weather," which was horrible to begin with, so the latter drove the car—a car headed for a rendezvous with destiny. "George had been down at a local tavern, and he was really rarin' to go—even if we missed the first half," McFadden recounted. "He was a fun-lover and, from the mood he was in that day, I should have guessed what might be in store for us."

According to the loquacious lumberman, who still tells his fascinating tale in the Cranford area and still finds many a fascinated listener, George Newcomer Larsen, known as "Guzz" to those who were familiar with his Danish ancestry, was "the type of fellow who was always getting into headlines with his antics. You know, he was often in a little trouble because he was devilish. It was never too serious, but, if there was a prank to play, 'Guzz' was there to play it. . . ."

Stu and George arrived in Princeton at halftime, whereupon "Guzz" started meandering all over his section of Palmer Stadium, paying little heed to the third-quarter action on the field. "He wouldn't sit still," McFadden explained. "He was a very sociable sort of fellow, especially that afternoon. When I went up to get him between the third and fourth periods, instead of returning

with me, he insisted on introducing me to a whole row of new-found friends. He was having a fine time."

Once Stu McFadden got back to his appointed seat, close behind the front-row fence, "Guzz" Larsen apparently decided to join him. Then, suddenly, he changed his mind, perhaps inspired by his first conscious sight of Dartmouth's eleven in defense of its goal, and merely kept on going. He hurdled the fence, after descending the stadium steps rapidly, threw off his telltale coat and hat (subsequently notarized by the "bouncer" who watched him strip, then, several minutes later, bounced him) and assumed his unscheduled role as the Big Green's "twelfth man."

"It was a short but scintillating performance," McFadden, truly the thirteenth man, admitted. "I climbed over the fence to retrieve George's coat and hat, and I didn't mind at all that I was obliged to leave with him. By then, I had seen it all anyhow, believe me."

WHAT'S IN A NICKNAME?

College football teams must have nicknames someone decreed back in the nineteenth century, something to define the ferociousness of a team, or its speed and agility, or its blithe spirit, or maybe just its uniqueness. Yale became the Bulldogs, Princeton the Tigers, Michigan the Wolverines, USC the Trojans, and Notre Dame the Fighting Irish.

When all the Lions, Tigers, Bears, Wildcats, Bulldogs, Mustangs, Wolf Packs, and Eagles were used up, the selections got creative, often strange, sometimes obscure.

FACING PAGE
Jubilant Michigan players and fans come together after the Wolverines defeated Washington State in the 1998 Rose Bowl game 21—16.

TOP LEFT
The University of Georgia Bulldog, and friend.

TOP RIGHT
Representing the Florida State Seminoles: Chief Osceola.

MIDDLE LEFT
The falcon, mascot of the U.S. Air Force Academy.

MIDDLE RIGHT
Ralphie, mascot of the University of Colorado Golden Buffaloes.

BOTTOM
The ferocious mascot of the University of Michigan, a wolverine (caged here), is introduced at the dedication of the school's new stadium before the Ohio State game of 1927. The Wolverines were equally ferocious that afternoon, defeating the Buckeyes 21—0.

Some Whose Meanings Are Often Lost on Most of Us:

Akron Zips (Could be positive or negative)

Furman Paladins (Knights in Charlemagne's court)

Knox Siwash (Either an Alaskan breed of dog or a North Pacific Coast Indian)

North Carolina Tar Heels (Those in the pine barrens of North Carolina apparently not careful enough to avoid stepping in the pine tar)

Oklahoma Sooners (People who occupied homestead land before the authorized time, thus gaining an unfair advantage in choice of location)

Southern Illinois Salukis (A breed of dog of the greyhound family, with long ears and silky hair)

Tennessee Volunteers (Those who enter the military of their own free will)

VMI Keydets (Perhaps they don't know how to spell Cadets?)

Wake Forest Demon Deacons (Something satanic)

Western Carolina Catamounts (Actually a puma or a cougar—"cat of the mountain"— get it?)

Some Not So Likely to Strike Fear in the Heart of an Opponent:

Amherst Lord Jeffs

Boston U. Terriers

Delaware Fightin' Blue Hens

Ohio Wesleyan Battling Bishops

Oregon Ducks

Pennsylvania Quakers

Swarthmore Little Quakers

Texas Christian Horned Frogs

Tufts Jumbos

VPI Gobblers

Williams Ephmen

Youngstown State Penguins

The Most Common (Among Major Colleges):

Tigers

Auburn

Clemson

Grambling

Jackson State

Louisiana State

Memphis State

Missouri

Pacific

Princeton

Tennessee State

Texas Southern

Bulldogs

Citadel

Drake

Fresno State

Georgia

Louisiana Tech

Mississippi State

South Carolina State

Yale

Wildcats

Arizona

Davidson

Kansas State

Kentucky

New Hampshire

Northwestern

Villanova

Weber State

A LITTLE OUT OF THE ORDINARY

The following are some feats and events that are unlikely to be repeated in the game of college football.

- Snooks Dowd of Lehigh, in college football's earlier days, ran 210 yards for a touchdown in a game against Lafayette. He ran the length of the field the wrong way, realized his mistake, circled the goal posts, and raced back the length of the field for a touchdown.

- In 1900, Kentucky won a football game without running a single offensive play during the contest. In defeating Louisville YMCA 12–6, Kentucky elected to kick on first down every time it received the ball and scored only on recovered fumbles.

- Coincidences: In 1966, Augustana (of South Dakota) played Augustana (of Illinois). In addition, both teams were nicknamed the Vikings, both had the same school colors, and both had an assistant coach named Kessinger. In case anyone is interested, Augustana of South Dakota won 27-0.

- In 1897, Georgetown College of Kentucky played its entire schedule against the University of Kentucky (three games).

- In 1958, the first year to allow 2-point conversions, Stanford scored two touchdowns and a field goal to California's two touchdowns, but still lost the game. The score: 16–15.

- Marquette lays claim to the longest punt ever. In a 1925 game against Navy at Farragut Field in Annapolis, Maryland, on an exceptionally blustery afternoon, their quarterback, Bob Demoling, took the snap on his own 20-yard line. He boomed one all the way to Navy's 19, where it bounced, was picked up by the gusting wind, and was carried not just into the end zone but 30 yards beyond it where it plopped into Chesapeake Bay and was swept out to sea. Total yardage has never been precisely determined.

- Jay Kelley of Santa Clara is credited with perhaps the worst kick ever. In a game during Prohibition days against highly favored California, Santa Clara had battled the Golden Bears to a scoreless tie. With only a few minutes remaining, Santa Clara, on fourth down with the ball on Cal's 39-yard line, elected to punt, hoping to strand California deep in its own territory and preserve the tie. Kelley put his foot to the ball, which sailed almost straight upward, arced a little backward, landed a yard behind Kelley, and then rolled 24 yards the wrong way. California got the ball on Santa Clara's 37 and proceeded to move it in for a touchdown just before time ran out. Kelley was credited with a punt of minus 25 yards.

- What's What Publishing Company of Omaha, Nebraska, once reported this novel kick: "In the 1926 game between Boston College and Haskell, the spectators were treated to a kick that will probably never be repeated again. Sun Jennings, Haskell's star halfback, who was also the kicker, tried a 50-yard drop kick. The ball soared high in the air and came down directly on the crossbar. It bounced straight up in the air again and fell back on the crossbar to bounce a second time only to again hit the crossbar falling back on the playing field. The ball actually hit the crossbar three times. The game ended in a 21–21 tie."

TWIST OF FATE

George Connor, All-America tackle from Notre Dame and a member of both the College and Pro Football Halls of Fame, remembers a fateful contest:

I played for Holy Cross before I came to Notre Dame [separated by military service in World War II] and we weren't all that good. Our biggest game in 1942, however, is one I'll never forget.

We went to Boston to play Boston College at Fenway Park. They were a real powerhouse that year, heavily favored against us, and were all set to accept the bid to the Sugar Bowl that year after they disposed of us. Well, it didn't happen that way. We annihilated them that day, 55–12. The first irony was that those figures, 55 and 12, were the jersey numbers of Holovak and Naumutz, Boston College's co-captains, pictured on the front cover of the game program. The second irony, and more important, was that they had scheduled a victory party to be held that night at the Cocoanut Grove nightclub in Boston. They were so embarrassed by the defeat that they cancelled [the party], and that was the night that the Cocoanut Grove burned down and almost 500 people were killed. I guess you could say that our beating them maybe saved their lives.

THE OLD COLLEGE CHEER

There's always something special about hearing the old college cheer, shouted out into the crisp autumn air. Here is a selection of some original college football rallying cries, as taken from a turn-of-the-(twentieth)-century program.

Alabama

Rah, hoo, ree! Universitee! Rah, boo! Wah, hoo! A.C.U.!

California

Ha-Ha-Ha-California—U.C. Berk-lee, Zip-Boom-ah!

Centre

Rackity-cax! Co-ax! Co-ax! (twice) Hurrah! Hurrah! Centre! Centre! Rah! Rah!

Colorado

Rah, rah, rah! Pike's Peak or Bust! Colorado College! Yell we must!

Franklin and Marshall

Hullabaloo, bala! (twice) Way-up! Way-up! F and M! Nevonia!

Heidelberg

Killi-killick! Rah, rah, Zik, sik! Ha! Ha! Yi! Hoo! Barn! Zoo! Heidelberg!

Nebraska

U, U, U, N-I-Ver-Ver-Ver-Sit-Y Oh My!

Ohio State

Wahoo, Wahoo, Rip, Zip, Baz, Zoo, I yell, I yell, for O.S.U.!

Washington and Lee

Chick-a-go-runk! go-runk! go-runk! ha, ho, hi, ho! Washing-ton and Lee!

SUPER FAN

The most loyal college football fan in the nation just had to be Giles Pellerin, whose devotion to the University of Southern California became a thing of legend. Only his death in 1998 could bring to an end the string of 797 *consecutive* Trojan games, at home and away, the retired telephone company executive from Pasadena, California, had attended. He did not miss a single game in 72 years, including 69 USC–Notre Dame games and 67 contests between the Trojans and UCLA.

Super Fan Pellerin began attending USC games as a sophomore there in 1926. His first game was the home opener, when a Howard Jones–led Trojan team trounced Whittier 74–0. Since that time Pellerin followed the team by plane, train, and automobile, more than 650,000 miles on the road, spending upward of $85,000 in so doing. Since that first game he witnessed USC win 532 games, lose 225, and tie 40.

He delayed his honeymoon eight months in 1935 so he could celebrate it at a game USC was playing in Hawaii that year. Pellerin came close to missing a game or two, however, especially one during the 1949 season, when he was hospitalized five days after an emergency operation to remove his appendix. On game day, Giles told the nurses he was going out for a walk on the hospital grounds. Instead he went to the Los Angeles Coliseum and returned to his bed several hours later after Southern Cal had beaten Washington 40–28.

He once explained his avocation, "I never played the game, but I love it. There's just a certain spirit about college football. I've always said that going to USC games is the thing that has kept me alive, young and happy." Well, it did for nearly three quarters of a century and Giles Pellerin died, appropriately enough, watching his beloved Trojans play UCLA in the Rose Bowl on November 21, 1998.

TEN GREAT THINGS ABOUT COLLEGE FOOTBALL, ACCORDING TO BEANO COOK:

Beano Cook, commentator for Saturday afternoon telecasts of college football games, speaking:

There are certain things people should do before they die. They should make out a will and make sure they see the following:

1. The dotting of the i at Ohio State.
   It's like seeing "Casablanca." You could see it 1,000 times but it still excites you. You know he's going to say, "We'll always have Paris" and that the i is going to be dotted. But it still sends a chill up your spine.

   A couple of years ago they invited former band members back to Ohio State for an Oldtimers Day. They had two bands on the field at the same time and two guys dotting the i at the same time. It had to be one of the greatest moments in college football.

   I'd rather dot the i before I die than be president. I think that's a greater honor.

2. Hearing the Victory March at Notre Dame.
   When the Victory March starts and the team comes out of the tunnel, it's kind of like hearing the National Anthem when you're in a foreign country. It does something to you. That is, of course, as long as your team isn't the one playing Notre Dame. If you happen to be the visiting team, it's no fun.

   Did you know the Victory March is the fourth most famous song in America? The National Anthem is No. 1, although nobody knows the words to the second verse. Then there's "God Bless America," "White Christmas" and the "Victory March." You have to have Kate

FACING PAGE
One of college football's revered moments, dotting the I at Ohio State.

Smith singing "God Bless America," Bing Crosby singing "White Christmas" and you have to be at Notre Dame to appreciate the Victory March.

3. Walking through the woods at the University of North Carolina.

There's a wonderful stadium there in a gulley, surrounded by woods. You're walking through the same woods that Thomas Wolfe and Charles Kuralt walked through. That's what makes it exciting.

4. An autumn afternoon at West Point.

The thing about pro football is that all the stadiums look the same now. One Stefanie Powers is great, but if every one looked like her, we would get bored. What makes college football different is its different settings, like at West Point, when the corps marches in. Even if you were just a private in the Army and had to pull KP, as I did, it's still a great scene.

5. The Yale Band.

They're very disorganized, but it doesn't matter. And what makes their fight song, "Bulldog, Bulldog," so extra special is that it was written by Cole Porter.

6. A night game at LSU.

Most tailgate parties start a few hours before the game. At LSU, they start Thursday afternoon.

7. The Florida–Georgia game.

This is one of the great spectacles in sport, the World's Largest Outdoor Cocktail Party.

I like it better than the Texas–Oklahoma game because there are too many rich people at that game. The Florida–Georgia game has more real fans. There might be more hard drinking at a Texas–Oklahoma game—more bourbon—but there's more real drinking by the average guy at Florida–Georgia.

Pageantry before the Army—Navy game. Traditionally the Cadets and Midshipmen march on field before each game in one of college football's most colorful rivalries.

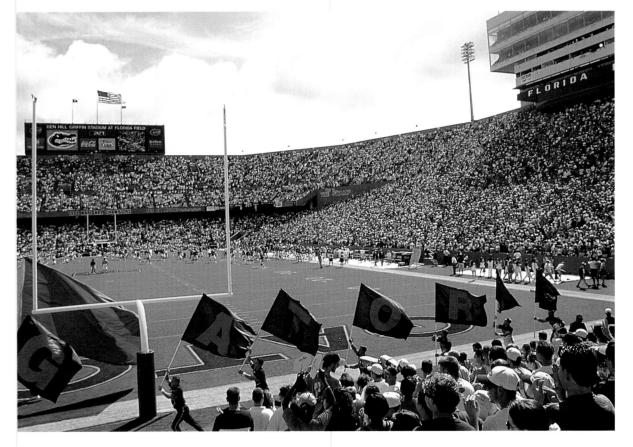

The Florida—Georgia game—this one being played at Florida Field in Gainesville—is one of the 10 Great Things About College Football, according to Beano Cook.

8. Nebraska fans.

I think Nebraska fans are as fair as anybody, and I like it when everybody is in red.

They keep telling me that all those farmers out there are broke. The price of hogs is down, bacon is down, and they're getting one cent to every 80 bushels of wheat. But when that team goes to Hawaii, as it seems to do every four years, 15,000 fans go along with them. How can they be broke?

9. The Trojan Horse at USC.

I don't like the Los Angeles Coliseum particularly, but that horse is great. When he charges around that track, it's the greatest performance since the '32 Olympics.

The USC cheerleaders, who incidentally might be just a little bit too pretty, are OK, but it's the horse that makes it special at USC.

10. The Michigan–Ohio State game.

This to me is the greatest rivalry in all sports. Maybe the North Central states are declining in industry, but this rivalry never will decline.

Army–Navy is a close second for me, because you know most of the players involved will graduate.

Rivalries are what college football has over pro football. In pro football, the rivalries change. Pittsburgh–Oakland was a stiff rivalry for a couple of years, especially after the Immaculate Reception. But if the Steelers and Raiders play next year, it'll be a good game, but you know it won't be Michigan–Ohio State.

"
Nobody ever got back-slapped

into winning anything. "

WALLACE WADE
University of Alabama
Head Coach, 1923—30

VICTORY

THE GREATEST GAMES

In the same way boxing has Dempsey–Tunney and Ali–Frazier, baseball its Yankee–Red Sox pennant race of 1949 or Giants–Dodgers playoff game of 1951, college football has its own outstanding encounters, games with excitement or consequence above all others. From that first soccerlike game played between Rutgers and Princeton in 1869 to the 2001 meeting between Oklahoma and Florida State at the Orange Bowl to determine the first national champion of the new millennium, the game has featured classic confrontations: cliff-hangers, remarkable come-from-behind wins, shocking upsets, and conflicts with the national championship hanging in the balance.

Perhaps no game illustrates what college football is all about more than the meeting between Michigan and Northwestern on November 4, 2000. A game so filled with ironies, it could have been scripted by Shakespeare; an ending so filled with suspense and surprise that it could have been the work of Alfred Hitchcock. Michigan, ranked No. 3 in the nation at the start of season and the unanimous pick to win the Big Ten, traveled to Evanston, Illinois, to take on Northwestern, a team absent from the early rankings and picked by many preseason prognosticators to finish 11th in the Big Ten (Penn State became 11th member of the Big Ten in 1993).

By early November, however, both teams were in contention for the conference title; both were ranked in the Top 25. Michigan was heralded for its great defense, Northwestern for its explosive offense. From the opening touchdown by Northwestern less than 3 minutes into the game, the lead changed hands with metronomic regularity down to the last score in the last half-minute of play. At game's end the two teams had scored a total of 105 points and were just 3 apart. The twists in the last 2 minutes

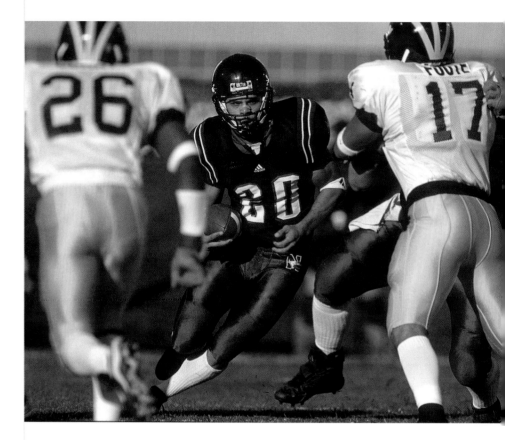

alone were staggering: with Michigan ahead 51–46 Northwestern All-America candidate Damian Anderson, alone in the end zone, drops a fourth-down, potentially game-winning touchdown pass; a Michigan All–Big Ten running back, Anthony Thomas, moments later fumbles the ball back; then redemption for Northwestern as quarterback Zak Kustok completes three straight passes, the last to Sam Simmons for the go-ahead touchdown with 26 seconds on the clock. Wildcats 52, Wolverines 51. A 2-point conversion, another Kustok pass, this time to Teddy Johnson, 54–51. Still, with 20 seconds remaining, Michigan moves into remote but possible field goal range . . . 57 yards; Michigan's kicker, Hayden Epstein, had booted a 52-yarder earlier . . . 5 seconds remain, but the hold is mishandled, the kick does

Damian Anderson carries the ball for Northwestern against Michigan in 2000, one of the most offensively explosive, exciting college football games ever. With twists and surprises in the last two minutes of the game worthy of O. Henry, Northwestern finally emerged victorious by the score of 54–51.

not get off. It was a game that will long be remembered, though its outcome did not in the end determine the Big Ten title, much less the national championship. This game was truly college football at its best.

In the long line of college football tradition leading up to the Michigan–Northwestern game in the first year of the new century, there has been a myriad of truly special Saturday afternoons: Jim Thorpe and his Carlisle Indians defeating mighty Army in 1912; Notre Dame and Army astonishing a nation by playing to a 0–0 tie in 1946; Nebraska and Oklahoma deciding the national championship of 1971; the list is long indeed. They have involved the greatest of players; the coaching genius of legends like Pop Warner, Frank Leahy, Bud Wilkinson, Bear Bryant, among many others.

Choosing *the* greatest games is a nearly impossible task, and the following selections will surely be controversial. Everyone has favorites, and arguments can be made for those great games not included here. Few will argue, however, that the games profiled in the following pages were no less than monumental events in the long and colorful story of college football.

The Poes of Princeton, one of the first families of college football, and all blood-related to the literary master Edgar Allan Poe. From the left, with their years of graduation: Arthur (1900), S. Johnson (1894), Nielson (1897), Edgar Allan (1891, grandnephew of his namesake), Gresham H. (1902) and John P. Jr. (1895). Edgar Allan, a halfback, was an All-America selection in 1889; end Arthur was an All-American in 1899.

PRINCETON–YALE

November 24, 1899

The following is from a newspaper account of this vintage college football game (the author of the "blue" prose remains to this day unidentified):

New Haven, Conn., Nov. 25, 1899 (Special)—Princeton has finally done it, and done it well. Of course, they always want to defeat Yale whenever they meet at football. Fate had not been kind to the boys from Old Nassau in this desire up to today. Then, when it was dollars to doughnuts that Yale would win by a score of 10 to 6, Fortune gave to the wearers of the orange and black a regular sunbeam of a smile.

Fifteen thousand people at least packed the Yale field. Five thousand of them cheered for Princeton and now joined in a paean of joy that Poe pater had sent his big family of boys to Princeton instead of Yale. It was the second time that this Poe—Arthur—had saved the day for his alma mater. He did it a year ago, on Brokaw Field, by making a phenomenal run of 90 yards after stealing the ball out of the hands of an opposing halfback, and so making the only score of that game in 1898. Yale was also the victim at that time, by 6 to 0.

[In 1899] there were but five minutes left in which to finish the second half of a game that had been most stubbornly contested on both sides. The sky was blue. Princeton's supporters, massed on the west stand, were bluer. The east stand was packed with thousands of men and women who kept a cloud of blue flags and banners in motion above their heads.

Princeton's original eleven had faded under the hammering until there was little of it left on the field. It looked as if all chances of making either a goal from the field or a touchdown—either of which would have been sufficient to win the game—had been lost to Princeton. Yale was "playing foxy," as is her wont under such circumstances.

As man after man of the regular Princeton team was hauled out of the line and a substitute sent in in his place, the lips and cheeks of the Princeton "rooters" blanched, and then turned blue. Victory, to all appearances, was about to perch on the blue banners of Old Eli once more, and the hopes of the Princeton aggregation that they could at last beat Yale two years running (which had never happened before) seemed to be blasted. It was a very blue outlook indeed.

Suddenly through a rift in the blue cloud burst the rich orange light of the dying sun. The Yale blue sky changed to a Princeton orange. Away to the east where were the blue waters of New Haven harbor, a golden light beamed down on them, and, with the shadow cast over the narrow bay, seemed, from the field two miles away, to cover the waters with a satin-like film of orange and black. Was it all an omen for Princeton?

Princeton's battered eleven, reinforced by new blood, took a sudden brace. Its backs seemed to suddenly get their "second wind," and they plunged into the solid line of blue in front of them as if they had seen nature promising victory in the magnificent transformation she was making. Princeton took on a new lease of life. Plunges into the line yielded her territory to put the ball on Yale's 20-yard line.

It was now do or die for Princeton. There was a moment's consultation of Princeton's players. Captain (Bill) Edwards called [Arthur] Poe into it, and the sharps suspected at once that there was to be a try for goal from the 35-yard line. [The quarterback] shouted the mystic numbers that meant "Protect Poe for a try for goal from the field." Bannard, at center, juggled the ball for an instant, and then, turning sharply, passed it nicely into the hands of Poe.

For an instant Poe gauged the distance to and direction of the goal posts. He dropped the ball carefully, caught it squarely on the toe of that good right foot of his, raised it in the air in a graceful curve, and the crowd held its breath as it sailed until the spheroid stopped its upward flight. Then it moved gracefully toward the ground, and a great shout went up from the Princeton stand. The ball had gone directly between the goal posts. Five points were added to Princeton's score, making the total 11 to 10, and the game was won by the representatives of Old Nassau with but one minute left for play.

Arthur Poe said later: "The ball was actually kicked from my instep deliberately, as I was wearing lightweight running shoes in order to increase my speed on getting down the field. It was the first drop kick that I had attempted in my college career."

CARLISLE–ARMY

November 9, 1912

In 1912, Carlisle Indian School, a tiny institution of about 250 students in Cumberland County, Pennsylvania, hardly seemed competition for the mighty U.S. Military Academy of West Point, which took its football very seriously. Army also had the home field advantage, with almost all the 3,000 fans at the game cheering for the once-defeated Cadets.

Despite its small student body, Pop Warner's football team was of Goliath proportions. The Indians of Carlisle had a thunderous offense, spearheaded by the legendary Jim Thorpe. Blocking for him were two other Indian greats, Joe Guyon and Pete Calac (Guyon would later become an All-American himself). Carlisle was considered one of the most difficult teams in the country to stop.

Army claimed an All-American tackle in Leland Devore, a near All-American in quarterback Vernon Prichard, and a promising halfback by the name of Dwight Eisenhower. But the Cadets were best known for their defense, the best in the nation, according to many. Army had allowed only 13 points that season and a mere 11 in eight games the year before.

It was a classic confrontation: Carlisle's bulldozing offense versus Army's stingy defense. Before the game few were willing to predict which would prevail.

Army held its own in the first half, and a touchdown by halfback Leland Hobbs kept Cadet hopes high. But as good as the Army defense was, it could not contain Jim Thorpe. The Sac and Fox Indian proved unstoppable. He took an Army punt and carried it back 45 yards for an apparent touchdown, a run in which virtually every Army defender had hands on him at one time or another. It was called back because of a penalty, however. But the Army defense was not so lucky after that. Four times Carlisle drove against Army's vaunted defense, Thorpe grinding out 10 yards on this carry, 5 on that. And each time he brought the Indians down to the Army goal line and then watched a teammate carry the ball in for the score. As described the day after in the *New York Times*, "Thorpe went through the West Point line as if it were an open door. . . . Thorpe tore off runs of ten yards or more so often that they became common."

In the second half, Army was virtually overwhelmed. Carlisle so dominated the game that the Cadets squeezed out only a single first down during the rest of the game.

The final score was 27–6, tiny Carlisle the titan of the day. Not since 1900, when Harvard scrubbed them 29–0, had a team scored as many points against Army. Carlisle's Pop Warner commented, "At least this day, we proved that an explosive offense can not only score points, but also can be the best defense a team might have."

When it was all over, Army coach Ernest Graves said that he had just witnessed the finest football offensive attack he had ever seen. When asked about Jim Thorpe in particular, he slowly shook his head as if to rid himself of a painful memory.

Thorpe shed his college cleats after that season, and Carlisle drifted out of football prominence, but Army was just beginning down a path that would culminate with three national championships (one shared with Notre Dame) in the 1940s.

CHICAGO– PRINCETON

October 28, 1922

Years after this desperately battled game, Chicago's coach Amos Alonzo Stagg and Princeton's Bill Roper were attending a meeting of coaches at which all were asked the most exciting contest they had participated in during their long careers. Neither Stagg nor Roper hesitated; both said unequivocally that it was their dramatic meeting in Chicago in 1922.

Before that game, Chicago was a 3–1 favorite, according to the oddsmakers of the day. But

Princeton, playing its first game ever in the Midwest, was nicknamed the "Team of Destiny." They were undefeated, although they had been an underdog in practically all their games that year. A sellout crowd of more than 32,000 gathered at Stagg Field to witness what one Midwest sportswriter dubbed "the battle of East and West."

Stagg, according to the same writer, "had fashioned a stone-cracking steamroller that hit an enemy line with the force of the Theban phalanx," and his Chicago Maroon lent credence to that as they pulverized Princeton in the first half. On their first possession, Chicago marched downfield, principally behind the plunges and end runs of fullback John Thomas and his brother Harry, a halfback. From the 2-yard line, John Thomas bucked in for the game's first score.

But Bill Roper's Tigers came back later in the period. Barr Snively connected with Howard Gray on a 45-yard pass play that brought the ball to the Chicago 7-yard line. A few plays later, Princeton fullback John Cleaves burst into the end zone. A successful conversion gave the Tigers a 7–6 lead.

Stagg's Theban phalanx, however, was unimpressed. They came right back, driving almost the length of the field. John Thomas carried the ball in to regain the lead for Chicago. Princeton battled, but the Maroon stopped them each time throughout the rest of the second period and all of the third quarter. In the meantime, Thomas scored his third touchdown of the day. Going into the last quarter, Chicago had a comfortable lead, 18–7.

In the final period, with Princeton backed up at its own 2-yard line, the game seemed over. A punt, the obvious play choice, would get the ball out perhaps only to their 40, and Princeton had not been able to contain Chicago's offense most of the day. It was morbidly quiet in the small Princeton cheering section.

John Cleaves lined up in punt formation at the back of his own end zone. The Maroon crowded the line of scrimmage, intent on a massive invasion to block the kick. Cleaves grabbed the snap, took a step as if to kick the ball, then suddenly pivoted and rolled to his right. He lofted a floating pass to quarterback Johnny Gorman, who raced with it all the way to midfield before being caught by a Chicago defender. But the Tigers could get no closer to the Chicago goal than the 42-yard line.

This time Cleaves did punt the ball. And on the next play, Chicago, deep in its own territory now, fumbled, and the ball bounced directly into the hands of Princeton end Howard Gray, who ran with it for the score (as rules permitted in those days). Princeton was now within 4 points of favored Chicago.

An inspired Princeton defense held the Maroon and got the ball back 58 yards from the goal line. Now it was the Tigers' turn to march. And they did, all the way to the Chicago 3-yard line. There, on fourth down, halfback Harry Crum hit the line in desperation. Several Chicago players had him in their grasp, but somehow he wriggled free and fell into the end zone. The conversion made the score Princeton 21, Chicago 18.

A stunned Stagg urged his team to come back. There were only two minutes left, and Stagg changed the attack from running to passing. It worked. Chicago moved swiftly to the Princeton 25-yard line. Another pass, grabbed by quarterback Otto Shohmeier at the 6, quieted the reinvigorated Princeton fans. And now the Maroon went back to their devastating running game. Three plunges got them to the 1-yard line. There were only a few seconds left now. Everyone looked for John Thomas to run for his fourth touchdown of the day, and it was no surprise when he got the call. Thomas hit the Princeton line full speed, but went down in a chaos of black-and-orange-clad bodies, still 2 feet from the goal. On the next play, Princeton punted out of danger as the whistle blew, a winner, 21–18.

Word of the great upset was telegraphed back to New Jersey where, according to the *New York Times*, "With bells tolling and bonfires burning on several parts of the campus, the Princeton undergraduates celebrated their team's victory over Chicago . . . the hundreds of students formed an enthusiastic parade down Nassau Street singing the old Princeton songs and the famous bell began to ring out the 'Glory of Old Nassau.' . . . When the team and its followers return to jungle land tomorrow, a glorious homecoming is being planned by the undergraduate body. A parade will be formed and the victorious warriors will be escorted from the station to their rooms in state."

The scene of the Stanford–California game of 1924, played at Memorial Stadium in Berkeley. At the time, the crowd of 76,000 was recognized as the largest ever to attend a college football game. At stake was the Pacific Coast Conference title and a trip to the Rose Bowl, but the game ended in a 20–20 tie (Stanford ended up getting the Rose Bowl bid).

STANFORD–CALIFORNIA

November 22, 1924

On November 22, 1924, the largest crowd to attend a college football game up to that time gathered at Berkeley, California. The event: the latest chapter in the already torrid rivalry between the Stanford Indians (they have since changed their nickname to the Stanford Cardinal) from the other side of San Francisco Bay and California's Golden Bears. A crowd of 76,000 filled California's Memorial Stadium, and another estimated 24,000 thronged Tight Wad Hill, a vantage that offered a clear view down into the stadium.

Both teams were undefeated, vying for the championship of the Pacific Coast Conference and a Rose Bowl bid. Stanford, under Pop Warner, would have been favored had not its star back Ernie Nevers been sidelined with a broken ankle. As a result, the game was rated a toss-up.

Carrying the team in Nevers's absence, halfback Murray Cuddeback guided Stanford to a 6–0 halftime lead by moving the team on offense and kicking two field goals himself. With some spectacular catches and dazzling runs, however, California's Tut Imlay turned the tide in the second half, leading coach Andy Smith's Bears to three unanswered touchdowns.

With the score 20–6 in the fourth quarter, Cuddeback and quarterback Ed Walker rallied the Indians to two touchdowns, the latter on a pass from Walker to Ted Shipkey. All that was needed for the tie was the

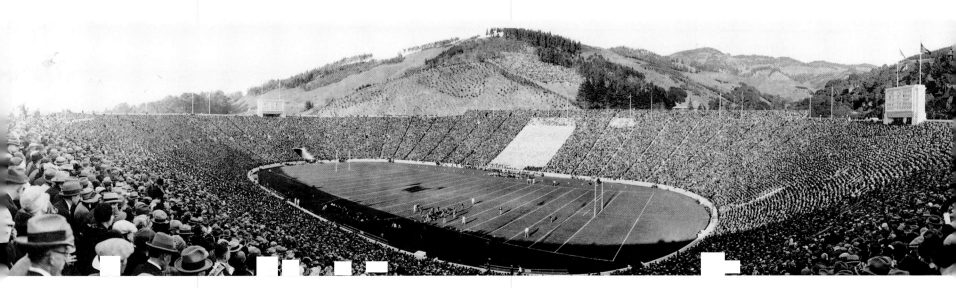

conversion, which Cuddeback kicked. The 20–20 tie was, in the words of Walter Camp, who was on the West Coast to watch the game, "one of the most exciting I've ever seen in any part of the country."

Stanford went on to the Rose Bowl that year and a hobbled Ernie Nevers came back to play for them, but they were demolished 27–10 in Pasadena by Knute Rockne's Notre Dame team, which featured the fabled Four Horsemen.

YALE–DARTMOUTH

October 31, 1931

Neither Yale nor Dartmouth was in contention for national recognition in 1931—that was to be fought out by Bob Neyland's Tennessee Volunteers and the USC Trojans under Howard Jones. Still, the most exciting game of that year, and many another for that matter, took place at the Yale Bowl on October 31, when the Dartmouth Indians, as they were called in those days (today they're the Big Green), came down from Hanover, New Hampshire, to face the Eli.

The Yale Bulldogs were the favorites. They had easily vanquished Dartmouth four times in the previous five years, the face-saver for the Indians a 0–0 tie the year before. Yale had a whirling dervish in its backfield by the name of Albie Booth, five-foot-six-inches tall and 144 pounds, combining speed and grit, and in the process making everyone, opponent and spectator alike, forget how small he was. Known as "Little Boy Blue" or the "Mighty Mite," he was the Eli captain and its superstar.

Dartmouth had two fine backs in quarterback Bill Morton and halfback Bill McCall. And they had an overwhelming desire to alter the cruel history of their confrontations with Yale.

Throughout the first quarter, Dartmouth controlled the ball, penetrating as far as the Yale 20-yard line once, but without a score. That was rectified at the start of the second period, however, when Morton kicked a field goal to give the Indians a 3–0 lead.

But unfortunately it served to ignite the little firecracker known as Albie Booth. He snared the ensuing kickoff at his own 6-yard line, shot up the middle, cut to the sideline, shook off several tacklers, and raced into the end zone. Dartmouth got the ball back, and Morton fired a pass over the middle that Booth picked off and returned to midfield. Booth passed on first down to end Herster Barres, who ran to Dartmouth's 22-yard line. Then Little Boy Blue slid through the Indians' secondary to catch a pass from halfback Kay Todd, and carry it in for still another Bulldog touchdown. After Booth kicked the extra point—he had missed the first two—he left the game mildly winded with the score Yale 19, Dartmouth, 3.

An undaunted Dartmouth came back, however. Bill McCall took a pitchout from Morton and ran 25 yards for a score. But Yale, even with Albie Booth on the bench, was unstoppable. Filling his lit-

Albie Booth, Yale captain in 1931. Known as "Little Boy Blue" (he was five-foot-six and 144 pounds), Booth was a triple-threat back who starred for Yale during the years 1929–31. Perhaps the only time it could be said he failed the Eli was in the 1931 game with Dartmouth.

tle shoes was halfback Bob Lassiter, who raced 53 yards to set up another touchdown and then tossed one to Barres for still another. A 33-point second quarter gave Yale a 23-point lead at the half.

Yale kicked off to start the second half, and Bill McCall grabbed the ball at his own 8-yard line. He raced with it the length of the field, and suddenly the momentum of the game changed. Dartmouth held Yale, and when the Eli attempted a punt on fourth down, Dartmouth's Roger Donner broke through and blocked it, picked the ball up on the run, and ran it in for another Indian touchdown. The score was now 33–24, Yale.

Albie Booth was back in the game for Yale, but Dartmouth was keying on him, and their defense proved impregnable. When he couldn't make it on the ground, Booth called for a pass play. He pitched out to Kay Todd, then took off downfield. Todd zeroed in on him and threw the ball, but seemingly from out of nowhere, Dartmouth's Bill McCall cut in front of Booth, snatched the ball away, and sped 60 yards with it to bring the Indians within 3 points of Yale.

The partisan crowd in the Yale Bowl was dismally quiet. Once again, Dartmouth contained Booth and his fellow Bulldogs. And again Dartmouth marched. With 4 minutes left and the ball on Yale's 14-yard line, Bill Morton lined up for a field goal. It was perfect, and the score was tied. With time running out Booth attempted a drop kick field goal from the Indians' 20-yard line, but failed and the game ended in a 33–33 tie.

Albie Booth sat on the bench after the game pondering what had happened. After such a flawless second quarter, how could they have had such a dismal second half, he asked himself. When a sportswriter approached, Booth said, "That's football," shook his head and added, "Crazy game, isn't it."

MINNESOTA–NORTHWESTERN

October 31, 1936

When Minnesota traveled to Evanston, Illinois, in 1936 to face the Northwestern Wildcats, Bernie Bierman's Golden Gophers, reigning national champions from the year before, had not a defeat since 1932—28 consecutive games without a loss.

Grantland Rice had written of Bierman's 1934 Gophers: "Football fans here are no longer discussing whether Minnesota's team is the best in the country today. They are taking that for granted. What they want to know is this: Shouldn't it be rated the greatest of all time?" Bernie Bierman said of his 1936 squad, "They would class right along with the 1934 team."

The Minnesotans had certified All-Americas in tackle Big Ed Widseth and halfback Andy Uram and a shrewd quarterback named Bud Wilkinson, who would later make the most of his voluminous football knowledge as head coach at Oklahoma. The Gophers had easily defeated Washington, Nebraska, Michigan, and Purdue, and predictably they were heavy favorites.

Lynn "Pappy" Waldorf's Wildcats, however, had a few things going for them, too. They were undefeated and underrated. They had an All-America in guard Steve Reid and near All-Americas in end John Kovatch and halfback Don Heap. And they had Mother Nature, who drenched the field of play and turned it into a quagmire, certainly aiding Northwestern's plans to dampen Minnesota's explosive offense.

Despite the slop, Minnesota's Andy Uram broke away in the first quarter, sloshing and sliding 48 yards all the way to Northwestern's 23-yard line. Three plays gained only a few yards, and then Bernie Bierman made a decision he would rue. He went for the first down instead of a field goal, and didn't make it.

Waldorf's Wildcats defied the mud as well in the first period. Don Heap ran for 16 and 26 yards on one drive, and then John Kovatch, on an end-around, picked up 22 more. But Northwestern's march fizzled and the remainder of the first half was merely an exchange of possessions.

In the second half, Minnesota dominated, but every time they appeared ready to score something went wrong. A shanked punt, costly penalties, fumbles—Minnesota hardly seemed the team that had rocketed through the four previous seasons without a loss. Still, the Wildcats could not capitalize on the Gophers' misfortunes, and the game went into the final period a scoreless stalemate.

Deep in their own territory, Minnesota halfback Julius Alfonse took a pitchout from Uram, but the wet ball skittered through his hands. Suddenly bodies with flailing arms and legs piled on top of each other, grabbing for the slippery football. When the referee pulled all the players off the pile, he found Northwestern's tackle DeWitt Gibson cradling the ball. The Wildcats took over just 13 yards from the Gophers' goal line.

On the first play reserve fullback Don Geyer hit the line and was smothered by Minnesota defenders. Once again there was a huge pile-up, suggesting another fumble. But as the referee stripped bodies away he did not find a scramble for the ball but instead Big Ed Widseth punching the ball carrier. A flag was thrown—15 yards against Minnesota, 12 of which were walked off—and the ball was placed on the 1-yard line (the rule in those days, instead of half the distance to the goal). The Gophers held for two downs, but then fullback Steve Toth charged in for the score. The 6 points were enough. Northwestern dug in and stopped Minnesota in the mud for the remainder of the game, and the Gophers' illustrious winning streak ended with the final gun.

PITTSBURGH–FORDHAM

October 16, 1937

Pitt was the No. 1 ranked team in the nation in 1937. The year before they had barely missed the national title and had demolished Washington in the Rose Bowl 21–0. They had just about everybody from that team back, including consensus All-American halfback Marshall Goldberg. Their coach, Jock Sutherland, later claimed they were the finest team he had fielded in his 20-year college coaching career.

But they also had a nemesis, the Maroon or Rams of Fordham, as they were alternately known, whose line, billed as the "Seven Blocks of Granite," was the most formidable defense in college football. In encounters during the two previous seasons, Fordham, coached by former member of Notre Dame's Four Horsemen Jim Crowley, had held the otherwise high-scoring Panthers to consecutive scoreless ties. In fact, during the entire 1936 season, the Rams had allowed only one touchdown.

Two of the Seven Blocks were All-Americans, center Alex Wojciechowicz and tackle Ed Franco; the other five, which included football legend-to-be Vince Lombardi, were just a string or two below them. And now with an improved backfield, Crowley's eleven from the Bronx had a shot of their own at the national crown.

For both teams, as they confronted each other at the Polo Grounds in 1937 before 53,000 spectators, this was the game of the year, the one in which one team would have to cede its claim to the nation's top ranking to the other.

Fordham moved the ball first, reaching the Pitt 40-yard line, where the drive stalled. After the punt,

Fordham's "Seven Blocks of Granite," as the Fordham line was known in 1936 and 1937. From the left, Johnny Druze, Al Barbartsky, Vince Lombardi, Alex Wojciechowicz, Nat Pierce, Ed Franco, and Leo Pasquin. Lombardi, of course, would go on to great fame as coach of the Green Bay Packers, and Wojciechowicz as a center for the Detroit Lions and Philadelphia Eagles; both are enshrinees of the Pro Football Hall of Fame. Ed Franco was an All-American in both 1936 and 1937.

Pitt ripped off 37 yards on four running plays until the Fordham defense shored itself up and stopped them.

At the start of the second quarter, Fordham again moved, this time behind the rushing of Angelo Fortunato and Dom Principe. But again Pitt managed to stifle the drive, regaining possession at their own 8-yard line. Shortly thereafter came what appeared to be the break of the game: the Panthers fumbled on their own 23, and Joe Granski recovered for Fordham. But three plunges into the Pitt line gained only 5 yards, and Fordham's John Druze missed the field goal attempt.

Pittsburgh got its big chance later in the quarter. Halfback Harry Stebbins ran a Fordham punt back 35 yards to the Maroon 40. Then the Panthers ground it out to the Fordham 5. A slick reverse to Marshall Goldberg, and he swept around left end and across the goal line for an apparent touchdown—the first score in three years of Pitt–Fordham games. But a holding call erased the play. The Rams' defense regrouped and held, leaving a scoreless tie at the end of the first half.

Further evidence that things were not going Pitt's way came on the first play of the second half when Stebbins fumbled and Fordham recovered on the Pitt 28. Fordham came up with a fancy reverse of its own, and Principe made it down to the Pitt 10-yard line. But it was now the Panthers' turn to hold. Druze tried an 18-yard field goal this time, but it was partially blocked. Marshall Goldberg picked up the bounding ball in his own end zone and ran it out to the 8. Two plays later, however, Goldberg fumbled, and Druze recovered, the ball still only 8 yards from the Pitt goal line. Principe bulled his way to the 3, and Fordham's rooters were on their feet, chanting "Score, Score, Score." But it was not to be. A 15-yard penalty moved them back and the Pittsburgh defense held. Druze tried another field goal, this one from his 30, but it, too, was wide.

A few minutes later, Pittsburgh had another chance to score when, on fourth down at the Fordham 23, end Bill Daddio tried a field goal, but his was also off the mark. On their next possession Pitt came back again, driving hard, and just when it seemed as though the mighty Fordham defense might be faltering, Alex Wojciechowicz smashed into Harry Stebbins, causing a fumble, which he recovered for the Rams.

Later in the fourth quarter, Wojie, as most called the Fordham great, forced another Stebbins fumble, but the Rams again could not take advantage of the turnover.

When the final gun sounded, there were still two large zeros on the scoreboard. For three years in a row the two great teams had been unable to score upon each other. The tie would be the only blemish on either team's record at the end of the 1937 season. Pittsburgh (9-0-1) was judged by the AP to be the best team in the nation because it played a tougher schedule, while Fordham (7-0-1) had to settle for the No. 3 berth, behind the University of California (10-0-1).

ARMY–NOTRE DAME
November 9, 1946

It was surely the game of the year; and many have said it was the college football game of the century. Army, unbeaten and untied in 25 games, had been national champs two years running and was aiming for a third title. Notre Dame, refurbished now that the war was over, was also unbeaten and untied in 1946. The neutral ground for their meeting was New York City's Yankee Stadium, and more than 74,000 fans filled it to overflow. Scalpers were getting as much as $200 a ticket, and more than $500,000 had to be returned to those who had tried to buy tickets through normal channels.

In the stands were such West Point alumni as Generals Dwight Eisenhower, Omar Bradley, Jacob Devers, and Maxwell Taylor, as well as Secretary of the Navy James Forrestal, Secretary of War Robert Patterson, and Attorney General Tom Clark. The uniformed Cadets, 2,100 strong, marched into the stadium with the precision of the world's largest drill

team before the opening whistle. The Fighting Irish band blared out "Cheer, Cheer for Old Notre Dame," accompanied by the voices of thousands of students and alumni.

Notre Dame had vengeance on their mind—Army had scorched them 59–0 and 48–0 in the two previous years when many of the Irish players were serving in the armed forces. Coach Frank Leahy was back from duty in the Navy, and he was indeed set upon regaining the Irish's self-esteem. On the other hand, Earl Blaik had his team thirsting for an unprecedented third national championship.

On the field, Army's dream backfield warmed up. Doc Blanchard was playing at right halfback instead of fullback for this game because Herschel "Ug" Fuson was injured. Glenn Davis was at the other halfback, while junior Rip Rowan filled in at fullback and Arnold Tucker handled the quarterbacking duties. Across the gridiron Notre Dame's gifted backs were loosening up: quarterback Johnny Lujack, halfbacks Terry Brennan and Emil Sitko, and fullback Jim Mello. Sportswriters and spectators alike were predicting a fast-paced, ferocious offensive game, despite the stalwart defenses of both teams.

In college football, things do not always turn out as the scribes and fans predict.

Army got the first chance to score early in the opening period. Emil Sitko fumbled the ball on his own 24-yard line, and Army tackle Goble Bryant fell on it. Arnold Tucker hit Glenn Davis with an 8-yard pass to the Notre Dame 16. Blanchard tried three times to get the first down, without success. But on fourth down, Blaik decided to go for it, calling for Blanchard once more. But when he hit the line, so did the Irish, and they stopped him a yard short.

Notre Dame picked up a pair of first downs on the running of Terry Brennan and Sitko, but then had to punt. Army appeared to live up to its reputation on the next possession. Blanchard went inside for a first down, and Davis swept outside for another. Davis then took a pitchout from Arnold Tucker and fired a pass to All-American end Barney Poole for another 5 yards. But then Notre Dame's line, with such greats as George Connor, Bill Fischer, Jim Martin, and George Strohmeyer, dug in and stopped the Cadets.

In the second quarter, Army had another chance to put some points on the board. From Notre Dame's 46-yard line, Glenn Davis, looking as though he were about to break off one of his patented end runs, suddenly pulled up and tossed a 23-yard pass diagonally across the field, which

Blanchard leaped high in the air to grab before tumbling out of bounds. The ball was at the Notre Dame 21-yard line. But again the Irish defense rose to the challenge. This time they not only stopped Army but drove them back to the 37, where the Cadets were forced to punt.

Notre Dame took over on their own 15 and began the longest drive of the game. Substitute halfback Gerry Cowhig burst off tackle and gained 20 yards. Lujack passed to end Bob Skoglund for another 25 yards. With Leahy platooning backs, the Irish worked their way down to the Army 4-yard line. With fourth down and 2 for a first, Leahy disdained

Notre Dame's Johnny Lujack makes a touchdown-saving tackle of Army's Doc Blanchard (35) in one of college football's most memorable games, played in 1946 at Yankee Stadium in New York. The Cadets and the Fighting Irish battled to a 0–0 tie that day; both remained undefeated at season's end but the national championship was bestowed on Notre Dame.

Second Thoughts

Terry Brennan, Notre Dame's left half-back in the classic scoreless tie that the Fighting Irish and Army played to in 1946, was the leading ground gainer that day, 69 yards on 14 carries, and had the longest run of the game, 22 yards. He remembers the game vividly:

> Thinking back on it, I believe both Blaik and Leahy choked. They both went conservative, ultra-conservative, and that was ridiculous with all the offensive talent on those two teams. We had Johnny Lujack and Emil Sitko in our backfield, they had Blanchard, Davis, and Tucker. In fact, Red Blaik told me much later that he felt they both blew it. They didn't coach for the win, they didn't go for it, neither one, that's what he told me.
>
> We had the best chance to win it. At one point we were down on their 5-yard line. It was third down and Leahy called for a quarterback sneak. Lujack only got a yard. On fourth down, we went for it. Bill Gompers was in the game at half-back and he tried to get around right end. I still don't understand why we ran the ball at Hank Foldberg, who was the best defensive end they had. We'd gone all the way down the field running to the other side where Barney Poole was the end; he was a slow, gumshoe type of a guy and we had been beating him. But we ran right at their best defense and Gompers only got a yard, Foldberg got him.
>
> They could have won the game at another point. Doc Blanchard broke into the clear, and the only one who had a chance at him was Lujack, who was as great a defensive back as he was a quarterback. Lujack made a helluva one-on-one tackle to bring him down and save the touchdown.

the field goal as Blaik had in the preceding quarter. The call was for a pitchout to halfback Bill Gompers, but he could only get to the 3-yard line.

Before the half ended, Army had still another shot at taking the lead. Notre Dame fumbled the ball away to Army reserve end Tom Hayes, who dropped on it at the Irish 35. But the Cadets could only muster 2 yards in four plays and turned the ball back to Notre Dame. Everyone in Yankee Stadium was surprised at the scoreless first half, but no one was saying that it was anything but an extraordinary game.

It was back and forth again in the third quarter. And then it was Army's turn to give Notre Dame the opportunity: a fumble on their own 34, recovered by Irish guard John Mastrangelo. But when Lujack rifled a pass over the middle, Arnold Tucker picked it off and raced 32 yards with it. With the ball now on the Army 42, Doc Blanchard broke through for 21 yards, and again Army was threatening. Blanchard and Davis picked up a few more yards, then Tucker hit Hank Foldberg at the 20, and the Cadets had a first down. The crowd from West Point rose to their feet, sensing that their attack had finally found its misplaced adrenaline. But the cheering came to a sudden halt, and the enormous block of Cadets slumped as one back into their seats when Terry Brennan leaped in front of an Army receiver to intercept a pass from Glenn Davis on the Notre Dame 8-yard line.

Neither team could put together another scoring threat until the final minute of play. With 48 seconds left, Davis rolled out and threw a long, arcing pass. Blanchard made a spectacular catch at the 20-yard line, only to be ruled out of bounds. The remaining seconds ticked off the clock, and when it was over neither team had scored, a shock to everyone.

Notre Dame won the battle on paper by outrushing the Cadets 173 yards to 138 and picking up 11 first downs to Army's 9, but Army had had the most chances to post some points, a fact not lost on Notre Dame coach Frank Leahy. "You escaped today," one writer mentioned to him after the game. "I suppose I should be elated over the tie," Leahy said to him. "After all, we didn't lose. But I'm not. There is no jubilation in this dressing room." There wasn't any in Army's either.

NOTRE DAME–SMU
December 3, 1949

The Notre Dame squad of 1949 was a truly gifted ball club. They had four consensus All-Americans on the starting team: quarterback Bob Williams, fullback Emil Sitko, tackle Jim Martin, and Heisman Trophy–winning end Leon Hart. They also had several future All-Americans in end Jim Mutscheller, center Jerry Groom, and tackle Bob Toneff. Besides Sitko, they had a depth chart of backs as polished as the dome that glistens above their South Bend campus: Bill Gay, Larry Coutre, Billy Barrett, Mike Swistowicz, John Petitbon, and Jack Landry.

They had not lost a game all season. In fact, they hadn't lost since the last game of the 1945 season, and were firmly at the top of the national rankings.

Southern Methodist was proud to have everybody's All-American halfback Doak Walker, but he was injured and forced to watch the game in street clothes from the sideline. Carrying Walker's normal load was junior tailback Kyle Rote, a player who would earn All-America honors the following year.

They had a blossoming quarterback in sophomore Fred Benners, a bulldog of a halfback with the perfect football name of Johnny Champion, and a potential All-American in center Dick Hightower. But the Mustangs had already lost that year to Rice, Baylor, Texas Christian, and had been tied by Texas A&M. The friendly atmosphere of the Cotton Bowl in hometown Dallas was a small advantage, but Mustang fans knew they would need much more than that if they were to upset the awesome Irish, who were a 28-point favorite.

"We come here to round off a perfect season," Frank Leahy said when his Notre Dame team arrived in Dallas. "We are confident of success." Perhaps they were overconfident, or perhaps they just underestimated the ability of Kyle Rote—it almost cost them the national championship.

Notre Dame lived up to their advance billing in the first half. Moving from his own 27-yard line, Williams led a ground attack to the SMU 42-yard line, then faked a handoff, dropped back, and threw to end Bill Wightkin, who took it in for the game's first score. The Mustangs came right back with a little razzle-dazzle. Rote handed off to Champion on what appeared to be an ordinary end run, but suddenly Champion stopped and tossed a long pass to end John Milam, who gathered it in at full speed 27 yards from the line of scrimmage and continued down the sideline until Mike Swistowicz knocked him out of bounds at the Notre Dame 6-yard line. In three plays, the Mustangs banged their way to the 1-foot line. On fourth down, Rote tried to bull it in, but the Irish dropped him at the line of scrimmage and took over.

In the second period, Bill Gay intercepted a Mustang pass. At the SMU 35, Notre Dame's Williams faded back and threw a Hail Mary type pass into the end zone, which several SMU defenders got

their hands onto, only to tap it directly into the arms of Irish halfback Ernie Zalejski. The score when the half ended was the Irish 13, the Mustangs 0.

The second half was one of the most exciting ever staged at the Cotton Bowl. Rote got it going in the third period, picking up 44 yards on his own rushing, finishing it off with a 3-yard touchdown run. On SMU's next possession, however, Rote was not so fortunate. A pass of his was picked off by Jim Mutscheller. Williams, always the capitalizer, immediately threw a short pass to Leon Hart, who lateraled to halfback Frank Spaniel, and suddenly the ball was on the SMU 10. A few plays later, Billy Barrett slid off tackle for a touchdown, and Notre Dame led 20–7.

In the fourth quarter, SMU played inspired football. Rote led another drive, this one 61 yards, including a pass to Champion, who bulldozed his way to the 1, where Rote carried it in for the touchdown. Then the Mustangs held—and in fact kept the Irish at their own 1-yard line. SMU's Bill Richards grabbed the subsequent punt, and ran it back to the Notre Dame 14. Rote carried the ball three straight times, the last crossing into the end zone for his third touchdown of the day. The score was 20–20, but SMU's chance for the lead was batted away when Jerry Groom blocked the extra point try.

Now Notre Dame revived. The gargantuan six-foot-five-inches-tall, 260-pound end Leon Hart was switched to fullback to hammer away at the Mustang line. He went inside. Emil Sitko, now at halfback, and Frank Spaniel went outside. They moved the ball 51 yards to the SMU 6-yard line. Billy Barrett, back in the game at halfback, swept left end for the score and Notre Dame led 27–20.

There was still plenty of time. Rote got the Mustangs moving immediately. And it truly was all Rote. Passing here, running there, he had SMU on

the move. From his own 29 he moved the Mustangs to the Irish 28, but there, a vicious tackle by Leon Hart sent him dazed to the sideline. Fred Benners took over and passed the Mustangs to the 5, but another bone-jarring tackle by Hart sent him to the bench as well. Rote came back, logy and battered, and moved the Mustangs to the Irish 4. Hoping to surprise the Irish, who were keyed for a Rote run, the tailback started for the line, then leaped to throw a jump pass over the line, but it was tipped by Bob Lally, and Notre Dame's Jerry Groom intercepted it.

And that's the way it ended, 27–20, Notre Dame. A relieved Frank Leahy said afterward, "This Notre Dame team was the greatest I ever coached." And SMU fans went home with the dignity of a great try to unseat the champs and the consolation that Kyle Rote would be back the following season.

MICHIGAN–ARMY
October 8, 1949

When Army traveled to Ann Arbor in October 1949, the oddsmakers had them as two-touchdown underdogs to powerful Michigan. After all, the Wolverines had not lost a single football game since 1946 (they were the national champion in 1948); they had the home field advantage with 97,000 fans in Michigan Stadium cheering for them; and Army's top ground-gainer, Gil Stephenson, was sidelined with an injury. On the line was Michigan's 25-game winning streak.

Gone were such Wolverine stars as Bob Chappius, Bump Elliott, and his brother Pete, but they were replaced in the backfield by such fine runners as tailback Charley Ortmann and fullback Don Dufek. Coach Bennie Oosterbaan reminded his team that Army had escaped playing the Wolverines in their two preceding years of glory but had battered and beaten them with Blanchard, Davis, Tucker & Company in 1945 and 1946. No other team in Michigan football history, Oosterbaan told them, had defeated the Wolverines three times in succession.

But disaster struck early. After the second play of the game, Michigan's triple-threat back Ortmann was carried from the field on a stretcher. When Army got the ball, they marched 89 yards to post the first score of the game. Karl Kuckhahn, filling in at fullback for Stephenson, had hammered away at the Michigan line, while quarterback Arnie Galiffa had thrown to ends Dan Foldberg and Bill Kellum to pick up 52 yards during the drive. It culminated with halfback Frank Fischl racing 5 yards around left end for the touchdown.

Michigan got a wonderful break later in the period when Army punted from their own end zone and the kick was deflected. Michigan had the ball at the Cadet 16-yard line. The Wolverines went to the air, but could not complete a pass and therefore were unable to capitalize on the Cadets' gift.

Michigan presented a little gift to Army in the second quarter, a fumble right into the arms of Army tackle Bruce Ackerson, who ran 5 yards to the Michigan 10. On the next play, halfback Jim Cain broke two tackles and carried it in for another Cadet touchdown, and Army led 14–0.

The Wolverines took advantage of a break in the third quarter, however. Army punter Tom Brown had booted a 62-yarder that was called back on a penalty. On his second attempt, Brown did not get

the punt off and was tackled on his own 31-yard line. Michigan resorted to their running game and moved the ball to the 1, where Don Dufek burst through to bring the Wolverines within a touchdown of the Cadets.

Now Michigan was fired up. On the first play after the kickoff, defensive back Walt Teninga intercepted a pass from Galiffa, which put the ball on the Cadet 42-yard line. A reverse to halfback Leo Koceski got the ball to the 25. An off-tackle plunge by Dufek brought it to the 17, and a wildly cheering Michigan crowd sensed that the Wolverines were finally asserting themselves. But then Michigan went back to the air, only to watch Army safety Tom Brown leap into the air in his own end zone to intercept for a touchback.

Late in the final period Army added another touchdown after Michigan surrendered the ball deep in their own territory. That was it; Army won the game 21–7. Not since Cornell, in the period from 1921 to 1924, had a team won 26 consecutive games. Michigan would have to settle for 25, equaling Army's streak in the years from 1944 through 1946.

PURDUE–NOTRE DAME

October 7, 1950

The Fighting Irish from South Bend, Indiana, and the Boilermakers from downstate Lafayette were intrastate rivals since the two teams first squared off back in 1896 (a game that Purdue won 28–22). Over the years, Notre Dame dominated the series, but Purdue was known for an occasional surprise.

In 1950, Notre Dame was the reigning national champion (10-0-0 in 1949) and had not lost a game in their last 39 encounters. During that period, which stretched from the first game of 1946 to the meeting with Purdue in 1950, only Army in 1946 and USC in 1948 had managed to tie Notre Dame. Facing them was a Purdue squad composed mostly of sophomores that took a 5-game losing streak into the contest. To make matters even worse, they were facing Notre Dame in South Bend, where the Irish had not lost a game since 1942. Not surprisingly, Notre Dame was a 20-point favorite.

But coach Stu Holcomb had his Boilermakers primed, and Frank Leahy, who was looking for his 63rd victory as a Notre Dame coach against only 4 defeats and 5 ties, saw early in the game how uninvincible his own team was.

Behind the passing of 160-pound sophomore quarterback Dale Samuels and the rushing of fullback John Kerestes and halfback Neil Schmidt, Purdue marched 74 yards in the first quarter. Kerestes bulled in for the score. Two other long Purdue drives were just barely stopped; one included a touchdown run called back because of a penalty, the other an 85-yard march that stopped at the 1-yard line.

Early in the ensuing quarter, Samuels hit Schmidt with a 35-yard pass to set up Purdue's second touchdown, again scored on a plunge by Kerestes. Later in the same quarter, Samuels went to Schmidt once more for a 30-yard touchdown play. The score at half: Purdue 21, a stunned Notre Dame 0.

Notre Dame finally got something going in the third period. Purdue fumbled on their own 10, and Dick Cotter gathered it up for Notre Dame. Moments later, Bob Williams rifled a 4-yard pass to

the punt off and was tackled on his own 31-yard line. Michigan resorted to their running game and moved the ball to the 1, where Don Dufek burst through to bring the Wolverines within a touchdown of the Cadets.

Now Michigan was fired up. On the first play after the kickoff, defensive back Walt Teninga intercepted a pass from Galiffa, which put the ball on the Cadet 42-yard line. A reverse to halfback Leo Koceski got the ball to the 25. An off-tackle plunge by Dufek brought it to the 17, and a wildly cheering Michigan crowd sensed that the Wolverines were finally asserting themselves. But then Michigan went back to the air, only to watch Army safety Tom Brown leap into the air in his own end zone to intercept for a touchback.

Late in the final period Army added another touchdown after Michigan surrendered the ball deep in their own territory. That was it; Army won the game 21–7. Not since Cornell, in the period from 1921 to 1924, had a team won 26 consecutive games. Michigan would have to settle for 25, equaling Army's streak in the years from 1944 through 1946.

PURDUE–NOTRE DAME

October 7, 1950

The Fighting Irish from South Bend, Indiana, and the Boilermakers from downstate Lafayette were intrastate rivals since the two teams first squared off back in 1896 (a game that Purdue won 28–22). Over the years, Notre Dame dominated the series, but Purdue was known for an occasional surprise.

In 1950, Notre Dame was the reigning national champion (10-0-0 in 1949) and had not lost a game in their last 39 encounters. During that period, which stretched from the first game of 1946 to the meeting with Purdue in 1950, only Army in 1946 and USC in 1948 had managed to tie Notre Dame. Facing them was a Purdue squad composed mostly of sophomores that took a 5-game losing streak into the contest. To make matters even worse, they were facing Notre Dame in South Bend, where the Irish had not lost a game since 1942. Not surprisingly, Notre Dame was a 20-point favorite.

But coach Stu Holcomb had his Boilermakers primed, and Frank Leahy, who was looking for his 63rd victory as a Notre Dame coach against only 4 defeats and 5 ties, saw early in the game how uninvincible his own team was.

Behind the passing of 160-pound sophomore quarterback Dale Samuels and the rushing of fullback John Kerestes and halfback Neil Schmidt, Purdue marched 74 yards in the first quarter. Kerestes bulled in for the score. Two other long Purdue drives were just barely stopped; one included a touchdown run called back because of a penalty, the other an 85-yard march that stopped at the 1-yard line.

Early in the ensuing quarter, Samuels hit Schmidt with a 35-yard pass to set up Purdue's second touchdown, again scored on a plunge by Kerestes. Later in the same quarter, Samuels went to Schmidt once more for a 30-yard touchdown play. The score at half: Purdue 21, a stunned Notre Dame 0.

Notre Dame finally got something going in the third period. Purdue fumbled on their own 10, and Dick Cotter gathered it up for Notre Dame. Moments later, Bob Williams rifled a 4-yard pass to

FACING PAGE
Michigan fullback Don Dufek catapults over the Army defenders in this memorable 1949 game at Ann Arbor. Michigan, unbeaten and the reigning national champion, had to settle for this lonely score that day, upset by the Cadets 21–7. It brought to an end Michigan's 25-game win streak.

165

VICTORY

Jim Mutscheller in the end zone, and Notre Dame finally had some points on the scoreboard. Meanwhile, the Irish defense began to contain both Samuels and the Boilermaker running attack. Late in the period, Notre Dame staged their first impressive drive of the game, 57 yards, highlighted by a 33-yard run by halfback Billy Barrett. Then, barely into the fourth quarter, John Petitbon carried on a slant for 6 yards and a second Notre Dame touchdown.

But Purdue was not finished. On their next possession, Samuels, facing a third and long yardage for a first down, threw to halfback Mike Maccioli, who was racing down the sidelines and didn't break stride as he gathered it in and raced into the end zone. It was the last score of the game: Purdue had shocked Notre Dame 28–14.

The loss did more than simply end a winning streak; the Irish would end 1950 with a record of 4-4-1, their poorest since 1933.

OKLAHOMA–NOTRE DAME

November 16, 1957

The 1957 Oklahoma Sooners, under the brilliant coaching of Bud Wilkinson, were the proud owners of college football's longest winning streak ever: 47 consecutive victories. That was 8 games more than the record of 39 established by Washington back in the period from 1908 through 1914. And for two years running the Oklahomans had been the undisputed national champions.

By mid-November the Sooners were in a hotly contested race with Ohio State, Auburn, and Michigan State for the national crown, lusting for an unprecedented three in a row. Four more wins, and they would register another perfect season. At home in Norman, they were hosting Notre Dame, coached by Terry Brennan, a team they had annihilated the year before 40–0. The Irish, with consecutive losses to Navy and Michigan State in the two weeks before the Oklahoma game, were not in the running for a title of any kind. The Sooners were 18-point favorites.

Oklahoma's biggest threat was halfback Clendon Thomas, an All-America who had inherited the backfield responsibilities of recently graduated Tommy McDonald. Guard Bill Krisher was another consensus All-American. Bob Harrison was a standout center who made All-America the following year, and Don Stiller and Ross Coyle were as good a pair of ends as a coach could hope for. They were the keys to providing Bud Wilkinson with what he hoped would be his 102nd victory at Oklahoma, not his ninth defeat.

Notre Dame had some standouts, too: All-America guard Al Ecuyer, fullback Nick Pietrosante, end Monty Stickles, and halfback Dick Lynch. Before the game, coach Terry Brennan reminded his Irish that Notre Dame was the last team to beat Oklahoma, back in 1953. He thought it would be very nice to put a win at the other end of the Sooners' string of victories.

Notre Dame thought otherwise, which became obvious from the outset. Or almost the outset. The Sooners marched on their first possession down to the Irish 13-yard line, but there Notre Dame held. From that point on, the Irish defense was overwhelming, and Oklahoma couldn't get anything going on the ground or in the air during the remainder of the first half. The team that had been averaging 300 yards a game that year would not gain even half that against Notre Dame that afternoon.

"At the half, I knew we were in for a game of it," Bud Wilkinson said later. "At the end of the third quarter, I was willing to settle for a scoreless tie. We had just never been so shut down and Notre Dame was getting stronger as they went along."

But there wouldn't be a scoreless tie. In the final period, Notre Dame's offense decided to give the defense something to protect. It took them 20 plays to go 80 yards after a Sooner punt was downed in the end zone. The drive was engineered by quarterback Bob Williams (not to be confused with the Bob Williams who quarterbacked Notre Dame from 1948 to 1950). With Williams throwing short passes, and some key plunges for first downs from Nick Pietrosante, Notre Dame moved steadily down the field.

With less than 5 minutes remaining in the game, Notre Dame had a first down on the Oklahoma 8-yard line. Pietrosante picked up 4 more yards on a plunge straight into the middle. On the next play, Dick Lynch tried to go off tackle but got nowhere. Williams himself carried up the middle on third down and gained another yard. With fourth down and 3 yards for the score, Williams decided to surprise the Sooners. As he later explained, "They were in tight, real tight, just waiting for me to give the ball to Pietrosante. Well, I just faked to him and tossed out to Lynch and it worked like a charm. He went in standing up." Monty Stickles booted the extra point.

Notre Dame halfback Dick Lynch carries it in for the game-winning touchdown in 1957, bringing to an end Oklahoma's 47-game winning streak, the longest in college football history. The Sooners, playing at home in Norman, were an 18-point favorite, but they fell to the Irish that day 7–0.

Oklahoma came back in desperation, reaching the Irish 24 with less than a minute to go, but Notre Dame stopped them for the last time that day with an interception. The final score was 7–0, Notre Dame. It was the first time in 123 games that Oklahoma had failed to score a point.

A jubilant Notre Dame team carried Terry Brennan off the field on their shoulders. They had proved to be the spoilers, as Brennan hoped they would. "The greatest thrill of my athletic career," Brennan later called it.

Bud Wilkinson would have to wait another week for his 102nd triumph. "Well, we couldn't go on winning forever," he said after the game.

NOTRE DAME– MICHIGAN STATE

November 19, 1966

Ara Parseghian was in his third year as head coach at Notre Dame when he brought the undefeated, No. 1 ranked Irish to East Lansing to face Duffy Daugherty's No. 2 ranked Michigan State Spartans. The year before, State had been UPI's number one team, though AP gave Alabama the national championship. With this, the next-to-last game of the college football season, the stakes were very high indeed.

Both teams sparkled with All-America-caliber players. Notre Dame had defensive end Alan Page, halfback Rocky Bleier, linebacker Jim Lynch, defensive tackles Kevin Hardy and Pete Duranko, guard Tom Regner, and two superbly talented sophomore starters in quarterback Terry Hanratty and end Jim

Seymour. Michigan State could boast a mountain of a man in the six-foot-seven-inch, 280-pound defensive end Bubba Smith, end Gene Washington, quarterback Jimmy Raye, halfback Clint Jones, and defensive back George Webster.

Notre Dame's first serious setback came before the game. Nick Eddy, their most productive running back, slipped getting off the train in East Lansing and aggravated an already injured shoulder to a degree that would keep him out of the game. Then in the first period of play center George Goeddeke left the game for good with an injured ankle; shortly after, Hanratty, victim of a savage tackle administered jointly by Bubba Smith and linebacker Charlie Thornhill, suffered a shoulder separation and was also through for the afternoon.

To add to the dismal turn of events, Michigan State marched downfield late in the first quarter and at the beginning of the second, going 73 yards on 10 plays. The score came when fullback Regis Cavender smashed in from the 4. Notre Dame

A fumble in the great Michigan State–Notre Dame game of 1966. With Irish coach Ara Parseghian choosing to run out the clock and settle for a 10–10 tie, it remains controversial to this day; but Parseghian and Notre Dame ended up No. 1 in the nation at season's end while Michigan State had to settle for the No. 2 ranking. The Michigan State player in the picture is Frank Waters (43).

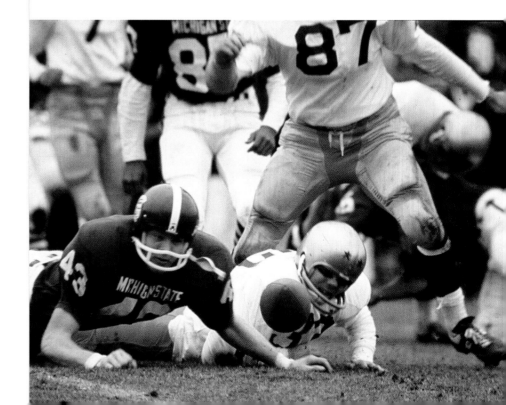

could not move the ball in several ensuing possessions. But the Spartans could, at least far enough to enable their barefoot kicker from Hawaii, Dick Kenney, to boot a 47-yard field goal and give MSU a 10–0 lead.

Coley O'Brien, a sophomore, directed the Irish offense in the absence of Hanratty, and he finally got it moving by going to the air. Three completed passes covered 54 yards and gave Notre Dame its first score of the game. The payoff pass was a 34-yarder into the end zone to halfback Bob Gladieux, who was filling in for the injured Eddy.

From that point on, the vaunted Irish defense took over. They had allowed only four touchdowns in their preceding eight games and had shut out five of their opponents. Michigan State ran at them and threw into them, but for the remainder of the first half and all of the second, they could not come up with one legitimate scoring opportunity. The Spartans gained yardage, but mostly in their own territory.

But Notre Dame was going nowhere on offense either, at least until the end of the third quarter when O'Brien orchestrated a drive that took the Irish from their own 20 to the Spartan 12, where it faltered. Onto the field trotted Joe Azzaro to kick the game-tying field goal; the score 10–10.

A big break came Notre Dame's way a little later in the final period when safety Tom Schoen picked off one of Jimmy Raye's passes in Spartan territory and ran it down to the 18. But in three plays the Irish managed to lose 6 yards. Azzaro came back out to attempt a 41-yarder, but it drifted to the right.

With little more than a minute left, Notre Dame got the ball back again on their own 30-yard line, but fearing a turnover in his own territory, Parseghian chose to run out the clock. The partisan

Spartan fans showed their displeasure with a volley of boos. Afterward, some thought it was the prudent thing to do, others thought it was a real cop out; if nothing else it remains one of the most remembered and controversial decisions in college football lore.

Parseghian said in the locker room to reporters, "We'd fought hard to come back and tie it up. After all that, I didn't want to risk giving it to them cheap. You get reckless and it could cost the game. I wasn't going to do a jackass thing like that at this point."

Notre Dame had one more game to play that year, against tough arch-rival USC. They destroyed them 54–0 the following week and as a result of that, and the fact that they had outscored their opponents that season 362–38, Notre Dame was awarded its first national title since 1949. Duffy Daugherty and his Spartans had to settle for second place.

TEXAS–ARKANSAS
December 6, 1969

The Texas Longhorns in 1969, under Darrell Royal, were an explosive team, dominating the Southwest Conference. Going into the last game of the season against Arkansas, they were undefeated and in a race with similarly undefeated Penn State for the national championship. In their previous nine games, the Texans had collectively drubbed their opponents 399–88, running up scores like 69–7 over Texas Christian, 56–14 over Baylor, 56–17 over Navy, and scoring 49 points each in wins over Texas A&M and Texas Tech.

Arkansas, under the tutelage of Frank Broyles, was also undefeated but ranked only seventh by AP and third by UPI. "Everything to win and hardly anything to lose," Broyles told his Razorbacks. By everything he meant a definite shot at the national title, the conference championship, a Cotton Bowl bid, and the opportunity to serve as spoiler to a longtime rival.

Both Texas and Arkansas had only one All-American apiece, Longhorn tackle Bob McKay and Razorback center Rodney Brand. But both teams had a number of highly respected ballplayers. Texas halfback Steve Worster, tackle Bobby Wuensch, and defensive end Bill Atessis would receive All-American honors the following year. And they had a fine end in Cotton Speyrer and a feared linebacker in Glen Halsell. Arkansas also had several future All-Americans: end Chuck Dicus, linebacker Cliff Powell, and running back Bill Burnett.

There were more than 44,000 fans, a capacity crowd, at Razorback Stadium in Fayetteville, Arkansas, including President Richard Nixon, to witness, as one writer put it, "the most important battle in the southwest since the Alamo."

Texas took the opening kickoff, but on their second play from scrimmage they fumbled and Arkansas recovered on the Texas 22-yard line. The Razorbacks battered their way to the 1, where Bill Burnett slashed through for the first score of the game. The Longhorns, used to scoring almost at will—they averaged 44 points a game that season—were thwarted every time they had the ball, not just in that first quarter but in the first three quarters of the game.

Arkansas capitalized on another Texas fumble in the third quarter. Behind the passing of quarterback Bill Montgomery, and some grind-it-out rushing, the Razorbacks moved the ball down to the Longhorns' 29-yard line. From there, Montgomery dropped back and hit Chuck Dicus, his favorite receiver, for another touchdown.

But if the first three quarters belonged to Arkansas, the final period turned out to be totally Texas. It began on the opening play of that quarter. With the Longhorn running game shut down, quarterback James Street went to the air, or at least tried to, but when he could not find a receiver he took off out of the pocket and zigzagged his way 42 yards for a touchdown.

Coach Darrell Royal decided against kicking the extra point. "We felt that was the time for a two-point conversion," he explained later. "If we missed it, we still could have gone for two again and gotten a tie. But if we had kicked after the first touchdown and gone for two after the second, then the pressure is really on us." It proved a fortuitous decision. Street carried to his left on an option, then sliced in for the 2 points.

Appropriately named Texas placekicker Happy Feller boots the game-winning extra point in the Longhorn's 15–14 victory over Arkansas in 1969.

Late in the period, Street had the Texans on the move again. But at their own 43 the drive stalled. It was fourth down, a little more than 2 yards for the first, with just less than 5 minutes to play. Royal sent in a play and, seeing the formation, the Arkansas punt returner hustled up to join the defense. Texas was going for it. They lined up tight, and Arkansas dug in, expecting the run. Street took the snap, faked a handoff, dropped back, and threw toward the sideline where tight end Randy Peschel was a step ahead of the Arkansas defenders. It was right on the mark, and Peschel carried it all the way to the Razorback 13. Texas then moved the ball to the 2, where moments later Jim Bertelsen burst through for the touchdown. With the score tied at 14, Texas placekicker Happy Feller came on and drilled the go-ahead point.

Arkansas bounced back, but now in desperation. Behind Montgomery's passing they moved from their own 20 to the Texas 39. There was just over a minute left. The partisan crowd was in an uproar, screaming for the Razorbacks to pull it out. And for a moment it looked as if they just might do it. Montgomery faded back, spotted Dicus streaking toward the goal line, and rifled the ball to him, but as the end reached for it Texas defensive back Tom Campbell snatched it away, along with any hope of victory for the Razorbacks.

Frank Broyles said afterward, "I'm proud, we played a winning game. We lost on the scoreboard, lost really on just that one play," referring to the surprise fourth-down bomb by Street. Regarding the same play, Darrell Royal, who looked on the passing game at best as a last resort, added, "Every now and then you just have to suck it up and pick a number. You don't use logic and reason, you just play a hunch. I never considered punting."

NEBRASKA– OKLAHOMA

November 25, 1971

Millions of Thanksgiving turkey dinners were rescheduled or postponed in 1971 so that college football fans could watch the national telecast of the battle of the unbeatens, Nebraska and Oklahoma. The No. 1 ranked Cornhuskers had been AP's choice for the national championship the year before (UPI picked Texas), and coach Bob Devaney had guided them thus far through a perfect season in 1971. Second-ranked Oklahoma, under Chuck Fairbanks, had their eyes on removing Nebraska from the race, and the Sooners had the advantages of the home field and the raucous fans who filled the stadium.

Both teams were loaded with All-American-quality players. Nebraska was led by the quarterbacking of Jerry Tagge, the running of Jeff Kinney, and the running and pass catching of future Heisman Trophy winner Johnny Rodgers. They also had Outland Award winner Larry Jacobson at defensive tackle and All-American Willie Harper at defensive end. Oklahoma was paced by a dazzling runner, Greg Pruitt, and had a consensus All-American in center Tom Brahaney, an outstanding quarterback in Jack Mildren, and two fine defensive linemen, Derland Moore and Raymond Hamilton. Oklahoma was averaging 45 points a game (they had scored 75 against Kansas State; their closest call a 33–20 win over Southern Cal); Nebraska, almost as volatile, had averaged 42.8.

The game started out with a bang. The Sooners, shortly after receiving the opening kickoff, had to punt, and Johnny Rodgers took it at his own 28-yard line, cut up the middle, weaved his way through defenders, and carried the ball 72 yards before depositing it in the end zone. Then a truculent Nebraska defense, rated the finest in the nation that year, geared itself to stop Oklahoma's formidable wishbone offense.

But they were not going to be able to do that this Thanksgiving Day. They did manage to bottle up the usually electrifying Greg Pruitt, but they could not stem all the Oklahoma options. Jack Mildren brought the Sooners right back with a 70-yard march, although they had to settle for a field goal.

Now it was Nebraska, as Jerry Tagge led a Cornhusker drive of 54 yards, crowned when Kinney bucked in from the 1-yard line.

Then came Oklahoma again. Mildren engineered an 80-yard drive this time, carrying it in himself from the 3-yard line. Late in the second quarter, he moved the Sooners 78 yards for still another touchdown, this one by tossing a 24-yard pass to wide receiver Jon Harrison with 5 seconds left in the half. By intermission, Oklahoma had already chalked up 311 total yards and a 17–14 lead.

Nebraska, however, took control in the third quarter. Jeff Kinney was almost unstoppable on the ground, and Tagge was effective in the air when he had to be. Kinney, who would gain 154 yards rushing in the second half alone, gave the lead back to the Cornhuskers with a 3-yard plunge, and with the extra point Nebraska claimed a 21–17 lead. Another touchdown and it was 28–17.

Now it was Oklahoma's turn. The Sooners ate up chunks of yardage, 75 in all, and reached the Nebraska 3, where Mildren ran it in for his second touchdown of the day. It was a dogged battle in the fourth quarter, but Oklahoma still had the momentum. Mildren again was the focal point of a major drive, this one 69 yards, and he capped it with a 16-

yard touchdown pass, again to Harrison, and the lead passed to the Sooners 31–28. Nebraskans could not remember when a team had scored so many points against their tremendous defense, which had given up an average of just over 8 points a game that year.

This game, however, the Cornhuskers now knew, would have to be won by their offense. There were about 6 minutes left when they launched a drive from their 26-yard line. Relying on Kinney carrying the ball, it took 12 plays, and it was suspenseful. On third down and 1 at their own 35-yard line, Kinney broke for a 17-yard gain. Then on another third down, this one with 8 yards to go at the Oklahoma 46, Tagge was forced out of the pocket, scrambled wildly, then threw to Johnny Rodgers, who was practically on the ground, sandwiched between two Oklahoma defenders, but he held on to it to keep the drive alive. Nebraska continued to battle their way downfield to the 2, where Kinney exploded into the end zone for his fourth touchdown.

All-American flanker Johnny Rodgers is shown here returning a punt 72 yards for a touchdown to give Nebraska its first score of the game in 1971 that pitted the No. 1 ranked Cornhuskers against No. 2 Oklahoma. In what turned out to be one of the most exciting offensive games ever in college football, Nebraska came from behind in the fourth quarter to eke out a 35—31 victory.

It was enough, and Nebraska won 35–31, one of the great offensive games in college football annals. Nine touchdowns were scored, and a grand total of 829 yards gained by the two teams. Even in defeat Sooner coach Chuck Fairbanks saw it as "a classic game, the greatest one I've ever been involved in." Nebraska coach Bob Devaney had no arguments about that.

ALABAMA–USC

September 23, 1978

It was the third game of the season, and Alabama held the No. 1 ranking in the nation, while USC languished in seventh place. The year before, the Trojans' 15-game winning streak had been decisively terminated in Los Angeles by Bear Bryant's visiting Alabamans. A turnabout would be poetic justice, or something to that effect, as John Robinson told his players.

The 1978 meeting of the two teams was held at Legion Field in Birmingham, Alabama, before more than 77,000 avid 'Bama fans and a national television audience. The Crimson Tide was listed as a 14-point favorite. But perhaps the oddsmakers were not taking into account the productivity of USC tailback Charles White, the latest in a line of Trojan tailbacks that included Mike Garrett, O. J. Simpson, Anthony Davis, and Ricky Bell. Or what a fine passer left-handed quarterback Paul McDonald could be when John Robinson wanted to mix things up.

McDonald explained the Trojan game plan: "We'd throw on second down, run on third and long, and screw 'em up with motion. Sometimes I'd call two or three plays in the huddle and then choose one when we got to the line." Coach

Robinson described it with a shrug as "a wheeling-dealing offense that could self-destruct at any minute if we start making mistakes."

It didn't destroy itself, however, but it did dismantle favored Alabama. Throughout the first half, USC controlled the line of scrimmage and the momentum of the game. They led off with a beautifully executed drive down the field, mostly on carries by Charles White, but it fell flat on the Tide's 2-yard line when White got separated from the football. On the Trojans' next possession, however, White made everyone forget the miscue when he followed his blockers around right end, suddenly broke by them and the defenders, and raced 40 yards for a touchdown.

The usually productive Alabama offense, which averaged almost 29 points a game that season, spearheaded by running back Major Ogilvie and quarterback Jeff Rutledge, was unable to put more than an occasional dent in the USC defense during either of the first two periods of play. The thousands of 'Bama fans were forced to spend most of their time watching the USC offense at work. For almost 9 minutes in the second quarter, in fact, USC put together a

Tailback Charles White carries for Southern Cal in their 1978 battle with Alabama. White, rushing for 199 yards, led the Trojans to an upset victory that day 24–14. The following year he would win the Heisman Trophy.

plodding 23-play drive, which eventually resulted in a field goal. The score at intermission was 10–0.

Bryant roused his Alabamans during the break, and in the third quarter the Tide got on the scoreboard when Ogilvie wove his way through the USC defense for 41 yards and a touchdown.

It failed to daunt Southern Cal. Back they came behind White's running: 6 yards on one carry, 4 on the next, picking up needed first downs one after the other. At the Tide's 6-yard line, with the defense keying on White, McDonald went to the air, a little pass over the line of scrimmage to flanker Kevin Williams, who carried it in; the score was now USC 17, Alabama 7.

Later, in the fourth quarter, McDonald again found Williams, this time for a 40-yard touchdown play. As time wore down, 'Bama got on the board once more with a 41-yard touchdown pass from Jeff Rutledge to Barry Krauss. Although they had several more possessions, the Tide, however, never got back in the game. Southern Cal won it 24–14. The game had been all USC: 417 total yards gained, with 199 of those accounted for by Charles White's rushing.

Bear Bryant faced the sportswriters after the game, held up his thumb and forefinger about an inch apart, and said, "We been at it six weeks and we ain't improved this much. You don't win championships if you don't improve." A gleeful John Robinson said to his team, "We're not number one. I'm voting us number six. But you're going to be a great team, I sense it. We're not number one now . . . but in January, who knows."

Alabama did improve, however, and did not lose another game in 1978. USC did lose another, to Arizona State. Ironically, at the end of the season the wire service polls put once-defeated Alabama at the No. 1 spot, with once-defeated USC ranked No. 2.

USC–STANFORD

In mid-October 1979, USC had easily won their first five games, residing at the top of both the AP and UPI polls. Now, on homecoming weekend at the neighborhood Los Angeles Coliseum, they were facing Stanford, a team that had already lost two games. The Trojans were 22-point favorites.

And USC got 21 of those 22 points in the first half, blithely entertaining the students, alumni, and other loyal Angelenos with neatly executed drives featuring some exciting runs. All-American and Heisman Trophy winner-to-be Charles White scored two Trojan touchdowns, one on an 8-yard power sweep and the other on a 1-yard plunge. The third score was on a 15-yard run by White's heir apparent, sophomore Marcus Allen. USC led 21–0 when the teams left for the locker room at halftime, and White had already amassed 169 yards rushing.

But then something happened. The Cardinal from Palo Alto suddenly came alive. As Rod Dowhower, one of Stanford's coaches, later said, "I can't explain it. I guess we called some plays they didn't expect. We threw long on fourth and five, converted a lot of third- and fourth-down plays."

That they did, and it was all under the masterful manipulation of Stanford quarterback Turk Schonert. Stanford took the opening kickoff of the second half and started from their 20. Switching to a passing game (completing three of his first four) as well as running at the gaps, Schonert moved his team to the Trojan 19-yard line, then passed to Mike Dotterer for Stanford's first touchdown.

The Stanford defense suddenly became a stone wall to White and Allen and a pursuing, sacking menace to quarterback Paul McDonald. In the

FACING PAGE
USC back Charles White (12) fumbles the ball at the 12-yard line as he is being tackled by Stanford's Steve Foley in the 1979 meeting between the two intrastate rivals. Other Stanford defenders are Chuck Evans (89) and Craig Zellmer (52). Southern Cal was a 22-point favorite and scored 21 unanswered points in the first half at the Coliseum in Los Angeles, but Stanford staged a miraculous second-half rally and brought the game to a 21–21 tie, costing the Trojans a share of the 1979 national championship. White went on to win the Heisman Trophy that year, however.

fourth quarter, a jarring tackle caused White to fumble, a costly turnover. Schonert took quick advantage of it by marching the Cardinal 52 yards, then throwing his second touchdown pass of the game, this one to wide receiver Ken Margerum.

Stanford continued to shut down USC's offense, which had averaged almost 36 points in the first five games of that year. Schonert started again from his own 13-yard line and before long a disillusioned homecoming crowd watched as the Turk rolled out, faked a pass, found a hole, and raced in for the touchdown from the Trojan 10-yard line. The extra point tied the game at 21 apiece with four and a half minutes left.

Then, with 38 seconds on the clock, Stanford had a remote chance to win it, but a fourth-down, 53-yard field goal fell short. A desperate USC frantically moved the ball and, with 3 seconds left, lined up for a 39-yard field goal, but the snap was juggled and the kick was blocked.

The 21–21 stalemate proved disastrous to USC at season's end. Their record was 11-0-1, including a Rose Bowl victory over Ohio State, but the Stanford blemish left them just short of Alabama's perfect record. And for the second year in a row, John Robinson's Trojans ran second in the national rankings to Bear Bryant's Crimson Tide.

PENN STATE– NEBRASKA

September 25, 1982

Nebraska arrived in University Park, Pennsylvania, with a strong resemblance to at least six of the biblical ten plagues. A week earlier, the Cornhuskers and their incendiary offense had set an NCAA record by amassing 883 total yards in the 68–0 humiliation they dealt to New Mexico State. The week before that they had decimated Big Ten title contender Iowa by a score of 42–7.

Tom Osborne's Nebraskans had two fabulous running backs in Mike Rozier and Roger Craig and a quarterback named Turner Gill who could throw from the pocket or on the run, execute the option, and run the ball himself with equal skill. All that behind a first-rate offensive line, keyed by two-time Outland Award winning center Dave Rimington.

They were ranked second in the nation when they came to play Penn State. But the Nittany Lions were hardly laggards either, with Heisman candidate Curt Warner and Jon Williams running the ball and Todd Blackledge throwing it. They had already beaten Temple, Maryland, and Rutgers.

Predictably Nebraska was the pregame favorite, but they did not play like it in the first half. Penn State's defense controlled the line of scrimmage, consistently stopping Rozier and Craig, who was playing with an injured leg. And late in the first quarter, State's Blackledge iced an 84-yard drive—the highlight of which had been a 43-yard pass to Curt Warner—with a 14-yard touchdown pass to tight end Kirk Bowman, who only recently had been converted from an offensive guard and had acquired the ignoble nickname "Stonehands."

In the second period, Paterno tried out his ground game and found Nebraska could not handle Warner, who broke one for 31 yards and then burst in from the 2, giving the Nittany Lions a 14–0 advantage.

Nebraska finally got on the board with less than a minute to go in the half when Gill threw a 30-yard touchdown pass to wide receiver Irving Fryar.

But the second half began much like the first, with Penn State in control. Blackledge increased the score to 21–7 with a pass to flanker Kenny Jackson. That, however, proved to be the end of Penn State's dominance.

It was now Turner Gill's turn to shine. He directed the Cornhuskers downfield, finally tossing to Rozier for a score and bringing Nebraska within a touchdown. A field goal in the fourth quarter cut the Penn State lead to four. Then Nebraska held and got the ball back late in the quarter at their own 20-yard line. Passing with deadly precision, two key third-down conversions among them, Gill advanced the Cornhuskers all the way to the Penn State 1, where he dove in with the ball to give Nebraska the lead.

The lead was short-lived, however, thanks to Todd Blackledge's masterful performance in the game's remaining 1 minute and 18 seconds. Penn State should have had the ball on their own 20 after the kickoff, but an unnecessary roughness call against Nebraska gave it to them at the 35. Blackledge first threw to halfback Skeeter Nichols, a screen pass that picked up 16 yards. Two plays later he hit Jackson at the sideline for another 16. A running play lost a yard, and then Blackledge's magic appeared to vanish as he threw two incompletions. It was fourth and 11 yards to go at the Nebraska 34. There were 28 seconds on the clock. Paterno sent in word to go for the first down. His freshman kicker,

FACING PAGE
Nebraska's great center Dave Rimington holds off a Penn State defender in the clash between the two powerhouses of 1982. Penn State came out on top 27–24. Rimington won the Outland Trophy, honoring the outstanding interior lineman in the nation, in both 1981 and 1982.

Massimo Manca, had failed on three field goal tries earlier in the game, and Paterno had little faith in a 51-yard attempt.

Blackledge dropped back, spotted Kenny Jackson buttonhooking just past the first-down marker, and drilled it to him. On the next play, Blackledge faced a ferocious rush and had to scramble, but he managed to pick up 6 yards and call a time-out. With 13 seconds now left in the game, Blackledge stayed in the pocket and found tight end Mike McCloskey on the sideline at the 2-yard line. It was close, but the referee ruled he was in bounds when he caught the ball. Seven seconds now remained. Two passes maybe, or one run. Penn State came to the line of scrimmage with two tight ends bunched up. Blackledge faded back and, under heavy pressure and waiting until the last possible second, finally glimpsed "Stonehands" Bowman at the back of the end zone. Throwing off balance, Blackledge's pass was low, but the former lineman made a spectacular shoestring catch for the touchdown. The final score was Penn State 27, Nebraska 24, but as Joe Paterno observed, "There was enough glory out there for both teams."

NOTRE DAME–MIAMI
October 15, 1988

This was a game that started out with special bitterness. Three years earlier, on November 30, 1985, Miami had come to Notre Dame Stadium and humiliated the Irish 58–7, the largest margin of defeat since they had been crushed by Army 59–0 back in 1944. Two years later the Hurricanes shut out the Irish 24–0 down in Florida; in their last four encounters Miami had outscored the Irish 133–20.

Notre Dame, under Lou Holtz, who took over in 1986, craved revenge. Miami, coached by Jimmy Johnson, was 4-0 and bent on continuing their domination over the Irish as well as preserving a 16-game winning streak and their ranking of No. 1 in the national polls. Holtz had reversed the decline that had afflicted Notre Dame under his predecessor, Gerry Faust, and turned them into a contender—they were 5-0 in 1988 and ranked fourth in the nation when Miami arrived.

Hostilities broke out before the game even started. As the two teams passed each other near the end zone tunnel during pregame warm-ups, taunts were exchanged, some fists flew, and suddenly a full-scale brawl was underway. Coaches and security personnel broke it up, tempers cooled, and what followed was one of the most exciting games in either team's history.

Notre Dame jumped out to a 7–0 lead in the first quarter after quarterback Tony Rice carried it in from the 7. Miami quarterback Steve Walsh, on his way to a record day passing, threw for a touchdown early in the second period to tie the game. Rice responded with a touchdown pass of his own, and soon after Notre Dame safety Pat Terrell picked off a Walsh pass and returned it 60 yards for a touchdown, giving the Irish a 21–7 lead. Now it was Walsh's turn to retaliate: with less than two and half minutes to play in the half he threw for two touchdowns. The score at the half was 21–21.

In the third quarter, it was all Notre Dame, a touchdown and a field goal giving them a 10-point lead, not a cushion by any means, however, against defending national champion Miami. And what followed was a truly memorable fourth quarter. Walsh marched the Hurricanes down the field but Notre Dame's defense finally held at the 6-yard line, forcing Miami to settle for a field goal. Several minutes later, Miami was on the move again, reaching the Notre Dame 11 this time. With fourth down and 7 yards needed for a first down, Johnson decided against the field goal this time. Walsh rolled out and threw to fullback Cleveland Gary at the 5, who lunged for the goal line, ball thrust out in front of him, but Irish safety George Streeter knocked the ball out of his hands and linebacker Mike Stonebreaker recovered the fumble for Notre Dame.

With just under 4 minutes remaining in the game, Miami again moved the ball deep into Notre Dame territory. From the 24-yard line Walsh dropped back to pass but blitzing linebacker Frank Stams smashed into him, knocking the ball loose, which was recovered by Notre Dame's All-American tackle Chris Zorich. Now, with 2:10 remaining and Notre Dame in need of a first down, the situation was reversed, Rice dropped back and Miami blitzed,

defensive back Randy Shannon knocking the ball loose, and the Hurricanes recovering at the Irish 15.

Notre Dame's defense again rose to the occasion and allowed only 4 yards in three plays, bringing up a fourth down at the 11-yard line, 51 seconds on the clock. Walsh was successful this time, finding Andre Brown in the end zone, who made a diving catch for the touchdown. With the score 31–30, Notre Dame, Johnson decided against playing for the tie and lined up for a 2-point conversion. Walsh dropped back again, looking for what seemed like an eternity for an open receiver, then throwing to running back Leonard Conley only to see Notre Dame safety Pat Terrell flash in front of his intended receiver and knock the ball away.

Notre Dame had its revenge. And more. The Fighting Irish remained undefeated that year and won the national championship; the Hurricanes did not lose another game either and ended up second in the final polls.

Notre Dame safety Pat Terrell (15) leaps to bat away the 2-point conversion attempt in the last seconds of the Miami—Notre Dame game of 1988 to preserve a 31—30 victory for the Irish. No. 28 is Miami's intended receiver, Leonard Conley.

FLORIDA STATE–
NOTRE DAME

November 13, 1993

BOSTON COLLEGE–
NOTRE DAME

November 20, 1993

A double-header. Seven days apart, these two cliff-hangers would be instrumental in determining the 1993 national championship. After nine games in the 1993 season both Florida State, coached by Bobby Bowden, and Notre Dame, under Lou Holtz, remained undefeated, with the Seminoles ranked No. 1 in the nation and the Fighting Irish No. 2. They met at Notre Dame Stadium, with the national championship potentially in the balance.

Once the game got underway, it appeared that the top rankings in the national polls should have been reversed. Notre Dame dominated through the first three quarters and most of the fourth, leading 31–17 with just under two and a half minutes remaining in the game. With fourth down and 20 for a first, Seminole quarterback and that year's Heisman Trophy winner Charlie Ward threw a desperation pass into the end zone, tapped away by Notre Dame safety Brian Magee but grabbed before it hit the ground by Seminole receiver Kez McCorvey. The conversion brought Florida State within 7 points.

Bowden, with faith in his defense, chose not to try an onside kick, and his defense responded by stopping the Irish on three plays and forcing a punt. With 51 seconds remaining, no time-outs left, and the ball on the Florida State 37, Ward went to work. Forty-one seconds later he had the Seminoles at the

Notre Dame 10-yard line. Ward, looking to the end zone, threw but Irish defensive end Thomas McKnight got a hand up and batted the ball away. Three seconds on the clock now, Ward rolled out and threw again for the end zone and this time Notre Dame cornerback Shawn Wooden got a hand in front of intended receiver Kevin Knox and knocked it away; the final score 31–24, Notre Dame.

Boston College had lost two of their nine games before coming to South Bend to meet now No. 1 ranked Notre Dame the next week. The year before the Eagles had been embarrassed by Holtz's Irish 54–7, and the memory of that horror story was all too fresh.

As motivated as Boston College was, Notre Dame was complacent. Four minutes into the fourth quarter, the Eagles, led by quarterback Glenn Foley, who was having a Doug Flutie–like day, held a commanding 38–17 lead in an eerily quiet Notre Dame Stadium. Foley had thrown three touchdown passes in the first half and another early in the fourth quarter. But finally the Irish caught fire. First running back Lee Becton broke away on a 29-yard touchdown run, and the Irish successfully went for a 2-point conversion. On the BC next possession Foley fumbled the ball over to Notre Dame, and the Irish marched, capping the drive with fullback Ray Zellars carrying it in from the 4. With just over 4 minutes left the Irish had pulled to within 6, 38–32.

Notre Dame held, forcing the Eagles to punt. Irish quarterback Kevin McDougal completed a 46-yard bomb to wide receiver Derrick Mayes, who was brought down on the BC 4-yard line; McDougal then passed to Lake Dawson in the end zone. The extra point, the 22nd point the Irish had scored in 9 minutes of the fourth quarter, gave them their first lead of the day, 39–38, with a mere 1:09 left to play.

Starting from his own 10-yard line, Foley once again took control for the Eagles. Two quick passes got the ball out to the Boston College 43-yard line with less than a half-minute to go. Then he scrambled and hit tight end Pete Mitchell, who reached the Notre Dame 33-yard line. Only 18 seconds remaining now. Foley found Ivan Boyd open on the next play and he was brought down at the Notre Dame 24. With 5 seconds left, BC took a time-out.

The game now rested on the foot of placekicker David Gordon, a left-footed kicker who was a walk-on that year at Boston College. His longest field goal ever was 39 yards; he was facing a game-winning 41-yarder. Foley held, Gordon kicked a career-long field goal, and a stunned Notre Dame team fell from first place in the nation.

Both Notre Dame and Florida State were 11-1 when bowl time came around. The Irish took on seventh-ranked Texas A&M in the Cotton Bowl and beat them 24–21; in the first year of the Bowl Coalition the Seminoles faced top-ranked Nebraska at the Orange Bowl and prevailed 18–16. The national championship went to Florida State, Notre Dame was ranked No. 2, and Nebraska No. 3.

NEBRASKA–MISSOURI

November 8, 1997

Nebraska was nearing the end of a nine-year dynasty when they traveled to Columbia to take on Missouri in 1997. The Cornhuskers were 8-0 and ranked No. 1 in the nation; they were four-touchdown favorites. Missouri was 6-3, not a contender for anything but at least appeared to be on the way to their first winning season in 14 years. It was an important game for

Tom Osborne's Nebraska team, who were in a tight race for the national title with Michigan, Florida, and Penn State; for the Tigers, under Larry Smith, it was more a matter of just beating a team they had lost to in each of the previous 19 seasons.

Missouri set the tone for the day on their first possession. Quarterback Corby Jones marched them down the field, including a 17-yard scramble, to set up the first touchdown of the afternoon. The lead went back and forth through the first half. Jones threw two touchdown passes while Nebraska quarterback Scott Frost scored two on running plays. Missouri added a field goal and took a 24–21 lead into the locker room.

Nebraska regained the lead in the third quarter when Frost carried it in for his third rushing touchdown of the day. Jones brought the Tigers right back, capping it himself with a 6-yard touchdown run. It was Missouri 31, Nebraska 28 at the end of the third. Early in the fourth quarter, Nebraska tied it with a 44-yard field goal. Jones, having the best game of his college career, led another Tiger march and with just over four and a half minutes to go in the game passed to tight end Eddie Brooks for the go-ahead touchdown: Missouri 38, Nebraska 31.

Both teams exchanged punts, but Nebraska finally got the ball back with 1 minute remaining. It was now Corby Jones's time to shine. Four completions later he had the Cornhuskers at the Missouri 12-yard line with just 7 seconds on the clock. The last play in regulation was one of the most bizarre in college football history.

Nebraska lined up in the shotgun formation. Corby took the snap, looked for an open receiver but couldn't find one. At the last possible second he spotted Shevin Wiggins cutting across the middle and rifled the ball to him at the goal line. Wiggins had his

Nebraska's Shevin Wiggins (on his back) manages to kick the ball out of the hands of Missouri's Harold Piersey (top right) in the end zone in the final seconds of this classic 1997 game. Before the ball hit the turf, another Cornhusker (not in the picture), scooped it up for a touchdown. The ensuing extra point sent the game into overtime, from which Nebraska emerged victorious 45–38.

hands on the football just as Missouri safety Julius Jones tackled him and the ball popped into the air. As it was about to hit the ground, Missouri's Harold Piersey scooped it in only to have Wiggins, who had been knocked violently to the ground, somehow kick it out of Piersey's hands. The ball floated lazily toward the back end line when suddenly a diving Matt Davidson, one of Nebraska's receivers, snatched it only just inches from the turf. There was no time on the clock when Nebraska kicked the game-tying extra point, and the Cornhuskers were saved from what appeared certain defeat.

In overtime, Frost scored for Nebraska. Missouri was unable to respond. And the Cornhuskers, with a 45–38 win, managed to save their unbeaten record and their No. 1 ranking, for a few weeks anyway. Nebraska finished with a record of 12-0 in 1997; so did the University of Michigan. Nebraska defeated Tennessee in the Orange Bowl 42–17; Michigan beat Washington State in the Rose Bowl 21–16. The AP poll picked Michigan No. 1, Nebraska, No. 2, the USA Today/ESPN coaches poll selected Nebraska tops with Michigan right behind them. Missouri was just pleased to post a winning season, 7-5.

7

"We've done so much with so
little for so long,
we believe we can do anything
with nothing."

MARINO CASEM
Alcorn State
Head Coach, 1964—85

CONFLICT AND CHANGE

COLLEGE FOOTBALL COMES OF AGE

College football was a major force in the sports world throughout much of the first half of the twentieth century. It grew from a game that filled rickety grandstands with perhaps a few thousand students and townspeople at the start of the century to one that by the mid-1920s was at some schools entertaining 50,000, even as many as 70,000, fans in a stadium on a fall Saturday afternoon.

By the time Americans were listening to jazz, dancing the Charleston, and reading Fitzgerald and Hemingway, college football had become a spectator sport with audiences comparable to those of baseball and boxing. The biggest names in the game—Grange, Nagurski, Nevers—were as prominent in the sports headlines as those of Ruth, Dempsey, Tilden, and Jones.

Even the Great Depression did not impede interest in the game, nor even much affect attendance at games in any area of the country. Marquee stars of the 1930s like Hutson, Baugh, and Harmon certainly helped the cause; so did increasing alumni loyalty and the visceral need for an uplifting diversion from the troubles of the time. The entire extravaganza was in place at the start of the 1940s: heated rivalries, exciting games, Saturday's heroes, bands and cheerleaders, mascots and fight songs, pregame rituals and postgame parties.

But the war came along, and with it the draft, swiftly depleting the store of athletes who might otherwise have been playing football for the college of their choice. Army and Navy were not affected, and soon became the nation's powerhouses. Service teams took shape, just as they had in World War I, packed with some of the best football players to be found and fielded by such places as the Great Lakes Naval Training Center just outside Chicago and the Army Air Corps' Randolph Field. College football, although still breathing and moving, was during the first half of the 1940s only a shadow of what it had been.

After the war, however, the game did more than just pick up where it left off. With the veterans' return to college and the arrival of a new crop of young stars just coming of college age, the game took on a uniform quality nationwide that had never been seen before. With dynasties like those developing at Notre Dame and Michigan and super-teams coming out of Georgia, Texas, and most of the major schools in the Midwest and in California, college football entered into a golden age.

It was a time, too, when the first steps were taken on America's long road to civil rights; from the

War was being waged in Europe and the Pacific; a friendlier battle, however, was about to take place between Army and Navy in 1942 at Thompson Stadium in Annapolis, Maryland. Captains Henry Mazur of Army (left) and Alan Cameron of Navy (45) wish each other luck before the game. The Midshipmen won 14—0, and they would win again the following year, but then Army would dominate for the rest of the 1940s (except for 1948 when Navy spoiled the Cadets' perfect season with a 21—21 tie in the last game of the season).

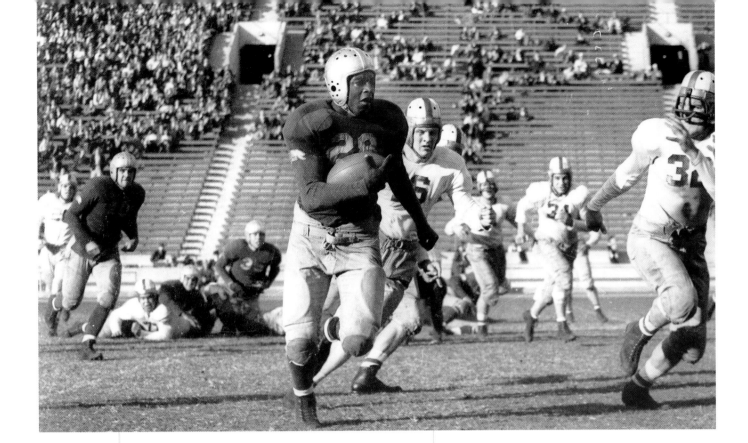

Halfback Jackie Robinson gains a good chunk of yardage for UCLA in a 1940 game. Robinson spent three years at UCLA, where he was a member of the baseball, basketball, and track teams as well as a football star. Drafted into the army in 1942, he went to Officer Candidate School, was commissioned a second lieutenant, and served until 1945. After the war, Robinson became the first black to play Major League Baseball, signed by the Brooklyn Dodgers on October 23, 1945; in 1947 he made his debut in Brooklyn, where he would attain legendary status. He was inducted into baseball's Hall of Fame in Cooperstown, New York in 1962.

time Truman desegregated the armed forces in 1948 to the Supreme Court ruling in *Brown* v. *Topeka Board of Education*, the black experience in college football suddenly came to the forefront. Much earlier, mostly before the Roaring Twenties, a few blacks had made a mark in the game, All-Americas like Fritz Pollard at Brown, Paul Robeson at Rutgers, and Duke Slater at Iowa. After that, however, a kind of tacit agreement excluded blacks from all the college football fields, just as they were from those of the NFL (which didn't begin to integrate until after World War II, and even then it was prompted by the teams of a rival league, the AAFC, most notably the Cleveland Browns).

After the war, however, the players returned and made their presence known: Buddy Young at Illinois, Kenny Washington at UCLA, George Taliaferro at Indiana, Len Ford at Michigan, although the South remained strictly segregated. It

was not without incident, however, and many a black player found himself a marked man on fields of play in the North, the Midwest, and the Far West, the victim of ugly and hate-riddled acts.

It was also a time for football to flourish in the black schools of the South, under such now legendary coaches as Eddie Robinson at Grambling and Jake Gaither at Florida A&M, and with milestone players like Tank Younger from Grambling, Maryland State's Johnny Sample, Willie Galimore of Florida A&M, and, of course, later superstars like Walter Payton of Jackson State and Jerry Rice from Mississippi Valley State.

Led by great stars like Syracuse's Jim Brown and Ernie Davis and Ohio State's Jim Parker in the 1950s, blacks soon became not only mainstays but quite often the stars of teams throughout the nation, until they finally emerged as one of the truly dominant forces in the modern-day game of college football.

Of course, the emergence of blacks was only one of many trends and events that altered the game of college football after World War II. The range is broad: from such general influences as the rapid suburbanization of America to the more specific, like the increasing impact of television to the growth of the enforcement powers of the NCAA. If indeed one other postwar trend in football, both college and professional, is to be singled out, however, it would have to be the advent of television coverage. The press had long been reporting the game's events. Some of the prewar sportswriters would make huge names for themselves later in other areas of writing, like Damon Runyon, Ring Lardner, and Paul Gallico. One would become an immortal in his profession, Grantland Rice. Radio had been there almost as long as press coverage. But it was television that would make the biggest impact after the war. The first game to be televised actually took place before the war, 1940, Maryland vs. Pennsylvania, but almost no one had a television set then. Later, however, television would bring the sport to tens of millions of people on Saturday afternoons and now on Thursday nights and Saturday nights; on New Year's Day and now on days just preceding it and those just following it.

College football met the conflicts that arose in the second half of the twentieth century, adapted to the changes . . . and came out all the better for it.

THE BLACK EXPERIENCE

No one, it is safe to say, understands the history of blacks and college football better than Marino Casem. He coached at Alcorn State for 22 years where his record was 132-65-8. When he took over in 1964, only two Alcorn players had ever made it to the NFL; by the time he retired in 1985, 57 of his players could claim professional football credentials. He said: "We've done so much with so little for so long, we believe we can do anything with nothing." He spoke for a lot of people when he said that.

The experience Coach Casem introduces is a storied one . . .

Fred Kent was a photographer in Iowa City, Iowa, and one of his duties was to photograph University of Iowa football games. Against undefeated Notre Dame in the biggest game of the 1921 season, Fred got himself quite a picture . . . it showed one whole side of the Irish line being collapsed by just one Hawkeye player, Duke Slater.

Duke could do that. He was from Clinton, Iowa, a large man, with huge hands and feet. He played tackle on offense and on defense, from 1919 through 1921, and he became an All-American.

Slater's college coach was Howard Jones, himself a football legend, although a less than loquacious one, it seems. Asked if he had ever seen a better tackle than Duke Slater, Jones's answer was brief: "No, I don't believe I ever did." Had he been a little less reserved, Jones might have added that Slater was one of the most important factors in carrying his Iowa team to an undefeated season in 1921, on the way ending a three-year, 20-game Notre Dame win streak.

After a successful four years at Iowa, both on the football field and in the classroom, Slater went on to law school, eventually to sit as a municipal judge in Chicago. They've got a dormitory now at Iowa called Slater Hall, but its namesake never lived there—blacks weren't allowed to live on campus when Duke Slater was in school.

Indeed, there weren't many blacks playing football in largely white Northern colleges in Slater's time. But there were some prominent ones. Paul Robeson, an All-American end in 1917 and 1918, was one; Fritz Pollard, halfback for Brown, was another, earning the same national recognition in 1916.

Pollard, a tiny fellow, was, in fact, the first black to win All-America honors. A true pioneer, Pollard was also the first black to play in the Rose Bowl, and later the first black to coach in professional football. Underscoring the fact that amateur status may have been more loosely defined in earlier times, Fritz Pollard, who was from Evanston, played semiprofessional football in Illinois before he ever went away to become a star at Brown University. But a college football star he became, then went on to play for four different NFL teams in the league's infancy, and eventually became a successful businessman.

His son, Fritz Jr., won a silver medal in the high hurdles, representing the United States in the 1936 Berlin Olympics, the year Jesse Owens, Fritz Jr., and a group of other talented black athletes ran over Hitler's theory of a master race.

Fritz Pollard was nothing new to college football, however. By the time he arrived at Brown, black colleges had been fielding teams for more than 20 years. Livingstone and Biddle Colleges played on the Livingstone campus in North Carolina in 1892. Pregame news reports said the Livingstone men were "sanguine of success, while the boys from Biddle were quite confident they wouldn't be beaten." The Biddle boys weren't, winning 4–0 (in those days, touchdowns counted for four points). W. J. Trent coached and played for Livingstone. Later he would become Livingstone's president.

LEFT

Duke Slater, one of the first great blacks to play college football, starred as a tackle on offense and defense for Iowa from 1919 through 1921. After graduating, he earned a law degree and later served as a municipal judge in Chicago, Illinois. Today a dormitory is named after him at Iowa; ironically, when he attended the school blacks were not allowed to live in the dorms on campus.

BELOW

Fritz Pollard, at five-feet-eight and 150 pounds, played halfback for Brown from 1914 through 1916, and has the distinction of being the first black to be named to Walter Camp's All-America team (1916). He went on to play for several NFL teams in the first half of the 1920s before pursuing a successful business career.

The team Hampton Institute of Hampton, Virginia, fielded in 1900. Today the Hampton Pirates play in the Mid-Eastern Athletic Conference of the NCAA's Division 1-AA.

Football blossomed in black schools through the first half of the twentieth century, the majority of those schools in the South where blacks had otherwise long been denied educational rights. For years, nobody knew the program—both on the field and in the classroom—better than Jake Gaither at Florida A&M.

Before he became a football coach, Gaither dug ditches, shined shoes, bell-hopped, and mined coal. He coached football for 36 years, taking over as head coach at A&M in 1945; he also coached track and basketball, served as athletic director, and taught classes every semester. His teams won 203 games, lost 36, and tied 4, a remarkable .844 winning percentage. Gaither sent 42 players to the NFL and produced 36 All-Americans.

Gaither's "Split-line T" formation was a bold new concept. Coach Gaither was explaining his formation at a clinic when Paul "Bear" Bryant, who coached just up the road at Alabama, questioned Jake at length, then said he doubted the formation would work in big-time football. Irritated, Gaither challenged Bryant. "I'll tell you what. I'll take my players and beat yours with it, and take your players and beat mine with it."

IN THE LATE 1970S, the Chicago Bears—like other NFL clubs—hosted the football coaching staff of a black college in their training camp. Such visits were sometimes valued as much for their social opportunities as for football recruitment possibilities, but the men at the Bear camp in Lake Forest, Illinois, were all business. After the second practice of the day, Bear coaches would ordinarily grab a beer before dinner. Their visitors would meet to review notes taken during the day. After dinner, the visitors attended Bear team meetings, then attended their own, where they evaluated what they'd learned, as it might apply to their program.

A Bear employee teased one of the college coaches during a practice, noting they had scarcely been off campus.

The assistant smiled, then nodded. "Coach Robinson made it real clear we're here to work."

Coach Robinson . . .

One writer, Bill McGrane, summed it up: "You say Bobby Bowden or Tom Osborne or Joe Paterno. Or Vince Lombardi or Tom Landry or Don Shula. I'll say Eddie Robinson, and we'll be saying the same thing." Dominant football coaches. Winners.

Eddie Robinson was named football coach at Louisiana Negro Normal and Industrial Institute in 1941. Happily, the school's president, "Prez" Jones, talked the legislature into changing the name of the school. Prez told the legislators about a big game the previous year when the opponent had the ball at the LNN&II 7-yard line.

"Our students were cheering for us to hold that line," Prez explained, "but by the time they could get the school name out, the other team had scored."

Well, the name problem went away. The school took the name of the town in which it was situated, Grambling, and the team became the G-Men. And Grambling's football program became the goal to which every black program in the country aspired. Three men made it possible: school president Jones, publicist/promoter Collie Nicholson, and Robinson. But Eddie was the key, and the name Grambling soon became a household word in the domain of college football.

Eddie Robinson coached at Grambling for 55 years, retiring in 1997. His teams won 408 games, lost 165, and tied 15. He won more games than any other college football coach. His teams captured 17 Southwestern Athletic Conference championships, nine Black College national championships, and had 27 straight winning seasons (1960–86). More than 200 of Robinson's players advanced to the NFL. Robinson won more awards than any coach in history. Not bad for a man who, when he started coaching at Grambling, also mowed the grass and

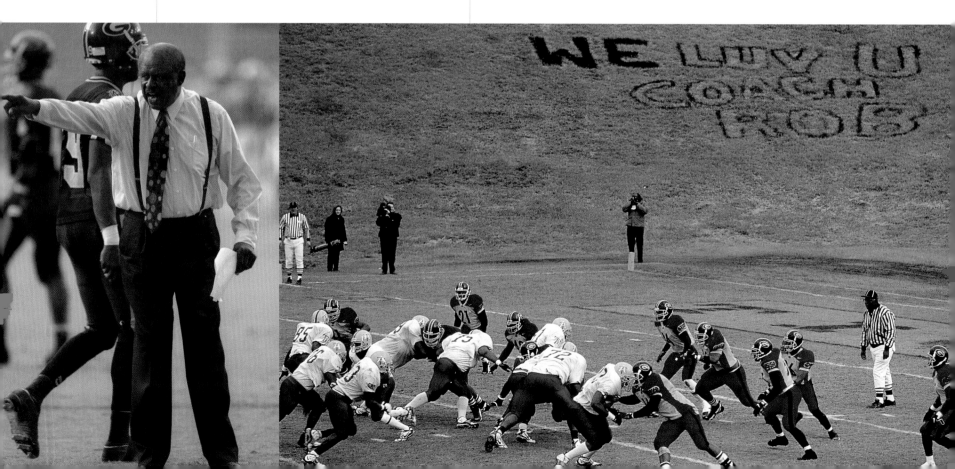

ABOVE

Leading the heralded Grambling Band, the Drum Major. One of the most colorful and famous bands in college football, Grambling's was launched in Louisiana in 1926 when Ralph Waldo Emerson Jones secured a line of credit from Sears, Roebuck & Company to purchase 17 instruments.

RIGHT

The Grambling trombones, not quite 76, but part of a band that grew from 17 marching members in 1926 to 250 by the 21st century.

lined the field, sewed torn uniforms, taped ankles, directed the band, and wrote game accounts for Louisiana newspapers.

Coach Robinson, it was said, "practiced the daylights out of his teams." Pro scouts knew they could visit with Eddie before practice, then nip on over to Ruston and watch Louisiana Tech work, then return to Grambling and still see plenty of practice there.

Winning began early for Eddie: he was a running back at McKinley High School in Baton Rouge, Louisiana, where his teams went 27-0, and at Leland College, where his teams went 18-1. Robinson also worked on a coal truck and was the campus barber at Leland.

Albert Armour, a teammate both in high school and college, said of Robinson, "He had enough personality to make you run through the line, even when you knew you couldn't. You just wanted to do it for him."

GAITHER AND ROBINSON were only two of many successful coaches in black college football. Billy Nicks coached at Prairie View, called "the

Black Notre Dame," because everybody wanted to play for coach Nicks. NFL Hall of Famer Ken Houston said of Nicks, "He didn't play any favorites. If we were going on a trip and there were star players missing when we got ready to leave, Coach would say, 'We got eleven? Let's roll this bus.'"

Joe Taylor at Hampton. "My goal is to reach a national championship in an all-black setting, and it's possible, but I can't be the only one to think that. I have to convince guys that it's okay to be good in the 'hood, but don't be afraid to go uptown. And not just in football season, but year round."

Ace Mumford coached at Jarvis Christian College, Bishop College, Texas College, and Southern University. His 36-year career was 235-82-25. Emory Hines, former Southern athletic director who played guard for Mumford at Texas College, said Mumford's strategies were admired by prominent white coaches of the day, among them Bear Bryant and Frank Broyles. "I can recall coach Mumford sitting down with those men here at Southern, moving soda-water tops in offensive and defensive patterns

until the wee hours of the morning." Another of Hines's reminiscences: "We didn't have lights on the practice field, but Coach Mumford would get the players down by the end of the field near the streetlights and work until he got what he wanted."

Big John Merritt's teams went 172-33-7 at Tennessee State. Billy Joe, at Central State, turned the Marauders into a National Association of Intercollegiate Athletics power. Archie Cooley's nickname is "Gunslinger." He runs wide-open offenses. Archie's coached at Mississippi Valley, Arkansas Pine Bluff, and Norfolk State. Willie Totten and Jerry Rice made Archie's offense sizzle at Mississippi Valley. The Delta Devils once beat Kent State 86–0. Archie's defensive coaches complained, saying, "You're going to have to quit scoring so fast, you're killing the defense."

"I just told them they'd better get those boys in shape," Cooley responded.

Walter Highsmith grew up wanting to play for Jake Gaither at Florida A&M. He did, as an offen-

sive lineman and middle linebacker on the Rattlers' 1961 Southern Intercollegiate Athletic Conference championship team. "When Jake would come in to meet the freshmen, he'd say, 'If you come to Florida A&M for anything other than a degree, get the hell out of here!'" Highsmith makes the same speech now as head coach at Texas Southern.

And there have been many more . . . the list is a long and honored one, and we must mention another . . . although his college playing days might not have indicated his future coaching success.

Or maybe they did.

After World War II, the University of Iowa didn't have a bad football team, it had a terrible team. Nile Kinnick and the Iron Men were but a memory as the postwar Hawkeyes, a mismatch of returning veterans and youngsters, bumped along near the bottom of the Big Ten.

But one player quickly became a favorite of Iowa fans, a roly-poly guard whose helmet was often twisted over half his face at the conclusion of a play. Fans loved that he played with fury, but usually had a grin on his face. Atop a body that stood five-foot-seven-inches and weighed 220 pounds, it was a wide grin.

Earl Banks was from Chicago's South Side. Growing up, kids in his neighborhood played football with a tin can. One of those kids Earl played with was Buddy Young, who would go on to track and football All-America honors at Illinois. Banks won All-State honors at Chicago's Wendell Phillips high school. At Iowa, he became an All-American.

But the best was yet to come. After serving as a high school coach and college assistant, Banks replaced Eddie Hurt as coach at Morgan State in Baltimore in 1960. It was a tall order—Hurt's 31-year record was 173-51-19. Banks coached at Morgan for 14 years. His teams never had a losing record. His

The Grambling trumpets. Besides playing at all its school's football games, the Grambling Band has entertained at Super Bowls and U.S. presidential inauguration ceremonies, as well as on television and at jazz festivals throughout the United States.

career mark was 94-30-2. Between 1965 and 1967, Morgan State won 32 consecutive games. In his 14 years as head coach, 90 percent of the young men who played for Banks graduated from Morgan State.

"You have to be lucky," Banks said after his career ended. "I attribute a lot of that to Eddie [Robinson]. He gave a lot of us credibility by letting us play Grambling. And if there was some banquet to speak at, Eddie would say he was too busy to go, then say, 'Why don't you get a guy like Earl Banks?'"

ALTHOUGH more than 200 of Eddie Robinson's players went on from Grambling to play in the National Football League, it was the first one—indeed, the first player from any black college to play in the NFL—who was perhaps the most memorable: Paul "Tank" Younger.

Younger was a devastating runner. At Grambling, he scored 60 touchdowns, 25 of them as a freshman. The nickname "Tank" came from Robinson's publicist-crony, Collie Nicholson. A Marine combat photographer in the Pacific, Nicholson said, "I watched him run over people he couldn't get around. I'd been in the South Pacific, and it reminded me of what I'd seen those tanks doing there."

Younger, at age 20, signed as a free agent with the Los Angeles Rams in 1949. "Coach Robinson said to me, 'Listen, Tank, this is a great opportunity for black college football. You're the outstanding player in black college football. If you fail, it's no telling when another player will get the opportunity. They'll say we took the best you had and he failed.'"

Tank didn't fail. He was a five-time Pro Bowl selection with the Rams and the first black to play in that game honoring the very best.

The late Howard Cosell said of Younger: "He opened the door to a new talent source and gave pro football a new dimension. Tank Younger was a great player. No matter what criteria they use in the selection process, the NFL has diluted its Hall of Fame in bypassing Younger."

Younger needed to be a man of resolve. As a rookie, he and teammate Willie Steele almost missed a preseason game in San Antonio because a stadium security officer didn't believe they played for the Rams.

"He wanted to know, 'Where'd you niggers steal those passes?'" Tank recalled. A Ram assistant coach was nearly arrested, trying to aid the two players. Finally, the game promoter assured the guard the men were players. Younger didn't limit his trailblazing to the playing field. In 1975, Tank became the first black to be named a club's assistant general manager. He held that post both with the Rams and the San Diego Chargers. Tank Younger wasn't the only black player to encounter racial challenges.

James Nathaniel Brown was another. Many will tell you he was the greatest football player ever. It seemed like Jim ran angry, like he was heading out there, football under his arm, to hurt someone. Carrying the ball, turning upfield, Brown was mayhem in cleats. He would go around you, but if around wasn't handy, right over you would be just fine. Until Walter Payton spun out his legendary journey nearly three decades later, Jim Brown had rushed for more yards than any man in the history of the National Football League.

But before he did that he played at Syracuse.

Jim Brown grew up poor on St. Simons Island, off the south Georgia coast. He didn't know his father, Sweet Sue Brown. Sweet Sue (Swinton, actually) left two weeks after Jim was born and Jim never saw him more than three or four times in his life. His mother left, too, heading north where she could

make a decent wage. His great-grandmother Nora Peterson raised Jim, who called her Mama. Gradually, as he grew up, the way he lived troubled young Brown. White kids on St. Simons swam off the pier at Port Allen, but blacks walked three miles through the woods to the Negro beach. Whites bused to a handsome school. Blacks walked to a two-room school set in the backwoods.

Brown recalled becoming angry at the picture of Jesus his grandmother had hanging on the wall of her cabin—a blond, handsome, blue-eyed, pink-skinned Jesus. "I said 'Jesus don't look like that! Why is he blond and blue-eyed? Nobody knows what he looks like . . . ' We got into a row over that."

Mama sent Jim north at age eight to live with his birthmother, Teresa, a domestic for a Jewish couple on Long Island. Jim grew up on the Island, eventually attending Manhasset High School. He was a star in sports and in other school activities. He was accepted in the community. Wooed by Ohio State, Brown instead chose Syracuse University where his high school coach, Kenny Molloy, had

gone. Molloy was under the impression that Syracuse had a scholarship for Brown.

Not really, he found out. Molloy pleaded, but Syracuse wouldn't offer a scholarship because they had never scouted Brown. Molloy wouldn't give up. He appealed to Manhasset's leading citizens and established a fund for Jim's education. Molloy's deal with Syracuse provided that the fund would pay for Jim's freshman year, but if his play as a freshman was good enough, Syracuse would offer a scholarship.

If that wasn't awkward enough, Brown was never told he really wasn't on scholarship. He didn't live in a dorm with other players, he lived three miles away in old university housing. Players had meal tickets for one dining hall, Jim's was for another. The players got more to eat. Eventually, Jim and a friend forged phony meal tickets so that he might eat with the team. Factor in that he was the only black on the freshman team, and you have a sense of the freshman's concern. Things weren't much better on the field, as Brown was viewed with distrust by some in the Syracuse program.

Prior to Brown's arrival, Syracuse had a black quarterback named Vada Stone, a flashy young man who partied hard, dated white women, and eventually quit college for the Canadian Football League. Brown, who had never heard of Vada Stone, was promptly measured against him, and told he'd better not be like Stone. When Jim learned the basis of comparison was the color of his skin, he was furious. In retrospect, however, he felt his anger did become a benefit to him—it made him work harder. And he got that scholarship his mentor Molloy had fought for.

Brown began his sophomore season as a fifth-team running back. Against Cornell, in the sixth game, and with two other backs hurt, Jim played.

Jim Brown, one of the greatest ballcarriers ever to run on a college (and pro) football field. The Syracuse All-American running back, who played in the Cotton Bowl in Dallas, Texas, on January 1, 1957 (contributing three touchdowns and three extra points), was a milestone player in the history of blacks in college football.

He ran for 150 yards, including 54 for a touchdown. He started every game, the rest of his career.

At the end of Brown's senior season, Syracuse played Texas Christian in the Cotton Bowl in Dallas, the first game Jim would play in the South. His coaches wanted Jim to stay in a private home, but he would have none of it: he was part of the team, he would stay with the team. Syracuse settled for a small hotel outside Dallas, where Jim was encouraged to spend as little time in the lobby as possible.

Brown was an All-American in lacrosse as well as football at Syracuse. He was also in the Army ROTC, and the summer after his graduation, while training at Fort Benning, Georgia, Jim and two local black friends were pulled over by a sheriff's car after they had passed a car on a dirt road. Brown was driving.

Two plainclothes officers told Brown to get out of the car. "Boy, why did you throw dust up on those white people?" one officer asked. "Huh, nigger?"

Brown blurted that he was no nigger. One of his friends got down on his knees, saying, "Sir, he's not from here. He doesn't understand. Please, don't shoot him." The other officer, older, eventually steered the moment past danger. "I'll tell you what you do, boy," he said. "You get back in that car and get outta here. And don't be throwin' dust up on white folks no more."

During his football career at Syracuse, Brown gained 2,091 yards rushing and accounted for 187 points, which included 25 touchdowns. In his senior year, Jim scored 43 points in a game against Colgate—six touchdowns and seven extra points— then an NCAA record. His contributions to the Syracuse athletic program were not limited to football and lacrosse, however. He played basketball for the Orangemen as well, scoring 563 points in 43 games, and also participated on the track team.

After Jim had left for the pros, Brown's coach at Syracuse, Ben Schwartzwalder, became a focal point of racial tension. The issue at Syracuse was unrest over the desire by some players that a black coach be added to the football staff. Reluctantly, Schwartzwalder spoke to his team about the issue of discrimination, but his remarks only added to the problem: blacks thought their coach patronizing and whites thought the staff was giving preferential treatment to blacks.

With nine black players boycotting over the issue, Schwartzwalder eventually hired a black assistant, then dismissed eight of the nine dissenters from the squad. The situation simmered for a year, but eventually dissipated. Schwartzwalder remained.

Perhaps ironically, no school in the middle years of the century produced finer black running backs than Syracuse, a list that includes Brown, Ernie Davis, Floyd Little, and Jim Nance.

Ernie Davis follows a pair of Syracuse blockers in a 1961 game. Davis, who broke all of Jim Brown's rushing records at Syracuse, won the Heisman Trophy that year, the first black to be so honored. He was selected first in the NFL's 1962 draft but never played a professional game. Stricken with leukemia, he died at the age of 23.

CONFRONTATION was common in the 1960s and 1970s. In football, it spread west to Oregon State University where football Coach Dee Andros sparked a flame of protest quite by chance. Walking across the Oregon State campus, Andros passed one of his black players, Fred Milton. Andros is said to have told Milton to shave off his mustache and Vandyke beard by the following Monday, or be dismissed from the team. Milton refused, and was dismissed from the team although his scholarship remained in place.

Andros pointed out it was athletic department policy that athletes not have facial hair; he said the policy had nothing to do with discrimination, but was aimed at presenting an image all could be proud of.

Black students united in Milton's defense. The university community was divided. The two causes were unable to yield to one another. Andros, on the one hand, saw Milton's refusal as undermining a most basic need in athletics—discipline. Milton—and the rest of Oregon State's black community—believed Milton had the same right of expression as any student on campus, so long as it was within good taste. It was a bitter struggle. Black athletes left the university; Milton relocated to Portland State. The "beard blowup," as the incident was called, eventually brought into focus the general resentment black students had for their acceptance in the city of Corvallis. Eventually the university and the Black Student Union agreed on forming a Commission on Human Rights and Responsibilities. Lengthy delays presaged a committee report that appeased neither side: while the athletic department acted in the best interests of the school and its students, it would do well to review its policies, especially as they affected the reasonable rights of black student-athletes.

Minor appearance code changes were implemented and Andros hired a black assistant coach.

It's a safe assumption that Andros came out of the Milton affair sure as ever that his way was the right way. Of the school's 17 black athletes, 11 stayed in school. Not surprisingly, recruitment of black athletes suffered at Oregon State for the next few years. Fred Milton would have been able to wear his mustache and Vandyke after the dust settled, but only in the off-season. But by then, Milton was gone.

Then there was Jack Trice.

Trice played tackle for Iowa State in 1923, the first African-American to play for that school. The night before a game at Minnesota, Trice's first as a Cyclone, he wrote a note to himself. The note read: "The honor of my race, family and self are at stake. Everyone is expecting me to do big things. I will!" Trice went on to say he would play with abandon, without thought of risk.

Trice suffered a broken collarbone early in the game, but insisted on staying in. In the second half, knowing he could not stop the big Minnesota linemen, Trice tried to throw a roll block into three blockers leading a ball-carrier. He was thrown to the ground and run over by the three linemen. Carried from the field, Trice was taken to a Minneapolis hospital where, on the advice of doctors, he was discharged. He returned to Iowa with his team, lying on a bed of straw in a Pullman car. The day after the team's return to Ames, Iowa, Trice died in a hospital. He had hemorrhaging in the lungs and other internal bleeding.

In Trice's day, black athletes faced the humiliation of having to sit out games because of their color, as it was not uncommon for a team to refuse to play against blacks. Trice, so intent upon succeeding, played far beyond his capabilities that day and died as a result; an unnecessary victim of the racial hatred of that day.

When Iowa State built a new stadium in 1980, they named it for Jack Trice.

Acceptance of black football players in major college programs was in motion, but still in a patchwork fashion as the nation moved away from World War II. Jackie Robinson—who would become baseball's black pioneer—and Kenny Washington starred at UCLA, with never an incident, but Chester Pierce and the Harvard team on the other side of the country endured an ugly episode in 1947.

Harvard played at Virginia. Virginia officials were opposed to Harvard's Pierce playing, but players on both sides were good with it, so the school relented. But not its fans. In Charlottesville, Pierce was told he would have to stay in a segregated annex at a town hotel, and that he would have to enter the dining room by a separate entrance.

To a man, the Harvard team insisted on staying in the same accommodations, and entering the dining room through the same door as their black teammate. And so they did, without incident.

Where inclusion of black players moved briskly in the North, it took much longer for it to move at all in the South and the Southwest, and it moved at best at a measured pace in those border states that separated North and South during the Civil War. Indeed, some have described that pace as "glacial." And menacing.

In 1951, Drake University had a remarkable black athlete named Johnny Bright. Bright went to Drake on a split scholarship—basketball and track. Bright was an incredible fast-pitch softball pitcher. His no-hitters were routine. At Drake, he competed in basketball and track, but his stardom came in football. As a sophomore tailback, he led the nation in combined rushing and passing offense with 1,950 yards. He led the nation again as a junior—2,400

yards. And he was on pace to repeat as a senior until Drake played at Oklahoma A&M, a border state school.

On the first play of the game, Bright handed off to a teammate and was standing, hands at his sides, 5 yards behind the play, when A&M defensive lineman Wilbanks Smith broke Bright's jaw with a windup blow with his forearm. Bright's jaw was shattered. He played 7 minutes more and gained 70 yards, but had to leave the game in pain. His jaw had to be wired.

A&M officials first denied any deliberate roughness, but when game films showed the hit to be obvious and deliberate, they apologized. But the Missouri Valley Conference did nothing to penalize A&M despite Drake protests. Drake eventually dropped out of the conference in further protest.

COLLEGE football coaches, it will surprise no one to learn, are avid in their pursuit of blue-chip high school players. The only thing worse, in fact, than failing to recruit a blue-chipper is seeing him in the uniform of a team you're likely to play. Thus it was that, in 1959, Jim Tatum, the coach at North Carolina, called his friend Murray Warmath, the coach at Minnesota. Tatum told Warmath he had a player for him. Tatum told Warmath he'd like to see this young man playing for Minnesota and, especially, he *wouldn't* like to see him playing for a North Carolina opponent. Freely translated: I can't have him, so I sure don't want to have to play against him.

And that's how Bobby Bell got to Minnesota.

Bell played for the Gophers from 1960 through 1962. It is no accident that the sharp improvement in the Gophers' record coincided with Bell's arrival. Bobby played defensive tackle. He could also pass a football 80 yards, but was never called on to do so. He won two varsity letters on Minnesota's basketball

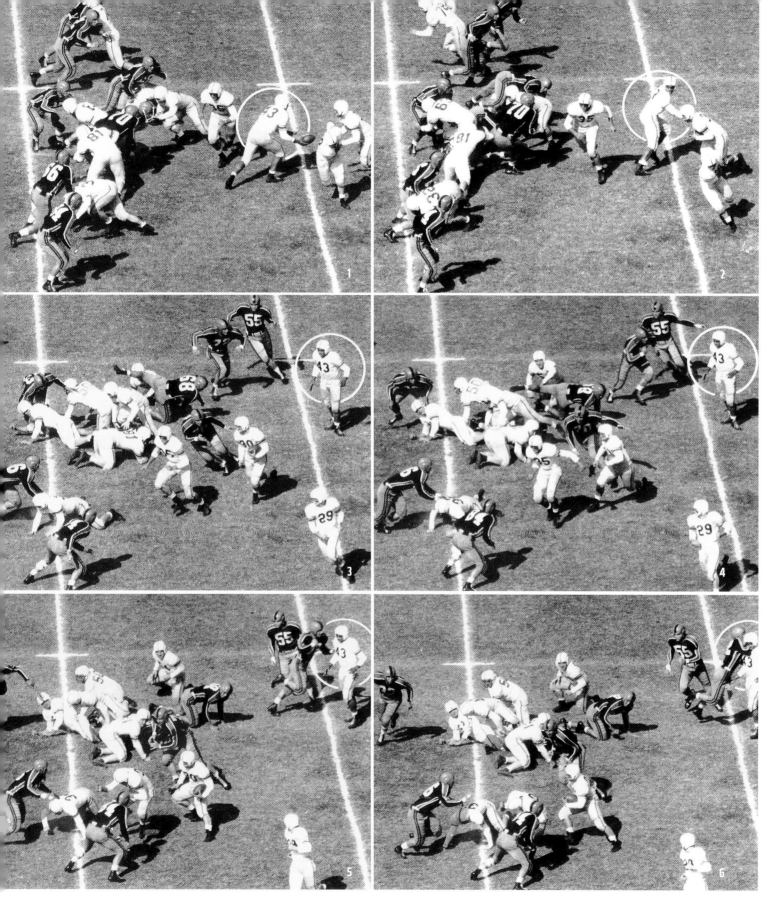

The hit on Johnny Bright. This dramatic sequence shows Drake quarterback Johnny Bright handing off in the upper left frame in a 1951 game against Oklahoma A&M. Five frames later (bottom right) it records him taking a blind-side forearm punch to the face from A&M defensive lineman Wilbanks Smith long after he was out of the play. Bright suffered a broken jaw in the racially inspired incident. Photo by photographers John Robinson and Don Ultang, copyright 1951, The Des Moines Register and Tribune Company. Reprinted by permission.

team. One night at indoor track practice, Bell was hanging around, waiting for a pal on the team. Bored waiting, he took off his shoes and socks and eyed the high jump bar. It was set at six feet. Bobby, with no training in that discipline, cleared it on his second try. He'd even put on skates and work out with the Gopher hockey team. Bobby Bell went on from college to a Hall of Fame pro career with the Kansas City Chiefs, one of the best outside line-backers in the history of the game.

And he fell in Minnesota's lap, because he couldn't play in his home state.

With Bell, a Minnesota pipeline opened. Carl Eller was next, Charlie Sanders would follow. Stars, all.

In 1965, Jerry Levias of Southern Methodist became the first black player in the Southwest Conference. Opponents spit in his face and made flagrant roughness penalties that officials ignored for the most part. Off the field, Levias received hate mail and a death threat. All that, while he was leading the Mustangs to a conference championship.

Crawford, Mississippi, has 668 residents and is about 15 miles from Starkville, the site of Mississippi State University. But in 1981, Crawford's Jerry Rice

Jerry Rice, one of the game's greatest receivers, leaps to haul in a pass for Mississippi Valley State. Catching passes for the Delta Devils from 1981 through 1984, Rice set 18 NCAA Division II records before going on to become one of the NFL's all-time great pass receivers.

went on further west to Itta Bena, population 2,377, where he attended Mississippi Valley State. With Archie "Gunslinger" Cooley as his coach, and Willie Totten as his quarterback, Rice broke 18 NCAA Division II career records and gained 4,693 yards on pass receptions. With the San Francisco 49ers, Rice later became the model all teams look for in a receiver.

EDDIE ROBINSON may be black football's most powerful spokesman. Most of his stories were delightful and homespun, but they were football stories and football's core is neither delightful nor homespun. Eddie liked to recall when he was a boy, and he and his chums played football with a blown-up pig's bladder or a torn-up tire.

"When we played a tough team across town, we used their real ball and got beat real bad. Then a white player from the high school said he'd coach us, and he taught us blocking and tackling and real plays. The next time, we killed those other kids."

No, it is not a homespun game. Not soft. Football is an enamel-hard game; beneath its color and pomp, it is brutal and not very far removed from the time of gladiators. It teaches hard lessons.

"When I went from fifth-string to All America, I made myself a promise," said Jim Brown. "For the rest of my life, I will never let anyone tell me what I can and cannot do."

Joe Taylor, the Hampton University coach, said it more simply, maybe even more eloquently. "Don't let other people decide your world. It'll be too small."

Paul Robeson

"The artist must elect to fight for freedom or slavery. I have made my choice. I had no alternative."

PAUL ROBESON

Football fans and sportswriters referred to him as the "Giant Negro." They were right, although for reasons then largely beyond their vision.

Paul Bustill Robeson played end at Rutgers from 1915 through 1918. He earned 15 varsity letters in four sports. When "Robey" was a sophomore, his football coach, G. Foster Sanford, caved in and benched his star player when Washington & Lee College refused to take the field against a black player. Later that season—regretting his decision—Sanford played Robeson when West Virginia made a similar demand.

Robeson was named to Walter Camp's All-America team in 1918. Away from Rutgers athletic fields, he was the school's star in other venues: scholar, orator, and a singer of great talent. He was admitted to the Phi Beta Kappa honor society as a junior. As a senior, he was the Rutgers class valedictorian. His graduation message was a stirring plea for a government where "character shall be the standard of excellence."

Robeson paid his way through law school by tutoring students in Latin and playing professional football with the Akron Pros. He played through 1922. His law career was even briefer. Assigned to prepare his first brief for a New York law firm, a white secretary refused to take dictation from him. Robeson resigned from the firm and the practice of law.

Paul Robeson, however, would gain America's ear, then the world's, although too often the world found that message nettlesome. His marvelous singing voice quickly won him followings in America and in Europe, but even as he gained star stature, Robeson chafed at the lack of opportunity for other black artists. He and his wife, Essie, preferred London to New York because, as Essie noted, they could "dine as respectable human beings at any public place." In the 1930s, Robeson's voice soared, both in song and social protest, not only for blacks, but for all that were oppressed. He identified with folk music of all races, he said, as "an emotional product developed through suffering." He spoke against Nazi persecution of the Jews and against Fascism in Spain. Bitter that a film he played in depicted blacks as savage children, Robeson shocked Western followers when he accepted an invitation to perform in the Soviet Union. There Robeson perceived all races as being treated equally.

Still popular as a performer, Robeson's ties to communism turned many Americans against him. In 1943, as he was being honored with the Lincoln Medal for service in human relations, the FBI began targeting him for communist sympathies. By the end of World War II Robeson was a trailblazer in civil rights efforts and the rights of dissidents. He addressed pro baseball owners and Commissioner Kenesaw Landis, asking that the ban against black players be removed. In 1947, ignoring threats, Robeson said, "I must raise my voice, but not in pretty songs." Accordingly, his professional career waned as promoters decided he was too controversial. Although he eventually denounced communism, Robeson's protests against racial inequality continued, resulting in increasing tension and penalties. Several attempts were made on his life.

Paul Robeson. Extraordinary athlete and scholar, brilliant performer, blazing reformer, he most wanted the hot, bright light of equality to shine across a dark sky of fear and ignorance. He died in 1976. At his funeral, 5,000 mourners listened to recorded spirituals, sung in Robeson's rich baritone.

End Paul Robeson moves out after catching a pass for Rutgers. Robeson played for the Scarlet Knights from 1915 through 1918 and won All-America honors in 1917 and 1918. A Phi Beta Kappa graduate, he went on to make an even bigger name as an internationally acclaimed singer and actor.

The Press

Sportswriting was more than a craft in the early days of college football. Walter Camp was among the first to report on the game when he wasn't playing, coaching, establishing rules, or picking All-Americas. Following him were the likes of Damon Runyon and Ring Lardner before they turned their hands to literature and humor. Grantland Rice, who nicknamed the 1924 Notre Dame backfield "The Four Horsemen" and Red Grange "The Galloping Ghost," used rich rhetoric and poetry to describe the action of a game or a skilled performance or a coach or player who managed to impress him. Many others filled the newspapers of the 1920s, 1930s, and 1940s with exciting, carefully written accounts of games and the events surrounding college football, fine writers such as Westbrook Pegler, Paul Gallico, Ford Frick, Allison Danzig; later Red Smith, Jimmy Cannon, Dan Jenkins, Frank Deford, and Dave Anderson.

Television came along and brought the action of college football to millions of people who otherwise could not get into a stadium to watch it firsthand. There is little question that the medium of television has had a monumental impact on the popularity of the game of college football. Today, between network television and ESPN cable, no game of consequence goes unrecorded or unbroadcast. On a given Saturday afternoon during the regular season in the twenty-first century, more than seven million homes in America are tuned in to watch a college football game; in the season's grand finale, fans in more than 12 million homes watch the bowl games on television.

TOP ROW
When writing was the name of the game in college football coverage: legendary sportswriters Grantland Rice, Damon Runyon, Ring Lardner.

BOTTOM ROW
When television took over: legendary broadcasters Paul Christman and Curt Gowdy, Chris Schenkel, Keith Jackson.

"When you're playing for the national championship, it's not a matter of life or death. It's more important than that."

DUFFY DAUGHERTY
*Michigan State
Head Coach, 1954–72*

DYNASTIES
ENDURING EXCELLENCE

Caesar . . . Charlemagne . . . William the Conqueror . . . well, college football has had its own dynasty builders: Rockne, Bierman, Blaik, Leahy, Wilkinson, Bryant . . . The dynasties arising from college football's autumn rites have reigned over all areas of the United States. In the East was Army; the Midwest had Notre Dame, Nebraska, Minnesota; the South, Alabama, Florida State, and Miami; the Southwest, Oklahoma; and the Far West, Southern Cal.

Teams from what is known today as the Ivy League compete in the NCAA's Division I-AA—its high minor leagues. But in the 1800s and the first decade of the twentieth century, the nation's powerhouse college football teams were Yale, Princeton, Harvard, and Pennsylvania, the only interloper in that exalted circle perhaps being mighty Michigan under Fielding Yost.

Yale was certainly the preeminent force. In the years from 1876 through 1909, many of them under the leadership of Walter Camp, the Elis or Bulldogs, call them what you will, sustained the first and longest dynasty in college football. During those 34 years, Yale won 315 games while losing only 14 and tying 18, a phenomenal winning percentage of .934, featuring memorable players like Frank Hinkey and Pudge Heffelfinger. Princeton, with stars like Edgar Allan Poe and Knowlton Ames, however, was not far behind; from 1877 through 1903 they won 90 percent of their games, turning in an overall record of 233-21-11 for those 27 years. Pennsylvania won 168 games while losing 21 and tying 7 during the period from 1894 to 1908, a win percentage of .875, while its roster claimed such stars of the day as Truxton Hare, Charles Gelbert, and George Brooke. Harvard, which blossomed a little later, was most successful

In the 1800s, Yale was perhaps the first team that produced a dynasty. Granted there was not as much competition in the early days of college football, but the Elis took it seriously and after first playing intercollegiately in 1872 they never had a losing season during that century (although they were 2-2-0 in 1875). The 1888 team pictured here was 13-0, not only undefeated but unscored upon as well, defeating their rivals 698—0.

in the eight years beginning with 1908 and ending after the 1915 season, posting a record of 64-4-5, for an impressive .911 winning percentage. The Crimson got a lot of help during that time from great performers like Hamilton Fish, Percy Wendell, Eddie Mahan, and Charles Brickley.

In the Midwest, Fielding Yost's Michigan teams were invincible. From 1901 through 1909, the Wolverines won 75 games against only 6 losses and 2 ties, an extraordinary .916 percentage. Just how invincible? In 1901 they outscored their opponents 550–0; in 1902, 644–12; in 1903, 565–6: that invincible. Michigan had an impressive roster of greats to help achieve those feats, foremost among them Willie Heston, the first truly great running back in the game, and Germany Schultz, one of the game's premier lineman.

We have chosen to profile here twelve of the most dramatic college football dynasties of the twentieth century. They illustrate above all others, we believe, the enduring excellence that has been achieved on college football fields by only the rare few. All have won at an extraordinary rate, and all have captured multiple national championships. What constitutes a dynasty in college football? Sustained success over a period of years, at least seven or eight. Often a dynasty is associated with a single coach—a Rockne, a Wilkinson, or a Bryant— but it is more than that. A coach, good as he may be, does not produce dominating teams year after year merely by his sideline genius. It is a unique combination of great coaching and awesome talent, inextricably woven together. And in college football, the talent changes from year to year; the life span of a star—or any starter, for that matter—is no more that three years. But the domination goes on, the enduring excellence of that special pact between coaches and their players.

Dynasties of a slightly lesser stature also deserve recognition, and so we list them here:

Pittsburgh	1913—20	55-5-4 (.891)
Southern Cal	1919—33	129-18-3 (.870)
Tennessee	1938—46	72-9-2 (.880)
Michigan	1940—48	68-13-2 (.831)
Michigan State	1950—66	117-37-4 (.753)
Ohio State	1954—61	56-14-4 (.784)
Texas	1961—72	107-21-2 (.831)
Nebraska	1969—76	79-14-4 (.835)
Penn State	1980—87	76-19-1 (.797)
Florida	1990—99	102-22-1 (.820)

Now on to the very best that college football has had to offer.

THE DYNASTIES

NOTRE DAME (1918—30)

In 1918, Knute Rockne, who had been an assistant coach at Notre Dame since 1914, succeeded Jesse Harper as the head coach and launched a 13-year era of sustained excellence unmatched in the school's long and distinguished football history. The Rock, as he came to be known, was born in Voss, Norway, and was 26 years old when he took charge of the Fighting Irish.

During the Rockne era, Notre Dame teams compiled a record of 105 wins against only 12 losses and 5 ties, a winning percentage of .881, the highest recorded by a coach in college football history. It prompted fellow coaching legend Pop Warner to observe in an article he wrote for the *Saturday Evening Post* in 1934, "No one ever asked me to pick the greatest football coach of all time, but if I were asked I would unhesitatingly name Rockne. . . . It

LEFT
Notre Dame's 1924 team, which featured the Four Horsemen: quarterback Harry Stuhldreyer, right halfback Don Miller, fullback Elmer Layden, and left halfback Jim Crowley. The line, from the left: Ed Hunsinger, Rip Miller, Noble Kizer, Adam Walsh, John Weibel, Joe Boch and Chuck Collins. This Fighting Irish team was 9-0 in the regular season, defeated Stanford 27—10 in the Rose Bowl, and was acclaimed national champions of 1924.

BELOW
Knute Rockne (left) goes one-on-one with a Notre Dame blocker in a practice at South Bend in the 1920s. The Rock guided Notre Dame from 1918 through 1930, and his entire career is considered a dynasty. His Notre Dame teams won 105 games while losing only 12 and tying five and captured three national titles.

who shone for Notre Dame during Rockne's dynastic rule were end and captain of the 1921 team Eddie Anderson, end Rodge Kiley, guard Heartley "Hunk" Anderson, fullback Johnny Mohardt, halfback Paul Castner, tackle Buck Shaw, center and captain of the 1924 team Adam Walsh, halfback Christy Flanagan, guard and captain of the 1927 team John "Clipper" Smith, tackles Bull Polisky, Fred Miller, and Ted Twomey, guard Jack Cannon, quarterback Frank Carideo, fullback Joe Savoldi, halfbacks Marty Brill and Marchy Schwartz, and end and captain of Rockne's last team (1930) Tom Conley.

The longest winning streak during that period was 22 games, begun in 1918 when Gipp was at his prime. During those years, Notre Dame also posted three other unbeaten streaks of 15 games or more. Rockne's fiery and eloquent pep talks worked, but he also had quite a bit to work with.

MINNESOTA (1933—41)

The nine-year period just before America's entry into World War II was the greatest in the history of the University of Minnesota, producing one of the

was Rockne's personality and ability as a coach, together with his willingness to depart from the merely orthodox and traditional, that gave Notre Dame successful football seasons."

Rockne, of course, did not create a dynasty by himself. He was aided by a magnificent cast of players that ranged from the talented (and quite unorthodox himself) halfback George Gipp to the fabled Four Horsemen, the Seven Mules (the line that blocked for them), and the Watchcharm Guard (the 145-pound Bert Metzger). Among the other stars most impressive dynasties in all college football. Bernie Bierman, dubbed "The Silver Fox of the Northland" for his prematurely gray hair, was captain of the 1915 Minnesota team and coached at Montana, Mississippi State, and Tulane before returning to his alma mater as head coach in 1932.

During that prewar period, Bierman's Golden Gophers won six Big Ten titles and four national championships (1934, 1936, 1940, 1941). His Minnesota teams were unbeaten in 1933 (although they were tied four times that year), 1934, 1935, 1940, and 1941. The 1935 Gophers shared the national title with Louisiana State. Defense was the hallmark of Bierman-coached teams, and during the nine-year dynasty Minnesota defenses shut out 25 opponents in their 72 games. Their record through those years was 58 wins, 9 defeats, and 5 ties. Despite Minnesota's overwhelming dominance during that period, however, they were never invited to a bowl game.

The most honored player on Bierman's teams during that era was halfback Bruce Smith, who won the 1941 Heisman Trophy. Other Minnesota All-Americas in the years from 1932 through 1941 were

Minnesota coach Bernie Bierman. The dynasty that Bierman spearheaded at Minnesota came earlier in his career, 1933–41, a period in which his Gophers won four national championships and shared another.

end Frank Larson, guard Bill Bevan, triple-threat back Pug Lund, and tackles Ed Widseth, Urban Odson, and Dick Wildung.

Bierman, a quiet, shy man, made it a practice to avoid speaking engagements, was the antithesis of fellow dynasty-builder Knute Rockne. According to *New York Times* sportswriter Allison Danzig, "He did not believe in whipping up his men into an emotional state before they went on the field. . . . He thought a group of calm, determined men was more effective. He is said never to have shouted at any of his players. . . . During intermission it was his custom to read to the team from a paper on which he had noted their mistakes in the first half, rather than to give a fiery pep talk." It certainly worked well for him through the seasons of 1933 through 1941.

ARMY (1943–50)

The lyrics "On brave old Army team" were never more lustrous than when the Cadets sang them out in the 1940s. Not since Ollie Oliphant carried the ball for Army in the 1910s or Chris Cagle in the 1920s had the Cadets experienced such football grandeur as they did with the great teams that came out of the war years and continued through the remainder of the 1940s.

Earl Blaik had taken over as head coach in 1941 and by 1943 he had the beginning of a dynasty. World War II, of course, had depleted the rosters of most schools while Army was attracting the finest football talent in the nation. So dominant was Army in 1944 that they not only went unbeaten, they collectively defeated their nine opponents 504 to 35, including a 59–0 annihilation of Notre Dame, and easily captured the national championship. Equally awesome the next year, Army again went 9-0, this

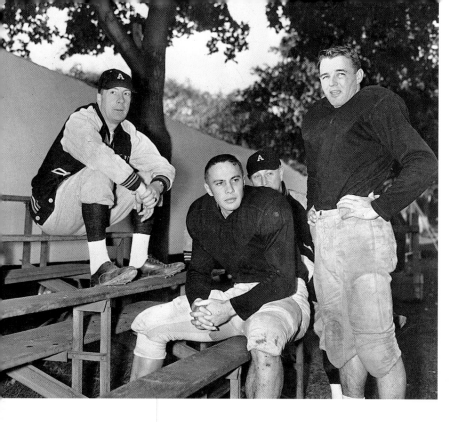

time outscoring their victims 412 to 46, and humiliating Notre Dame 48–0, while recording a second national title. In 1946, the Cadets were 9-0-1, the tie, 0–0, with a refurbished Notre Dame team costing Army that year's national championship.

The Cadets fielded in those three years what became the most famous backfield duet in college football history, fullback Doc Blanchard and halfback Glenn Davis, aka Mr. Inside and Mr. Outside, who respectively won the Heisman Trophies for 1945 and 1946. In 1948 and 1949, led by quarterback Arnold Galiffa, Army also went undefeated. In 1950, a bid for a third consecutive unbeaten season, however, was thwarted when the Cadets fell to arch-rival Navy in the last game of the year 14–2, the loss also signaling the end of Army's dynasty.

During those eight years of glory, Army had a record of 64-5-5 for a winning percentage of .899. The teams were laced with truly outstanding players: quarterback Arnold Tucker, halfbacks Shorty McWilliams

and Bobby Stuart, fullback Rip Rowan, ends Barney Poole and Hank and Dan Foldberg, Outland Award winning guard Joe Steffy, center Jim Enos, tackles Tex Coulter and Goble Bryant, guards John Green and Joe Henry, linebacker Elmer Stout, and defensive linemen Charles Shira and J. D. Kimmel.

Earl Blaik continued on at Army through most of the 1950s, but Army would never regain the eminence it commanded in the 1940s.

NOTRE DAME (1946–53)

Frank Leahy had played for Knute Rockne, as a lineman in 1929 until a knee injury ended his playing career, so he knew what a dynasty was when he returned to Notre Dame as head coach in 1946. The eight-year period in which he guided the Fighting Irish destiny was a half-decade short of Rockne's dynasty, but it was as dramatically successful. His Notre Dame teams were victorious in 87 of the 107 games they played, a win percentage of .855 (overall, including his two-year tenure at Boston College, Leahy was .864; Notre Dame *lowered* his career winning percentage), just short of Rockne's .881. Among the long history of college coaches, Rockne and Leahy rank No. 1 and 2 in winning percentage.

Leahy's first stint coaching at Notre Dame, 1941–43, was superb: 24-3-3. But his greatest years— his dynasty—did not truly begin until the 1946 season, when he returned from serving with the Navy in the Pacific during World War II. That first postwar team was one of the greatest of all time. With Johnny Lujack at quarterback, Terry Brennan and Emil Sitko at halfbacks, Jim Mello at fullback, Jim Martin and Jack Zilly at the ends, and a line that consisted of tackles George Connor and Ziggy Czarobski, guards Bill Fischer and John

Mastrangelo, and center George Strohmeyer, they went undefeated and in one of the college game's most classic matchups played the equally great Army team to a 0–0 tie.

The 1946 Notre Dame team, who outscored their opponents 271–24, was awarded the national championship (even though Army's record, 9-0-1, was slightly better than the Irish's 8-0-1), and they took that coveted honor again in 1947 and 1949. Over the next seven years Leahy's Irish would compile a record of 63 wins against just 8 losses and 6 ties, for a win percentage of .857. Their unbeaten streak of 39 games stretched over a five-season period (1946–50), during which they won 37 games and tied 2. It is the ninth longest in college football history.

Notre Dame produced three Heisman Trophy winners during that era—Johnny Lujack in 1947; Leon Hart, 1949; Johnny Lattner, 1953—and a host of All-Americas: tackles George Connor, Ziggy Czarobski, Bob Toneff, and Art Hunter; guards Bill Fischer, Marty Wendell, and John Mastrangelo; ends Jim Martin, Leon Hart, and Jim Mutscheller; halfback/fullback Emil Sitko; quarterback Bob Williams; and center Jerry Groom. Leahy, it could be said, had a lot to work with.

As Arthur Daley wrote in the *New York Times* just before Leahy's retirement after the 1953 season, "Rock gave Frank his start, but everything else that Leahy attained is his own. Notre Dame can be proud of him."

OKLAHOMA (1948–58)

No team in college football history has won as many consecutive games as the 47 strung together by the Oklahoma Sooners from 1953 to 1957; no school has even come close. Bud Wilkinson, who took over as

head coach in 1947, generated teams that were just the opposite of those he played on under Bernie Bierman at Minnesota in the mid-1930s. Where Bierman stressed defense, Wilkinson's teams were typified by an explosive offense; Bierman's grind-it-out style of offense from the single wing was a far cry from Wilkinson's ground attack, which worked out of the split T and was based on speed and quickness.

During the 11-year dynasty that Wilkinson controlled from 1948 through 1958, his Sooners won 107 games, losing only 8 and tying 2, for a phenomenal win percentage of .923—like Joe DiMaggio's 56-game hitting streak a record unlikely ever to be broken. Oklahoma won three national championships during those years: 1950, 1955, and 1956. They went to eight bowl games and triumphed in six of them.

No one facilitated Wilkinson's offense more than halfback Billy Vessels, the 1952 Heisman Trophy winner. But he was just one of the great running backs who helped Wilkinson's cause over those years, others were halfbacks Tommy McDonald, Clendon Thomas, and George Thomas and fullbacks Leon

Coach Bud Wilkinson oversees the celebration as his Sooners raise the bronze Cowboy Hat, possession of which goes each year to the winner of the Oklahoma–Texas game, after defeating the Longhorns 20–14 in 1949. It was Wilkinson's first victory over arch-rival Texas, a highlight of his first undefeated season. The Oklahoma dynasty covered the period from 1948 to 1958 and included three national titles.

Heath and Buck McPhail. Among the other outstanding Oklahoma players of that era were quarterbacks Jack Mitchell, Eddie Crowder, and Darrell Royal; ends Jimmy Owens, Frankie Anderson, and Max Boydston; guards Buddy Burris, Stanley West, J. D. Roberts, and Bo Bollinger; tackles Wade Walker, Jim Weatherall, and Ed Gary; and centers Tom Catlin, Kurt Burris, and Jerry Tubbs.

No school in college football history has put together a success story greater than the one Bud Wilkinson wrote with his wide-open, fast-paced attack in the 11-year dynasty at Oklahoma. As it was described in an official NCAA publication, "Many felt this particular span featured the greatest accomplishment in modern-day college football."

ALABAMA (1959—67 AND 1971—80)

Coach Paul "Bear" Bryant, who attained well-deserved legendary status at Alabama, is the only coach credited with putting together *two* dynasties. It took him only a year after taking over the head coaching job at Alabama in 1958 to launch the first, which would last nine years. During that period, the Bear's Crimson Tide posted a record of 83-10-6, a winning percentage of .869, capturing three national championships along the way: 1961, 1964, and 1965. And in five of those nine years, 1963 through 1967, his teams never lost a single home game in Tuscaloosa.

Only Bryant's 1962 team did not receive an invitation to a bowl game, and of the eight they did attend during that era Alabama triumphed in six. Two of the most memorable quarterbacks in modern college history helped Bryant maintain his dynastic run, Joe Namath, 1962–64, and Kenny Stabler, 1965–67. There was also consensus All-American Lee Roy Jordan, who played both center

Bear Bryant leads his Crimson tide onto the field. Bryant is credited with two distinct dynasties while coaching at Alabama: the first, 1959—67, during which the Tide won three national championships and posted a record of 83-10-6; and 1971—80, when they won 107 games while losing only 13 and capturing another three national titles.

and linebacker, and such other outstanding players as split ends Ray Perkins and Dennis Homan; halfback David Ray and fullback Steve Bowman; offensive linemen Wayne Freeman, Dan Kearley, Paul Crane, and Cecil Dowdy; defensive linemen Billy Neighbors and Richard Cole; and defensive back Bobby Johns.

There followed a three-year interlude between dynasties, although all three seasons were above .500. The second Bryant dynasty began in 1971 with Alabama winning its first SEC championship since 1966, an 11-1 season, and a trip to the Orange Bowl. During this 10-year span the Bear's Crimson Tide compiled an even better record than the first dynasty, winning 107 of 120 games to post a win percentage of .892. They again won three national

championships: 1973, 1978, and 1979, and went 28 consecutive games without a loss or a tie during a period from 1978 to 1980.

The stars in Bryant's cast during this golden era were not of the marquee quality perhaps of Namath and Stabler, but they did help him win more games. Among such outstanding players were quarterbacks Terry Davis and Richard Todd; running backs Johnny Musso, Wilbur Jackson, Willie Shelby, and Major Ogilvie, and fullback Johnnie Davis; and split ends David Bailey, Wayne Wheeler, and Ozzie Newsome. The team also featured such certified All-Americas as offensive guard John Hannah; offensive tackles Buddy Brown and Jim Bunch; center Dwight Stephenson; defensive tackle Marty Lyons; and defensive ends Leroy Cook and E. J. Junior.

Bear Bryant, as it turned out, won more games as a major college coach—Eddie Robinson's Grambling teams play in the NCAA's Divison I-AA—than anyone in history. He recorded his 323rd and final victory in 1982, 232 of which he won for Alabama. Two dynasties, one of nine years' duration and the other of 10, put together during his 25 years at the helm of the Crimson Tide, was the Bear's legacy to Alabama. Not bad.

SOUTHERN CAL (1967–79)

It was the age of the great running back in sunny Southern California, the late 1960s and the 1970s. Trojan teams under the guidance of two coaches, John McKay and John Robinson, virtually ran over almost every opponent in the 13 years from 1967 to 1979. First, it was Heisman Trophy winner O. J. Simpson carrying the ball in 1967 and 1968; then it was Clarence Davis in 1969 and 1970, Anthony Davis in 1972 and 1973, Ricky Bell in 1975 and 1976,

and finally Charles White from 1977 to 1979 (who won the Heisman in 1979).

John McKay, who had come to USC as head coach in 1960, guided the Trojans through the first nine years of the dynasty, John Robinson the last four. During those 13 years, Southern Cal won 122 games, losing just 23 and tying 7, a win percentage of .826. Three of the McKay-led teams won national championships: 1967, 1972, and 1974; John Robinson captured another in 1978. Robinson's Trojans also put together an unbeaten streak of 28 games that began in 1978 and extended into 1980.

The Trojans turned in three undefeated seasons: 10-0-1 in 1969, 12-0 in 1972, and 11-0-1 in 1979, and in five other years they lost only a single game. Eight times during the dynasty Southern Cal represented the Pac-10 in the Rose Bowl, winning six times (teams of 1967, 1969, 1972, 1974, 1976, and 1978). The 1975 team went to the Liberty Bowl and beat Texas A&M, and the Trojans of 1977 visited the Bluebonnet Bowl where they again defeated the Texas Aggies.

John McKay, pictured here, was one of two coaches who put together the Southern Cal dynasty that ran from 1967 to 1979; the other, John Robinson. Under McKay, who coached the Trojans from 1960 to 1975 and the first nine years of the dynasty, Southern Cal won three national titles; Robinson coached the remaining four years and added another national title.

The Oklahoma dynasty under Barry Switzer, 1971–80, was highlighted by a 37-game unbeaten streak, back-to-back national championships (1974, 1975), and 10 consecutive Big Eight titles.

Besides Heisman honorees Simpson and White, Southern Cal produced 13 other consensus All-Americas during that 13-year run: running backs Anthony Davis and Ricky Bell; offensive tackles Ron Yary and Booker Brown; offensive guard Brad Budde; linebackers Adrian Young and Richard Wood; defensive ends Tim Rossovich, Jimmy Gunn, and Charles Weaver; flanker Lynn Swann; and defensive backs Artimus Parker and Dennis Thurman. Yary won the Outland Trophy in 1967, and Budde the Lombardi Trophy in 1979.

And perhaps a more enduring mark, one far dearer to the hearts of diehard Trojan fans, Southern Cal triumphed over long-standing rival Notre Dame nine times during those 13 years, tied them twice, and lost only twice.

OKLAHOMA (1971–80)

Bud Wilkinson had been gone from Oklahoma's sidelines for eight years, but still cast an enormous shadow when Barry Switzer arrived in Norman, Oklahoma, in 1966. For the next seven years Switzer would serve as an assistant coach under Chuck Fairbanks before taking over the head coaching job The starting point for the Sooner dynasty of the 1970s began while Switzer was still the team's offensive coordinator in 1970 when he convinced head coach Fairbanks to change to the wishbone offense, which had been serving so well Oklahoma's fiercest rival, Texas, in recent years.

With the wishbone, a triple-option attack, in place, the Sooners turned in an 11-1 season for 1971, scoring a Sooner record high 534 points. In 1973, Switzer began a head coaching career that would sustain the dynasty and eventually make him Oklahoma's all-time winningest coach.

During the 10-year run that ended with the 1980 season, Oklahoma compiled a record of 102 wins against 14 losses and 2 ties, for a winning percentage of .873, and won back-to-back national championships in 1974 and 1975. They won the Big Eight conference title in each of those 10 years, and put together a 37-game unbeaten streak in which they were tied only once from 1972 to 1975 (Switzer's teams accounted for 28 of those wins).

Fairbanks and Switzer had some pretty spectacular help in winning all those games. Fairbanks had All-American Greg Pruitt carrying the ball for him, while Switzer had Joe Washington and later Billy Sims. And on defense were two-time All-American defensive tackle Lee Roy Selmon, Lee Roy's brothers Dewey and Lucious, both noseguards; linebackers Rod Shoate and George Cumby; defensive end Jimbo Elrod; and defensive back Zac Henderson. Other honored Sooner players of the 1970s included quarterback Jack Mildren; center Tom Brahaney; split ends Tinker Owens and Billy Brooks; tackles Derland Moore, Eddie Foster, and Mike Vaughn; center Kyle Davis; guards John Roush, Terry Webb, Greg Roberts, and Terry Crouch; linebacker Daryl Hunt; and noseguard Reggie Kinlaw.

MIAMI (FLORIDA) (1983–92)

The dynasty developed in the south of Florida during the 1980s and early 1990s was the work of three head coaches: Howard Schnellenberger, Jimmy Johnson, and Dennis Erickson. The first year belongs to Schnellenberger, the last four to Erickson; the five in between are Johnson's.

It was quite a first year, too. The Hurricanes were 11-1 at the end of the regular season and an 11-point underdog when they met Nebraska in the Orange Bowl, but they beat the Cornhuskers that New Year's Day 31–30 in one of the most exciting bowl games ever; the victory earned Miami its first national championship. The Hurricanes would win three more national titles during their years of dynasty, one under Jimmy Johnson, 1987, and two behind Dennis Erickson, 1989 and 1991.

During the 10-year run, Miami triumphed in 107 of the 121 games they played, a winning percentage of .884. They went to a bowl game for each of the 10 seasons. Besides Schnellenberger's famous victory in the Orange, Johnson took the Hurricanes to the Sugar, twice to the Fiesta, and twice to the Orange, while Erickson led them to the Sugar and Fiesta once and twice to the Orange.

Two Heisman Trophies went to Hurricanes during the dynasty, both quarterbacks, Vinny Testaverde in 1986 and Gino Torretta in 1992. Defensive tackle Russell Maryland won the Outland Award in 1990. All-America honors were also earned by wide receiver Eddie Brown; tight end Willie Smith; quarterback Steve Walsh; linebackers Maurice Crum and Michael Barrow; defensive backs Bennie Blades, Darryl Williams, and Ryan McNeil; defensive linemen Jerome Brown, Daniel Stubbs, Bill Hawkins, and Greg Mark; and placekicker Carlos Huerta.

Miami of the 1980s and early 1990s stands as living proof that college football dynasties are not made of one coach alone.

ABOVE

(left) Jimmy Johnson stalks the sideline; (right) Dennis Erickson proclaims victory. Miami won four national championships during their dynastic reign from 1983 through 1992, under three different coaches: Howard Schnellenberger (1983, one national title), Jimmy Johnson (1984–87, one national title), Dennis Erickson (1988–92, two national titles).

NEBRASKA (1988—97)

This was the most impressive segment of Tom Osborne's 25-year career as head coach of Nebraska, a 10-year run during which his teams had a record of 108-15-1, posting a win percentage of .875. On the other hand a case could be made that his *entire* career leading the Cornhuskers, from 1973 through 1997, was a dynasty because he was .836 over all those years (255-49-3) and not one of his 25 teams ever won fewer than nine games in a season. Nor did one of his teams ever miss going to a bowl game (only Penn State's Joe Paterno has taken his team to more bowl games than Osborne).

In the last quarter of the twentieth century, no team in college football was as consistently successful as Nebraska, and their record of attending 32 consecutive bowls, beginning with the 1969 team and still going in the twenty-first century, stands as a college football milestone.

Tom Osborne, here on the Cornhuskers sideline, spent 25 years as head coach of Nebraska, 10 of which constituted a dynasty (1988—97), although diehard Cornhusker fans claim his entire career at the school was a dynasty. Winning 108 games in those 10 years against only 15 losses and one tie, he claimed two national titles for Nebraska and shared another.

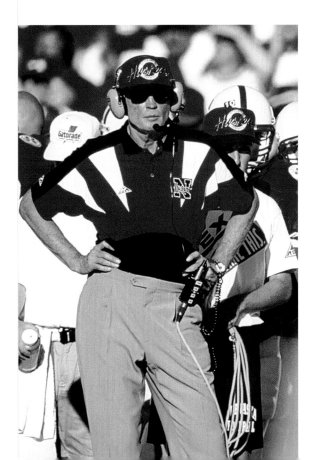

During the period from 1988 through 1997, Osborne's Cornhuskers won back-to-back national championships, 1994 and 1995, and they shared the 1997 national title with Michigan, both teams going undefeated that year. Only a last-second field goal by Florida State in the Orange Bowl deprived Osborne's otherwise undefeated 1994 Nebraskans of a fourth national championship during that era. The Cornhuskers also ran a win streak of 26 games from 1994 to 1996, and a 47-game victory streak at home in Lincoln from 1991 to 1998.

A host of All-Americas played for Nebraska during those years: quarterback Tommie Frazier, linebackers Broderick Thomas, Ed Stewart, and Trev Alberts, center Jake Young, offensive linemen Will Shields, Zach Wiegert, Brenden Stai, and Aaron Taylor, and defensive linemen Grant Wistrom and Jason Peter. In years outside the dynasty, Osborne also coached such shining stars as running back Mike Rozier, wide receiver Irving Fryar, and two-time Outland Award–winning center Dave Rimington.

FLORIDA STATE (1987—)

Four hundred twenty-five miles north of Miami is the state capital of Tallahassee, home to the Florida State Seminoles. It is here that Bobby Bowden established his own Florida dynasty—one that began in the middle of Miami's and has yet to come to an end. Bowden's was longer and just a little more successful than the one established by Miami's triumvirate of coaches: the Seminoles won 152 games against 18 losses and 1 tie over the 14 years from 1987 through 2000, a win percentage of .892, a scant .008 ahead of the mark posted by the Hurricanes during their 10-year run.

Bowden and the brilliant teams he coached during those years accomplished one feat that no other NCAA Division I-A school has in the long history of college football: they won 10 or more games in 14 consecutive seasons, a record still ongoing as of this writing. Just how consistently Florida State was at the top of the polls during those years is evidenced by the fact that the Seminoles ended each of those 14 years within the top five teams in the Associated Press national rankings.

They went to a bowl each year during that period as well, and won 11 of them, between 1985 and 1996, a college football record. The Seminoles were able to post just one undefeated season—1999—but they lost only one game during each of eight other years and never lost more than two. They won the national championship in 1993 and 1999, and were runners-up twice, in 1987 and 1992.

The biggest names found on the back of Florida State jerseys were undoubtedly those of defensive back Deion Sanders and Heisman Trophy—winning quarterbacks Charlie Ward (1993) and Chris Weinke

(2000). Quite a few others, however, earned consensus All-America status: cornerbacks Leroy Butler, Terrell Buckley, and Clifton Abraham; linebackers Marvin Jones, Derrick Brooks, and Sam Cowart; center Clay Shiver; defensive ends Peter Boulware and Andre Wadsworth; wide receiver Peter Warrick; defensive tackle Corey Simon; offensive guard Jason Whitaker; and placekicker Sebastian Janikowski.

Florida State is the only school to take its dynasty into the twenty-first century.

Like the Duracell battery: And still going strong . . .

THE GREATEST TEAMS OF THE TWENTIETH CENTURY

As arbitrary perhaps as a selection of the greatest players in the history of the game is a presumptuous list of the greatest teams. Citing great teams is fairly obvious; but *the* greatest, that's where the controversy enters, the arguments open, and often the impartiality ends. However, it has never stopped sportswriters and broadcasters, fans and followers, even coaches.

We—the author and the experts from the ESPN television series *Rites of Autumn*—are no different, and have listed the most outstanding teams of each decade. Beyond that we have taken it upon ourselves to select *the* team of each decade: let the arguments begin.

The 1900s
MICHIGAN, 1901

All of Fielding Yost's Michigan teams in the early 1900s were great. From 1901 to 1905, they lost only 1 game and tied another, while winning 55. The 1901 squad, undefeated in 11 games, outscored its opponents 550—0 (Buffalo fell to them 128—0, and their closest game was a 21—0 win over Ohio State). On New Year's Day 1902, the Wolverines played in the first Rose Bowl game and routed Stanford 49—0. Willie Heston was only a freshman that year but he was already spectacular, and Neil Snow, who played both tackle and fullback, was another great one. As good as Stagg's 1905 Chicago team, spearheaded by Walter Eckersall, was, they would still fall short of Yost's "Point-a-Minute" Wolverines of 1901.

And who could forget . . .

SCHOOL/YEAR	RECORD	COACH	STARS	
Michigan/1902	11-0-0	Fielding Yost	Willie Heston	HB
			Boss Weeks	QB
			Tug Wilson	G
			Dan McGugin	G
			Al Herrinstein	HB
Chicago/1905	9-0-0	Amos A. Stagg	Walter Eckersall	QB
			Mark Catlin	E
			Hugo Bezdek	FB
			Fred Walker	HB
Yale/1907	9-0-1	Samuel Morse	Tad Jones	QB
			Clarence Alcott	E
			Ted Coy	HB
			Horatio Biglow	T
Yale/1909	10-0-0	Howard Jones	Ted Coy	HB
			John Kilpatrick	E
			Henry Hobbs	T
			Hamlin Andruss	G
			Carroll Cooney	C
			Steve Philbin	HB

The 1910s
NOTRE DAME, 1919

Knute Rockne used to lapse into euphoria when he described the 1913 Notre Dame team, the one with which he and back Gus Dorais startled the football world with the forward pass. But the team he coached in 1919 to a perfect season, 9-0-0, was certainly the best of that decade. George Gipp was a junior, fast becoming one of the most famous names in the game. With Dutch Bergman at the other halfback, Pete Bahan at quarterback, and Johnny Mohardt at fullback they vanquished their opponents 229—47 that year. Among other notables on the 1919 Irish squad were end Eddie Anderson and guard Hunk Anderson.

And who could forget . . .

SCHOOL/YEAR	RECORD	COACH	STARS	
Carlisle/1911	11-0-0	Pop Warner	Jim Thorpe	HB
Carlisle/1912	12-1-1	Pop Warner	Joe Guyon	HB
Harvard/1912	9-0-0	Percy Haughton	Charley Brickley	HB
			Sam Felton	E
			Stan Pennock	G
			Percy Wendell	HB
Notre Dame/1913	7-0-0	Jesse Harper	Gus Dorais	QB
			Ray Eichenlaub	FB
			Knute Rockne	E
			Joe Pliska	HB
Georgia Tech/1917	9-0-0	John Heisman	Joe Guyon	HB
			Ev Strupper	HB

The 1920s
ILLINOIS, 1923

A very tough choice. Notre Dame of 1924, with the Four Horsemen, is one of the most famous football teams of all time. But they also played weaklings like Lombard, Wabash, and Carnegie Tech. Bob Zuppke's Illinois team in 1923 was a masterpiece, with consensus All-American sophomore Red Grange; Earl Britton, a marvelous blocking back and kicker; Harry Hall at quarterback; plus a tremendous line anchored by All-American guard Jim McMillen. Undefeated in eight games in 1923, they never even came close to losing one. Their single wing with a split line, Grange's sweeping end runs, and novel trap blocking made the Illini unbeatable, and better, we believe, than Rockne's dynamic team of 1924.

And who could forget . . .

SCHOOL/YEAR	RECORD	COACH	STARS	
Iowa/1921	7-0-0	Howard Jones	Aubrey Devine	QB
			Gordon Locke	HB
			Duke Slater	G
Cornell/1922	8-0-0	Gil Dobie	George Pfann	QB
			Eddie Kaw	HB
Notre Dame/1924	10-0-0	Knute Rockne	Harry Stuhldreyer	QB
			Jim Crowley	HB
			Elmer Layden	FB
			Don Miller	HB
			Adam Walsh	C

The 1930s
ALABAMA, 1934

This may have been the best Alabama team ever, outshining even the Bear Bryant—coached powerhouses a few decades later. Under Frank Thomas, the Crimson Tide crushed opponent after opponent; 9-0-0 in the regular season, and outscoring their opponents 316—45, they capped the year with a 29—13 victory over Stanford in the Rose Bowl. Thomas's Tide had three consensus All-Americans: triple-threat back Dixie Howell; Don Hutson, whose pass receiving and end-arounds dazzled everyone; and Bill Lee, one of the most savage blockers and tacklers in the game. Alabama's other end that year was, coincidentally enough, Bear Bryant. Jock Sutherland's 1937 Pittsburgh Panthers, with everybody's All-American Marshall Goldberg, were also a great team, but they couldn't beat Fordham and its Seven Blocks of Granite.

And who could forget . . .

SCHOOL/YEAR	RECORD	COACH	STARS	
Tennessee/1931	9-0-1	Bob Neyland	Beattie Feathers	HB
			Herman Hickman	G
			Bobby Dodd	QB
			Gene McEvery	HB
Minnesota/1935	8-0-0	Bernie Bierman	Bud Wilkinson	QB
			Andy Uram	HB
			Ed Widseth	T
			Frank Larson	E
			Bill Bevan	G
Pittsburgh/1937	9-0-1	Jock Sutherland	Marshall Goldberg	HB
			Frank Patrick	HB
			Tony Matisi	T
Tennessee/1938	11-0-0	Bob Neyland	George Cafego	HB
			Bowden Wyatt	E
			Bob Suffridge	G
			Ed Molinski	G

-WESTERN CHAMPIONS-

ABOVE
Knute Rockne's 1919 Notre Dame national championship team.

LEFT
Red Grange, star running back for Illinois, 1923–25.

RIGHT
Willie Heston, Michigan's star halfback, 1901–4.

The 1940s

ARMY, 1945

What a decade for college football: the dominant Army teams of the war years with Mr. Inside, Doc Blanchard, and Mr. Outside, Glenn Davis; Notre Dame of 1947, with Johnny Lujack and George Connor; then Michigan of 1948, showcasing Bob Chappius and Bump Elliott, were outstanding. But the Army team of 1945, coached by Earl "Red" Blaik, stands as one of the most outstanding teams ever. Granted Army's competition was not that severe in 1944 and 1945 because of the war, but they were an undeniably marvelous team. Besides Blanchard and Davis in the backfield there was quarterback Arnold Tucker and halfback Shorty McWilliams; and on the line such stalwarts as Tex Coulter, John Green, and Jim Enos; and Barney Poole and Hank Foldberg were two of the best ends in the nation.

Fullback Doc Blanchard (35) gains some yardage for Army in their game against Michigan in 1945, played at Yankee Stadium in New York. Army was that year's undefeated national champion; and Blanchard won the Heisman Trophy. Army won 28–7. No. 17 is Army quarterback Arnold Tucker.

And who could forget . . .

SCHOOL/YEAR	RECORD	COACH	STARS	
Stanford/1940	10-0-0	Clark Shaughnessy	Frankie Albert	QB
			Hugh Gallarneau	HB
			Pete Kmetovic	HB
			Norm Standlee	FB
			Bruno Banducci	G
			Charlie Taylor	G
Georgia/1942	9-1-0	Wally Butts	Charlie Trippi	HB
			Frankie Sinkwich	HB
Army/1946	9-0-1	Earl Blaik	Doc Blanchard	FB
			Glenn Davis	HB
			Arnold Tucker	QB
			Hank Foldberg	E
			Barney Poole	E
			Joe Steffy	G
			Goble Bryant	T
Notre Dame/1947	9-0-0	Frank Leahy	Johnny Lujack	QB
			Emil Sitko	HB
			Terry Brennan	HB
			Leon Hart	E
			Jim Martin	E
			Bill Fischer	G
			Ziggy Czarobski	T
Michigan/1947	10-0-0	Fritz Crisler	Bob Chappius	HB
			Bump Elliott	FB
			Pete Elliott	QB
			Len Ford	E
			Al Wistert	T
			Dick Rifenberg	E

The 1950s
MARYLAND, 1951

As great as Bud Wilkinson's Oklahoma teams were, especially the teams of 1950, with Billy Vessels, and 1955, with Tommy McDonald, no team was more well rounded or more intimidating than Jim Tatum's Maryland Terrapins. Using a split-T with Jack Scarbath handling the ball, the 1951 Terps combined Scarbath's pinpoint passing, Ed Modzelewski's pulverizing plunges into the line, and one of the stingiest defenses ever, which included Ed's brother Dick Modzelewski at tackle and All-American Bob Ward at guard, Maryland had little trouble marching through the regular season (10-0-0). Then they trounced Tennessee, a team that had been rated No. 1 at season's end, 28—13, in the Sugar Bowl.

And who could forget . . .

SCHOOL/YEAR	RECORD	COACH	STARS	
Oklahoma/1950	10-1-0	Bud Wilkinson	Billy Vessels	HB
			Leon Heath	FB
			Jim Owens	E
			Jim Weatherall	T
Kentucky/1950	11-1-0	Bear Bryant	Babe Parrilli	QB
			Wilber Jamerson	FB
			Bob Gain	T
			Walt Yowarsky	T
Oklahoma/1955	11-0-0	Bud Wilkinson	Tommy McDonald	HB
			Clendon Thomas	HB
			Jerry Tubbs	C
			Bo Bollinger	G
LSU/1958	11-0-0	Paul Dietzel	Billy Cannon	HB
			Johnny Robinson	HB
			Warren Rabb	QB
Syracuse/1959	11-0-0	Ben Schwartzwalder	Ernie Davis	HB
			Gerhard Schwedes	FB
			Roger Davis	G

The 1960s
SOUTHERN CALIFORNIA, 1967

The Trojans lost a game in 1967, a 3—0 slip-up in the mud at Oregon State, but they can be forgiven that. They drubbed a host of highly ranked teams on other Saturdays that year, including Texas, Michigan State, Notre Dame, and UCLA, and ended up with the national championship. John McKay's explosive offense centered around O. J. Simpson, who averaged 5.3 yards a carry and gained 1,543 yards rushing through the season. The defense was outstanding with stars like linebacker Adrian Young, defensive end Tim Rossovich, and defensive back Mike Battle. All-American tackle Ron Yary was on the offensive line. Southern Cal triumphed in the Rose Bowl as well that year, 14—3 over Indiana. Close behind the Trojans is Woody Hayes's best Ohio State team ever, the 1968 Buckeyes, who defeated Southern Cal and O.J. on New Year's Day 1969 in the Rose Bowl.

And who could forget . . .

SCHOOL/YEAR	RECORD	COACH	STARS	
Texas/1963	11-0-0	Darrell Royal	Tommy Nobis	LB
			Duke Carlisle	QB
			Phil Harris	RB
			Scott Appleton	T
Ohio State/1968	10-0-0	Woody Hayes	Rex Kern	QB
			Jim Otis	FB
			Dave Foley	T

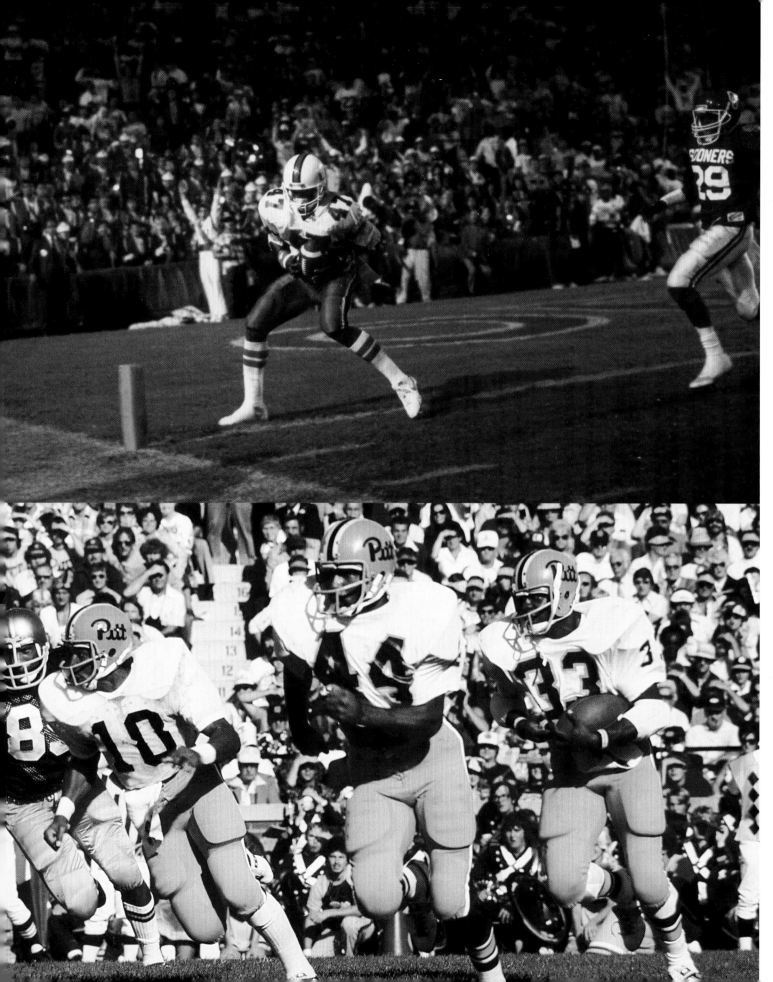

The 1970s
PITTSBURGH, 1976

Johnny Majors had a lot to smile about on the sidelines in 1976. Pitt's defense, with such pillars as middle guard Al Romano and tackle Randy Holloway, overwhelmed every offense it faced, while Heisman Trophy winner Tony Dorsett led the nation in both rushing (1,948 yards, 177.1 per game) and scoring (134 points, including 22 touchdowns). Consensus national champs and victors over highly ranked Georgia in the Sugar Bowl 27—3, the Panthers were the class of the 1970s. Close behind is Nebraska of 1971, paced by the quarterbacking of Jerry Tagge and the breakaway runs of Johnny Rodgers; the Cornhuskers disposed of 12 strong teams during the regular season and then demolished second-ranked Alabama in the Orange Bowl 38—6. But the nod still goes to Pittsburgh.

And who could forget . . .

SCHOOL/YEAR	RECORD	COACH	STARS	
Nebraska/1971	13-0-0	Bob Devaney	Jerry Tagge	QB
			Johnnie Rodgers	RB
			Willie Harper	DE
			Larry Jacobson	DT
US/1972	12-0-0	John McKay	Anthony Davis	RB
			Sam Cunningham	FB
			Lynn Swann	WR
			Charles Young	TE
			Rich Wood	LB
			Pete Adams	T
			John Grant	DT
Alabama/1979	12-0-0	Bear Bryant	Major Ogilvie	RB
			E. J. Junior	DE
			Dave Hannah	DT
			Don McNeal	DB
			Tommy Wilcox	DB
			Dwight Stephenson	C
			Jim Bunch	T

The 1980s
MIAMI, 1987

It is hard to imagine a better team than the Miami Hurricanes of 1987. Coached by Jimmy Johnson, they were undefeated in 12 games during a season that saw the Oklahoma Sooners and Nebraska Cornhuskers 1-2 in virtually every weekly poll. When Miami and Oklahoma, the only two undefeated teams remaining, met in the Orange Bowl, the Hurricanes cleanly displaced the Sooners as the No. 1 team in the nation that year, beating them 20—14. Behind the quarterbacking of Steve Walsh, who threw two touchdown passes at the Orange Bowl, and a defense that was exceptional all year long, the underrated Hurricanes are the choice for the best of the decade—a decade in which four other national champions posted undefeated seasons: Georgia (1980), Clemson (1981), Brigham Young (1984), and Notre Dame (1988).

And who could forget . . .

SCHOOL/YEAR	RECORD	COACH	STARS	
Nebraska/1983	12-1-0	Tom Osborne	Mike Rozier	RB
			Turner Gill	QB
			Irving Fryar	WR
			Dean Steinkuhler	G
			Mike Knox	LB
Oklahoma/1985	11-1-0	Barry Switzer	Jamelle Holieway	QB
			Brian Bosworth	LB
			Keith Jackson	TE
			Anthony Phillips	T
			Tony Casillas	NG
			Kevin Murphy	DE
Penn State/1986	12-0-0	Joe Paterno	D. J. Dozier	RB
			John Shaffer	QB
			Shane Conlan	LB
			Michael Zordich	DB
Notre Dame/1988	12-0-0	Lou Holtz	Tony Rice	QB
			Mark Green	RB
			Raghib Ismail	WR
			Micheal Stonebreaker	LB
			Frank Stans	DE
			Todd Lyght	DB

The 1990s

NEBRASKA, 1995

Nebraska had won the national championship the year before, but in the 1995 polls they trailed Florida State through the first half of the season. As October came to a close, however, the Cornhuskers ascended to the No. 1 position and never looked back. Tom Osborne was nearing the end of his Nebraska coaching career, which at that time had run 23 years, and said that this might well be the finest all-around football team he had ever been associated with. Quarterbacked by consensus All-American Tommie Frazier (runner-up for the Heisman that year), it certainly was one of the most explosive offenses the Cornhuskers ever fielded. To prove just how good they were, they took on the nation's No. 2 ranked team, Florida, in the Fiesta Bowl and humiliated them 62–24. Other major contributors to Nebraska's excellence that year were: running back Ahman Green, linebackers Grant Wistrom and Jarad Tomich, center Aaron Graham, wide receiver Coester Johnson, and tackles Chris Dishman and Eric Anderson.

And who could forget . . .

SCHOOL/YEAR	RECORD	COACH	STARS	
Alabama/1992	13-0-0	Gene Stallings	Derrick Lassic	RB
			David Palmer	WR
			Antonio Langham	DB
			Jay Barker	QB
			John Copeland	DE
			Eric Curry	DE
			George Teague	DB
Tennessee/1998	13-0-0	Phillip Fulmer	Jamal Lewis	RB
			Tee Martin	QB
			Al Wilson	LB
			Raynoch Thompson	LB
			Peerless Price	WR
Florida State/1999	12-0-0	Bobby Bowden	Chris Weinke	QB
			Peter Warrick	WR
			Travis Miner	RB
			Corey Simon	DT
			Jason Whitaker	G
			Tommy Polley	LB
			Sebastian Janikowski	PK
Oklahoma/2000	13-0-0	Bob Stoops	Josh Heupel	QB
			J. T. Thatcher	DB
			Rocky Calmus	LB
			Torrance Marshall	LB
			Quentin Griffin	RB
			Bubba Burcham	C
			Roy Williams	DB

FACING PAGE
Tom Osborne gets a Gatorade shower after his Nebraska team defeated Tennessee in the 1998 Orange Bowl 42–17, giving the Cornhuskers a share (with Michigan) of that year's national championship. Osborne's Nebraska team won outright two other national titles in the 1990s (1994 and 1995).

THE LONGEST WINNING STREAKS

These are the longest winning streaks in college football history, and include both regular season and bowl games.

SCHOOL	WINS	YEARS
Oklahoma	47	1953—57
Washington	39	1908—14
Yale	37	1890—93
Yale	37	1887—89
Toledo	35	1969—71
Pennsylvania	34	1894—96
Oklahoma	31	1948—50
Pittsburgh	31	1914—18
Pennsylvania	31	1896—98
Texas	30	1968—70
Michigan	29	1901—03
Michigan State	28	1950—53
Oklahoma	28	1973—75
Alabama	28	1978—80
Alabama	28	1991—93
Nebraska	27	1901—04
Michigan	26	1903—05
Cornell	26	1921—24
USC	25	1931—33
Army	25	1944—46
Michigan	25	1946—49
San Diego State	25	1965—67
Brigham Young	25	1983—85

THE LONGEST UNDEFEATED STREAKS

These schools ran the longest streaks without losing a game; bowl games are included.

SCHOOL	NUMBER	WINS	TIES	YEARS
Washington	63	59	4	1907—17
Michigan	56	55	1	1901—05
California	50	46	4	1920—25
Yale	48	47	1	1885—89
Oklahoma	48	47	1	1953—57
Yale	47	42	5	1879—85
Yale	44	42	5	1894—96
Yale	42	39	3	1904—08
Notre Dame	39	37	2	1946—50
Yale	37	37	0	1890—93
Minnesota	35	34	1	1903—05
Toledo	35	35	0	1969—71
Princeton	34	29	5	1877—82
Princeton	34	32	2	1884—87
Nebraska	34	33	1	1912—16
Pennsylvania	34	34	0	1894—96

THE WINNINGEST SCHOOLS

The Top 25. The following schools have won the most games in major college football (NCAA's Division I-A), through the year 2000. Included in the totals are regular season, playoff, and bowl games.

SCHOOL	WINS
Michigan	805
Notre Dame	776
Nebraska	753
Texas	744
Penn State	739
Alabama	737
Ohio State	724
Tennessee	707
Oklahoma	702
Southern Cal	678
Georgia	641
Syracuse	638
Army	618
Louisiana State	618
Washington	617
Colorado	611
Auburn	610
Texas A&M	609
West Virginia	603
Georgia Tech	601
North Carolina	600
Miami (Ohio)	597
Pittsburgh	596
Arkansas	594
Minnesota	587

THE NATIONAL CHAMPIONS

Over the past 130 years there have been many selectors of college football's annual national champion. In 1936, the Associated Press became the first truly nationwide poll for ranking college football teams, its weekly and year-end rankings voted on by sportswriters and broadcasters. United Press International began its poll of football coaches in 1950 and published it through 1990 when it was taken over by *USA Today*/Cable News Network. In 1997, ESPN replaced Cable News Network. Today the two best known and most widely circulated college football polls are those by the AP and *USA Today*/ESPN.

In 1998 the NCAA adopted the Bowl Championship Series for the purpose of matching the top two teams in the nation in a postseason bowl game. The system the BCS uses to determine the top two teams takes into account four elements: polls (AP and *USA Today*/ESPN), computer rankings, strength of schedule, and won-lost record. A point system for each of the four components is specified and then the points are added together for a total rating from which the top two teams are determined.

The following lists the consensus national champions. If, however, the AP and UPI or *USA Today*/ESPN disagreed on the national champion, both top-rated teams are cited.

YEAR	SCHOOL	RECORD	COACH	YEAR	SCHOOL	RECORD	COACH
1936	Minnesota	7-1-0	Bernie Bierman	1971	Nebraska	13-0-0	Bob Devaney
1937	Pittsburgh	9-0-1	Jock Sutherland	1972	USC	12-0-0	John McKay
1938	Texas Christian	11-0-0	Dutch Meyer	1973	Notre Dame (AP)	11-0-0	Ara Parseghian
1939	Texas A&M	11-0-0	Homer Norton		Alabama (UPI)	11-1-0	Paul Bryant
1940	Minnesota	8-0-0	Bernie Bierman	1974	Oklahoma (AP)	11-0-0	Barry Switzer
1941	Minnesota	8-0-0	Bernie Bierman		USC (UPI)	10-1-1	John McKay
1942	Ohio State	9-1-0	Paul Brown	1975	Oklahoma	11-1-0	Barry Switzer
1943	Notre Dame	9-1-0	Frank Leahy	1976	Pittsburgh	12-0-0	Johnny Majors
1944	Army	9-0-0	Earl Blaik	1977	Notre Dame	11-1-0	Dan Devine
1945	Army	9-0-0	Earl Blaik	1978	Alabama (AP)	11-1-0	Paul Bryant
1946	Notre Dame	8-0-1	Frank Leahy		USC (UPI)	12-1-0	John Robinson
1947	Notre Dame	9-0-0	Frank Leahy	1979	Alabama	12-0-0	Paul Bryant
1948	Michigan	9-0-0	Bennie Oosterbaan	1980	Georgia	12-0-0	Vince Dooley
1949	Notre Dame	10-0-0	Frank Leahy	1981	Clemson	12-0-0	Danny Ford
1950	Oklahoma	10-1-0	Bud Wilkinson	1982	Penn State	11-1-0	Joe Paterno
1951	Tennessee	10-1-0	Bob Neyland	1983	Miami (Fla.)	11-1-0	Howard
1952	Michigan State	9-0-0	Biggie Munn				Schnellenberger
1953	Maryland	10-1-0	Jim Tatum	1984	Brigham Young	13-0-0	LaVell Edwards
1954	Ohio State (AP)	10-0-0	Woody Hayes	1985	Oklahoma	11-1-0	Barry Switzer
	UCLA (UPI)	9-0-0	Red Sanders	1986	Penn State	12-0-0	Joe Paterno
1955	Oklahoma	11-0-0	Bud Wilkinson	1987	Miami (Fla.)	12-0-0	Jimmy Johnson
1956	Oklahoma	10-0-0	Bud Wilkinson	1988	Notre Dame	12-0-0	Lou Holtz
1957	Auburn (AP)	10-0-0	Shug Jordan	1989	Miami (Fla.)	11-1-0	Dennis Erickson
	Ohio State (UPI)	9-1-0	Woody Hayes	1990	Colorado (AP)	11-1-1	Bill McCartney
1958	Louisiana State	11-0-0	Paul Dietzel		Georgia Tech (UPI)	11-0-1	Bobby Ross
1959	Syracuse	11-0-0	Ben Schwartzwalder	1991	Miami (Fla.) (AP)	12-0-0	Dennis Erickson
1960	Minnesota	8-2-0	Murray Warmath		Washington (UPI)	12-0-0	Don James
1961	Alabama	11-0-0	Paul Bryant	1992	Alabama	13-0-0	Gene Stallings
1962	USC	11-0-0	John McKay	1993	Florida State	12-1-0	Bobby Bowden
1963	Texas	11-0-0	Darrell Royal	1994	Nebraska	13-0-0	Tom Osborne
1964	Alabama	10-1-0	Paul Bryant	1995	Nebraska	12-0-0	Tom Osborne
1965	Alabama (AP)	9-1-1	Paul Bryant	1996	Florida	12-1-0	Steve Spurrier
	Michigan State (UPI)	10-1-0	Duffy Daugherty	1997	Michigan (AP)	12-0-0	Lloyd Carr
1966	Notre Dame	9-0-1	Ara Parseghian		Nebraska	13-0-0	Tom Osborne
1967	USC	10-1-0	John McKay		(USA Today/ESPN)		
1968	Ohio State	10-0-0	Woody Hayes	1998	Tennessee	13-0-0	Phillip Fulmer
1969	Texas	11-0-0	Darrell Royal	1999	Florida State	12-0-0	Bobby Bowden
1970	Nebraska (AP)	11-0-1	Bob Devaney	2000	Oklahoma	13-0-0	Bob Stoops
	Texas (UPI)	10-1-0	Darrell Royal				

THE PERFECT TEAMS

This rare group of teams managed to go an entire season without losing or being scored upon.

YEAR	SCHOOL	RECORD
1901	Michigan	11-0
1911	Utah State	5-0
1917	Texas A&M	8-0
1919	Texas A&M	10-0
1932	Colgate	9-0
1938	Duke	9-0
1939	Tennessee	10-0

MOST CONSECUTIVE WINNING SEASONS

Some schools make a tradition of winning, or at least of producing winning seasons. These are the Top 10 schools consecutively turning in seasons with a winning percentage of .500 and above.

NUMBER OF SEASONS	SCHOOL	YEARS
46	Penn State	1939—87
42	Notre Dame	1889—1932*
40	Texas	1893—1932
39	Nebraska	1962—2000
38	Alabama	1911—50
33	Michigan	1968—2000
29	Oklahoma	1966—94
29	Texas	1957—85
28	Virginia	1888—1915
27	Michigan	1892—1918

* Did not field teams in 1891 and 1892.

HOME FIELD ADVANTAGE

These teams have posted the longest winning streaks at home.

TEAM	WINS	YEARS
Miami (Fla.)	58	1985—94
Alabama	57	1963—82
Harvard	56	1890—95
Michigan	50	1901—07
Nebraska	47	1991—98
Texas	42	1968—76
Notre Dame	40	1907—18
Notre Dame	38	1919—27
Harvard	33	1900—03
Nebraska	33	1901—06
Yale	31	1890—93
Texas A&M	31	1990—95
Marshall	31	1995—
Florida	30	1994—

9

> "What is it?" he would ask rhetorically. "A prolate spheroid, an elongated sphere," he would answer himself, "one in which the outer leathern casing is drawn up tightly over a somewhat smaller rubber tubing." Then, after a melodramatic pause, "Better to have died as a small boy than to fumble this football."
>
> JOHN HEISMAN,
> *a football in hand, as he traditionally addressed recruits*
> *at the beginning of the football season*

THE NATION'S BEST
HEISMAN TROPHY WINNERS

In 1935, the Downtown Athletic Club of New York decided to offer an annual award for the most outstanding college football player "east of the Mississippi River" in the United States. The man behind the idea was Willard Prince, one of the club's administrators. A trophy was designed, the now familiar bronze figure of a ball carrier with a menacing stiff-arm, and it was agreed that the first would be awarded after the conclusion of that football season.

It was originally known as the DAC Trophy, an acronym for Downtown Athletic Club, and was presented that first year to Jay Berwanger, a halfback from the University of Chicago. In October of 1936, John W. Heisman, one of college football's most famous coaches and an organizer and the director of athletics for the Downtown Athletic Club, died. In his honor the award was renamed the Heisman Memorial Trophy, and eligibility was extended to include football players west of the Mississippi River.

The sculptor of the Heisman Trophy was 23-year-old Frank Eliscu, a, recent graduate of Pratt Institute, and it was his first commission. He submitted samples and the final design was approved by a panel appointed by the DAC, which included Jim Crowley, one of Notre Dame's Four Horseman, who was then the coach of Fordham, Lou Little, coach of Columbia, and John Heisman.

Traditionally, the winner of this prestigious award has been selected by a poll of sportswriters and sportscasters who, according to the Downtown Athletic Club, "in order to balance sectional favoritism have been divided evenly among geographic regions." Most recently there have been 870 media voters, 145 from each of six regions. Since 1988, former Heisman recipients have also been eligible to vote. In the nearly seven decades of its existence the Heisman has almost always been awarded to either a running back or a quarterback, on a few occasions to an end, and only once to a defensive player (Michigan defensive back Charles Woodson in 1997)—though, of course, during the first two decades of the Heisman's existence, the rule prohibiting platooning required that all players play both offense and defense.

The Heisman Memorial Trophy remains college football's ultimate accolade, a symbol of excellence honoring only the very best.

JOHN HEISMAN: THE MAN BEHIND THE TROPHY

John William Heisman was born the same year that the first intercollegiate football game was played, in 1869, when Princeton faced Rutgers in New Brunswick, New Jersey. He played in his first football game 17 years later for Titusville High School in western Pennsylvania (against the wishes of his father, incidentally, who described the game as "bestial").

That introduction began a love affair with the sport that would last almost 50 years. Heisman enrolled at Brown in 1887, starred as a lineman there for three years, then went on to the University of Pennsylvania to study law and play another two years of varsity ball. In 1892, he abandoned his studies to coach football at Oberlin College. It was the beginning of a 36-year career that would take him to eight different colleges. As a grand strategist and innovator, his name would come to rank in football lore with those of Camp, Stagg, and Warner.

John Heisman, an early innovator in American football, best remembered for the trophy named in his honor, left his biggest mark at Georgia Tech, where he coached from 1904 to 1919. He was also the head coach at Oberlin (1892, 1894), Akron (1893), Auburn (1895–99), Clemson (1900–03), Pennsylvania (1920–22), Washington & Jefferson (1923), and Rice (1924–27).

Heisman, who stood five-foot-ten-inches and weighed about 155 pounds when he played as well as when he later coached, usually wore a high turtleneck sweater and a baseball cap when he walked the sidelines (and never showing anything that might possibly be construed as a smile). At Oberlin, his team won all seven of their games that first year. Then he moved to Akron for the 1893 season but returned to Oberlin in 1894.

He experimented with the hidden ball trick, instituted a shouted signal (sometimes "Hike," sometimes "Hep") to snap the ball from center, and developed a double-lateral pass that was much copied. To the Rules Committee, he advocated the division of the game into quarters and campaigned for three years for the legalization of the forward pass, a campaign that came to fruition in 1906.

After coaching at Oberlin, he moved to Auburn for a five-year stint, then to Clemson for four seasons, and finally to Georgia Tech in 1904 where, over the next 16 years, he made his biggest impact. At Tech he was a noted taskmaster: long practices, tight training rules (including no hot-water baths or use of soap during the week because they were, in his opinion, "debilitating"), and stern dealings with players. He often lectured his team in booming stentorian tones, replete with Shakespearean quotes.

It was also at Georgia Tech that he coached one of the game's all-time greats, Joe Guyon, who had earlier blocked for Jim Thorpe at Carlisle and then replaced him as the Indian school's star ball-carrier. Besides remembering Guyon as a wonderful football player, Heisman always liked to tell the story of taking Guyon to New Orleans to play Tulane. He told Guyon that the oysters in that town were a special treat. The afternoon of the game Heisman noticed his star back sitting in a corner of the dressing room and looking a little ill. "The oysters," he told Heisman when the coach asked him what was the matter. "Raw oysters," he said, grimacing.

"They didn't agree with you?" Heisman asked.

"Well, the first four or five dozen did. I think I got some bad ones after that."

At Georgia Tech, Heisman also gained a legitimate reputation for running up the score against weak opponents. In 1916, tiny Cumberland College traveled to Atlanta to face Tech and was beaten by Heisman's team 222–0, the most points ever scored in a college football game. Thirty-two touchdowns and 30 extra points were all that Heisman needed that afternoon. Tech, in fact, did not record a first down all day, having scored on each possession within three downs. He was roundly criticized at the

Insurance

With John Heisman's Georgia Tech Bulldogs ahead 126–0 at halftime of their 1916 game with Cumberland College (a team with only 19 players that had been assembled just a week before the game), the coach had this to say to his team: "Men, don't let up. You never know what those Cumberland players have up their sleeves." Not much as it turned out, and Heisman's boys added another 96 points to the score in the second half.

time, which he often said was not only "ungrounded and unfair" but "frivolous and without merit." Victory was his goal, and what was left in its wake was of no consequence to him. And success he achieved: during his 16 years at Georgia Tech the Yellow Jackets claimed a national championship in 1917, and went unbeaten in 33 consecutive games during a period from 1914 into 1918 (31 wins, 2 ties).

The innovative Heisman also lent his name to a shift, one he invented while at Georgia Tech. It was described in the *New York Sun* by sportswriter George Trevor this way: "On the ingenious shift Heisman originated in 1910, the entire team, except the center, dropped behind the scrimmage zone. The four backs took their post in Indian file at right angles to the rush line, forming the letter T." The Heisman shift, along with the Minnesota shift, developed by Dr. Harry Williams, and the Notre Dame shift of Knute Rockne, became the most famous shifts in the early years of organized American football. Heisman's was unorthodox, although, everyone agreed, it was effective. As Trevor noted with enthusiasm, "one virtue of the balanced formation was that it could attack either

flank with equal force. There were no strong- or weak-side plays as the shift swung left or right. At the shift signal the phalanx deployed with the startling suddenness of a Jeb Stuart cavalry raid, catching the defense off balance. No pause was required by the more lenient rules of that period, the absence of any momentary stop making it difficult for the defense to countershift in time."

Heisman himself shifted to Pennsylvania in 1920 and remained there three seasons before moving on to Washington & Jefferson in 1923. The following year he took the head coaching job at Rice and held it until 1927, when he retired at the age of 60.

Running up scores on hapless opponents was bad enough; during his coaching years Heisman was described varyingly as "arrogant," "contentious," and "irascible." Writer William N. Wallace noted that "Heisman had warts and poultices all over his career," and pointed out in particular that the last eight years of that career "were marred by squabbles with his superiors, his associates and his players."

When his coaching career ended, Heisman had a record of 185 victories against 70 defeats and 17 ties, and remains to this day one of the 25 winningest coaches in college football history. He served as president of the American Football Coaches Association twice, was one of the founders and the first president of the Downtown Athletic Club of New York, and, after retiring from coaching, regularly contributed articles on college football to *Collier's* magazine and the *New York Evening Journal*.

The year he died, 1936, the Downtown Athletic Club of New York named their annual award for excellence, begun the year before, in honor of their accomplished member, and Larry Kelley of Yale was given the first trophy bearing the name Heisman.

University of Chicago halfback Jay Berwanger, striking a Heisman pose here, was the first to win the trophy, inaugurated in 1935 by the Downtown Athletic Club of New York but not named the Heisman until the following year. A two-time All-American, Berwanger was also the first player taken in the first ever National Football League draft, held in 1936, but he chose instead to go into business.

THE HEISMAN MEMORIAL TROPHY: THE WINNERS

YEAR	WINNER	POSITION	SCHOOL	RUNNERS-UP	YEAR	WINNER	POSITION	SCHOOL	RUNNERS-UP
1935	Jay Berwanger	HB	Chicago	Monk Meyer (Army) Bill Shakespeare (Notre Dame)	1951	Dick Kazmaier	HB	Princeton	Hank Lauricella (Tennessee) Babe Parilli (Kentucky)
1936	Larry Kelley	E	Yale	Sam Francis (Nebraska) Ray Buivid (Marquette)	1952	Billy Vessels	HB	Oklahoma	Jack Scarbath (Maryland) Paul Giel (Minnesota)
1937	Clint Frank	HB	Yale	Byron White (Colorado) Marshall Goldberg (Pittsburgh)	1953	Johnny Lattner	HB	Notre Dame	Paul Giel (Minnesota) Paul Cameron (UCLA)
1938	Davey O'Brien	QB	TCU	Marshall Goldberg (Pittsburgh) Sid Luckman (Columbia)	1954	Alan Ameche	FB	Wisconsin	Kurt Burris (Oklahoma) Howard Cassady (Ohio State)
1939	Nile Kinnick	HB	Iowa	Tom Harmon (Michigan) Paul Christman (Missouri)	1955	Howard Cassady	HB	Ohio State	Jim Swink (TCU) George Welsh (Navy)
1940	Tom Harmon	HB	Michigan	John Kimbrough (Texas A&M) George Franck (Minnesota)	1956	Paul Hornung	QB	Notre Dame	Johnny Majors (Tennessee) Tommy McDonald (Oklahoma)
1941	Bruce Smith	HB	Minnesota	Angelo Bertelli (Notre Dame) Frankie Albert (Stanford)	1957	John David Crow	HB	Texas A&M	Alex Karras (Iowa) Walt Kowalczyk (Michigan State)
1942	Frank Sinkwich	HB	Georgia	Paul Governali (Columbia) Clint Castleberry (Georgia Tech)	1958	Pete Dawkins	HB	Army	Randy Duncan (Iowa) Billy Cannon (LSU)
1943	Angelo Bertelli	QB	Notre Dame	Bob Odell (Pennsylvania) Otto Graham (Northwestern)	1959	Billy Cannon	HB	LSU	Richie Lucas (Penn State) Don Meredith (SMU)
1944	Les Horvath	QB	Ohio State	Glenn Davis (Army) Doc Blanchard (Army)	1960	Joe Bellino	HB	Navy	Tom Brown (Minnesota) Jake Gibbs (Mississippi)
1945	Doc Blanchard	FB	Army	Glenn Davis (Army) Bob Fenimore (Oklahoma A&M)	1961	Ernie Davis	HB	Syracuse	Bob Ferguson (Ohio State) Jimmy Saxton (Texas)
1946	Glenn Davis	HB	Army	Charlie Trippi (Georgia) Johnny Lujack (Notre Dame)	1962	Terry Baker	QB	Oregon State	Jerry Stovall (LSU) Bobby Bell (Minnesota)
1947	Johnny Lujack	QB	Notre Dame	Bob Chappius (Michigan) Doak Walker (SMU)	1963	Roger Staubach	QB	Navy	Billy Lothridge (Georgia Tech) Sherman Lewis (Michigan State)
1948	Doak Walker	HB	SMU	Charlie Justice (North Carolina) Chuck Bednarik (Pennsylvania)	1964	John Huarte	QB	Notre Dame	Jerry Rhome (Tulsa) Dick Butkus (Illinois)
1949	Leon Hart	E	Notre Dame	Charlie Justice (North Carolina) Doak Walker (SMU)	1965	Mike Garrett	HB	USC	Howard Twilley (Tulsa) Jim Grabowski (Illinois)
1950	Vic Janowicz	HB	Ohio State	Kyle Rote (SMU) Reds Bagnell (Pennsylvania)	1966	Steve Spurrier	QB	Florida	Bob Griese (Purdue) Nick Eddy (Notre Dame)

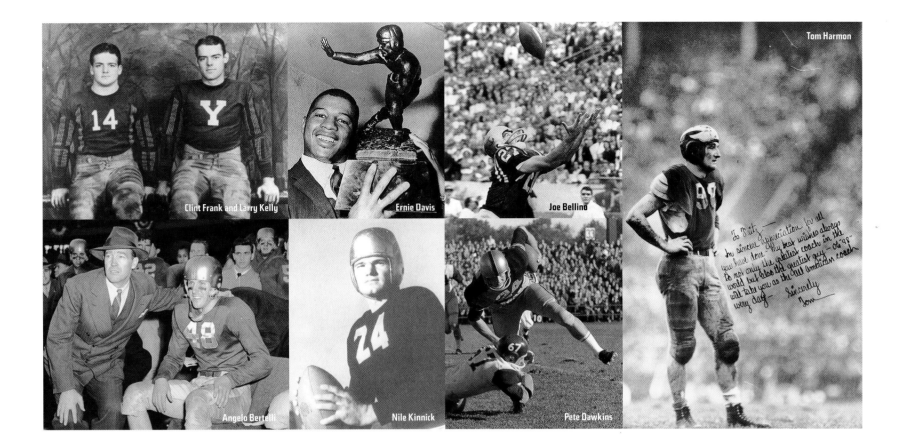

Clint Frank and Larry Kelly

Ernie Davis

Joe Bellino

Tom Harmon

Angelo Bertelli

Nile Kinnick

Pete Dawkins

*To Fritz —
In sincere appreciation for all
you have done — My best wishes always
to not only the greatest coach in the
world but also the greatest guy — as "98"
will take you as the best American coach
every day —
Sincerely
Tom*

ABOVE, CLOCKWISE FROM LEFT
Yale's two Heisman Trophy winners: Clint Frank (left), who won it in 1937, and Larry Kelley, the 1936 recipient. A great running back, Frank was also a top-flight passer, called by Greasy Neale, an assistant coach at Yale then, "the finest all-around back I've ever seen." Kelley, an end, was Yale's captain in 1936 and the favorite target of Frank's passes. According to *New York Times* columnist Allison Danzig, "etched indelibly in the minds of all . . . is the almost phenomenal genius of Larry Kelley of Yale as a headlined hunter, who always got his ball and touchdown regardless of the odds."

Syracuse great Ernie Davis poses with the Heisman Trophy after being awarded it in 1961. The six-foot-eight-inch, 210-pound running back broke all the school rushing records that had been held by Jim Brown and became the first black to be honored with the Heisman. The No. 1 pick in the 1961 NFL draft (chosen by the Washington Redskins and then immediately traded to the Cleveland Browns where

he was to join Jim Brown in the backfield), Davis never played pro ball; stricken with leukemia, he died two years later at age 23.

Navy halfback Joe Bellino, about to gather in a touchdown pass here against Missouri in the Orange Bowl on January 2, 1961, was the 1960 winner of the Heisman Trophy. Only five-feet-eight-inches and 180 pounds and often described as "built like a fireplug," Bellino led Navy to one of its finest regular seasons ever in 1960, 9-1-0, including a 17—12 win over arch-rival Army, but the Midshipmen lost to Missouri at the Orange Bowl 21—14.

Tom Harmon, a true triple-threat and two-time All-American at Michigan, won the Heisman Trophy in 1940. In the last game of his career, against arch-rival Ohio State, he ran for 139 yards and two touchdowns, completed 11 of 12 passes for 151 yards and another two touchdowns, kicked four extra points, and averaged 50 yards on his punts; on defense, he intercepted three passes, returning one for a

touchdown (Michigan, not surprisingly, won 40—0). After enlisting in the Army Air Corps in World War II, Harmon survived two airplane crashes and was awarded the Silver Star.

Halfback Pete Dawkins gains a few yards for Army against Colgate in 1958. Dawkins, one of West Point's most illustrious graduates, was awarded the Heisman Trophy (and the Maxwell) that year; but at Army he was also the senior class president, first captain of the corps of cadets (highest ranking member of the student body), football team captain, and a "star man" (academically in the top 5 percent of his class). Dawkins is the only Cadet in West Point history to have earned all four honors. He was also the first Heisman winner to win a Rhodes scholarship, and went on to became a brigadier general in the regular army.

Nile Kinnick, great running back and passer for Iowa, as well as a Phi Beta Kappa graduate, won both the Heisman and the Maxwell Trophies in 1939 and was named Male Athlete of the Year by the Associated

Press (beating out, among others, Joe DiMaggio and Joe Louis, who also had pretty good years in 1939). A Navy pilot in World War II, he was killed when his fighter plane crashed in the Caribbean off South America in 1943.

Notre Dame quarterback Angelo Bertelli (48) watches the action from the sideline with his coach Frank Leahy during the last game of his career, against Navy on October 30, 1943. A member of the Marine Corps Reserve, he was activated the next day and eventually saw duty on Iwo Jima where he won the Bronze Star and the Purple Heart. Despite his shortened season, he still won the Heisman Trophy for 1943.

THE HEISMAN MEMORIAL TROPHY: THE WINNERS

YEAR	WINNER	POSITION	SCHOOL	RUNNERS-UP
1967	Gary Beban	QB	UCLA	O. J. Simpson (USC) Leroy Keyes (Purdue)
1968	O. J. Simpson	HB	USC	Leroy Keyes (Purdue) Terry Hanratty (Notre Dame)
1969	Steve Owens	HB	Oklahoma	Mike Phipps (Purdue) Rex Kern (Ohio State)
1970	Jim Plunkett	QB	Stanford	Joe Theismann (Notre Dame) Archie Manning (Mississippi)
1971	Pat Sullivan	QB	Auburn	Ed Marinaro (Cornell) Greg Pruitt (Oklahoma)
1972	Johnny Rodgers	FL	Nebraska	Greg Pruitt (Oklahoma) Rich Glover (Nebraska)
1973	John Cappelletti	RB	Penn State	John Hicks (Ohio State) Roosevelt Leaks (Texas)
1974	Archie Griffin	RB	Ohio State	Anthony Davis (USC) Joe Washington (Oklahoma)
1975	Archie Griffin	RB	Ohio State	Chuck Muncie (California) Ricky Bell (USC)
1976	Tony Dorsett	RB	Pittsburgh	Ricky Bell (USC) Rob Lytle (Michigan)
1977	Earl Campbell	RB	Texas	Terry Miller (Oklahoma State) Ken MacAfee (Notre Dame)
1978	Billy Sims	RB	Oklahoma	Chuck Fusina (Penn State) Rick Leach (Michigan)
1979	Charles White	RB	USC	Billy Sims (Oklahoma) Marc Wilson (Brigham Young)
1980	George Rogers	RB	South Carolina	Hugh Green (Pittsburgh) Herschel Walker (Georgia)
1981	Marcus Allen	RB	USC	Herschel Walker (Georgia) Jim McMahon (Brigham Young)
1982	Herschel Walker	RB	Georgia	John Elway (Stanford) Eric Dickerson (SMU)
1983	Mike Rozier	RB	Nebraska	Steve Young (Brigham Young) Doug Flutie (Boston College)
1984	Doug Flutie	QB	Boston College	Keith Byars (Ohio State) Robbie Bosco (Brigham Young)
1985	Bo Jackson	RB	Auburn	Chuck Long (Iowa) Robbie Bosco (Brigham Young)
1986	Vinny Testaverde	QB	Miami (Fla.)	Paul Palmer (Temple) Jim Harbaugh (Michigan)
1987	Tim Brown	WR	Notre Dame	Don McPherson (Syracuse) Gordie Lockbaum (Holy Cross)
1988	Barry Sanders	RB	Oklahoma State	Rodney Peete (USC) Troy Aikman (UCLA)
1989	Andre Ware	QB	Houston	Anthony Thompson (Indiana) Major Harris (West Virginia)
1990	Ty Detmer	QB	Brigham Young	Raghib Ismail (Notre Dame) Eric Bieniemy (Colorado)
1991	Desmond Howard	WR	Michigan	Casey Weldon (Florida State) Ty Detmer (Brigham Young)
1992	Gino Torretta	QB	Miami (Fla.)	Marshall Faulk (San Diego State) Garrison Hearst (Georgia)
1993	Charlie Ward	QB	Florida State	Heath Shuler (Tennessee) David Palmer (Alabama)
1994	Rashaan Salaam	RB	Colorado	Ki-Jana Carter (Penn State) Steve McNair (Alcorn State)
1995	Eddie George	RB	Ohio State	Tommie Frazier (Nebraska) Danny Wuerffel (Florida)
1996	Danny Wuerffel	QB	Florida	Troy Davis (Iowa State) Jake Plummer (Arizona State)
1997	Charles Woodson	DB	Michigan	Peyton Manning (Tennessee) Ryan Leaf (Washington State)
1998	Ricky Williams	RB	Texas	Michael Bishop (Kansas State) Cade McNown (UCLA)
1999	Ron Dayne	RB	Wisconsin	Joe Hamilton (Georgia Tech) Michael Vick (Virginia Tech)
2000	Chris Weinke	QB	Florida State	Josh Heupel (Oklahoma) Drew Brees (Purdue)

Archie Griffin

O. J. Simpson

Tim Brown

Herschel Walker

Roger Staubach

Ricky Williams

Marcus Allen

ABOVE, CLOCKWISE FROM LEFT
Stepping out here is the only two-time winner
of the Heisman Trophy, Ohio State's Archie Griffin.
At five-feet-eight-inches and 182 pounds he was less
than imposing, but he was one of college football's
most productive running backs; as a sophomore he
rushed for 1,428 yards, as a junior for 1,620 yards, and
as a senior for 1,450 yards. He was also considered
one of the best blocking backs in the game.

Southern Cal's O. J. Simpson, carrying the ball here,
will go down as one of the greatest running backs ever
to play college football. A two-time All-American, he
was runner-up for the Heisman Trophy in 1967 and the
winner of it in 1968. Simpson set an NCAA record for
rushing in 1967 with 1,415 yards and then broke it the
next year with 1,709; scoring 34 touchdowns in those
two years, he led the Trojans to two Rose Bowls and
a national championship in 1967.

Notre Dame wide receiver Tim Brown heads out on an
end-around in this 1987 game against Navy. That year
he became only the fourth player who was not a back to
win the Heisman Trophy, following ends Larry Kelley
and Leon Hart and flanker Johnny Rodgers; Brown also
became the seventh Notre Dame player to win the
award. As great a kickoff and punt returner as he was a
receiver, Brown compiled 1,937 all-purpose yards as a
junior; as a senior he gained 846 yards on 39 receptions
and averaged 19.7 yards on kickoff returns and 11.8 on
punt returns, including three returned for touchdowns.

Not since Frank Sinkwich and Charlie Trippi in the
1940s had Georgia seen a back so dominating as Herschel Walker, winner of the 1982 Heisman Trophy. He
set an NCAA rushing record for a freshman in 1980 when
he gained 1,616 yards, and was third in the voting for
the Heisman that year, another first for a freshman.
As a sophomore he was the first runner-up; as a junior
the award was his. After that he left for the fledgling
USFL, signing a $5 million, 3-year contract with the
New Jersey Generals.

Tailback Marcus Allen carries the ball for Southern Cal
in 1981, the year he earned the Heisman Trophy. He
became the fourth Trojan running back to win the Heisman, following Mike Garrett, O. J. Simpson, and Charles
White. Allen rushed for 1,563 yards as a junior; as a
senior he became the first running back in college history to gain 200 or more yards each in eight games. He
also became the first to rush for more than 2,000 yards
in a season (2,342); all told that year he set 14 NCAA
records and tied two others.

Texas running back Ricky Williams, breaking away
here, was a consensus All-American in both 1997 and
1998, and won the Heisman Trophy in 1998 as well as
the Maxwell Award and the Walter Camp Award.

Navy quarterback Roger Staubach, shown here lining
up behind the Middies' line in 1963, was the winner,
as a junior, of that year's Heisman Trophy. In his three-
year career (1962—64) with the Middies, Staubach
produced 4,253 yards of total offense, 3,571 of them
passing, and brought Navy to a national ranking of
No. 2 at the end of the 1963 regular season, their highest ever. Staubach was plagued by injuries his senior
year, then spent four years on active duty for the Navy,
one in Vietnam, before joining the Dallas Cowboys,
where he became one of the greatest quarterbacks in
NFL history.

UNDERCLASSMEN WHO HAVE WON THE HEISMAN (ALL JUNIORS)

PLAYER	SCHOOL	YEAR
Doc Blanchard	Army	1945
Doak Walker	SMU	1948
Vic Janowicz	Ohio State	1950
Roger Staubach	Navy	1963
Archie Griffin	Ohio State	1974
Billy Sims	Oklahoma	1978
Herschel Walker	Georgia	1982
Barry Sanders	Oklahoma State	1988
Andre Ware	Houston	1989
Ty Detmer	Brigham Young	1990
Desmond Howard	Michigan	1991
Rashaan Salaam	Colorado	1994
Charles Woodson	Michigan	1997
Ricky Williams	Texas	1998

FACING PAGE
UCLA quarterback Gary Beban, Heisman Trophy recipient of 1967, running with the ball here against USC, was better known as a master of the great play, his long touchdown passes becoming a trademark. As a sophomore he led the Bruins to a 14–12 victory over No. 1 ranked Michigan in the 1966 Rose Bowl by scoring both touchdowns himself, even though in this game the Bruin's lost to the Southern Cal Trojans 21–20. In the words of his coach, Tommy Prothro: "He has no weaknesses. Maybe some quarterbacks can run or throw better. But I don't know anyone else who can do it all like he can."

RIGHT
John Cappelletti, described as "a fullback at a tailback's position," became the first Penn State player to win the Heisman after a magnificent 1973 season during which he rushed for 1,522 yards and led the Nittany Lions to an Orange Bowl victory over LSU. Cappelletti was honored with the Heisman Trophy in New York, where he gave his memorable acceptance speech.

A HEISMAN FOR JOSEPH

Penn State's great tailback John Cappelletti was awarded the Heisman Trophy in 1973 and his acceptance speech was one of the most memorable ever delivered. In the audience when the award was presented by then U.S. Vice President Gerald Ford were his parents and his 11-year-old brother, Joseph. As he accepted the trophy, his eyes swept the gathering of people and then came to rest on his little brother.

"The youngest member of my family, Joseph, is very ill," he said. "He has leukemia. If I can dedicate this trophy to him tonight and give him a couple of days of happiness, this is worth everything. A lot of people think that I go through a lot on Saturdays and during the week as most athletes do. You get your bumps and bruises, and it is a terrific battle out there on the field. Only for me it is on Saturdays, and it's only in the fall. For Joseph, it is all year round, and it is a battle that is unending with him. He puts up with much more than I'll ever put up with, and I think that this trophy is more his than mine because he has been a great inspiration to me."

KENNEDY AND THE HEISMAN

Robert F. Kennedy, who played varsity football while at Harvard and was the U.S. attorney general in 1962, was asked to present the Heisman Trophy for that year to Terry Baker of Oregon State. Kennedy was happy to make the appearance, but apparently somewhat reluctant to hand over the trophy. The following is excerpted from his speech:

> It is a singular pleasure to be present at this award of the John W. Heisman Football Trophy. For some of us former aspirants, it is a great pleasure just to see the trophy.

When I received the letter from the Heisman Award Committee, I thought for a second that it had been delayed in the post office for 15 years.

In fact, I would prefer to believe that I am here, not as Attorney General, but rather as a senior who once got the "short end of the stick" from the Heisman Trophy Selection Committee in 1947.

Some of you sports enthusiasts may have wondered about the origin of that sports expression the "short end." Well, I was the "short end" at Harvard.

With respect to the Heisman Awards and the Big Three—Harvard, Yale, and Princeton—the name of the Yale winner started with "K," Larry Kelley. So, also, the Princeton winner, Dick Kazmaier. The "K's" at Harvard are still dying with suspense.

Grantland Rice's All-Time Team

Just before the first half of the twentieth century ended, Grantland Rice, who had been selecting All-America teams since the demise of Walter Camp almost 25 years earlier, was asked to publish his "All-Time" team. Who were the absolute greatest players at their positions, from the time the game emerged in the Ivy League in the late 1800s up to 1950?

Rice complied, saying, "This side of a house full of ghosts, nothing could be more mythical, but I'll give it a whirl . . ." and added these remarks:

"Who were the best men [backs] I have looked at . . . Jim Thorpe, Red Grange, Bronko Nagurski, Ernie Nevers, Ken Strong, Benny Friedman, Steve Van Buren, Cliff Battles, Dutch Clark, Bill Dudley, Norm Standlee, and such great passing quarterbacks as Sammy Baugh, John Lujack, Sid Luckman, Otto Graham, and Frankie Albert . . . with Bobby Layne coming up in a hurry and Bob Waterfield in close consideration."

Rice explained that all these players went on to play professional football, and therefore enhanced their football reputation. He added that it would be interesting to select an all-time backfield of players who played *only* in college. His selection:

QB	Walter Eckersall	Chicago
HB	George Gipp	Notre Dame
HB	Clint Frank	Yale
FB	Eddie Mahan	Harvard

He also gave special mention to such college-only backs as Elmer Oliphant of Army, Ted Coyle, Yale; Willie Heston, Michigan; George Pfann, Cornell; and Albie Booth, Yale.

Rice's All-Time, Pre-1950 Team:

E	Don Hutson	Alabama
E	Bennie Oosterbaan	Michigan
T	Joe Stydahar	West Virginia
T	Pete "Fats" Henry	Washington & Jefferson
G	Pudge Heffelfinger	Yale
G	Herman Hickman	Tennessee
C	Germany Schultz	Michigan
QB	Sammy Baugh	Texas Christian
HB	Red Grange	Illinois
HB	Jim Thorpe	Carlisle
FB	Bronko Nagurski	Minnesota

The Greatest Players

In 1950, the Associated Press conducted a poll of 391 sportswriters and broadcasters to determine the greatest college football player of the first half of the twentieth century. The results:

PLAYER	SCHOOL	NO. OF VOTES	PLAYER	SCHOOL	NO. OF VOTES
Jim Thorpe	Carlisle	170	Charley Brickley	Harvard	1
Red Grange	Illinois	138	Pete Henry	Washington & Jefferson	1
Bronko Nagurski	Minnesota	38			
Ernie Nevers	Stanford	7	Bennie Oosterbaan	Michigan	1
Sammy Baugh	Texas Christian	7	Nile Kinnick	Iowa	1
Don Hutson	Alabama	6	Frankie Albert	Stanford	1
George Gipp	Notre Dame	4	Glenn Dobbs	Tulsa	1
Charlie Trippi	Georgia	3	Glenn Davis	Army	1
Willie Heston	Michigan	2	Doc Blanchard	Army	1
Chic Harley	Ohio State	2	Bulldog Turner	Hardin-Simmons	1
Sid Luckman	Columbia	2	Doak Walker	Southern Methodist	1
Steve Van Buren	Louisiana State	2			

This is not the time or the place to cry "discrimination" . . . I mean "foul." But why do the Heisman winners always have to be big guys??? Why did 26 of the 28 winners have to be backs??? Why do they have to be regulars all the time???

It's about time they recognized good, short substitutes!

And only four of the 28 winners had three syllables in their names.

The whole thing seems top heavy or something.

There are two things I keep in mind about the late John Heisman. One: he was enthusiastic about the smaller players. He was really teed off when Albie Booth was not chosen All America. He once compiled a list of All Americans who weighed less than 150 pounds—I was 147 myself. This list included Poe, Pollard, Hinkey, Casey, Daly, Weekes, Maulbetsch, Eckersall, Stevenson, Steffen, Strupper, Stinchcomb, and Stuhldreyer. No "K's" here either . . . and only a few with three syllable names.

The second thing I keep before me about the great John Heisman. He was courageous enough to *change* his selections, even years later. He picked his first all-time All-American team in 1920. He changed it drastically in 1932.

I'm not hinting, and I don't want to cause next year's Selection Committee a lot of trouble. But these things aren't necessarily final. All this old watchcharm wants is justice. And I don't mean "Choo Choo" Justice of North Carolina either.

I salute Terry Baker and congratulate him and Oregon State University on the national recognition and honor they are accorded here tonight.

Even though he is a back, a regular, and tall, and rangy, he fully deserves the Heisman Trophy. *This year* . . .

What a United States Marshal he'd make! It is said that he can switch as fast and often as his fellow Oregonian, Senator Wayne Morse. I regret the possibilities of this dexterity since Terry's Jefferson High School team in Portland was known as the Jefferson "Democrats."

OTHER MAJOR AWARDS

Outland Trophy

The Outland Trophy, first presented in 1946 by the Football Writers Association of America, honors the outstanding interior lineman of the year. The award is named for its benefactor, Dr. John H. Outland, who played for the University of Kansas as a tackle and a halfback, winning All-America honors in 1897 and 1898. He later coached at Kansas as well as at Franklin & Marshall, Haskell, and Washburn. Outland also earned a medical degree from the University of Pennsylvania, and was a surgeon when he wasn't coaching college football. Outland Trophy winners are:

YEAR	PLAYER	POSITION	SCHOOL
1946	George Connor	T	Notre Dame
1947	Joe Steffy	G	Army
1948	Bill Fischer	G	Notre Dame
1949	Ed Bagdon	G	Michigan State
1950	Bob Gain	T	Kentucky
1951	Jim Weatherall	T	Oklahoma
1952	Dick Modzelewski	T	Maryland
1953	J. D. Roberts	G	Oklahoma
1954	Bill Brooks	G	Arkansas
1955	Calvin Jones	G	Iowa
1956	Jim Parker	G	Ohio State
1957	Alex Karras	T	Iowa
1958	Zeke Smith	G	Auburn
1959	Mike McGee	T	Duke
1960	Tom Brown	G	Minnesota
1961	Merlin Olsen	T	Utah State
1962	Bobby Bell	T	Minnesota
1963	Scott Appleton	T	Texas
1964	Steve DeLong	T	Tennessee

YEAR	PLAYER	POSITION	SCHOOL
1965	Tommy Nobis	G/LB	Texas
1966	Loyd Phillips	T	Arkansas
1967	Ron Yary	T	Southern California
1968	Bill Stanfill	T	Georgia
1969	Mike Reid	DT	Penn State
1970	Jim Stillwagon	MG	Ohio State
1971	Larry Jacobson	DT	Nebraska
1972	Rich Glover	MG	Nebraska
1973	John Hicks	OT	Ohio State
1974	Randy White	DE	Maryland
1975	Lee Roy Selmon	DT	Oklahoma
1976	Ross Browner	DE	Notre Dame
1977	Brad Shearer	DT	Texas
1978	Greg Roberts	OG	Oklahoma
1979	Jim Ritcher	C	North Carolina State
1980	Mark May	OT	Pittsburgh
1981	Dave Rimington	C	Nebraska
1982	Dave Rimington	C	Nebraska

YEAR	PLAYER	POSITION	SCHOOL
1983	Dean Steinkuhler	OG	Nebraska
1984	Bruce Smith	DT	Virginia Tech
1985	Mike Ruth	MG	Boston College
1986	Jason Buck	DT	Brigham Young
1987	Chad Hennings	DT	Air Force
1988	Tracy Rocker	DT	Auburn
1989	Mohammed Elewonibi	OG	Brigham Young
1990	Russell Maryland	DT	Miami (Fla.)
1991	Steve Emtman	DT	Washington
1992	Will Shields	OG	Nebraska
1993	Rob Waldrop	MG	Arizona
1994	Zach Wiegert	OT	Nebraska
1995	Jonathan Ogden	OT	UCLA
1996	Orlando Pace	OT	Ohio State
1997	Aaron Taylor	OG	Nebraska
1998	Kris Farris	OT	UCLA
1999	Chris Samuels	OT	Alabama
2000	John Henderson	DE	Tennessee

One of the game's greatest two-way players, Notre Dame tackle George Connor (81) was a two-time All-American (1946 and 1947) and the first winner of the Outland Trophy honoring the most outstanding college football interior lineman (1946). Connor went on to an illustrious career in the NFL with the Chicago Bears and a berth in the Pro Football Hall of Fame. No. 60 on Notre Dame is center George Strohmeyer.

Maxwell Award

The Maxwell Award honors the nation's most outstanding football player of the year. It was first presented in 1937 by the Maxwell Memorial Football Club of Philadelphia, and is named for Robert "Tiny" Maxwell, a lineman who played for the University of Chicago in 1902 and for Swarthmore in 1904–05. A photograph of a beaten-up Maxwell that appeared in the newspapers after a game with Penn in 1905 prompted President Theodore Roosevelt to call for legislation to control the violence in football. Maxwell was later a noted sports journalist and editor with the *Philadelphia Evening Public Ledger*. Maxwell Award winners are:

YEAR	PLAYER	POSITION	SCHOOL	YEAR	PLAYER	POSITION	SCHOOL	YEAR	PLAYER	POSITION	SCHOOL
1937	Clint Frank	HB	Yale	1959	Rich Lucas	QB	Penn State	1980	Hugh Green	DE	Pittsburgh
1938	Davey O'Brien	QB	Texas Christian	1960	Joe Bellino	HB	Navy	1981	Marcus Allen	RB	Southern California
1939	Nile Kinnick	HB	Iowa	1961	Bob Ferguson	FB	Ohio State				
1940	Tom Harmon	HB	Michigan	1962	Terry Baker	QB	Oregon State	1982	Herschel Walker	RB	Georgia
1941	Bill Dudley	HB	Virginia	1963	Roger Staubach	QB	Navy	1983	Mike Rozier	RB	Nebraska
1942	Paul Governali	QB	Columbia	1964	Glenn Ressler	C	Penn State	1984	Doug Flutie	QB	Boston College
1943	Bob Odell	HB	Pennsylvania	1965	Tommy Nobis	G/LB	Texas	1985	Chuck Long	QB	Iowa
1944	Glenn Davis	HB	Army	1966	Jim Lynch	LB	Notre Dame	1986	Vinny Testaverde	QB	Miami (Fla.)
1945	Doc Blanchard	FB	Army	1967	Gary Beban	QB	UCLA	1987	Don McPherson	QB	Syracuse
1946	Charlie Trippi	HB	Georgia	1968	O. J. Simpson	HB	Southern California	1988	Barry Sanders	RB	Oklahoma State
1947	Doak Walker	HB	Southern Methodist	1969	Mike Reid	DT	Penn State	1989	Anthony Thompson	RB	Indiana
1948	Chuck Bednarik	C	Pennsylvania	1970	Jim Plunkett	QB	Stanford	1990	Ty Detmer	QB	Brigham Young
1949	Leon Hart	E	Notre Dame	1971	Ed Marinaro	HB	Cornell	1991	Desmond Howard	WR	Michigan
1950	Reds Bagnell	HB	Pennsylvania	1972	Brad VanPelt	DB	Michigan State	1992	Gino Torretta	QB	Miami (Fla.)
1951	Dick Kazmaier	HB	Princeton	1973	John Cappelletti	RB	Penn State	1993	Charlie Ward	QB	Florida State
1952	Johnny Lattner	HB	Notre Dame	1974	Steve Joachim	QB	Temple	1994	Kerry Collins	QB	Penn State
1953	Johnny Lattner	HB	Notre Dame	1975	Archie Griffin	RB	Ohio State	1995	Eddie George	RB	Ohio State
1954	Ron Beagle	E	Navy	1976	Tony Dorsett	RB	Pittsburgh	1996	Danny Wuerffel	QB	Florida
1955	Howard Cassady	HB	Ohio State	1977	Ross Browner	DE	Notre Dame	1997	Peyton Manning	QB	Tennessee
1956	Tommy McDonald	HB	Oklahoma	1978	Chuck Fusina	QB	Penn State	1998	Ricky Williams	RB	Texas
1957	Bob Reifsnyder	T	Navy	1979	Charles White	RB	Southern California	1999	Ron Dayne	RB	Wisconsin
1958	Pete Dawkins	HB	Army					2000	Drew Brees	QB	Purdue

> "We met an old grad who didn't care whether you roasted or boosted his college football team . . . or whether you even mentioned it. It was the first funeral we had attended in years."

GRANTLAND RICE
Sportlight,
October 17, 1924

FINAL GLORY
THE BOWL GAMES

10

The postseason bowls are the dessert tray to each year's college football feast. Each has its own personality, distinct pageantry, and something special to offer fans—most notably, exciting football between the best teams in the nation who ordinarily have not faced each other during the regular season.

In the earlier days of the bowls, the Rose was the premier New Year's Day festival, the most coveted invitation of all. Even after it was restricted to representatives of the Big Ten and Pac-8 (later Pac-10) in 1947, the Rose remained the focal point of postseason play for another decade. By the mid-1950s, however, the Sugar, Cotton, and Orange classics began to take on equal prominence. When many of the best college teams in the country started coming out of the South, Southwest, and Plains states, the biggest game of the college football year was often played now in New Orleans, Dallas, or Miami instead of Pasadena on New Year's Day.

The Rose Bowl actually had no competition until 1935 when the Sugar and Orange Bowls were launched (the Cotton Bowl arrived two years later and the Gator Bowl in 1946). Many bowls have come and gone over the years (there was a Bacardi Bowl played in Havana, Cuba, in 1937; a Shrine Bowl in Little Rock, Arkansas, in 1948; and a Mercy Bowl in Los Angeles in 1961—all of which lasted only a year). The 1960s and 1970s saw a proliferation of lesser bowls, some of which proved only slightly more durable than the Bacardi Bowl.

The four major bowl games, however, have always garnered media attention. Newspapers throughout the country carried the story of the first Rose Bowl game back in 1902, informing the reading public that Fielding Yost and his "Point-a-Minute"

Michigan Wolverines desecrated a mismatched Stanford team 49–0. On January 1, 1927, NBC Radio first broadcast the Rose Bowl nationally, and America listened as Wallace Wade's Alabama battled Pop Warner's Stanford to a 7–7 tie. In 1953, television began its coverage for the first time, allowing football fans throughout the nation to watch the Rose, Sugar, Cotton, and Orange Bowl games.

Over the years, the bowls have hosted dozens of great games, outstanding performances and just memorable moments—none more so than Roy Riegels's wrong-way run at the 1929 Rose Bowl. Then there was the Cotton Bowl game of 1954 when Tommy Lewis jumped off the Alabama bench to tackle Rice's Dicky Moegle as he was racing for a touchdown, an incident which more scribes remember than the fact that Moegle rushed for 265 yards that afternoon, more than anyone had previously in *any* bowl game, a record that would stand for almost a quarter-century. At the 1947 Rose Bowl Al Hoisch of UCLA ran a kickoff back 103 yards against Illinois; and in the same stadium, in 1963, Wisconsin's Ron VanderKelen passed for 401 yards against USC (the Badgers still lost 42–37). To this day fans can remember the day in 1946 when Bobby Layne astounded the Cotton Bowl crowd by completing 11 of 12 passes and scoring 28 points by himself to lead the Longhorns to a 40–27 victory over Missouri. And it is unlikely anyone will top Archie Griffin's "familiarity" standard, set in 1976 when he made a fourth consecutive appearance in the Rose Bowl (his Ohio State team, however, won only the 1974 game). Even the so-called lesser bowls have had their moments: Terry Baker's record-setting run of 99 yards from scrimmage for Oregon State in the 1962 Liberty Bowl, Florida State's Fred Biletnikoff

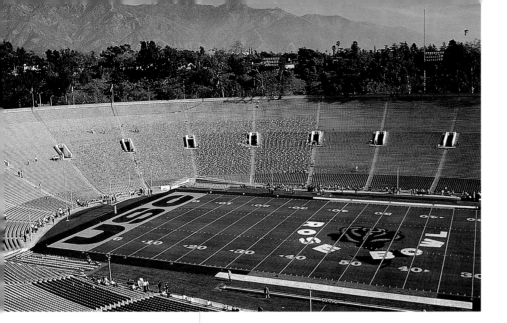

THE ROSE BOWL

The Rose Bowl in Pasadena, California, home to a true New Year's Day classic. The first Rose Bowl game was played in 1902, when Michigan vanquished Stanford 49–0. The largest crowd ever to attend a Rose Bowl game gathered in 1973, when 106,869 watched Southern Cal trounce Ohio State 42–17.

catching four touchdown passes in the 1965 Gator Bowl, Russell Erxleben kicking a booming 55-yard field goal for Texas in the 1976 Astro-Bluebonnet Bowl, Texas Tech's James Gray breaking Moegle's record by gaining 280 yards rushing at the 1989 All-America Bowl.

Today bowl time (no longer just New Year's Day) has a significance granted by the Bowl Championship Series, which was launched in 1998 to match the nation's No. 1 and No. 2 ranked teams in a bowl game to determine the national championship. The BCS, as it is commonly called, is a coalition of the Rose, Orange, Sugar, and Fiesta Bowls, who alternately host the designated championship game in rotation. The first was in January 1999 at the Fiesta Bowl where Tennessee defeated Florida State 23–16. The following year the Sugar Bowl hosted, with Florida State trouncing Virginia Tech 46–29; and in 2001 Oklahoma claimed the national championship when they prevailed over Florida State at the Orange Bowl.

Some of the very best college football is today reserved for the last week in December and the first week of January when each season climaxes in a dazzle of bowl games.

A bearded, bespectacled zoology professor at Throop College of Technology (now the California Institute of Technology) by the name of Charles Frederick Holder deserves credit for launching the Tournament of Roses, as it was christened in 1890. There was no football game to go along with it that year, but it was indeed a celebration in which the people of Pasadena could take pride.

Holder and other members of Pasadena's fashionable Valley Hunt Club organized it as a New Year's Day festival to celebrate the sunshine, fruits, and flowers that flourished in Southern California while most of the rest of the nation shivered and sloshed through the winter. Everyone in town was invited and most of them, about 3,000 then, showed up at Sportsmen's Park for the gala, and most brought roses, as requested in the invitation, for a gigantic floral display. It was a picnic of magnificent proportions, with everything from rose-decorating competitions to burro races.

The following year, 1891, the festival was expanded to include an official Tournament of Roses parade, which took approximately the same route it does today. In its earliest days, horses, carriages, bicycles, and practically anything that could move were festooned with roses for the parade, the noble predecessors of the elaborate floats of today.

The festival grew quickly in popularity, and soon people came from all over the country to attend it. To establish the festival as a truly national one, James H. Wagner, president of the Tournament of Roses Association, which had been formed to run the burgeoning festival, proposed that the parade of 1902 be followed by a college football game match-

GAMES WORTH REMEMBERING

1902 | MICHIGAN 49 STANFORD 0

The two teams that queued up at Tournament Park in Pasadena before a crowd of about 8,000 for the very first Rose Bowl game were undoubtedly mismatched. But then any team Michigan played that year was mismatched. Not only had the Wolverines won all 10 of their games, but no team had scored a single point against them, while Michigan had racked up 501 points. Fielding Yost's Wolverines had aptly been nicknamed the "Point-a-Minute Team."

For the first 23 minutes of the game, the Indians (Stanford's nickname then before it was changed to Cardinal) played their best football of the year, holding Michigan scoreless, even rebuffing them three times from the 1-foot line. But finally Michigan powered in for a score, and then the demolition began. Not only was Stanford beaten up on the scoreboard, the team was also brutalized physically. Guard William Roosevelt, a second cousin of

It appears the Michigan team, shown here en route, found a unique method of travel to reach the 1902 Rose Bowl in Pasadena, Michigan defeated Stanford that New Year's Day, 49—0, capping a season in which they outscored their 11 opponents 550—0.

ing the best team from the East with the best of the West. Fielding Yost's great Michigan team was invited to come out to play Stanford, and the Rose Bowl was born. After Michigan annihilated Stanford 49–0, however, the California festival organizers were less enthusiastic about cross-country football competition and decided to offer different post-parade extravaganzas. Over the next 14 years, such things as chariot races, rodeo events, and races that involved everything from ostriches to camels were staged. Finally, football was reinstated in 1916 when Brown traveled from Providence, Rhode Island, to face Washington State. This time the West Coast triumphed, and from that New Year's Day forward, the Rose Bowl has become an annual institution.

A Dirty Story

Michigan played the same 11 men the entire game in 1902. Their All-American halfback Willie Heston told this story about it afterward: "The night after the game we had our dinner at the Raymond House in Pasadena and were sitting in the lobby enjoying ourselves. Coach Yost suddenly became aware that our three substitutes were missing. He asked Dan McGugin, our left guard, and me to look them up. We found them in back of the hotel turning a garden hose on each other and rolling in the dirt—in full uniform. They told us they were ashamed to go back to Michigan and have the folks think they hadn't played."

Halas at the Rose Bowl

George Halas, sometimes called the Father of Pro Football, played at Illinois and later for Great Lakes during World War I. While with the latter he went to the Rose Bowl in 1919, and described the game in his own inimitable way:

The Mare Island Marines, led by Biff Bangs and a great center, Jake Risley, had emerged as the best team in the West . . . [they] fumbled early. We recovered. Paddy Driscoll kicked to put us ahead 3–0. A pass intercep-tion by Lawrence Ecklund set up a touchdown by Blondy Reeves, a 215-pound plunger. [Hugh] Blacklock kicked for the extra point. After a sec-ond interception Driscoll threw to me on the 10 and I zipped my way to the goal. Later I intercepted a pass and re-turned it 77 yards. A determined Ma-rine, Jim Blewitt, caught me on the 3-yard line. I should have scored. After I took up coaching, I told the [ball-] carriers that when they reach the three, they should dive across the goal.

Anyone who can't dive three yards should play Parcheesi.

Later Paddy threw a pass to me in the end zone. It was short. I ran for it, bending low. My hands were only an inch off the ground. The ball came in and I held it. But the ref-eree, Walter Eckersall, ruled the ball had touched the ground. It had not. He cheated me out of a touchdown. And Walter came from Chicago! I would have expected a little more civic mindedness.

President Theodore Roosevelt, played the entire game and afterward retired for treatment of a broken leg and two broken ribs. Two other Indians also found they had broken bones.

When it was mercifully over, Michigan's stats were overwhelming. Fullback Neil Snow had rushed for five touchdowns; All-American halfback Willie Heston had rushed for 170 yards on 18 carries; and Michigan as a team outrushed Stanford 503 yards to 67.

1919 | GREAT LAKES 17   MARE ISLAND 0

World War I had ended nearly two months before, but the Tournament of Roses Association in 1918 decided to invite teams from military institutions rather than colleges. Great Lakes represented the naval station just outside Chicago, and Mare Island the Marine training base in California. The sailors had three future NFL Hall of Famers on their squad: end George Halas and backs Paddy Driscoll and Jimmy Conzelman.

Great Lakes controlled the game, striking in the first quarter when Driscoll drop-kicked a 25-yard field goal. The Marines never got going, and Halas clinched it when he grabbed a 22-yard pass from Driscoll and lugged the ball 10 yards into the end zone for the game's final score.

1925 | NOTRE DAME 27   STANFORD 10

The Notre Dame team that Knute Rockne brought to the Rose Bowl in 1925 was the top team in the nation and already a legend. Its backfield consisted of the famed Four Horsemen—Harry Stuhldreyer, Elmer Layden, Jim Crowley, and Don Miller—and they were undefeated.

But Stanford was no slouch. Coached by another immortal, Glenn "Pop" Warner, they had the best fullback in the nation, Ernie Nevers. But Nevers had fractured bones in both ankles during the regular sea-son and was not playing at full strength.

More than 53,000 people crowded into the Rose Bowl to watch the two powerhouses. Rockne started his second string, a ploy he often used, in order to wear down his opponent before putting in his lustrous first-stringers. The subs could not contain Nevers, however, and, after the Indians marched steadily down the field, Rockne pulled them and got down to business.

But it took a while. After a fumble by Crowley, Stanford halfback Murray Cuddeback kicked a 17-yard field goal, the lone score in the first quarter. After that, however, it was almost all Notre Dame. Elmer Layden bucked in for a touchdown in the second quarter, and a few minutes later he snatched a pass Ernie Nevers threw into the flat and raced with it 78 yards for another Irish touchdown. Layden

Rockne and Warner

After Notre Dame and the Four Horsemen defeated Stanford 27–10 in the Rose Bowl on January 1, 1925, Stanford's coach, Pop Warner, fumed about the outcome because his team had outgained Knute Rockne's triumphant 11 and toted up more first downs. In an interview after the game, Warner stormed about, then said that a new scoring system should be instituted immediately, in which a team would get point credits for its first downs and yardage gained.

When victorious coach Rockne was asked if he had a comment on Warner's proposal, he said: "Sure, but I'll not say it until they start giving baseball victories to the teams that have the most men left on base."

repeated the feat in the fourth quarter, this time for a 70-yard touchdown.

Stanford gave Rockne's Irish another touchdown in the third quarter when safety Fred Solomon fumbled a Notre Dame punt, and Ed Hunsinger picked it up and toted it 20 yards for a score. Nevers said after the game, "They lived up to their reputation." And Rockne said, "The Four Horsemen have the right to ride with the gridiron great."

1926 | ALABAMA 20 WASHINGTON 19

Both Alabama and Washington had certified superstar backs in 1926. The Crimson Tide boasted Johnny Mack Brown, who later would become a well-known movie star, featured in dozens of westerns. Washington had George "Wildcat" Wilson.

Alabama, coached by the famed Wallace Wade, was undefeated going into the Rose Bowl and notorious for its stingy defense. On the other hand, Washington was an explosive offensive team that

The Rose Bowl parking lot, January 1, 1925. College football fans were there that day to watch Notre Dame in its first appearance in a bowl game. Coached by Knute Rockne and featuring the Four Horsemen in the backfield, the Fighting Irish defeated Stanford 27–10.

had scored 450 points during the regular season. And, at least in the first half, it appeared offense would prevail.

Wildcat Wilson was uncontrollable, running, passing, and intercepting 'Bama passes. The Huskies racked up two touchdowns, but they couldn't convert the extra points, which would prove to be their downfall.

Washington's 12–0 halftime lead seemed comfortable, but Wilson was hurt and on the sidelines. Alabama took quick advantage of it, scoring three touchdowns in the first 7 minutes of the third quarter. Quarterback Pooley Hubert, after carrying the ball on every play of the drive, snuck in from the one for the first score. Then Johnny Mack Brown streaked down the field and without losing a step gathered in a long, lofty pass from Grant Gillis, a picture-perfect, 59-yard touchdown play. On Alabama's next possession, Hubert hit Brown on

Washington's 3-yard line, and Brown carried two Washington defenders into the end zone with him. Wilson came back into the game for the Huskies and led them to another touchdown but couldn't get them any closer than the 1-point margin by which they finally lost.

1935 | ALABAMA 29 STANFORD 13

Frank Thomas was coach of Alabama when they made their fourth appearance in the Rose Bowl. And at each end of his offensive line, he had a man destined to become a football legend, each in a different way: Don Hutson, the greatest pass-catcher of his time, and Paul "Bear" Bryant, who would gain his fame as a coach. Besides those two, 'Bama had one of the best tailbacks anywhere in Dixie Howell, whom Grantland Rice called the "Human Howitzer" because of his powerful arm and pinpoint passing.

Wrong-Way Riegels

In the most infamous run in college football annals, Roy Riegels, California's center, scooped up a Georgia Tech fumble in the 1929 Rose Bowl game and began running laterally across the field (you could run with a fumble in those days), turned the corner, and streaked off toward the goal line. Only it was his own goal he was racing toward. More than 66,000 fans sat dumbfounded as Riegels ran 80 yards the wrong way with his teammate

Benny Lom in desperate pursuit. Riegels made it into the end zone but Lom pulled him back out to the 1-yard line where Georgia Tech tacklers brought him to the turf. On the ensuing play, California tried to punt out of danger (Riegels centered the ball) but it was blocked and the ball bounced out of the end zone.

The 2-point safety proved to be the margin of victory at day's end, the final score Georgia Tech 8, California 7.

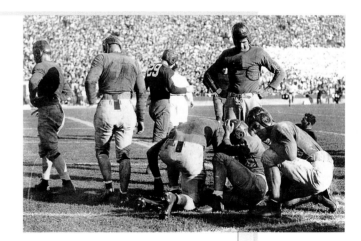

California center Roy Riegels (hand on helmet) sits in consternation amid his equally dismayed teammates after running with a fumble 79 net yards the wrong way in the 1929 Rose Bowl against Georgia Tech.

The Fiery Red

Mel Hein, who after his Hall of Fame college football career forged another with the New York Giants (he was named the All-Pro center an unprecedented eight consecutive times), got to the Rose Bowl in 1931, the last time Washington State appeared in the classic until New Year's Day 1998. He tells about the experience:

Our coach, a fine man, Babe Hollingberry, was somewhat of a showman and he was superstitious. In the showman role he bought a lot of new uniforms for our appearance in the Rose Bowl—bright crimson red. The headgear was red, the shoes were red, the stockings were red, everything was red. I think it scared us more than Alabama because we didn't play too good a ball game.

They walloped us 24–0. They simply had a better team than we had.

The superstitious part of Babe Hollingberry came out when we got back to Pullman after the game. No one ever saw those uniforms again, and the story was that Babe had a big bonfire and burned them all. He didn't want any of his teams ever to wear those uniforms again.

The Crimson Tide, sporting a 10-0 record and ranked No. 1 in the nation, was a favorite, but in the first quarter they barely resembled a national champ. Stanford totally dominated, and the Tide was held to a mere 4 yards during the entire quarter. But then Howell and Hutson came alive before the crowd of more than 85,000, and Alabama erupted with 22 points in the second quarter.

Dixie Howell ended the day with a total of 160 yards passing and another 111 rushing (67 of which were earned on a dazzling touchdown run). But sitting up in the stands, Curly Lambeau, coach of the Green Bay Packers, was more impressed with the fleet-footed end who seemed to be able to catch anything thrown within 10 feet of him, and made a silent vow that he was going to put Don Hutson in a Packer uniform the next year.

Triple-threat back Dixie Howell scores for Alabama in the 1935 Rose Bowl game. Howell scored two touchdowns that day and teamed with his favorite receiver, Don Hutson, for another two as the Crimson Tide defeated Stanford 29–13.

1949 | NORTHWESTERN 20 CALIFORNIA 14

California and its coach, Lynn "Pappy" Waldorf, really wanted to play Michigan, the nation's top-ranked team, in the Rose Bowl of 1949. But the Wolverines had been there the year before and under the terms of the agreement between the Pacific Coast Conference and the Big Ten, a team could not appear in successive years. So Northwestern, the second-place team, went to Pasadena instead.

One of the more controversial touchdowns in Rose Bowl history is this one in 1949, where Northwestern fullback Art Murakowski (30) loses the ball as he is crossing the California goal line. The official, however, ruled that Murakowski had crossed the goal line before losing possession of the ball; the touchdown proved to be the margin of victory in Northwestern's 20—14 win. Tackling Murakowski is California end Norm Pressley.

The Golden Bears from Berkeley, with their All-American back Jackie Jensen, were the decided favorites, but Waldorf, who had coached at Northwestern earlier in his career, was wary of the Wildcats. His concern was justified in the first quarter when halfback Frank Aschenbrenner zigzagged through the California defense on a 73-yard touchdown run. Not to be outdone, however, Jackie Jensen on the first play from scrimmage after the ensuing kickoff raced 67 yards to tie the game.

In the second quarter, Northwestern fullback Art Murakowski bucked in from the 1, only to fumble the ball in the end zone, but field judge Jay Berwanger (who at the University of Chicago in 1935 won the first Heisman Trophy) ruled that he had crossed the goal before the fumble and allowed the touchdown to stand.

Jackie Jensen left the game in the third quarter with an injury and never returned, but California still moved the ball and finally regained the lead 14–13. But then, with a Frank Merriwell ending, Northwestern pulled it out. With less than 3 minutes left in the game, the Wildcats had the ball on the Golden Bears' 43-yard line, second down and 8 yards to go for a first down. Northwestern came out of the huddle, lined up in their typical T formation, with quarterback Don Burson behind the center calling signals. Suddenly halfback Frank Aschenbrenner went into motion to the right, and Burson shifted over a man. The snap went directly to halfback Ed Tunnicliff, who charged toward the slot at right tackle, then veered off to follow Aschenbrenner's interference around right end. Cal was totally taken in, and Tunnicliff raced for the game-winning touchdown.

1956 | MICHIGAN STATE 17 UCLA 14

Duffy Daugherty's Michigan State 11 was ranked second in the nation at the end of the 1955 season, only undefeated Oklahoma having fared better. And UCLA was No. 4. Their meeting in Pasadena produced one of the most chaotic endings in Rose Bowl history.

The Spartans were quarterbacked by consensus All-America Earl Morrall, but he had a tough time getting going. His first pass of the game was intercepted deep in his own territory, and a few plays later UCLA turned it into the game's first score.

Morrall redeemed himself in the following period of play, leading an 80-yard march down the field and icing it with a 13-yard touchdown pass to halfback Clarence Peaks. The game remained tied at 7 into the fourth quarter, but then Peaks took a pitchout from Morrall, pulled up, and heaved a long pass to end John Lewis, who shook off a tackler and carried the ball into the end zone for a 67-yard touchdown.

Then it was UCLA quarterback Ronnie Knox's turn, engineering his own march, which culminated when substitute fullback Doug Peters bucked in from the one. But Morrall moved the Spartans again, and it appeared the game was Michigan State's when, with just over a minute and a half left, kicker Gerry Planutis lined up for a try from the UCLA 22. But he missed and the Bruins took possession of the ball. That's when the chaos started.

On the first play of their possession, UCLA was penalized 15 yards for coaching from the sideline, called when an assistant coach shouted to Knox to pass the ball. Then, from the 5, Knox faded back to pass and, under a heavy Michigan State rush, threw the ball away, but UCLA was penalized again, this time for having an ineligible receiver downfield. The ball was moved back to UCLA's 1-yard line. The Bruins decided to punt it out of danger. Seemingly determined to force a win on Michigan State, UCLA got off a short punt and then drew a 15-yard penalty when Hardeman Cureton bumped into Clarence Peaks, who had signaled for a fair catch. Michigan State ended up on the UCLA 19-yard line.

Michigan State, seemingly as reluctant as UCLA to win, fumbled the ball twice, recovered both times, then incurred a 10-yard penalty for illegal use of the hands, and used up all their time-outs. But fi-

Michigan State coach Duffy Daugherty with quarterback Earl Morrall (top) and end Dave Kaiser savor the moment of victory after the 1956 Rose Bowl game. Kaiser kicked the game-winning 41-yard field goal in the last seconds of the game. Daugherty coached the Spartans from 1954 to 1972, guiding them to a national championship in 1965 and three Rose Bowl appearances.

nally they worked their way back to the UCLA 19, and with only seconds left Daugherty pulled off a desperate but decisive move. He sent a substitute in, drawing a 5-yard, delay-of-game penalty, which stopped the clock, enabling his team to line up for a field goal try. But it wasn't regular placekicker Planutis, who had missed three attempts earlier in the game, standing behind the holder—instead it was end Dave Kaiser, who boomed the ball 41 yards straight through the uprights for a last-second victory.

1963 | USC 42 WISCONSIN 37

This particular Rose Bowl game matched No. 1 USC, undefeated in 11 games, and No. 2 Wisconsin, and the result was a display of passing pyrotechnics unprecedented in the bowl's history.

Led by All-American candidate quarterback Pete Beathard, USC was a decided favorite, and they played like one as they transformed a 21–7 halftime lead into a 42–14 mauling by the fourth quarter. Beathard was unstoppable, setting two Rose Bowl records with 401 yards gained passing, including four touchdowns, and completing 33 of 48.

Many of the more than 100,000 fans had already left the stadium when suddenly Wisconsin erupted, and USC was very nearly overwhelmed. A pair of touchdowns, one on a run by Badger halfback Lou Holland and another on a pass from Ron VanderKelen to halfback Gary Kroner, diminished the score to 42–28. A safety gave Wisconsin another 2 points and possession of the ball. Again VanderKelen moved the Badgers, capping the drive with another touchdown pass, this time to end Pat Richter, and the score was now 42–37 with a little over a minute to play. But an onside kick failed, and time finally ran out on Wisconsin.

1972 | STANFORD 13 MICHIGAN 12

Stanford and Michigan had met in the Rose Bowl once before, 70 years earlier in the very first contest for the roses.

The Cardinal, as Stanford was now known, had waited a long time to avenge that original 49–0 shellacking. Stanford had been to the classic the year before, drubbing a favored Ohio State team 27–17 behind the passing of Heisman Trophy winner Jim Plunkett. Plunkett was gone by New Year's Day 1972, but in his place was Don Bunce, who would rise to the occasion. Michigan was undefeated, winning 11 games and the Big Ten title, and was favored to beat Stanford.

The Wolverines had led 3–0 at the half and 10–3 at the start of the fourth quarter. Then Johnny

Ron Bedsole (19) leaps to grab the fourth touchdown pass thrown by Pete Beathard for Southern Cal in the 1963 Rose Bowl. Along with another touchdown, it was enough to give the Trojans a 42–37 win over Wisconsin, despite the Badgers' 23-point fourth quarter. Wisconsin defenders are Fred Reichardt (48) and Jim Nettles (26).

Ralston, Stanford's adventuresome coach, took a gamble that paid off. With fourth and 10 on his own 33-yard line, he called for a fake punt and Jackie Brown swept around right end for 31 yards. Moments later, the same swift back cut off tackle and broke free—24 yards and a touchdown.

Michigan got within range of a field goal, but the 46-yard try fell short, and into the hands of safety Jim Ferguson, who tried to run it back, only to be tackled in the end zone for a safety.

Losing by 2 points, Stanford had the ball on their own 22-yard line with 1 minute and 48 seconds left. Now it was Don Bunce's moment to glimmer under the California sun. He threw for 13 to tight end Bill Scott, picked up 16 and then another 12 on tosses to flanker John Winesberry, plus 11 more when he hit split end Miles Moore, and 14 on a strike to fullback Reggie Sanderson. Suddenly Stanford stood on the Michigan 14-yard line with 14 seconds to go. On came Rod Garcia to boot the game-winning field goal, giving Stanford both long-awaited revenge and back-to-back Rose Bowl victories.

1975 | USC 18   OHIO STATE 17

The confrontation between the Buckeyes of Ohio State and the Trojans of Southern Cal brought together two of the best running backs in college football, both consensus All-Americas: Heisman Trophy winner Archie Griffin and Anthony Davis, runner-up for that award. But the Trojans would hold Griffin to a mere 76 yards, the first time in 23 games that he had not collected over 100 yards rushing, while Davis had to leave the game injured in the second period after gaining 71 yards for the Trojans.

The two highly ranked teams were at their defensive best in the first half. The Trojans got a

field goal in the first quarter but lost the lead in the second when Buckeye fullback Champ Henson bulled in from the 2. There was not another score until the fourth quarter.

Pat Haden, USC's All-America candidate quarterback and a Rhodes Scholar, regained the lead for his Trojans when he found tight end Jim Obradovich in the end zone. But Ohio State came right back in one of Woody Hayes's patented plodding drives, which climaxed when quarterback Cornelius Greene carried it in from the 3. The Buckeyes got the ball again and increased their lead to 17–10 with a field goal by Tom Skladany.

But then it was time for some frenetic last-minute action by Southern Cal. Pat Haden guided the Trojans down the field 83 yards, climaxed by a

Pete Johnson carries the ball for Ohio State in a 1975 game against Michigan State. Ohio State went to the Rose Bowl that year but lost to UCLA 23—10. The Buckeyes have represented the Big Ten in 13 Rose Bowls and won six times.

38-yard touchdown pass to wide receiver John McKay, the son and namesake of Southern Cal's coach. A kicked extra point would tie it, but coach McKay would have none of that. "We didn't come to play for a tie," he said later. So Pat Haden took the snap, rolled to his right, and rifled one to Shelton Diggs in the end zone for a 2-point conversion and a 1-point lead. In the last seconds of the game, Skladany tried for a record 62-yard field goal for Ohio State, but it fell short. An unhappy Woody Hayes said after the game: "We got beaten by a better team. One point better."

1976 | UCLA 23   OHIO STATE 10

The Bruins were a decided underdog this New Year's Day, having lost 41–20 in the regular season to Woody Hayes's Buckeyes, who featured two-time Heisman Trophy winner Archie Griffin. It was, however, to be a near replay of the Rose Bowl of 1966 when UCLA faced favored Michigan State, a team they had fallen to 13–3 earlier in the season.

Losing 3–0 at the half in 1976, UCLA exploded in the third quarter with 16 unanswered points behind the passing of John Sciarra, who threw two touchdown passes to flanker Wally Henry, and a field goal by Brett White. Ohio State got a touchdown in the final period, but the Bruins came right back with one of their own on a breakaway 54-yard run by halfback Wendell Tyler, who led all rushers that day with 172 yards.

The 23–10 victory was a stunning surprise, just as memorable as the 14–12 upset over Michigan State in 1966. In that game, too, it was the quarterback who sparked the Bruins to victory: Gary Beban threw two touchdown passes that day, enough for the win (UCLA incidentally had never won a bowl game before that one).

1992 | WASHINGTON 34   MICHIGAN 14

There was the possibility of a national championship for undefeated Washington if they triumphed over Michigan in Pasadena. The Huskies were ranked just beneath similarly undefeated Miami (Florida), who was playing Nebraska in the Orange Bowl. Michigan, who had lost only once during the season, to Florida State, was bent on being the spoiler.

The Wolverines certainly had the talent: wide receiver Desmond Howard had won the Heisman Trophy, linebacker Erick Anderson was honored with the Butkus Award, quarterback Elvis Grbac and freshman running back Tyrone Wheatley were nationally recognized for their performances during the 1991 season. The Washington Huskies, however, boasted college football's top-ranked defense.

And as so often happens, it was defense that prevailed. Washington held the Wolverines' ordinarily explosive offense to a single touchdown in the first half and took a 13–7 lead into the locker room. The Huskies shut out Michigan in the third quarter and added another 8 points. In the fourth quarter, it was all Washington—two more touchdowns for the Huskies, giving up only a meaningless score near the end of the game when Wheatley broke loose on a 53-yard touchdown run.

The day belonged to Washington's defense and the play of quarterback Billy Joe Hobert, who passed for two touchdowns and ran for another. But the Huskies had to settle for a shared national title because the Miami Hurricanes drubbed Nebraska in Miami 22–0.

2000 | WISCONSIN 17 STANFORD 9

Wisconsin had won at Pasadena the previous year, defeating UCLA 38–31, and had their sight set on becoming the first Big Ten team to ever win back-to-back Rose Bowls. Stanford had not been to a Rose Bowl in 28 years. Wisconsin had running back Ron Dayne, the Heisman Trophy winner for 1999 and college football's all-time leading rusher (6,397 yards).

Neither team was in contention for the national championship; Wisconsin had lost two of their 11 games in 1999 and Stanford was 8-3. The interest in the game centered around the volatile offenses of both teams: Dayne carrying the ball for the Badgers and the always dangerous Stanford passing attack, this year led by quarterback Todd Husak.

What the fans got, however, was the lowest-scoring Rose Bowl game in 23 years. In the first half, Dayne was held to 46 yards rushing, Wisconsin's only touchdown coming on a 1-yard quarterback sneak by Brooks Bollinger. Stanford could only post a field goal before intermission.

On the second play of the third quarter, however, Dayne burst through the Stanford line, broke two tackles, and carried the ball 64 yards before being brought down at the Stanford 11-yard line. Two plays later he carried it in for the touchdown (his fifth career Rose Bowl touchdown, a record). From that point on, Dayne was virtually unstoppable and ended the day with 200 yards rushing.

Husak passed for 258 yards (17 of 34), but the Cardinal was minus 5 yards rushing (another Rose Bowl record, although a rather undistinguished one). The final score was 17–9, but Ron Dayne ended his college football career on a high note, and Wisconsin had the distinction of becoming the only Big Ten team to prevail in the Rose Bowl two years in a row.

THE ORANGE BOWL

If sunny Southern California could have a New Year's Day football spectacle, why couldn't sunny South Florida? So speculated a group of businessmen and civic officials in the early 1930s. They had no trouble selling the idea in tourist-happy Miami.

It was 1933, and the pageant that emerged was called the Palm Festival. To be featured was a football game that would pit the University of Miami, just then beginning to compete in intercollegiate athletics, against any respectable team it could entice to come down to Florida. New York's Manhattan College agreed.

The game was actually played on January 2, at a local field by the name of Moore Park, and 3,500 showed up for it. Manhattan was favored but perhaps could not adapt to the January warmth and was unable to score. Miami's one touchdown was enough. The next year Duquesne came down from Pittsburgh and demolished Miami 33–7.

In 1935, the Palm Festival was renamed the Orange Bowl Festival. A new charter was drawn up, and the first official Orange Bowl game was played on the site of what is today the Orange Bowl Stadium. In 1935, however, it was merely a small field with wooden bleachers that accommodated just over 5,000 spectators that New Year's Day when Bucknell, from Lewisburg, Pennsylvania, clashed with the Miami Hurricanes. And once again it was not Miami's day, wiped out by a score of 26–0.

Over the years, the Orange Bowl festival has included such other sporting events as a regatta, tennis and golf tournaments, and, of course, a parade. It also became the first major bowl to stage a game at night, when more than 80,000 fans clustered under the lights to watch Nebraska beat Louisiana State 17–12 on New Year's Eve 1971.

GAMES WORTH REMEMBERING

1944 | LOUISIANA STATE 19 TEXAS A&M 14

Steve Van Buren, one of the best running backs in the nation in 1943, almost single-handedly won this game for LSU. It was also one of the more unusual bowl games in that the war had depleted the college football ranks, so 17- and even 16-year-olds were escalated to the college level. One writer referred to this game as the "Teenage Bowl."

The A&M Aggies had beaten Louisiana State during the regular season and were favored. The Aggies displayed a strong passing attack, but Van Buren set the tone of the game in the first period, running the ball in from the 11 for one touchdown and tossing a pass for another. Then in the third quarter, he ripped off a dazzling 63-yard run, and that provided the winning margin.

LEFT
A Miami player shows his exuberance with a kiss for a cheerleader after the Hurricanes triumphed over Oklahoma in the 1988 Orange Bowl 20–14. Miami has been to eight Orange Bowls, the first in 1935, and come out on top in five of them.

RIGHT
Louisiana State halfback Steve Van Buren gains some yardage against Texas A&M in the 1944 Orange Bowl. Van Buren scored two touchdowns that New Year's Day and kicked an extra point as LSU beat the Aggies 19–14. No. 18 for Texas A&M is Earl Betsley.

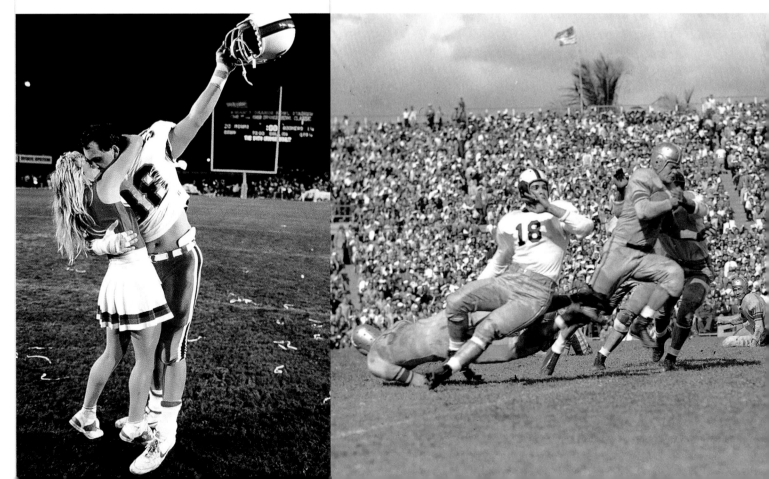

1949 | TEXAS 41 GEORGIA 28

Georgia was a weighty favorite, undefeated in the regular season and led by running back Joe Geri. Texas had lost three games during the regular season and tied another; the only name of consequence on the roster would not become famous in football until a number of years later, and then it would be as a coach—Tom Landry, the Texas quarterback and star defensive back.

The game was entertaining, with the lead changing hands five times during the four quarters until Texas tacked on two touchdowns at the end, giving the final score a more lopsided appearance than the game warranted.

The longest run of the day was the first touchdown, a 71-yard jaunt by Georgia's Al Bodine with an intercepted pass. And the 69 points scored that day still stands as a record Orange Bowl high, although it was matched by Oklahoma's 48–21 victory over Duke in 1958 and Michigan's 35–34 win over Alabama in 2000.

1956 | OKLAHOMA 20 MARYLAND 6

Bud Wilkinson's Sooners had treated Oklahoma fans to 29 consecutive victories by the time they took the field at the Orange Bowl on the first day of 1956. They were an easy choice for the No. 1 berth at the end of the regular season. But Maryland had gone undefeated that season as well. Not only that, coach Jim Tatum and a lot of others around Maryland remembered the humiliation two years earlier when the Terrapins came to the Orange Bowl as undefeated national champs, only to be upset by Oklahoma.

Maryland played a determined first half, their defense shutting down the running of All-American

Tommy McDonald and the rest of the famed Oklahoma offense as well. On top of that, they held the lead with a touchdown from end Ed Vereb. "The sweet spoils of revenge are but a half away," one broadcaster noted.

But they were much further away than that, as Oklahoma proved quickly in the second half. On their first possession the Sooners drove down the field, and finally Tommy McDonald raced around end to score. On their next possession, Oklahoma marched downfield again, this time with quarterback Jay O'Neal carrying it in for a 14–6 lead. The final blow came in the last quarter when Carl Dodd snatched a Maryland pass and raced 82 yards for the game's final score.

1965 | TEXAS 21 ALABAMA 17

Texas had been to the Orange Bowl only once (1949) prior to 1965, obviously much more accustomed to the Cotton Bowl, where they had already won six times.

Bear Bryant's Crimson Tide, quarterbacked by All-American Joe Namath, were ranked No. 1 when they arrived in Miami, after a perfect season. Texas had lost only to unbeaten Arkansas.

In the first quarter, Texas had the ball on their own 21-yard line when halfback Ernie Koy broke loose and sprinted 79 yards for a touchdown, at the time the longest run from scrimmage in Orange Bowl history. A few minutes later, and just into the second quarter, Longhorn quarterback Jim Judson hit streaking split end George Sauer (later Namath's teammate on the Super Bowl Champion New York Jets) on a 69-yard touchdown pass. Alabama fumbled not too many minutes later, and Ernie Koy carried the ball in for the Longhorns' third touchdown of the half.

After the intermission, Alabama fought back with a touchdown and a field goal to make a game of it. Their chance to win came in the fourth quarter. Inches from the goal line, on fourth down, a pained, gimpy Joe Namath tried to sneak it in but was turned back by an inspired Texas defense.

1968 | OKLAHOMA 26 TENNESSEE 24

Tennessee rated a little higher than Oklahoma at the close of the 1967 regular season, both trailing USC, which sat in the top spot. A national championship was not riding on the game, but it promised to be the best of the bowl matchups that year.

Oklahoma was now under the tutelage of Chuck Fairbanks, and they had a bull of a fullback in Steve Owens. They also were aiming for a higher ranking, perhaps even a No. 1, if USC were to fall to Indiana in the Rose Bowl.

The Sooners came out on a roll, racking up 19 points in the first half and holding the Volunteers from Tennessee scoreless. But Tennessee came alive

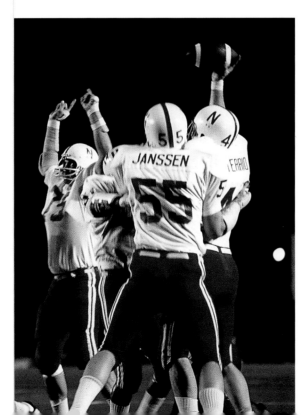

Nebraska players celebrate their victory in the 1972 Orange Bowl, after defeating Alabama 38–6. The Cornhuskers made their first appearance in a bowl game in 1941, but lost to Stanford 21–13. By 2001, Nebraska had played in 39 different bowl games, winning 20 and losing 19.

in the third quarter, and a pair of touchdowns put them right back in the game, trailing by a mere 5 points. In the fourth quarter, Tennessee added another 10 points, but Oklahoma, leading all the way, got 7 when defensive back Bob Stephenson picked off a Volunteer pass and ran it back for a touchdown.

Tennessee fought all the way, moving the ball as the clock worked against them. Then finally, with 14 seconds remaining and behind by 2 points, they got within field goal range. There was hardly a sound in the Orange Bowl as Karl Kremser tried a 43-yarder; then, as it veered off, the Oklahoma partisans erupted. There was no national championship for the Sooners, however, who remained in the shadow of USC, a team also victorious that New Year's Day.

1975 | NOTRE DAME 13 ALABAMA 11

Notre Dame had been the national champion the year before, but after two losses during the 1974 season they had no chance for a repeat title; all that remained was to be a spoiler to No. 1 ranked Alabama. It was Ara Parseghian's last game as Notre Dame's head coach, and he wanted to leave on a better note than the 55–24 trimming his Irish had taken from Southern Cal in the last game of the regular season.

Across the field was Bear Bryant's team, eager to solidify its claim to the national title, and reverse their dismal recent history in bowl appearances— they had lost seven in a row.

But it was not to be. The star-crossed Crimson Tide were as lackluster as they had been in any of the preceding seven bowl games. Notre Dame got off to a fast start, and fullback Wayne Bullock put them on the board when he bulled his way into the Alabama end zone in the first quarter. In the next period, Mark McLane ran another one in from the 9, a missed extra point leaving the score at 13–0.

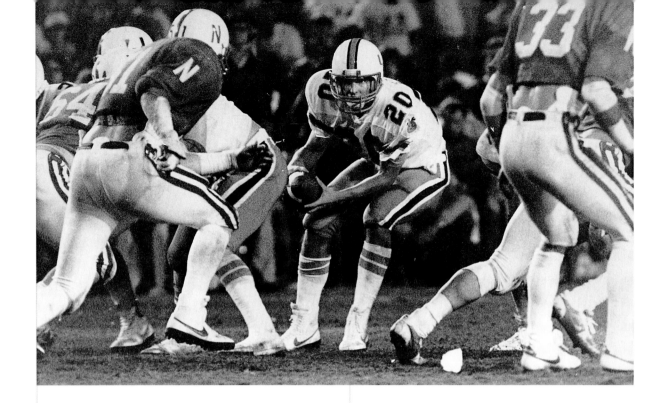

That was enough. The Irish gave up a field goal, and in the fourth quarter a touchdown when Richard Todd unleashed a long one to Russ Schamun. Alabama threatened in the closing minutes, getting close to field goal range, but then their bowl demons took over as Todd was intercepted. Ara Parseghian departed Notre Dame just as he had come in 11 years earlier, with a win.

1984 | MIAMI (FLORIDA) 31   NEBRASKA 30

The Miami Hurricanes had not won an Orange Bowl contest since 1946, when they barely edged out Holy Cross; in fact, they had not been to the classic since 1951, when they lost to Clemson by a point. But this was to be their year, and they unseated undefeated Nebraska, the nation's top-ranked team.

The Nebraska Cornhuskers were an 11-point favorite according to the bookmakers, to which Miami coach Howard Schnellenberger said, "I doubt they know what a bunch of alley cats Nebraska is about to run into."

Besides a confident coach Miami had quarterback Bernie Kosar, a drop-back passer with the finesse of a pro, and a defense that was obsessed with stopping Nebraska's All-American running back, Mike Rozier.

The Hurricanes lived up to their nickname in the first quarter. Kosar passed them down the field, then threw a short one to tight end Glenn Dennison for the score. A field goal and another strike to Dennison made the score 17–0 at the end of the period.

In the second quarter, it was Nebraska's turn. The Cornhuskers, who had averaged 52 points a game during the regular season, came back and put 10 on the board. Then a minute into the second half, they tied it. But Kosar went back to the air to set up first one touchdown and then another, and Miami took a 31–17 lead into the fourth quarter.

Nebraska fought back gamely, driving 76 yards to narrow the lead to 7 points. There were just under 2 minutes left in the game when the Cornhuskers got the ball back, and again they marched. At Miami's 24-yard line, fourth and 8, coach Tom

Miami (Florida) quarterback Bernie Kosar (20), with the ball, in the 1984 Orange Bowl game against Nebraska. Behind the passing of Kosar, the Hurricanes upset the top-ranked, undefeated Cornhuskers that day 31—30.

Osborne called for a pitchout to Jeff Smith, who had replaced Mike Rozier, out with a foot injury. Smith not only passed the first-down marker but made it all the way in for the score.

One point would tie it, and that would almost certainly be enough to maintain Nebraska's grip on the national championship. A 2-point conversion would win the game. Osborne, subscribing to the dictum that a true champion only plays to win, went for the 2, a roll-out pass that defensive back Kenny Calhoun batted away to give Miami its first national championship.

1988 | MIAMI (FLORIDA) 20   OKLAHOMA 14

This game was for the national championship. Oklahoma had been ranked No. 1 in the nation throughout most of the 1987 season, winning all 11 of their games. Miami, also undefeated in 11 games, was ranked second when the two squared off on New Year's Day at the Orange Bowl. The Hurricanes were looking for a repeat of their 1983 Orange Bowl performance when they knocked off No. 1 ranked Nebraska to win the national title.

With that in mind, Miami marched 65 yards down the field on their first possession, capping it with a 30-yard touchdown pass from Steve Walsh to Melvin Bratton. But then everything slowed down for the Hurricanes. Oklahoma similarly was going nowhere until late in the second quarter when Ricky Dixon intercepted a pass from Walsh; the Sooners ground it out, scoring after a 15-play drive with just 9 seconds left on a 1-yard plunge by Anthony Stafford. The score at the half was 7–7.

Miami's offense came to life in the third quarter. Walsh led drives that resulted in two scores: a 56-yard field goal by Greg Cox (an Orange Bowl record) and a 23-yard touchdown pass from Walsh to

Michael Irvin. Cox added another field goal, a 48-yarder, in the final period. With just over 2 minutes remaining Miami had a 20–7 lead. Oklahoma countered with a trick play: quarterback Charles Thompson deliberately fumbled the ball to offensive guard Mark Hutson, who carried it 29 yards for the score. But it was too little, too late.

Just as they had five years earlier, the Miami Hurricanes upset the nation's No. 1 team and captured the national championship.

1994 | FLORIDA STATE 18   NEBRASKA 16

It was the 60th anniversary of the Orange Bowl. And it was quite a celebration. The two top-ranked teams in the country—Bobby Bowden's Florida State Seminoles and Tom Osborne's Nebraska Cornhuskers—met to determine the national championship, and it was not decided until the very last second of the game.

As exciting a game as it became, it did not start out that way. Neither team scored in the first quarter, and defense continued to dominate in the second. The Seminoles managed two field goals, however, countered by a 34-yard touchdown pass by Tommie Frazier that was was tipped off the hand of a Florida State defender into the arms of Nebraska wide receiver Reggie Baul. The Cornhuskers led at the half 7–6.

On the opening possession of the second half, however, Florida State marched, a 67-yard drive, led by quarterback and that year's Heisman Trophy winner Charlie Ward and highlighted by a 41-yard Ward pass to Kevin Knox and culminated with a 1-yard touchdown plunge by fullback William Floyd. One possession later, the Seminoles were on the move again, capped by Scott Bentley's third field goal of the game, this one a 39-yarder. Florida State led 15–7.

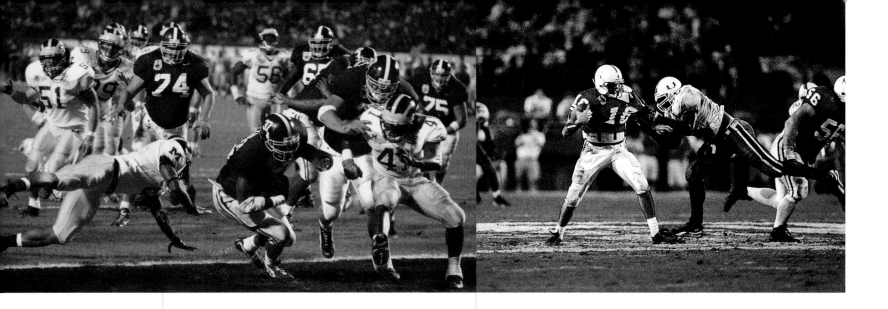

Behind the passing and running of Frazier, Nebraska came back with a drive of their own; from the 12-yard line, Lawrence Phillips danced his way in for the touchdown. A 2-point conversion attempt to tie the game at 15 failed. Then, with less than 5 minutes remaining in the game, Frazier engineered a 76-yard march to the Florida State 4-yard line. But there it stopped and the Cornhuskers had to settle for a 27-yard field goal from Byron Bennett, but they had the lead 16–15.

Now it was Charlie Ward's turn and, with the aid of two 15-yard penalties, he led the Seminoles to the Nebraska 5-yard line. With 21 seconds left in the game, Bentley kicked his fourth field goal of the day to regain the lead for Florida State. But it was not over. After a kickoff return to the 43, Frazier threw a 29-yard pass to Trumane Bell and called a time-out with 1 second on the clock and the ball at the Seminole 28-yard line. Bennett came on to try a 45-yard field goal, but it veered to the right, and Florida State escaped with the win and a national title.

2001 | OKLAHOMA 13 FLORIDA STATE 2

This was the third in the Bowl Championship Series, pitting the top two teams in the nation in a bowl game to determine the national champion.

Oddly enough, Oklahoma, the only undefeated team in the nation in 2000 and ranked No. 1 in both the AP and *USA Today*/ESPN polls, was as much as a two-touchdown underdog to No. 3 Florida State (11-1) according to the handicappers. It was also only the third time ever that a Heisman Trophy winner (quarterback Chris Weinke of Florida State) faced the runner-up for that award (Josh Heupel, Oklahoma's quarterback) in a bowl game. The other two: Ohio State's Archie Griffin against USC's Anthony Davis at the Rose Bowl in 1975, and South Carolina's George Rogers going up against Pittsburgh's Hugh Green in the 1980 Gator Bowl.

Florida State was playing in its third consecutive game for the national title, having lost two years earlier to Tennessee but prevailing the next year over Virginia Tech. The Sooners hadn't played for a national championship since 1987. Oklahoma's strong suit was its defense; Florida State's was its offense, which had averaged 42.4 points a game during the regular season.

Defense triumphed. Oklahoma shut out Florida State in the first half and took a 3–0 lead to the locker room on a 27-yard field goal by Tim Duncan. Again in the third quarter, Weinke and his Seminoles were stifled time after time (they would

ABOVE LEFT
Alabama running back Shaun Alexander scores for the Crimson Tide in the 2000 Orange Bowl game against Michigan. Alexander scored three touchdowns that New Year's Day, the most in Alabama history by an individual in a bowl game. But Michigan still won in overtime 35–34.

ABOVE RIGHT
Miami (Florida) quarterback Frank Costa is corraled by a Nebraska defender in the 1995 Orange Bowl game. Nebraska prevailed that day 24–17 before the largest crowd in Orange Bowl history, 81,753.

convert only one of 13 third-down chances in the game). Heupfel moved the Sooners in the third quarter, however, a 39-yard pass to Curtis Fagan setting up another Duncan field goal.

In the fourth quarter, Oklahoma's All-American linebacker Rocky Calmus burst through and knocked the ball out of Weinke's hand deep in Seminole territory. The Sooners recovered the fumble and Quentin Griffin carried it in from the 10-yard line moments later. Florida State was saved from the ignominy of a shutout when Oklahoma's punter took a safety with less than a minute to play in the game. The final score, 13–2, was the lowest scoring Orange Bowl game since Penn State defeated Missouri 10–3 back in 1970.

THE SUGAR BOWL

It took almost eight years for the Sugar Bowl to become a reality, from its inception in 1927 in the minds of Colonel James M. Thompson, publisher of the *New Orleans Item*, and one of his sports columnists, Fred Digby, until the first kickoff of the classic on January 1, 1935.

The two members of the New Orleans journalism community campaigned lustily for a football game to rival the Rose Bowl. Digby actually wanted the game to be the highlight of a midwinter sports carnival, one that would include a variety of athletic competitions. New Orleans was the ideal site for such a pageant, they argued: the climate was pleasant, the city was a popular winter tourist destination, the residents of the area were avowed football fans, it would focus positive publicity on the city. And would it be successful? Look at the Rose Bowl, Digby pointed out—despite the Depression, it was drawing about 60,000 spectators each year.

The city and factions within it, however, did not leap on the Thompson-Digby bandwagon. Instead they listened and hedged and postponed action on the project. But finally in 1934 enough support was garnered, and a Mid-Winter Sports Association was founded, a charter was drawn up, and plans for a New Year's Day college football game were laid.

The charter described the game as a "nonprofit civic enterprise" and specified that any and all proceeds would be distributed to charitable and educational institutions in the area. The site of the game was to be Tulane Stadium, with a seating/standing capacity in 1935 of about 24,000.

Fred Digby's dream had come to life, and it was only appropriate that he name his prodigy. He came up with Sugar Bowl not merely because the state was then the leading sugar producer in the United States but also because the site of Tulane Stadium was a former sugar plantation.

A crowd of 22,026 showed up for the first Sugar Bowl game, which featured Tulane and Temple, and the largely partisan crowd was treated to a Tulane win, 20–14. It was an exciting game. Temple, coached by the immortal Pop Warner, jumped out to a 14–0 lead, but saw it washed away in the second half by Tulane's relentless Green Wave. The play of the day was tallied by Tulane's Monk Simons when he ran back a Temple kickoff 85 yards for a touchdown.

From that first game until the 1975 contest, all Sugar Bowl games were played in Tulane Stadium (long since known as the Sugar Bowl), which was sequentially enlarged over the years until it could accommodate about 81,000 spectators. In 1976, the game was moved to the Louisiana Superdome, its home ever since.

GAMES WORTH REMEMBERING

1945 | DUKE 29 ALABAMA 26

The Sugar Bowl crowd of some 72,000 that year caught a glimpse of budding greatness when Alabama's 18-year-old freshman quarterback Harry Gilmer took the field. Gilmer, who would make the jump pass famous and later lead the Crimson Tide to an undefeated season in 1945 and a 1946 Rose Bowl victory, completed all eight of his pass attempts against Duke and nearly won the game in the last seconds.

But the Duke Blue Devils were a tenacious bunch. They were losing 12–7 at the end of the first quarter and 19–13 at halftime. Their game was running the ball, and they did it well. To take the lead in the third quarter, they marched 64 yards on 10 consecutive carries by fullback Tom Davis.

Alabama turned it around in the fourth quarter when Hugh Morrow intercepted a Duke pass and raced 75 yards with it for a touchdown. With the Crimson Tide ahead 26–20 and 3 minutes remaining, Alabama, on their own 1-yard line, made what turned out to be a terrible decision: an intentional safety, which ceded 2 points but gave them a free kick, on which they hoped to send the ball deep into Duke territory. Only the kick wasn't very good, leaving the ball on Alabama's 40-yard line. Duke rattled off two 20-yard runs and a touchdown; the score was now 29–26 in favor of the Blue Devils.

Still, with Gilmer guiding them, Alabama had a chance, and everyone in Tulane Stadium knew it. Gilmer got the Tide out to their own 42-yard line. Then, with time for only one more play, he faded back, eluded several Duke tacklers, and spot-

ted end Ralph Jones downfield. Gilmer lofted a long pass that dropped into Jones's hands at the 25-yard line, but the lone trailing Duke defender lunged and got hold of Jones's jersey, hung on, and wrestled him to the ground, preserving the Blue Devil victory.

1947 | GEORGIA 20 NORTH CAROLINA 10

The game was billed as the battle of the halfbacks, appropriately enough, considering that Charlie Trippi was at right half for Georgia and Charlie "Choo Choo" Justice was North Carolina's left half. Both were legitimate All-Americans in a year gilded with running backs the likes of Doc Blanchard and Glenn Davis at Army, Doak Walker of Southern Methodist, Clyde "Smackover" Scott of Arkansas, Buddy Young of Illinois, Bob Chappius of Michigan, and Emil Sitko at Notre Dame.

Georgia was favored, undefeated in the 1946 regular season and ranked only behind the magnificent Army and Notre Dame teams. But during the first half, defense prevailed and a crowd that had come to watch the dazzle of the two premier halfbacks was disappointed. The score at intermission was North Carolina 7, Georgia 0.

The Bulldogs must have gotten a bit of inspiration from coach Wally Butts before coming back on the field because they played a much better game in the second half. A concerted drive resulted in one touchdown, and a 67-yard pass play from Trippi to end Dan Edwards in the third quarter gave them a lead they would not relinquish.

As it turned out, it was not to be the day of the heralded halfbacks. Instead it was Georgia quarterback Johnny Rauch who scored two touchdowns and led the Georgia Bulldogs to victory that day.

1951 | KENTUCKY 13 OKLAHOMA 7

By the end of the 1950 season Bud Wilkinson's Sooners had run their amazing winning streak to 31 games, at the time the longest in modern football history. Bear Bryant's Kentucky team had lost only to Tennessee, who in turn had lost only to a much weaker Mississippi State team. While No. 1 ranked Oklahoma had already been awarded the national championship for the year, Kentucky hoped to claim a piece of the title by defeating the nation's best team on New Year's Day.

It was a star-studded cast. Favored Oklahoma had halfback Billy Vessels, fullback Buck McPhail, and tackle Jim Weatherall; Kentucky could boast quarterback Babe Parilli and tackles Bob Gain and Walt Yowarsky, all players of All-America caliber.

But Oklahoma was star-crossed that day. In the opening period quarterback Claude Arnold fumbled on his own 25, and Walt Yowarsky came up with the ball for Kentucky. On the next play, Parilli passed to halfback Shorty Jamerson for the game's first score.

Kentucky's defense was awesome that day as well. Oklahoma got virtually nowhere throughout the first three quarters; in all they had seven fumbles, five of which the Kentuckians recovered.

Parilli passed the Wildcats to the Oklahoma 1-yard line in the second half, and then handed off to Jamerson for the score. That would prove to be enough. Kentucky gave up a touchdown in the fourth quarter, earned for the most part by the rushing of Billy Vessels, the score coming when Vessels tossed a pass to halfback Merrill Green. But that was all for the Sooners, a far cry from the usual five or six touchdowns they ordinarily posted in games that year.

With characteristic class, Wilkinson said after the game, "We knew it had to come sometime. When it did we wanted it to come from a team we had respect for. I can state sincerely that we lost to a great team, a great school, a great coach, and a great state."

1959 | LOUISIANA STATE 7 CLEMSON 0

LSU was a unanimous choice as the best team in the United States in 1958. In its backfield were such luminaries as halfback Billy Cannon, who would win the Heisman Trophy the next year, halfback Johnny Robinson, and quarterback Warren Rabb; roving its sideline was Coach of the Year Paul Dietzel. In addition, LSU used a three-platoon system capable of wearing down the strongest of opponents. And twice-beaten Clemson fell short of that category. As a result, some oddsmakers were favoring the Tigers from Baton Rouge by as much as 17 points.

But for all that, there was only a single score in the entire game, and that was hardly earned. Clemson shut down the running attack of Cannon and Robinson and harassed Rabb throughout the game. The Tigers played their best game of the year, but they made one fatal mistake. In the third quarter, Clemson was forced to punt from their own 20, but the snap was bad and LSU tackle Duane

Kentucky quarterback Babe Parilli (10) carries the ball for the Wildcats in the 1951 Sugar Bowl against Oklahoma. Parilli, living up to his All-America billing, led Kentucky to a 13–7 upset, which also ended the Sooner's 31-game unbeaten streak.

Leopard broke through to fall on the ball on Clemson's 11-yard line. In two plays LSU could only advance the ball to the 9, but then Cannon took a pitchout on an end-around option and passed to Mickey Mangham in the end zone.

1966 | MISSOURI 20 FLORIDA 18

Neither Missouri nor Florida was ranked in the top five when the 1965 season came to a close, but the two teams put on the best display of football in any of the major bowls on New Year's Day 1966.

Missouri, under coach Dan Devine, appeared to have an easy win with a 20–0 lead going into the fourth quarter. Florida could not stop Missouri's hard-charging running game, especially Charlie Brown, who picked up 120 yards on 22 carries. But Florida had Steve Spurrier at quarterback, an All-American candidate who the next year would become only the sixth quarterback to win the Heisman Trophy. And in the fourth quarter he put on as dazzling a display as was ever performed in the closing quarter of any bowl game.

He rallied a disheartened Florida offense, marched them down the field, and tossed a touchdown pass to put them on the scoreboard, but a 2-point conversion try failed. He goaded the defense from the sideline to stop Missouri, and they did. Back on the field again, Spurrier moved the Gators,

passing flawlessly, finally carrying the ball in for another touchdown. With the score 20–12, there was little choice but to go for a 2-point conversion, but again it didn't work. Florida's defense held, however, and soon Spurrier was passing them down the field again, culminating with a touchdown toss. A 2-pointer would tie it, but for the third consecutive time, the attempt failed. Finally, time ran out on Spurrier and his fellow Floridians.

After the final gun, Spurrier lay claim to five Sugar Bowl records: completed passes, 27; attempted passes, 45; yards gained passing, 352; yards gained passing and rushing, 344; most plays passing and rushing, 52; but not the mark he sought the most—victory.

1973 | NOTRE DAME 24 ALABAMA 23

The national championship was on the line when Ara Parseghian's Fighting Irish took to the AstroTurf at Tulane Stadium to battle Bear Bryant's Crimson Tide on December 31, 1973. Both teams had gone through the regular season undefeated, although Alabama claimed the No. 1 ranking.

No Fighting Irish team had gone undefeated since 1949. It was the kind of situation Parseghian loved, the ultimate opportunity to stir his players to greatness.

Alabama was a slight favorite, but that was soon discounted as quarterback Tom Clements, with pin-

Florida quarterback Steve Spurrier (11) barely gets this pass off in the 1966 Sugar Bowl game against Missouri. Spurrier turned in a remarkable performance that day, setting five Sugar Bowl records, but the Hurricanes still lost to Missouri 20—18.

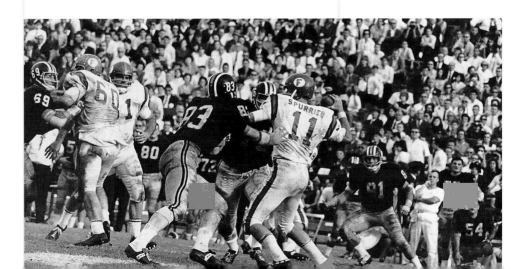

point passing, marched Notre Dame down the field, then gave the football to fullback Wayne Bullock at the 1 to blast in with the game's first score. The Irish failed to make the conversion. The Tide came back in the second quarter when Wilbur Jackson scored, and the successful conversion gave Alabama a 1-point lead. But Notre Dame was explosive. Al Hunter grabbed the Alabama kickoff on his 7-yard line and scampered for a bowl-record 93-yard touchdown return. A 2-point conversion gave Notre Dame a 14–7 lead, which was narrowed before the half by an Alabama field goal.

Alabama regained the lead in the third quarter, slogging out a concerted drive that had begun deep in their own territory, climaxing it with a touchdown. Alabama then held, got the ball back, but fumbled, and the Irish recovered just 12 yards shy of the Tide's goal line. On the first play from scrimmage Earl Penick took advantage of the turnover and carried the ball in to give Notre Dame a 21–17 lead.

In the fourth quarter, however, Notre Dame turned the ball over on a fumble, and Alabama capitalized on it with a touchdown of their own, giving them a lead of 23–21. They missed the extra point, however, and this would prove fatal to Bear Bryant's Alabamans. Notre Dame marched and with time running down Bob Thomas kicked a 19-yard field goal to regain the lead for the Irish. An inspired Notre Dame defense held and, with the narrow victory that day in the Sugar Bowl, Notre Dame wrested the 1973 national title from Alabama.

1979 | ALABAMA 14 PENN STATE 7

Penn State, under Joe Paterno, came to the Sugar Bowl with the expressed intention of winning the first national championship in the school's history. The Nittany Lions brought with them a 19-game winning streak and the No. 1 ranking in the polls. But a win for Bear Bryant's second-ranked Alabama team would give them the national title.

Penn State had Heisman Trophy runner-up Chuck Fusina at quarterback and a powerful fullback in Matt Suhey, as well as All-America linemen Keith Dorney and Bruce Clark, not to mention the nation's top-rated defense. Alabama was quarterbacked by Jeff Rutledge and had a fine running back in Tony Nathan.

The game, heralded as only the fifth major bowl matchup in history between the nation's two top-ranked teams, promised to be an explosive one, with two fine offenses and such high stakes. But it was defense that ruled; neither team scored in the first quarter. Late in the second quarter, the Crimson Tide got a drive going, moving the ball 80 yards, including a 30-yard gainer on a sweep by Tony Nathan, and culminating when Rutledge hit split end Bruce Bolton in the end zone.

In the third quarter, Penn State intercepted Rutledge and moved the ball to the Alabama 17-yard line, where Chuck Fusina passed to Scott Fitzkee for the score. But with time running out in the quarter, Lou Ikner returned a State punt 62 yards for a Tide touchdown.

Penn State had its chance in the fourth when it moved the ball to the Alabama 1-yard line. Three rushes at the fired-up Alabama defense gained nothing; it came down to fourth and inches. Mike Guman tried to vault over the Alabama line but was hurled back. It proved to be the last opportunity for a disheartened and disillusioned Penn State team, and gone with it was the crown Joe Paterno so coveted. After the game he commented: "Alabama has as much right to a national championship as anyone; I think they beat an awfully good team today."

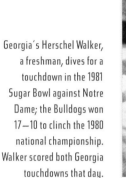

Georgia's Herschel Walker, a freshman, dives for a touchdown in the 1981 Sugar Bowl against Notre Dame; the Bulldogs won 17—10 to clinch the 1980 national championship. Walker scored both Georgia touchdowns that day.

1981 | GEORGIA 17 NOTRE DAME 10

It was said that the Georgia Bulldogs of 1980 were the luckiest team ever to win a national championship: lucky to have been ranked No. 1 at the end of the regular season when they hadn't played a team that finished in the top 20; lucky to have escaped with wins in at least three regular season games; and lucky to have come out on top in the Sugar Bowl.

Their luck in the Sugar Bowl bordered on the miraculous. They won the game by a touchdown, even though Notre Dame outgained them passing 138 yards to 7 and rushing 190 yards to 127. And the remarkable thing about Georgia's rushing statistic was that freshman sensation Herschel Walker ran for 150 yards, while his running mates totaled 23 yards in *lost* yardage.

Notre Dame took the lead in the first quarter when Harry Oliver booted a 50-yard field goal, but from then on it was nothing but a litany of blunders

for the Irish. First was a blocked field goal that Georgia then converted into a field goal of its own. When the Bulldogs kicked off after it, the two Notre Dame returners were confused about who was going to catch the ball and run it back, so neither did. The ball bounced around near the 1-yard line, where Georgia's Steve Kelly dove on it. A few moments later Herschel Walker vaulted into the end zone. Another Notre Dame fumble at their own 20 was recovered by the Bulldogs, and a few plays later, Walker skirted the end for still another Georgia score and a 17–3 halftime lead. In the second half, Notre Dame managed a touchdown, but was plagued by several interceptions and a missed field goal from the 13.

It was Dan Devine's last game as head coach of the Fighting Irish, only his 16th loss against 53 victories at Notre Dame; for Georgia it was their first national championship.

1983 | PENN STATE 27 GEORGIA 23

The Sugar Bowl on New Year's Day 1983 was again the site where the nation's two top-ranked teams met to decide the championship. Georgia, behind the running of Heisman Trophy–winner Herschel Walker, was ranked No. 1 at season's end, and Penn State, with a defense so deceptive and difficult to adjust to that it had earned the nickname "Magic," was just a notch beneath.

Penn State came out throwing, as quarterback Todd Blackledge passed his way to the Georgia 2-yard line, where All-American running back Curt Warner carried it in for the first score of the game. The Nittany Lions could virtually do nothing wrong in the first half. Kevin Baugh returned punts for 66, 24, and 10 yards; Blackledge completed nine of 16 passes for 160 yards; Warner ran for another touchdown; Nick Gancitano kicked two field goals. Georgia, which managed a field goal earlier, finally scored a touchdown with 5 seconds left in the half, when John Lastinger lobbed one to flanker Herman Archie in the end zone. Penn State had a 20–10 halftime lead.

The momentum shifted at the start of the second half, however, when Lastinger engineered a 60-yard drive that ended when Herschel Walker blasted in from the 1-yard line. Penn State's offense faltered, with the passing game shut down by a tight Georgia defense and Curt Warner severely hampered by leg cramps.

But when everything seemed to be falling apart, Joe Paterno sent in a little surprise from the sideline: a play-action fake to Warner, then Blackledge dropped back in the pocket and threw a 47-yard pass caught by a diving Gregg Garrity in the end zone.

Georgia came back with a touchdown in the fourth quarter, but after that an inspired Magic defense shut down the Bulldogs, giving Paterno and Penn State their long-sought national championship.

1993 | ALABAMA 34 MIAMI (FLORIDA) 13

Miami, coached by Dennis Erickson, headed the season-end polls going into the Sugar Bowl and was a decided favorite to defeat Gene Stallings's Crimson Tide. Miami quarterback Gino Torretta had won the Heisman Trophy that year and the Hurricanes' offense was awesome. Both teams had gone through the regular season undefeated.

Both teams also got off to a modest start, only a field goal apiece in the first quarter. Alabama's defense was playing the game of its life, however, and held the Hurricanes to just another field goal in the second period. Meanwhile the Tide put another 10 points on the scoreboard to lead at the half 13–6.

In the second half, 'Bama's defense put the game away quickly. On Miami's first play from scrimmage, Tommy Johnson intercepted a Torretta pass and returned it to the Hurricane 20-yard line; shortly thereafter Derrick Lassic scored from the 1. On Miami's next possession, George Teague picked off another Torretta pass and ran it 31 yards for a touchdown (two touchdowns in 16 seconds for the Tide). With a 27–6 lead going into the final period, Alabama continued to dominate. The Hurricanes managed a touchdown on a 78-yard punt return by Kevin Williams, but Alabama countered with another from Lassic.

The 34–13 Alabama victory was a huge surprise; credit went especially to the Tide's defense and the rushing of Derrick Lassic, who gained 135 yards on 28 carries.

1997 | FLORIDA 52 FLORIDA STATE 20

Florida State had beaten its intrastate rival Florida in the last game of the season 24–21, which secured the nation's No. 1 ranking for the Seminoles. Florida, who had headed the polls much of the season, dropped to No. 2. The national championship was on the line when they met at the Sugar Bowl.

It had all the makings of a nail-biter. And it was—until the second half. Florida got on the scoreboard first with a pass from Danny Wuerffel to Ike Hilliard after a 77-yard drive. On their next possessions the two teams exchanged field goals. Florida then erupted with a 73-yard touchdown drive, using just four plays. The Seminoles came right back, however, Thad Busby hitting Wayne Messam for 23 yards and then E. G. Green for 29 and a touchdown. Wuerffel's turn; he led the Gators on a 65-yard drive, capping it with a 31-yard touchdown pass to Hilliard. State's tailback Warrick Dunn responded with a 12-yard touchdown run. The score at the half, Florida 24, Florida State 17.

The Seminoles, adding a field goal, came to within 4 points early in the third period. But then disaster struck. Dunn, the heart of the Florida State offense, who had been suffering from the flu, was forced to leave the game. The Seminole attack came to a standstill, while the Gators' attack virtually exploded. Wuerffel hit Hilliard for the combination's third touchdown of the game; Wuerffel, never known for his running skills, then ran 16 yards for a touchdown, while running back Terry Jackson carried it in for two others.

With an astounding 52–20 victory, the Miami Gators were back on top, winning their first (and only) national championship.

2000 | FLORIDA STATE 46 VIRGINIA TECH 29

It was billed as the game of the quarterbacks: Florida State had 27-year-old Chris Weinke, Virginia Tech the 19-year-old freshman sensation Michael Vick. And they were meeting in the second national championship under the Bowl Championship Series. Both teams were undefeated; the Florida State Seminoles were ranked first at season's end with the Virginia Tech Hokies second.

The combination of Weinke and All-America receiver Peter Warrick proved unbeatable, however. They opened the scoring with a 64-yard touchdown pass play. A touchdown on a blocked punt gave Florida State a 14–0 lead in the first quarter. Vick responded with a 48-yard touchdown toss of his own. Then Weinke connected on a 63-yard touchdown pass to Ron Dugans; not long after Warrick returned a Hokie punt 59 yards for the last score of the first half, and a 28–14 Seminole lead.

Virginia Tech came back with three straight scores in the second half: a 3-yard run by Vick, a 29-yard run by Andre Kendrick, and a field goal. Despite having failed on a pair of 2-point conversions, Tech still claimed a 1-point lead going into the fourth quarter, 29–28.

As the third quarter belonged to the Hokies and Michael Vick, the fourth was the domain of Weinke and the Seminoles. Weinke connected again with Dugans for a touchdown and then with Warrick for a 2-point conversion. A 32-yard field goal from All-American kicker Sebastian Janikowski and another touchdown pass, 43 yards, Weinke to Warrick, put the game away.

The 46–29 victory gave Florida State the undisputed national title. Weinke had completed 20 of 34 passes for 329 yards and four touchdowns; Warrick had six receptions for 163 yards and two touchdowns and another on his 59-yard punt return. Michael Vick was 15 of 29 passing for 225 yards and one touchdown, and he gained 97 yards rushing on 23 carries.

THE COTTON BOWL

J. Curtis Sanford, a Texas oil magnate, was in Los Angeles one New Year's Day in the mid-1930s and went to Pasadena to take in the Rose Bowl festivities and game. He also heard talk that day about the two other cities that had just started similar New Year's Day pageants: Miami with its Orange Bowl, and New Orleans with the Sugar Bowl. Why not stage one in Dallas, his own hometown? He found the idea so appealing that he decided to finance it himself.

And so was born the Cotton Bowl in Dallas in 1937. It was not a success at the outset, even though it showcased Texas Christian's marvelous Sammy Baugh in his last college game. In fact, the benevolent Mr. Sanford lost several thousand dollars.

Marquette had come all the way from Milwaukee to face the Horned Frogs in a stadium on the Texas state fairgrounds in Dallas, but only about 17,000 fans showed up. Those who did were treated to a Sammy Baugh touchdown pass to L. D. Meyer, who proved to be the game's most glittering star. Meyer ran for another touchdown and kicked a field goal and an extra point to account for all 16 of the Horned Frogs' points. The final score was 16–6.

During the first four years of the Cotton Bowl, J. Curtis Sanford remained its patron, advancing money, promoting the event, and guiding its administration. He turned all his responsibilities over to a newly formed Cotton Bowl Athletic Association in 1940, which was instituted as an agency of the Southwest Conference. Two years later, it was agreed that the winner of that conference would automatically be invited to play in the Cotton Bowl.

GAMES WORTH REMEMBERING

1938 | RICE 28 COLORADO 14

Colorado College (now the University of Colorado) had gone undefeated through the 1937 season, but skeptics noted that they had not played any team of renown, and therefore would provide little competition for Southwest Conference champion Rice, which had played and defeated a number of nationally ranked teams.

What Colorado had, however, was a triple-threat back named Byron "Whizzer" White, who had earned All-America honors and a Rhodes Scholarship and would later become even better known as a U.S. Supreme Court justice. With White running and passing, Colorado moved down the field with relative ease in the first quarter. At Rice's 8-yard line, he dropped back and threw to halfback Joe Antonio for the game's initial score. When Rice got the ball, White anticipated a pass and picked it off, sprinting 47 yards to give Colorado a 14–0 edge.

But Rice was, in fact, a much stronger team, and in the second period the Owls asserted themselves. What got them going was sophomore quarterback Ernie Lain, who came off the bench to lead Rice's counterattack. In the second quarter, Lain threw for two touchdowns and ran another in himself, then passed for still another in the third period. In the meantime, Rice's defense thwarted Whizzer White, who, in effect, was the entire Colorado offense.

1946 | TEXAS 40 MISSOURI 27

If ever there was a one-man show in a bowl game, it was the performance put on by Texas quarterback Bobby Layne in the 1946 Cotton Bowl game. He played a role in every one of the Longhorns' 40 points that were scored that day.

The blond-haired All-American started the day with a 48-yard touchdown pass to halfback Joe Baumgardner. He followed that by scoring four touchdowns himself, three by running and one on a pass reception. For the last touchdown of the afternoon he threw again to Baumgardner. In between, he kicked four extra points for the Longhorns. At day's end he had completed 11 of 12 passes, mostly to

Byron "Whizzer" White takes off around end for Colorado in the 1938 Cotton Bowl against Rice. White, who would go on to become a U.S. Supreme Court justice, threw one touchdown pass and ran back an interception for another score, but the Rice Owls were too much for Colorado and triumphed 28–14.

All-American end Hub Bechtol, and accounted for 466 total yards.

Layne's four touchdowns, 28 points scored, four conversions, and completion percentage of .917 all became long-standing Cotton Bowl records. And the 67 points scored in the game was the highest total in a Cotton Bowl contest until 1985, when Boston College beat Houston 45–28.

1949 | SOUTHERN METHODIST 21 OREGON 13

There was a plentiful supply of present and future All-Americans on hand for the 1949 Cotton Bowl classic. Southern Methodist had Doak Walker and Kyle Rote in the backfield, while Norm Van Brocklin quarterbacked Oregon.

The Mustangs of SMU, whose campus was only a few miles from the Cotton Bowl, were the favorites both with the oddsmakers and the 69,000 fans who packed the recently enlarged stadium. They had reason to be happy from the opening kickoff, which SMU received and marched the length of the field, where Walker carried it in from the 1-yard line.

Oregon had no trouble gaining yards in the first half, but they could not score points. They fell behind further at the start of the second half when Kyle Rote broke loose on a 36-yard touchdown run. SMU scored again in the final period to provide the winning margin, overcoming Norm Van Brocklin's two touchdown passes in the same period.

1957 | TEXAS CHRISTIAN 28 SYRACUSE 27

Texas Christian had not won a Cotton Bowl game since the very first one back in 1937. And Syracuse had made only one appearance ever in a major bowl game, and that was its 61–6 humiliation at the hands of Alabama in the 1953 Orange Bowl.

In 1957, the TCU Horned Frogs had All-American Jim Swink at halfback, and the Syracuse Orangemen had All-American Jim Brown to carry the ball for them. The game was touted as a battle between the dazzling open-field running of Swink and the enormous power of Brown. Both lived up to their reputations that day, especially Brown. With Syracuse trailing by a touchdown in the second quarter, he blasted in twice for touchdowns and kicked two extra points to keep the Orangemen in the game. The Horned Frogs scored again, and the teams went to their dressing rooms deadlocked at 14–14.

TCU took the lead in the third period when quarterback Chuck Curtis swept left end for a touchdown, but Brown tied it up by running for another touchdown in the final quarter. Swink finally broke into the scoring column in the final period to give the Frogs a 28–21 lead.

Syracuse came right back. Brown pounded out yardage and then decoyed the Texas Christian defense to enable Chuck Zimmerman to loft a 27-

yard touchdown pass to halfback Jim Ridlon. There was only a little over a minute left when Brown lined up for the game-tying conversion. But a substitute end by the name of Chico Mendoza became the New Year's Day hero when he broke into the backfield to slap away Brown's kick and give Texas Christian a long-awaited Cotton Bowl triumph.

1970 | TEXAS 21 NOTRE DAME 17

Texas was the top-ranked team in the nation going into the 1970 Cotton Bowl, with a record of 10-0. (Only Penn State, similarly undefeated, threatened their crown.) Notre Dame, under Ara Parseghian, prided itself as a spoiler, and the Fighting Irish were at a bowl game for the first time since the Four Horsemen ran over Ernie Nevers and Stanford at the Rose Bowl 45 years earlier.

Texas fans, including former President Lyndon B. Johnson, thronged the Cotton Bowl to see their team clinch the national title. Coach Darrell Royal's Texas team had decimated Tennessee in the Cotton Bowl the year before, and from that squad remained quarterback James Street and running back Ted Koy (whose older brother Ernie had led Texas to an Orange Bowl triumph in 1965). The

Longhorns also had halfback Jim Bertelsen and All-American fullback Steve Worster. Royal's team had won 19 consecutive games.

On the other hand, Notre Dame had a quarterback named Joe Theismann and a gifted receiver in Tom Gatewood, a combination that could stun any team. Texas was a predictable 7-point favorite.

The Irish, however, dominated the game, taking a 3–0 lead at the end of the first quarter and a 10–7 margin at halftime, the touchdown coming on a 54-yard pass play from Theismann to Gatewood.

Nobody scored in the third period, but then in the final quarter Texas wrested the lead when Ted Koy ran for a touchdown. Notre Dame came right back, Theismann this time finding Jim Yoder for a go-ahead touchdown, the score 17–14.

In the end it was fourth-down gambles that Darrell Royal used to sink the Irish. The first one took place on the Notre Dame 20-yard line with about four and a half minutes left. A field goal would have tied the game, but Royal disdained that and ran the ball instead. The Longhorns picked up the first down, and seconds continued to tick off the clock. The drive continued to the 10-yard line, where again Texas faced fourth down, this time with 2 yards to go. And again the field goal kicker stayed on the Texas bench. James Street took the ball from center, rolled out on an option, and then threw a fluttery pass that Cotton Speyrer picked off his shoelaces at the 2, good enough for another first down. Notre Dame stopped the Longhorns on two plays, but finally, with just over a minute left, running back Billy Dale found a hole and raced into the end zone.

With the score now 21–17 in favor of Texas, the game was still far from over. Theismann moved the Irish quickly and deftly, all the way to the Texas 38-yard line. With a half-minute left he dropped back

Tempers flare with only 24 seconds remaining in the 1970 Cotton Bowl game: Notre Dame guard Gary Kos struggles with an unidentified but equally angry Texas player. Texas defeated Notre Dame 21—17.

again, and it appeared he had a receiver open at the 14, but Texas defensive back Tom Campbell leaped up and snatched the ball away. The interception killed Notre Dame's chance of being that year's spoiler.

"I forced the pass," Theismann said after the game. "They got the big plays," Ara Parseghian added, "but that's the name of the game. Maybe next time *we'll* ring up the big ones."

1971 | NOTRE DAME 24 TEXAS 11

Ara Parseghian was right, there was a next time: same time, same place, in fact, one year later. Texas was again No. 1 in the nation at the end of the regular season, undefeated in 10 games and now boasting a 30-game winning streak. Even the cast was almost the same: Notre Dame had Joe Theismann and Tom Gatewood, and Texas had Steve Worster and Jim Bertelsen, among other familiar faces.

Texas jumped out to a 3-point lead, but after that they were virtually overwhelmed by the vindictive

Fighting Irish. As he had the year before, Theismann teamed up with Tom Gatewood on a touchdown pass and then added a new twist by running for two additional touchdowns. With a field goal as well, Notre Dame had a 24–11 lead at the half.

As it turned out, the two teams could have donned their street clothes at that point and gone home. Not another point was scored in the remaining two periods. Swiftly and surely, the long Texas winning streak was over. Ara Parseghian's Irish made the big plays in 1971.

1983 | SOUTHERN METHODIST 7 PITTSBURGH 3

The SMU Mustangs had an extraordinary offense in 1982, led by the "Pony Express"—Eric Dickerson at tailback, alternating—with Craig James and Lance McIlhenny at quarterback. They were a running team of the first caliber, and they had not lost a single game that season. Pitt, on the other hand, was a team that could pass, and their fortunes hung on the arm of quarterback Dan Marino.

The game had all the potential of offensive bedlam: long breakaway runs, bombs, concerted drives, trick plays. And at the start it looked as though that would be the order of the day. Marino passed the Panthers down the field on their first possession, all the way to the Mustangs' 1-yard line. Fullback Joe McCall tried to bull it in from there, but there was a mix-up on the handoff from Marino, and the ball bounced around until Wes Hopkins fell on it for the Mustangs. SMU moved the ball to the other end of the field, to the Pitt 10. But then Dickerson fumbled a handoff from McIlhenny, and Pitt recovered.

In the second period, SMU drove to the Pitt 37, only to lose the ball again on a fumble. Marino went to the air with only a little over 2 minutes left. Five completions later, the Panthers were at the Mustangs' 10. But he couldn't get them any further than that. Eric Schubert tried a field goal on fourth down, but it was wide. And so the half ended without a score.

Southern Methodist's Bobby Leach hauls in a pass from Lance McIlhenny in the 1983 Cotton Bowl game against Pittsburgh. With Dan Marino passing for Pitt and SMU's running attack, which featured All-American Eric Dickerson, the game was anticipated to be a high-scoring thriller, but instead it turned into one of defense and offensive mishaps. The final score was SMU 7, Pitt 3.

In the third period, after Marino passed Pitt to the SMU 28-yard line, Schubert came and kicked a field goal. After the ensuing kickoff, the Mustangs' offense came to life. McIlhenny took to the air and threw two strikes to split end Bobby Leach that netted 62 yards. Dickerson then carried it to the Pitt 11-yard line. Two plays later, McIlhenny tried to pitch out to Craig James, found he couldn't, then pulled the ball back and carried it himself up the middle on an unintentional but successful quarterback draw for a touchdown. The conversion gave SMU the lead 7–3.

Pitt threatened once in the final period, reaching the Mustang 12-yard line, but then a Marino pass was picked off in the end zone, and that was it for the day. The anticipated offensive fireworks were a fizzle, but the victory ensured SMU the No. 2 ranking in the nation that year.

1991 | MIAMI (FLORIDA) 46 TEXAS 3

This game is joy to the memory of Miamians and, to say the least, less than treasured by Texas fans. The Longhorns were favored, ranked No. 3 in the nation when they went to the Cotton Bowl to face fourth-ranked Miami. The Hurricanes, however, scored on their first two possessions, two field goals by Carlos Huerta, one a Cotton Bowl record 50-yarder. Miami quarterback Craig Erickson added to that lead with a 12-yard touchdown pass to Wesley Carroll. Texas was held to minus 4 yards total offense in the first period.

The Longhorns got a field goal in the second period, but that was offset by another Erickson-to-Carroll touchdown pass, this one for 24 yards.

The second half was even worse for the Texans. They were shut out. Miami added two touchdowns in the third quarter, one on a 34-yard interception return by Darrin Smith and the other on a 48-yard pass from

Erickson to Randal Hill. Two more touchdowns in the fourth quarter completed Miami's embarrassment of the Longhorns. The final score of 46–3 stands as the most lopsided in Cotton Bowl history.

Craig Erickson set a Cotton Bowl record with his four touchdown passes, while Miami's All-American defensive tackle Russell Maryland recorded three sacks and nine individual tackles.

1994 | NOTRE DAME 24 TEXAS A&M 21

These two teams had met in the previous year's Cotton Bowl and No. 5 ranked Notre Dame had upset No. 3 Texas A&M 28–3. In 1994, the rankings were reversed with No. 4 ranked Notre Dame two places ahead of Texas A&M. The Aggies hoped they could counter with a Cotton Bowl upset of their own.

What the fans got was a much more exciting game than they had seen in 1993. Both teams scored on their opening drives. The Irish drove downfield, climaxing with a 19-yard touchdown run by Kevin McDougal. The Aggies moved the ball with equal ease, ending their drive with an 8-yard run by Greg Hill. The score stood at 7–7 at the end of the first quarter.

The defenses took over in the second quarter, but A&M managed a score just before the half when Corey Pullig connected with Detron Smith on a 15-yard pass play. Notre Dame drove for a touchdown at the outset of the second half to tie the score at 14–14. The Aggies regained the lead minutes later with a long drive and a 1-yard plunge by Rodney Thomas. Notre Dame came right back and scored a touchdown themselves, the score 21–21 as the third quarter came to an end.

During the final quarter, the ball was traded back and forth until late in the fourth when Notre Dame's Michael Miller returned a punt 38 yards to the A&M 22-yard line. In three downs the Irish managed to pick up 8 yards; faced with a fourth and 2 situation, the Irish brought on Kevin Pendergast to attempt a 31-yard field goal. He made it, and with the 24–21 victory Notre Dame made it two in a row over Texas A&M at the Cotton Bowl.

Defensive Battles

In the history of the four major bowls—Rose, Orange, Sugar, and Cotton—there have only been three scoreless ties. Two of them occurred in the Cotton Bowl: on a rainy, muddy New Year's Day in 1947, Arkansas and a Y. A. Tittle–led Louisiana State ended up 0–0; and in 1959 neither Texas Christian nor the Air Force Academy could post any points. The only other scoreless tie occurred in the Rose Bowl back in 1922, when California met Washington & Jefferson.

Notre Dame's Lee Becton finds a hole in the Texas A&M line in the 1994 Cotton Bowl game. The Fighting Irish emerged victorious that day, 24–21, making it two in a row over the Aggies at the Cotton Bowl (the year before they won 28–3).

INDEX OF NAMES

A

Abraham, Clifton, 219
Ackerson, Bruce, 164
Adams, Charles P., 132
Adams, Franklin P., 126–28
Adams, Pete, 227
Agase, Alex, 6, 82
Aikman, Troy, 242
Akers, Fred, 98
Albert, Frankie, 223, 240, 246, 247
Alberts, Trev, 8, 217
Alcott, Clarence, 220
Aldridge, Rikki, 109
Alexander, Bill, 82
Alfonse, Julius, 156
Allen, Marcus, 8, *11*, 174, 242, 243, 249
Alpert, Herb, 107, 126
Alvarez, Barry, 82
Ameche, Alan, 7, 240
Ames, Knowlton, 5, 12, 206
Anderson, Damian, 148, *148*
Anderson, Eddie, 6, 51, 61, 82, 208, 220
Anderson, Eric, 228
Anderson, Erick, 263
Anderson, Frankie, 213
Anderson, Heartley "Hunk," 100, 208, 220
Anderson, John, 105
Andros, Dee, 198
Andruss, Hamlin, 5, 220
Andrusyshyn, Zenon, 108–9
Antonio, Joe, 281
Applequist, H. A., 55, 62
Appleton, Scott, 224, 248
Archie, Herman, 278
Armour, Albert, 193
Arnold, Claude, 274
Arnsparger, Bill, 83
Arrington, Dick, 7
Arrington, LaVar, 8
Aschenbrenner, Frank, 259
Atessis, Bill, 170
Azzaro, Joe, 169

B

Bagnell, Reds, 240, 249
Bahan, Pete, 220
Bailey, David, 214
Baker, Eugene, 34
Baker, Johnny, 100
Baker, L. H., 35
Baker, Terry, 3, 240, 246–47, 249, 252
Banducci, Bruno, 223
Bangs, Biff, 255

Banks, Earl, 194–95
Barker, Jay, 228
Barnett, Gary, 82
Barnhart, Tony, 109
Barr, Chris, 7
Barres, Herster, 154–55
Barrett, Billy, 161–63, 166
Barrow, Michael, 216
Battle, Mike, 224
Battles, Cliff, 246
Baugh, Kevin, 278
Baugh, Sammy, x, 2, 6, *125*, 186, 246, 247, 280
Baul, Reggie, 269
Bauman, Charlie, 77
Baumgardner, Joe, 281
Beagle, Ron, 7, 249
Beamer, Frank, 82
Beathard, Pete, 261, *261*
Beban, Gary, 3, 107–9, 242, 245, 249, 263
Bechtol, Hub, 6, 282
Becton, Lee, 181, 286
Bednarik, Chuck, 6, 240, 249
Beedde, Brad, 7
Beinor, Ed, 6
Bell, Bobby, 199–201, 240, 248
Bell, Ricky, 173, 214, 215, 242
Bell, Todd, 105
Bell, Trumane, 270
Bellino, Joe, 3, 95, 240, *241*, 249
Benners, Fred, 161–63
Bennett, Byron, 270
Bentley, Scott, 269
Bergman, Dutch, 220
Bernard, Chuck, 6
Bertelli, Angelo, 240, *241*
Bertelsen, Jim, 171, 283, 284
Berwanger, Jay, 4, 6, 44, 236, 238, 240
Bevan, Bill, 209, 221
Bezdek, Hugo, 220
Bible, Dana Xenophon, 51
Bierman, Bernie, x, 51, 71, 155, 206, 209, *209*, 212, 221, 232
Biglow, Horatio, 5, 220
Biletnikoff, Fred, 252–53
Blackledge, Todd, 176–78, 278
Blacklock, Hugh, 255
Blades, Bennie, 8, 216
Blaik, Earl "Red," x, xi, 6, 66–67, *66*, 82, 83, 93, 95, 158, 160, 206, 209–10, 210, 223, 232
Blanchard, Felix "Doc," x, 2, 6, 67, 93, 94–95, 158–60, *159*, 164, 210, *210*, 223, 223, 240, 245, 247, 249, 273

Blanda, George, 72
Bleier, Rocky, 168
Blewitt, Jim, 255
Bodine, Al, 266
Bollinger, Bo, 213, 224
Bollinger, Brooks, 264
Bond, Ward, 107
Booth, Albie, 154–55, *154*, 246, 247
Bosworth, Brian, 8, 227
Boulware, Peter, 219
Bowden, Bobby, x, 8, 83, 181, 192, 217–19, 219, 228, 232, 269
Bowden, Terry, 82
Bowman, Kirk, 176–78
Bowman, Steve, 213
Boyd, Ivan, 182
Boydston, Max, 213
Boykin, Arnold "Showboat," 24
Bradley, Danny, 98
Bradley, Omar, 126, 158
Brahaney, Tom, 171, 215
Brand, Rodney, 170
Bratton, Melvin, 25, 269
Brees, Drew, 4, 9, 242, 249
Brennan, Terry, 158, 160, 167–68, 210, 223
Brickley, Charles, 5, 89, 91, 207, 220, 247
Bright, Johnny, 199, 200
Brill, Marty, 208
Britton, Earl, 221
Brooke, George, 5, 206
Brooks, Billy, 215
Brooks, Derrick, 219
Brooks, Eddie, 182
Brooks, Rich, 82
Brosky, Al, 9
Brown, Andre, 179
Brown, Booker, 215
Brown, Buddy, 214
Brown, Charlie, 275
Brown, Dave, 7
Brown, Eddie, 216
Brown, Jackie, 262
Brown, Jerome, 216
Brown, Jim, 2, 7, 23–24, *23*, 187, 195–97, *197*, 201, *241*, 282–83, *283*
Brown, Johnny Mack, 63, 126, 256–57
Brown, Paul, 83, 232
Brown, Tim, 8, 242, 243
Brown, Tom, 164–65, 240, 248
Brown, Warren, 17
Browner, Ross, 7, *11*, 248, 249
Broyles, Frank, 51, 82, 169–71, 193
Bruce, Earle, 82, 105

INDEX OF SCHOOLS

PHOTO CREDITS

Pp. vii (left), 168, 226 (top), copyright ©
James Drake, *Sports Illustrated.*
P. vii (right), copyright © Rich Clarkson,
Sports Illustrated.
Pp. 3, 10 (S. Baugh; F. Sinkwich;
C. Trippi), 11 (J. Rodgers; T. Dorsett; end
zone; K. Stewart), 13, 15 (left), 33, 36 (left),
44 (both), 45 (left), 48–49, 52, 54, 59, 63,
65, 66, 69, 71, 73, 75, 76, 79, 81, 87, 91, 117
(bottom), 124 (B. White), 131, 138 (top left),
149, 162, 175, 203 (top center & right), 208
(both), 209, 210, 211, 215, 218, 219, 222 (bot-
tom left), 223, 226 (bottom), 239, 241 (A.
Bertelli; P. Dawkins; J. Bellino), 243 (M.
Allen; T. Brown), 257, 258, 259, 260, 261,
265, 272, 282 (center), 284, copyright ©
AP/Wide World Photos.
P. 4, copyright © Brent Smith/
Reuters/TimePix.
Pp. 11 (J. Montana), 14, 19, 129, 159, 167,
222 (top), 248, copyright © University of
Notre Dame Archives.
Pp. 15 (right), 203 (top left), copyright ©
Culver Pictures, Inc.
Pp. 12, 26–27, 40, 88, 154, 206, 241 (C. Frank
& L. Kelly), copyright © Yale Athletic
Department Archives.
Pp. 132 (both), copyright © Yale University
Manuscripts and Archives.
P. 61, copyright © and courtesy of the
University of Illinois.
P. 21, copyright © and courtesy of
University of Minnesota Men's Athletics.
Pp. 22, 41, 56, 138 (bottom), 164, 222
(bottom right), 241 (Tom Harmon), 254,
copyright © Ivory Photograph Collection,
Bentley Historical Library, University of
Michigan.
Pp. 23, 241 (E. Davis), copyright © and
courtesy of Syracuse University
Department of Athletics.
P. 9 (left), copyright © and courtesy TCU
Athletics Department.
P. 9 (bottom), copyright © and courtesy of
Wisconsin Sports Information.
P. 9 (top), copyright © Mark A. Philbruck/
Brigham Young University.
P. 10 (D. Walker), copyright © James T.
Bradley.
P. 10 (B. Cannon), copyright © LSU Sports
Information.
P. 10 (S. Spurrier), 274, 275, 277,
copyright © Sugar Bowl Archives.
Pp. 11 (A. Davis), 57, 108, 124 (J. Wayne),
copyright © USC Sports Information.
Pp. 29, 42, 43, 125 (bottom left), copyright
© Richard Whittingham Collection.
Pp. 30, 202, copyright © Special
Collections and University Archives,
Rutgers University Libraries.
P. 32, copyright © N.Y. Public Library
Picture Collection.
P. 36 (right), copyright © University of Penn-
sylvania Archives.

P. 38, copyright © Georgia Tech Sports
Information.
Pp. 39, 114, 243 (H. Walker), copyright ©
and provided by UGA Sports Communi-
cations Office.
Pp. 47 (left), 72, 99, 253, copyright ©
Stephen Fleming/Crossroads
Communications.
P. 103, copyright © Detroit News Photo.
Pp. 106, 187, copyright © UCLA Photography.
Pp. 125 (top left & right), copyright ©
Harvard Sports Media Relations.
Pp. 47 (right), 216 (both), 270 (right),
copyright © University of Miami Sports
Information Department.
P. 53 copyright © and courtesy of
Springfield College, Archives and
Special Collections.
Pp. 196, 197, 214, copyright © Marvin E.
Newman.
Pp. 78, 115 (bottom), 118 (left), copyright ©
Photo by: Per Kjeldsen.
Pp. 96 (all), 97, 212, copyright © Western
History Collections, University of
Oklahoma Library.
Pp. 110, 113, 120–121, 122, 127, 138 (top right),
203 (bottom row), copyright © ABC
Photography Archives.
Pp. 115 (center), 135, copyright © Photo
by Glen Johnson, Bryan, Tex.
P. 116, copyright © Frank Ward/Amherst
College.
Pp. 117 (top), 119, copyright ©
M. Culler/Depauw University,
Depauw University Sports Information.
P. 118 (right), copyright © Purdue
University Athletic Public Relations and
Communications.
P. 138 (middle right), copyright © and
courtesy University of Colorado Athletics.
Pp. 141, 143, 243 (A. Griffin), copyright ©
Ohio State University Photo Archives.
P. 145, copyright © Jay Metz/University
of Florida.
P. 144, copyright © U. S. Military
Academy Public Affairs Office.
Pp. 124 (D. Eisenhower; G. Ford;
R. Nixon), 125 (L. Gehrig), copyright ©
College Football Hall of Fame.
P. 153, copyright © The Bancroft Library,
University of California.
P. 157, copyright © Fordham Sports
Information Office.
P. 166, copyright © *Chicago Tribune.*
P. 172, copyright © University of
Oklahoma Media Relations File Photo.
P. 179, copyright © Photo by Michael &
Susan Bennett, Lighthouse Imaging.
Pp. 184–185, copyright © Peter Stackpole/
Reuters/TimePix.
Pp. 186, 243 (R. Staubach), copyright ©
United States Naval Academy.
Pp. 188, 189, 256, copyright © Pasadena
Tournament of Roses Archives.
Pp. 190 (top), 241 (N. Kinnick), copyright ©
University of Iowa Photo Service Unit.
Pp. 190 (bottom), 237, copyright © Brown
University.

P. 191, copyright © and courtesy of
Hampton University Archives.
Pp. 193 (top & bottom), 194, copyright ©
Anthony Valentino.
P. 200 (all), copyright © Photo by photo-
grapher John Robinson and Don Ultang;
© 1951, The Des Moines Register and
Tribune Company, reprinted with
permission.
P. 213, copyright © Paul W. Bryant
Museum, University of Alabama.
P. 268, copyright © and courtesy of Orange
Bowl Committee.
P. 270 (left), copyright © Kent Gidley.
Pp. 280 (right), 281, 282 (left), 283, copyright
© Cotton Bowl Athletic Association.
Pp. xvi–1, 130, copyright © Robert Rogers,
Sports Illustrated.
Pp. 24, 173, 262, 267, copyright ©
Heinz Kluetmeier, *Sports Illustrated.*
P. 45 (right), copyright © John G.
Zimmerman, *Sports Illustrated.*
P. 46, copyright © Carl Iwasaki,
Sports Illustrated.
P. 92, copyright © Al Tielemans,
Sports Illustrated.
P. 112, copyright © Andy Hayt,
Sports Illustrated.
Pp. 116, 137, copyright © Robert Beck,
Sports Illustrated.
Pp. vii (center), 84–85, 123, 138 (center left),
146–147, copyright © Richard Mackson,
Sports Illustrated.
P. 170, copyright © Neil Leifer,
Sports Illustrated.
P. 177, copyright © Manny Millan,
Sports Illustrated.
P. 180, copyright © Tom Lynn,
Sports Illustrated.
P. 183, copyright © David E. Klutho,
Sports Illustrated.
P. 192 (both), copyright © William
Snyder, *Sports Illustrated.*
P. 201, copyright © Mark Perlstein,
Sports Illustrated.
P. 228, copyright © Damian Strohmeyer,
Sports Illustrated.
P. 234–235, copyright © Brian Masck,
Sports Illustrated.
P. 243 (R. Williams), copyright ©
Phil Huber, *Sports Illustrated.*
Title page and pp. 225, 243 (O. J. Simpson),
244, copyright © Walter Iooss, Jr., *Sports
Illustrated.*
P. 245, copyright © John Kenney,
Sports Illustrated.
Pp. 148, 204–205, 217, 263, 265 (left),
279, copyright © John Biever,
Sports Illustrated.
P. 250, copyright © George Long,
Sports Illustrated.
P. 280 (left), copyright © Bill Frakes,
Sports Illustrated.
P. 285, copyright © Peter Read Miller,
Sports Illustrated.
P. 286, copyright © Jim Gund,
Sports Illustrated.

Pearl Entertainment presents

RITES OF AUTUMN

THE STORY OF COLLEGE FOOTBALL

A TEN-PART SERIES PREMIERING

FALL 2001

NARRATED BY BURT REYNOLDS

Executive Producers | Don Sperling | Wayne Chesler

Production Coordinator | Brad Bernstein

Coordinating Producers | Stephen Fleming | Woody Freiman

Segment Producers | Adam Hertzog | Joe Lavine | Matt Maranz | Stephen Mintz |
George P. Pozderec | Charlie Sadoff | Jason Sealove | Josh Shelov | Brian Roth

Production Associates | Josh Kreitzman | Brian Fassel | Evan Fisher | Nelson Dellamaggiore |
Jason Schaefer | Robyn Short | Danielle Shelov

Production Support | Noah Coslov | Jesse Legon | Matt Bauer | Justin Roestenberg

Consultant | Richard Wittingham

Visit our website: ritesofautumn.com

Look for the Home Video and DVD release in stores everywhere Fall 2001